P9-CBM-342

Public Relations Cases

SEVENTH EDITION

Public Relations Cases

SEVENTH EDITION

Jerry A. Hendrix

American University

Darrell C. Hayes

American University

THOMSON
™
WADSWORTH

Australia • Brazil • Canada • Mexico • Singapore • Spain
United Kingdom • United States

THOMSON

WADSWORTH

Publisher: Holly J. Allen
Assistant Editor: Lucinda Bingham
Editorial Assistant: Meghan Bass
Senior Technology Project Manager: Jeanette Wiseman
Managing Marketing Manager: Kimberly Russell
Marketing Assistant: Alexandra Tran
Marketing Communications Manager: Shemika Britt
Project Manager, Editorial Production: Karol Jurado
Creative Director: Rob Hugel
Executive Art Director: Maria Epes
Print Buyer: Doreen Suruki

Permissions Editor: Roberta Broyer
Production Service: G&S Book Services
Text Designer: Lisa Devenish
Copy Editor: Kathy Finch
Cover Designer: Patrick Devine
Cover Images: Lester Lefkowitz/Getty Images (top),
    Photolibrary.com/Getty Images (bottom)
Cover Printer: Phoenix Color Corp
Compositor: G&S Book Services
Printer: R.R. Donnelley

© 2007 Thomson Wadsworth, a part of The Thomson
Corporation. Thomson, the Star logo, and Wadsworth
are trademarks used herein under license.

ALL RIGHTS RESERVED. No part of this work covered by the copyright hereon may be reproduced or used
in any form or by any means—graphic, electronic, or
mechanical, including photocopying, recording, taping,
Web distribution, information storage and retrieval systems, or in any other manner—without the written permission of the publisher.

Printed in the United States of America
1 2 3 4 5 6 7 10 09 08 07 06

Library of Congress Control Number: 2006920823

Student Edition: ISBN 0-495-05028-8

Thomson Arts and Sciences
10 Davis Drive
Belmont, CA 94002-3098
USA

For more information about our products, contact us at:
Thomson Learning Academic Resource Center
1-800-423-0563

For permission to use material from this text or product,
submit a request online at **http://www.thomsonrights.com.**
Any additional questions about permissions can be submitted
by e-mail to **thomsonrights@thomson.com.**

Contents

Preface / ix

PART I

SOLVING PUBLIC RELATIONS PROBLEMS / 1

1 Public Relations in Action / 2

Process / 4
Cases / 4
New Technology / 5
Ethics / 6
The Overall Plan of This Book / 8
General Public Relations Readings / 10
General Trends Affecting Public
    Relations / 11

2 A Public Relations Process / 12

Research / 13
Objectives / 25
Programming / 31
Evaluation / 43
Summary / 45
Notes / 46
Readings on the Public Relations
    Process / 47

PART II

REACHING MAJOR AUDIENCES / 51

3 Media Relations / 52

Research / 53
Objectives / 56
Programming / 57
Evaluation / 63
Summary / 64
Note / 64
Readings on Media Relations / 64

Media Relations Cases

CASE 3-1 *Promoting and Positioning the
    Grand Opening of the National
    Museum of the American
    Indian / 69*
CASE 3-2 *How Will You Remember
    September 11? / 78*
CASE 3-3 *Shedd Sharks Go Wild / 88*

4 Internal Communications / 95

Employee Relations / 96
Research / 96
Objectives / 97
Programming / 98
Evaluation / 100
Summary / 100
Readings on Employee Relations / 101

Employee Relations Cases

CASE 4-1 *The Bucket Brigade: Creating
    Employee Loyalty through
    Corporate Philanthropy / 105*
CASE 4-2 *Trinity Health Retirement
    Redesign: Communicating Benefit
    Changes / 115*
CASE 4-3 *Wheel of Fortune / 124*

Member Relations / 131
Research / 131
Objectives / 132
Programming / 133
Evaluation / 134
Summary / 134
Readings on Member Relations / 134

Member Relations Cases

CASE 4-4 *It's Up to Us. It's Up to You / 136*
CASE 4-5 *Driving for Quality Care / 143*

5 Community Relations / 151

Research / 152
Objectives / 154

Programming / 155
Evaluation / 156
Summary / 157
Readings on Community Relations / 157

Community Relations Cases

CASE 5-1   *Dr. Martin Luther King, Jr.
Library—Check It Out! / 160*

CASE 5-2   *Barberton Citizens Hospital: Keep
Barberton Healthy / 169*

CASE 5-3   *Dare to Care About the Air / 176*

**6   Public Affairs and Government
Relations / 183**

Research / 184
Objectives / 186
Programming / 187
Evaluation / 195
Summary / 196
Readings on Public Affairs / 197

CASE 6-1   *A Record Gift to NPR: Keeping
Good News from Going Bad / 201*

CASE 6-2   *Standing Up for Consumer
Choice—The SB 1648 Battle / 210*

CASE 6-3   *Save Our Doctors Protect Our
Patients: The Maryland Miracle /
219*

7   Investor and Financial Relations / 228

Research / 229
Objectives / 230
Programming / 230
Evaluation / 232
Summary / 232
Readings on Investor and Financial
Relations / 233

Investor Relations Cases

CASE 7-1   *New Beginnings: Recovering from
Tragedy; Unlocking the Value / 236*

CASE 7-2   *Navigating Through a Current of
Uncertainty: Getting Aquila Back
on Solid Ground / 242*

8   Consumer Relations / 250

Research / 251
Objectives / 252

Programming / 252
Evaluation / 254
Summary / 255
Readings on Consumer Relations / 255

Consumer Relations Cases

CASE 8-1   *A Stronger Way to Sell
Appliances / 258*

CASE 8-2   *Lay's Stax Challenge / 267*

9   International Public Relations / 274

Research / 275
Objectives / 276
Programming / 277
Evaluation / 279
Summary / 280
Readings on International Public
Relations / 280

International Public Relations Cases

CASE 9-1   *Convincing the World That Film
Processing Matters—The Launch
of Kodak Perfect Touch
Processing / 284*

CASE 9-2   *The Electronic Product Code:
From Concept to
Commercialization in One
Year / 299*

CASE 9-3   *IDRC Merges with NACORE: The
Launch of CoreNet Global / 309*

10   Relations with Special Publics / 317

Research / 319
Objectives / 320
Programming / 321
Evaluation / 322
Summary / 322
Readings on Special Publics / 323

Special Publics Cases

CASE 10-1   *A Fashionable Red Alert Warns
Women of The Heart Truth / 326*

CASE 10-2   *REBEL: New Jersey's New Youth
Antitobacco Movement / 340*

CASE 10-3   *The Shutterfly Soirée / 356*

PART III

EMERGENCY PUBLIC RELATIONS / 367

11 Emergency Public Relations / 368

Research / 369
Objectives / 369
Programming / 370
Evaluation / 374
Summary / 374
Readings on Emergency Public
    Relations / 375

Emergency Public Relations Cases

CASE 11-1   *Protecting Consumer Confidence
            in U.S. Beef: A Success Story /
            378*
CASE 11-2   *San Diego Wildfires 2003 / 387*

PART IV

BEYOND PUBLIC RELATIONS / 395

12 Integrated Marketing Communications / 396

Research / 397
Objectives / 398
Programming / 399
Evaluation / 400
Summary / 400
Notes / 400
Readings on Integrated Marketing
    Communications / 400

*Integrated Marketing
Communications Cases*

CASE 12-1   *Diabetes for Life Campaign / 403*
CASE 12-2   *The Healthy Potato—
            Relaunching America's Favorite
            Vegetable in the Atkins Era / 413*
CASE 12-3   *Break a Treaty, Break the
            Law / 424*

*Appendix I: Questions for Class Discussion
and Case Analysis / 435*

*Appendix II: PRSA Member Code of Ethics
2000 / 438*

Index / 447

Preface

In preparing this edition, we continue to believe that readers should encounter a clear set of guiding public relations principles accompanied by cases that generally illustrate those principles in a positive light and thus serve as models of effective management and practice.

The book is divided into four sections: Solving Public Relations Problems, Reaching Major Audiences, Emergency Public Relations, and Integrated Marketing Communications.

In Part 1, the introductory chapter begins with a philosophy we have held for a long time—that the best public relations is characterized by interaction, or better still, interactive participation among sources and receivers of communication. This philosophy is based on the underlying premise that public relations is mostly persuasion. Some years ago, communication researchers discovered that the most effective means of persuasion is self-persuasion. Audience involvement thus becomes a crucial ingredient of successful public relations.

Chapter 1 also includes a section on ethics in public relations. As in previous editions, we have included the Public Relations Society of America (PRSA) Member Code of Ethics in Appendix II, but you will also find some additional dimensions of ethics in this opening chapter.

In Chapter 2, you will encounter the "Hendrix process model," which involves initial research, the setting of objectives, programming, and evaluation. (The elements of this process model form a convenient mnemonic device, the acronym ROPE.) This model focuses special attention on the significance of objectives and their arrangement in a hierarchical order of output and impact functions. Another feature of this process model, reflecting a training and background in speech communication, is special emphasis on the role of interpersonal communication, including speeches, speakers bureaus, small-group and one-on-one formats, and nonverbal aspects of communication. In a word, the ROPE process model is interactive.

Part 2 consists of audience-centered applications of the process, with accompanying illustrative cases. The audience-centered forms of public relations included are media relations, employee and member relations, community relations, public affairs and government relations, investor relations, international public relations, and relations with special publics. Most of the cases were winners of the prestigious Silver Anvil Award contest, conducted annually by the Public Relations Society of America, and therefore constitute some of the finest examples of public relations practices available. The cases also follow the Silver

Anvil entry format, which is somewhat different from the format of the ROPE model. The major difference is that the ROPE model sets objectives apart as a separate category, and the Silver Anvil format does not. The ROPE programming phase includes planning and communication (execution), and both Silver Anvil and ROPE begin and end with research and evaluation. Thus, the two models have a difference mainly in format, not substance.

Part 3 includes both theory and illustrative cases for emergency or crisis public relations. This field of PR is not oriented to a particular audience, so we have set it apart in a separate section of the book.

Also set apart is the section on integrated marketing communications (IMC), the newest area of public relations. IMC is a combination of public relations and marketing techniques, so it is not really new. Though some practitioners, scholars, and the PRSA itself omit the word "marketing" and call it "integrated communications," our preference is to use the widely accepted term "integrated marketing communications."

Finally, the appendixes contain questions for class discussion and the PRSA Member Code of Ethics 2000, which contains guidelines for the ethical practice of public relations.

All but one case from the sixth edition have been replaced to give current examples of award-winning communication campaigns.

Many public relations practitioners have helped by granting permission to use their cases. We hope they will accept our gratitude and understand that space does not permit a list of all their names.

The Instructor's Manual for the seventh edition has been expanded with additional material from many of the cases and updated scenarios for class exercises and discussions. Instructors who adopt the book will have access to the online edition of the Instructor's Manual and may request a copy of the video material from the publisher.

We thank the American University graduate assistants who have helped us with the seventh edition, Jessica Awig and Ileana Schinder.

As with previous editions, we are indebted to administrators in the American University School of Communication for their encouragement, support, and financial assistance.

Authors work most closely with their production editors and it is a pleasure to thank Jamie Armstrong for the warm and outstanding work as production editor for this edition.

We also thank Holly Allen and Meghan Bass for their leadership, guidance, and patience on this edition.

Finally, we gratefully acknowledge the following reviewers, whose constructive comments helped in the development of this seventh edition: Susan Balter-Reitz, Montana State University–Billings; Sheridan Barker, Carson-Newman College; Zoltan Bedy, SUNY at Oswego;

Bruce K. Bell, Liberty University; Dan Berkowitz, University of Iowa; Bojinka Bishop, Ohio University; Ashley Fitch Blair, Union University; Linda Burkley, Slippery Rock University; Keith Cannon, Wingate University; Robert Carroll, York College of Pennsylvania; Shirley S. Carter, University of South Carolina; Rod Carveth, SUNY at Oswego; W. Timothy Coombs, Eastern Illinois University; Gael L. Cooper, University of Southern Indiana; Terri Cornwell, Liberty University; Jeffrey L. Courtright, Illinois State University; Donna W. Cunningham, Northern Arizona University; Richard Davis Jr., August State University; Lora De-Fore, Mississippi State University; Bruce Dorries, Mary Baldwin College; Jeanette Drake, University of Findlay; Cynthia Droog, Grand Valley State University; Bosah Ebo, Rider University; Thomas R. Flynn, Slippery Rock University; Karen Fontenot, Southeastern Louisiana University; Tom Gardner, Westfield State College; Amiso M. George, University of Nevada, Reno; Kelly Griffin, Rider University; Felicia LeDuff Harry, Nicholls State University; Christine Helsel, Eastern Illinois University; Dan Henrich, Liberty University; Sue Hinz, University of Idaho; Terri Lynn Johnson, Eastern Illinois University; LeeAnn Kahlor, University of Texas, Austin; Chi-Chung Keung, Biola University; Frank Klapak, PhD, Seton Hill University; Jerri Lynn Kyle, Southwest Missouri State University; S. Law, Texas A&M International University; Ann Liao, SUNY at Brockport; Lisa Lundy, Louisiana State University; Deborah Menger, University of Texas, San Antonio; April Mouser-Fatula, Harding University; M. Nadler, Miami University; Joy M. Newcom, Waldorf College; Richard A. Nida, Emporia State University; Troy Oldham, Utah State University; Michelle Recicar, Stonehill College; Hugh Reilly, University of Nebraska at Omaha; Dr. Freda L. Remmers, Kean University; Brent Roberts, Montana State University–Billings; Richard C. Robertson, University of Tennessee at Martin; Helen Schubert, Roosevelt University; Mohammad A. Siddiqi, Western Illinois University; Jay Silverman, Sage College of Albany; William Sledzik, Kent State University; S. Catherine Walsh, Mount Saint Mary College; Debra Worley, Indiana State University; Debbie van Tuyll, Augusta State University; and Sr. Rita M. Yeasted, La Roche College.

About the Authors

Jerry A. Hendrix, Ph.D., is professor emeritus of communication at American University in Washington, D.C., where he taught for 37 years. He is an accredited member of the Public Relations Society of America.

Darrell C. Hayes is an assistant professor at American University's School of Communication, Washington, D.C. Before joining the faculty, he had more than 15 years experience in public relations with technology firms, nonprofit associations, and as a government communication manager. He has also worked with a marketing research firm and been the managing director of the Aerospace Education Foundation. He is an accredited member of the Public Relations Society of America.

PART I

Solving Public Relations Problems

CHAPTER 1   **Public Relations in Action**

CHAPTER 2   **A Public Relations Process**

Public Relations in Action

One of the best ways to learn about public relations is through the study of contemporary examples of its practice. Such case studies can bring public relations to life in a way that theoretical textbooks and classroom lectures cannot. Here we will first examine the nature of public relations through its definition and a process model. Then we will look at various forms of public relations along with several cases to illustrate each form.

One way of defining public relations has been simply to invert the term so it becomes "relations with publics." An improved modification of this definition is *"interrelationships* with publics." This better reflects the nature of contemporary public relations as an *interactive* form of communication in which the targeted audiences yield information to the organization through its research efforts and often *participate* in the public relations programming itself. This interactive or mutual dimension of public relations is seen in the comprehensive description adopted by the Public Relations Society of America (PRSA) in 1982 (see Exhibit 1-a).

EXHIBIT 1-A *PRSA's Official Statement on Public Relations**

Public relations helps our complex, pluralistic society to reach decisions and function more effectively by contributing to mutual understanding among groups and institutions. It serves to bring private and public policies into harmony.

Public relations serves a wide variety of institutions in society such as businesses, trade unions, government agencies, voluntary associations, foundations, hospitals, and educational and religious institutions. To achieve their goals, these institutions must develop effective relationships with many different audiences or publics such as employees, members, customers, local communities, shareholders, and other institutions, and with society at large.

The managements of institutions need to understand the attitudes and values of their publics in order to achieve institutional goals. The goals themselves are shaped by the external environment. The public relations practitioner acts as a counselor to management, and as a mediator, helping to translate private aims into reasonable, publicly acceptable policy and action.

As a management function, public relations encompasses the following:

- Anticipating, analyzing, and interpreting public opinion, attitudes, and issues that might impact, for good or ill, the operations and plans of the organization.

- Counseling management at all levels in the organization with regard to policy decisions, courses of action, and communication, taking into account their public ramifications and the organization's social or citizenship responsibilities.

- Researching, conducting, and evaluating, on a continuing basis, programs of action and communication to achieve informed public understanding necessary to the success of an organization's aims. These may include marketing, financial, fund-raising, employee, community, or government relations, and other programs.

- Planning and implementing the organization's efforts to influence or change public policy.

- Setting objectives, planning, budgeting, recruiting and training staff, developing facilities—in short, *managing* the resources needed to perform all of the above.

---

*Formally adopted by the PRSA Assembly on November 6, 1982. Reprinted courtesy PRSA.

- Examples of the knowledge that may be required in the professional practice of public relations include communication arts, psychology, social psychology, sociology, political science, economics, and the principles of management and ethics. Technical knowledge and skills are required for opinion research, public issues analysis, media relations, direct mail, institutional advertising, publications, film/video productions, special events, speeches, and presentations.

In helping to define and implement policy, the public relations practitioner utilizes a variety of professional communication skills and plays an integrative role both within the organization and between the organization and the external environment.

PROCESS

The public relations process is a method for solving problems. It has four phases: research, objectives, programming, and evaluation. Each element may be modified by the demands of different audiences or publics, including employees, members, customers, local communities, shareholders, and, usually, the news media.

The *research* phase of the process involves identifying and learning about three key elements: (1) a *client* or institution that has (2) a *problem* or potential problem to be solved, which involves (3) one or more of its *audiences,* or publics.

The second phase of the public relations process involves the setting of *objectives* for a program to solve the problem. These objectives may include the kind of influence the client hopes to exert with the audiences, such as informing them or modifying their attitudes or behaviors. The objectives may also include statements about the program itself, such as its composition or how it will operate.

The third phase of the process consists of planning and executing a *program* to accomplish the objectives. The program comprises a central theme, messages, and various forms of communication aimed at reaching the audiences.

Finally, *evaluation,* as defined in this process, consists of two parts. First, it includes an ongoing procedure of program monitoring and adjustment. Second, evaluation refers back specifically to the objectives that were set in the second phase of the process and examines the practitioner's degree of success in achieving them.

CASES

The illustrations of this process in action—the cases—are grouped in this text according to the various audiences that public relations practitioners reach. Each audience calls for some modifications in the overall four-step process, and the cases illustrate the modified process in action.

Cases are presented to illustrate relations with the media, with internal audiences, with the community, with the government, with investors, with consumers, with international audiences, and with special groups.

Effective public relations cases serve as models for students and practitioners alike. They enhance public relations theory, making it come alive with illustrations and examples of the PR process in action. Moreover, audience-centered cases exemplify the constraints involved in conducting research, setting objectives, designing and executing a program, and evaluating what has been done. In sum, cases, especially audience-centered cases, effectively illustrate public relations principles and management and test theoretical applications in real situations and environments.

NEW TECHNOLOGY

The most striking aspect of the cases included here is the pervasiveness of new technology, most notably the use of the Internet.

First generation "brochure-ware" websites are becoming more interactive. Websites are regularly used to conduct relations with a variety of publics. Organizations keep their media kits on the website in the form of news releases, background information, photographs, executive speeches, quarterly and annual reports to shareholders, position papers, interviews, and so forth. The sites provide means for e-mail feedback, registration, or chat rooms for collaboration. *New York Times* columnist Thomas L. Friedman suggested the convergence of new technologies has made this a "horizontal world" where global collaboration has become the skill that differentiates the best in their businesses.

E-mail has become the dominant form of communication both internally and externally. E-mail has virtually replaced internal print materials, such as newsletters, written memos, and some face-to-face communication. Externally, e-mail has become the major means of communicating news releases, media alerts, and other forms of media relations. E-mail also provides instant communication with consumers, investors, and a variety of other targeted publics.

Many organizations have created *intranets*—internal Internets—to handle large volumes of internal communication with employees and members. Some organizations also have created *extranets*—selective external Internets—to reach targeted external groups, such as investors, journalists, consumers, and others. CD-ROMs and DVDs also have become a major public relations tool, with vast storage and the potential for interaction with targeted groups. Instant Messaging has made online collaboration immediate, speeding both the flow of information and decision-making loops in organizations. Cell phone text messaging made computer e-mail portable and has even led to the rapid mobilization of street protests in many countries. Viral messaging uses the natural propensity of people to share information with others to spread organizational information.

Web logs, or blogs, allow anyone to becoming a publisher and to share personal opinions or their own "news." It has blurred the distinction between traditional journalism and other information sources. Some senior managers in organizations have established their own blogs to make sure the organization's positions are posted on this wider tableau of public opinion. Podcasting emerged as another tool for reaching audiences. With the popularity of "personal on-demand" players, podcasts became another way to share news, special events or personal opinions via the Internet. The rapid exchange of information and messages in this digital universe affects not only the way organizations must more quickly respond to an emergency, but has also impacted the practice of public relations in a major, ever-expanding way. It has both cluttered the message channels, and yet opened new avenues for connecting with publics.

ETHICS

The PRSA Member Code of Ethics (see Appendix II), adopted by the Public Relations Society of America Assembly in 2000, provides a way that each member "can daily reaffirm a commitment to ethical professional activities and decisions." The code of ethics first presents a set of core professional values that should guide all ethical practitioners of public relations. These values include responsible advocacy; honesty; expertise; independence (objective and responsible counsel to clients); loyalty to clients while serving the public interest; and fairness in dealing with clients, employers, competitors, the media, and the general public.

The second part of the code consists of such ethical principles of conduct as "protecting and advancing the free flow of accurate and truthful information," "promoting healthy and fair competition" among professional public relations practitioners, disclosing honest and accurate information in all communications, protecting "the privacy of clients, organizations, and individuals by safeguarding confidential information," "avoiding real, potential or perceived conflicts of interest," and working constantly to "strengthen the public's trust in the profession." All students of public relations, as well as long-time practitioners, should read the entire code.

This commitment to ethical practices on the part of PRSA is intended to counter the image of public relations practitioners as "hired guns" who will say or do whatever it takes to accomplish the goals of their clients. There is some basis for this negative public perception of the profession. The following is a discussion of some of the practices that have earned public relations a sometimes-less-than-savory reputation.

On a continuum going from bad to worse we might begin with the relatively innocuous practice of *lowballing*. This consists of downplaying expectations for a program or project that may not be especially successful in its outcome. The mass media frequently accuse the White House of "lowballing" a presidential visit abroad, a peace initiative in some part of the world, or some other effort that may not yield much tangible results.

Closely related to lowballing is the ubiquitous *spin* that is used by governmental and corporate public relations practitioners to make their programs look good. The "spin" actually consists of the one-sided use of facts or data to create a desired impression. These practitioners are often referred to by the mass media as *spin doctors*. By selectively using only positive aspects of a program or a political campaign, practitioners can portray their clients' activities in a favorable light. Conversely, the endeavors of an opponent may be selectively portrayed only in the negative.

Next we might examine six types of *distortion* sometimes found in the practice of public relations. The first of these is commonly called *hype*. Hype is the use of hyperbole or magnification, sometimes referred to as the "blowing out of proportion" of the attributes of a person, event, or product. The mass media are fond of portraying various criminal acts as "the crime of the century." Advertising constantly uses hype in its exaggerated claims for products and services, and public relations practitioners have been known to "stretch the truth" about clients and their programs.

A second type of distortion is *minimizing*, the exact opposite of hype. Sometimes practitioners will play down the seriousness of a failure or the negative aspects of a product or other problems experienced by a client.

A third type of frequently used distortion is *overgeneralization*, or drawing sweeping conclusions based on one isolated case or example. If a candidate for the presidential nomination of a political party loses the New Hampshire primary, for example, the mass media, along with the candidate's opposition, usually conclude that the nomination is lost, based on the results of that one primary election. Similarly, singular successes have been used to draw sweeping positive conclusions. One case study should never be the sole basis for such generalizations.

Categorization is a fourth type of distortion sometimes found in the practice of public relations. An example of categorization may involve the portrayal of a person, event, or product as "good" or "bad" with no middle ground or shades of gray. Other frequently used categories include "successful," "unsuccessful," "useful," "useless," and the like.

Closely related to categorization is the practice of *labeling*. An individual or program may be labeled either a "winner" or a "loser," often on the basis of sketchy or nonexistent evidence. History is replete with the use of such labels as "witch," "communist," "limousine liberal," and "right-wing conservative." The list could go on endlessly.

A final form of distortion may be called *image transfer*. This involves the deliberate shifting of image from one person, event, or product to another, but dissimilar, person, event, or product. Such advertising techniques as the identification of a product with an attractive or sexy model is perhaps the most frequent use of image transfer. Public relations practitioners also seek to transfer the high-credibility images of popular paid spokespersons to low-credibility or unknown programs, causes, or events.

In addition to lowballing, spinning, and a variety of distortions, we should consider the even more offensive practices of using outright *lies* and *coverups*. One example of these practices is the manufacturer that knows its product is defective and potentially dangerous. Instead of making this information public, the company blames accidents on improper consumer use and handles resulting litigation on a case-by-case basis. These case-by-case settlements are usually substantially less expensive than staging a product recall. Meanwhile, the company's public relations office is busy denying product fault, issuing statements blaming the consumer. In regard to coverups the defining event *that has become generic* in its field was the Watergate affair, a major turning point in American political history and the coverup by which all subsequent coverups have been measured.

This is by no means an exhaustive list of unethical public relations practices. The PRSA Member Code of Ethics cites other activities such as corruption of communication channels and other deceptive practices. For an understanding of the ethical practice of public relations, the student of public relations should carefully study the Member Code of Ethics in Appendix II, along with the unethical practices discussed here.

In the public relations workplace, the best argument for ethical practices is that they are "good business." The positive side is that the company or organization can point with pride to its ethical practices. The negative side is that, if an organization or client is caught by the ubiquitous mass media in an unethical practice, this will become a headline news story and perhaps blot out all previous positive accomplishments. This study of applied ethics should therefore become an overriding concern in the education of public relations practitioners.

THE OVERALL PLAN OF THIS BOOK

Part I introduces you to public relations, with special emphasis on the process outlined above. The elements of this process are eclectic, but the arrangement of those elements forms the acronym ROPE (research, objectives, programming, evaluation). A major feature is a new emphasis on and a new way of classifying public relations objectives. Objectives are viewed as the central and guiding element in the process, and they are arranged in a hierarchical order.

Another feature of this public relations process, consistent with its interactive nature, is a heightened emphasis on interpersonal interaction as a form of controlled communication. The importance of speeches and speakers' bureaus as methods of public relations communication is recognized, but this book also advocates the extensive use of small-group and dyadic (one-on-one) interpersonal formats, along with a treatment of nonverbal communication. A recurring theme is that in truly effective communication there can be no substitute for direct interaction.

Part II explores how public relations reaches major audiences. It looks at media relations; internal communication, including employee and member relations; community relations; public affairs, or government relations; investor and financial relations; consumer relations; international public relations; and relations with special publics. Following a conceptual treatment of each form of relations are several example cases. Most of these illustrative cases have won Silver Anvil Awards from the PRSA. As such, they represent the very best among models of public relations.

Part III concentrates on emergency public relations, an important area in contemporary practice. Both students and professionals need to be reminded of the need to study crisis PR procedures. Unlike such audience-centered forms as media relations or community relations, emergency PR is an area in which no one specializes. Yet all practitioners need to be prepared for it.

Part IV focuses on the newest development in the field: Integrated Marketing Communications, the combination of both public relations and advertising to accomplish essentially marketing objectives.

Finally, the appendixes include the PRSA Member Code of Ethics.

GENERAL PUBLIC RELATIONS READINGS

Austin, Erica Weintraub, and Bruce E. Pinkleton. *Strategic Public Relations Management.* Mahwah, NJ: Erlbaum, 2001.

Botan, Carl H., and Maureen Taylor. "Public Relations: State of the Field," *Journal of Communication* 54 (Dec. 1, 2004): 645–661.

Caywood, Clarke L., ed. *The Handbook of Strategic Public Relations and Integrated Communications.* New York: McGraw-Hill, 1997.

Center, Allen H., and Patrick Jackson. *Public Relations Practice: Managerial Case Studies and Practice,* 6th ed. Englewood Cliffs, NJ: Prentice-Hall, 2000.

Cutlip, Scott M., Allen H. Center, and Glen M. Broom. *Effective Public Relations,* 9th ed. Englewood Cliffs, NJ: Prentice-Hall, 2006.

Grunig, Larissa A., James E. Grunig, and David M. Dozier. *Excellent Public Relations and Effective Organizations.* Mahwah, NJ: Erlbaum, 2002.

Guth, David W., and Charles Marsh. *Public Relations: A Values-Driven Approach,* 3d ed. Boston: Allyn & Bacon, 2006.

Heath, Robert L. *Handbook of Public Relations.* Thousand Oaks, CA: Sage Publications, 2000.

Hunt, Todd, and James E. Grunig. *Public Relations Techniques,* 2d ed. Fort Worth, TX: Harcourt Brace, 1997.

Lamb, Lawrence F., and Kathy Brittain McKee. *Applied Public Relations.* Mahwah, NJ: Erlbaum, 2005.

Ledingham, John A., and Stephen D. Bruning. *Public Relations as Relationship Management.* Mahwah, NJ: Erlbaum, 2001.

Lesly, Philip, ed. *Lesly's Handbook of Public Relations and Communications,* 5th ed. New York: AMACOM, 1998.

Mickey, Thomas J. *Deconstructing Public Relations.* Mahwah, NJ: Erlbaum, 2002.

Mogel, Leonard. *Making It in Public Relations.* Mahwah, NJ: Erlbaum, 2002.

Newsom, Doug, Judy VanSlyke Turk, and Dean Kruckeberg. *This Is PR: The Realities of Public Relations,* 8th ed. Belmont, CA: Wadsworth, 2004.

Seitel, Fraser P. *The Practice of Public Relations,* 9th ed. Englewood Cliffs, NJ: Prentice-Hall, 2004.

Smith, Ronald D. *Strategic Planning for Public Relations,* 2d ed. Mahwah, NJ: Erlbaum, 2005.

Thomsen, Steven R. "Public Relations in the New Millennium: Understanding the Forces That Are Reshaping the Profession," *Public Relations Quarterly* 42 (spring 1997): 11–17.

Toth, Elizabeth L. *Public Relations Values in the New Millennium.* Mahwah, NJ: Erlbaum, 2000.

Wilcox, Dennis L. *Public Relations Writing and Media Techniques,* 5th ed. Boston: Allyn & Bacon, 2005.

Wilcox, Dennis L., Glen T. Cameron, Phillip H. Ault, and Warren K. Agee. *Public Relations: Strategies and Tactics,* 8th ed. Boston: Allyn & Bacon, 2006.

Zappala, Joseph M., and Ann R. Carden. *Public Relations Worktext,* 2d ed. Mahwah, NJ: Erlbaum, 2004.

GENERAL TRENDS AFFECTING PUBLIC RELATIONS

Friedman, Thomas L. *The World Is Flat: A Brief History of the Twenty-first Century*. New York: Farrar, Straus and Giroux, 2005.

Gladwell, Malcolm. *The Tipping Point: How Little Things Can Make a Big Difference*. New York: Little, Brown and Co., 2000.

## Chapter 2

A Public Relations Process

As we saw in Chapter 1, the public relations problem-solving process involves four procedures. First, initial research is performed to establish the basic elements of the communication transaction. Second, objectives for the transaction are established. Third, programming, including all the methods of communication used, is planned and executed to carry out the objectives. Finally, ongoing and follow-up evaluation is conducted both to monitor and to measure how well the program accomplished its objectives.

Now for a detailed look at each of the elements in this process.

RESEARCH

Research consists of investigating three aspects of the overall public relations procedure: the client or organization for whom the program is being prepared, the opportunity or problem that accounts for the program at this time, and all audiences to be targeted for communication in the PR program.

Client Research

First, public relations practitioners must be thoroughly familiar with their clients. If the practitioner is working in an in-house PR department, the client will be the organization housing the department. An employee of a PR firm will obviously be independent of the client. In either case, background data about the client or organization—its financial status, reputation, past and present public relations practices, and public relations strengths, weaknesses, and opportunities—are an essential starting point for any program.

If the organization is a business, the practitioner needs to be familiar with its products and services as well as the overall competitive environment. The practitioner should also know about the marketing, legal, and financial functions of the organization in order to coordinate them with the public relations efforts. Interviews with key management personnel and documents such as annual and quarterly reports can provide this information. The location of the organization, whether in a single city or in multiple branches, the delivery system for the products or services (such as the use of a dealer network), the organization's major suppliers, and, of course, the identity and demographics of the customers are all necessary to understand the client.

If the organization is nonprofit, the practitioner must become acquainted with the services provided and the organization's clientele, including major donors.

Other important background information includes the precise mission of the organization, its management's goals, priorities, and problems, and how this proposed public relations program might help accomplish these overall objectives.

Along with this background information the practitioner needs a good working knowledge of the organization's personnel—its total workforce, both management and nonmanagement. Special attention must be given to key management people, not just the director of public relations, if there is one. How does top management view the role of public relations? Are PR people regarded as problem solvers and decision makers, or are they simply "hired guns"?

The financial status of a publicly owned corporation is easy to determine. Financial data for such organizations must be reported to the U.S. Securities and Exchange Commission (SEC), and this information is always available in the company's annual report or other financial publications.

Finally, the practitioner needs to raise questions that directly relate to public relations. What is the client's reputation in its field and with its customers or clientele? The answers to these questions constitute the organization's public image, an area of primary concern to PR practitioners. What image liabilities or assets does the organization possess? What are its present and past public relations practices? Does the organization have particular PR strengths, that is, practices or programs that would enhance its public image? What are its PR weaknesses, the practices or programs that might create an unfavorable image or negative public opinion? What opportunities exist for promoting favorable public opinion or behavior toward the organization?

Thus, the first requisite for effective research in the public relations process is an in-depth understanding of the client for whom the program is prepared.

Opportunity or Problem Research

The second aspect of research, a logical outgrowth of knowledge of the client, consists of clearly determining why the organization should conduct a particular PR program at a particular time. Is it because of a unique opportunity to favorably influence public opinion or behavior toward the client, or is it in response to the development of unfavorable opinion or behavior toward the client? If it is the latter, extensive research must be done on the source of the problem, whether it be an individual or an organization.

Public relations programs that arise out of opportunities are called *proactive* programs. In the short run, effective proactive programming may seem extravagantly expensive to management, but these programs often head off the need to respond to problems with even more expensive *reactive* programs. The proactive program is like preventive medicine, or the concept of "wellness" now being widely promoted by health maintenance organizations. Preventive medicine is far more desirable than surgery in response to a severe illness. Similarly, an organization should keep close tabs on its ongoing relations with its constituent audiences to avoid PR problems.

This is not to argue that proactive programs are good and reactive programs are bad. In spite of all efforts to avert them, problems may develop. The reactive program then becomes necessary and perhaps beneficial. When a fire breaks out, we must call the fire department. Public relations practitioners must be ready to extinguish "fires," but they should also be skilled in "fire prevention."

Because they are preventive, proactive programs are generally long range in nature. The organization cannot afford to let its guard down in maintaining good relations with important audiences. Reactive programs, on the other hand, are usually short range, often ending as soon as the immediate problem is cleared up. But a good, ongoing, proactive program with the same audience may prevent the recurrence of similar problems.

Thus, an investigation of why a public relations program is necessary, whether it should be proactive or reactive, and whether it should be ongoing or short range is the second aspect of research in the public relations process.

Audience Research

The third aspect of research in the public relations process involves investigating the target audiences, or "publics." This part of the research process includes identifying the particular groups that should be targeted, determining appropriate research data that will be useful in communicating with these publics, and compiling or processing the data using appropriate research procedures.

Audience Identification. All organizations have long-range, and sometimes short-term, "relations," or communications, with certain "standard" publics. The publics of principal concern to most organizations include the media, internal employees or members, the organization's home community, and the national, state, and local governments. A business that provides a product or service for customers is concerned with consumers as an important public. A publicly owned business has the additional, significant audience of its shareowners and the financial community. Finally, all organizations have unique groups of constituent audiences, or special publics. Nonprofit organizations are concerned with donors as a special public. Schools are interested in maintaining communications with parents. Large corporations may need to communicate regularly with their dealers and suppliers.

To address publics most effectively, we should segment each public into its diverse components, so each component may become a separate public to be targeted for special messages. The media, for example, should be segmented into mass and specialized groups. Of the two internal publics, employees should be segmented into management and nonmanagement, and members should be divided into organization employees, officers, members, prospective members, state or local chapters, and related or allied organizations (see Chapter 4). The organization's home community should be segmented into community media, community leaders, and community organizations. Government publics should be subdivided into federal, state, county, and city levels; then each of these levels should be further segmented into legislative and executive branches. Consumer publics can be subdivided into groupings that include company employees, customers, activist consumer groups, consumer publications, community media, and community leaders and organizations (see Chapter 8). Investor publics for financial relations should be segmented into shareowners and potential shareowners, security analysts and investment counselors, the financial press, and the SEC. (See Exhibit 2-a for suggested segmentation of these major publics.)

Targeting.   Once the publics have been identified and segmented into their components, the practitioner is ready for the more difficult task of targeting the most important publics on a priority basis. This *prioritizing* calls for a situational assessment of the significance to the client or organization of each potential public. The importance of a potential public is determined by its degree of influence, prestige, power, or perhaps need, and by its level of involvement with the client or organization. Four key questions to consider in targeting and prioritizing publics are:

- Who is this public (demographics, psychographics, and so on)?
- Why is it important to us?
- How active or involved is this public, relative to our interests?
- Which publics are most important to us, in priority rank order?

Desired Data.   Once target publics have been segmented into their key components, the practitioner is ready to assess informational needs for each public. Typically, the practitioner will want to know each targeted public's level of information about the organization; the image and other relevant attitudes held about the organization and its product or service; and past and present audience behaviors relevant to the client or organization. Researching the demographics, media habits, and levels of media use of each targeted audience will tell the practitioner how best to reach it. All these data are used to formulate objectives for the public relations program.

Research Methods

With this general framework of informational needs in mind, the practitioner must next decide which research procedures will yield the necessary data. Public relations people use two general methods of research: *nonquantitative* and *quantitative*.

Nonquantitative Research.   One source of nonquantitative data is organization or client *records* (business reports, statistics, financial reports, past public relations records) and communications (speeches by executives, newsletters, news releases, memorandums, pamphlets, brochures).

EXHIBIT 2-A   *Major Publics*

Media Publics

Mass media
   Local
      Print publications
         Newspapers
         Magazines
      TV stations
      Radio stations
   National
      Print publications
      Broadcast networks
      Wire services
Specialized media
   Local
      Trade, industry, and association publications
      Organizational house and membership publications
      Ethnic publications
      Publications of special groups
      Specialized broadcast programs and stations
   National
      General business publications
      National trade, industry, and association publications
      National organizational house and membership publications
      National ethnic publications
      Publications of national special groups
      National specialized broadcast programs and networks

Employee Publics

Management
   Upper-level administrators
   Midlevel administrators
   Lower-level administrators
Nonmanagement (staff)
   Specialists

EXHIBIT 2-A *Major Publics (continued)*

Clerical personnel

Secretarial personnel

Uniformed personnel

  Equipment operators

  Drivers

  Security personnel

  Other uniformed personnel

Union representatives

Other nonmanagement personnel

Member Publics

Organization employees

  Headquarters management

  Headquarters nonmanagement (staff)

  Other headquarters personnel

Organization officers

  Elected officers

  Appointed officers

  Legislative groups

  Boards, committees

Organization members

  Regular members

  Members in special categories—sustaining, emeritus, student members

  Honorary members or groups

Prospective organization members

State or local chapters

  Organization employees

  Organization officers

  Organization members

  Prospective organization members

Related or other allied organizations

Community Publics

Community media

  Mass

  Specialized

Community leaders
  Public officials
  Educators
  Religious leaders
  Professionals
  Executives
  Bankers
  Union leaders
  Ethnic leaders
  Neighborhood leaders
Community organizations
  Civic
  Service
  Social
  Business
  Cultural
  Religious
  Youth
  Political
  Special interest groups
  Other

Government Publics

Federal
  Legislative branch
    Representatives, staff, committee personnel
    Senators, staff, committee personnel
  Executive branch
    President
    White House staff, advisers, committees
    Cabinet officers, departments, agencies, commissions
State
  Legislative branch
    Representatives, delegates, staff, committee personnel
    Senators, staff, committee personnel
  Executive branch
    Governor

EXHIBIT 2-A *Major Publics (continued)*

        Governor's staff, advisers, committees

        Cabinet officers, departments, agencies, commissions

County

   County executive

   Other county officials, commissions, departments

City

   Mayor or city manager

   City council

   Other city officials, commissions, departments

Investor Publics

Shareowners and potential shareowners

Security analysts and investment counselors

Financial press

   Major wire services: Dow Jones & Co., Reuters Economic Service, AP, UPI, Bloomberg

   Major business magazines: *Business Week, Fortune,* and the like—mass circulation and specialized

   Major newspapers: *New York Times, Wall Street Journal*

   Statistical services: Standard & Poor's Corp., Moody's Investor Service, and the like

   Private wire services: PR News Wire, Business Wire

Securities and Exchange Commission (SEC), for publicly owned companies

Consumer Publics

Company employees

Customers

   Professionals

   Middle class

   Working class

   Minorities

   Other

Activist consumer groups

Consumer publications

Community media, mass and specialized
Community leaders and organizations

International Publics

Host country media
  Mass
  Specialized
Host country leaders
  Public officials
  Educators
  Social leaders
  Cultural leaders
  Religious leaders
  Political leaders
  Professionals
  Executives
Host country organizations
  Business
  Service
  Social
  Cultural
  Religious
  Political
  Special interests
  Other

Special Publics

Media consumed by this public
  Mass
  Specialized
Leaders of this public
  Public officials
  Professional leaders
  Ethnic leaders
  Neighborhood leaders
Organizations composing this public
  Civic
  Political

EXHIBIT 2-A *Major Publics (continued)*

Service

Business

Cultural

Religious

Youth

Other

Integrated Marketing Communications

Customers

New Customers

Old Customers

Potential Customers

Employees

Management

Nonmanagement

Media

Mass

Specialized

Investors

Shareowners and potential shareowners

Financial analysts

Financial press

Suppliers

Competitors

Government Regulators

A second source of nonquantitative data is *published materials*. These include news articles from mass media and trade publications, published surveys or polls, library references, government documents, directories, and published trade association data.

Third, nonquantitative research can be conducted through interviews or conversations with *key members of targeted publics*. Important civic leaders, elected officials, business leaders, religious leaders, educators, influential editors, reporters, and other key individuals in the community can provide invaluable background information for a public relations program.

Fourth, feedback from the client's *customers* or *clientele* can be helpful as a means of nonquantitative research. Customer responses may come via telephone, mail, e-mail, or face-to-face interactions.

Fifth, talking with *organized groups* with an interest in the client can be useful. These groups may include the organization's formal advisory boards, committees, commissions, or panels from inside or outside the organization.

Sixth, the World Wide Web has become an essential source of information for public relations practitioners. Among the most popular and useful of the Web's search sites are Google, Yahoo!, AltaVista, Excite, HotBot, Infoseek, and Lycos. Meta–search engines include Dogpile, Inference Find, MyExcite, Mamma Metasearch, Ask Jeeves, and MetaCrawler; and specialized search services include Deja News, which searches for newsgroups; Liszt, a directory of list servers; and Who Where for finding people.

Finally, groups created especially for research purposes can provide valuable insight. The most popular form of this procedure is the *focus group,* usually consisting of 8 to 12 people who are representative of the audience the client wishes to reach. A moderator who is skilled in interviewing and group-process management encourages the participants of the focus group to consider the client's image, products, services, and communication proposals, or other issues affecting the client. The focus-group meetings are usually videotaped and carefully studied to identify and analyze participants' reactions and comments.

Some researchers are experimenting with new ways to conduct surveys and focus groups using the Internet. For example, chat rooms provide a way to bring diverse audiences into a focus group setting.

It should be emphasized that although these seven methods of nonquantitative research may yield useful data regarding all areas of concern in the research process, the data will not be scientifically reliable. For a scientific level of reliability, statistical research methods must be used.

Quantitative Research.   Three methods of quantitative research are widely used in public relations: sample surveys, experiments, and content analysis. The key to each is the use of statistical methods.

The *sample survey* is the most frequently used quantitative research method in the public relations process. It is most useful in determining audience information levels, attitudes, behaviors, and media habits. Surveys can be conducted by mail, by telephone, or in person, with cost increasing in that order.

Mail questionnaires (both regular and e-mail) are the least expensive survey method because of lower staffing requirements. They can yield more data because length is no problem and respondents can give thorough answers. The major problem with such questionnaires is the low response rate. Unless the intended respondents have a high level of interest in the subject, mail questionnaires can be a big waste of the researcher's time and money.

Telephone interviews have become the most popular means of conducting surveys. Sampling can be done using the random digit dialing technique and an ordinary telephone directory. Although more expensive than mail questionnaires, telephone interviews provide a more economical use of staff time. The limitations of communicating by voice alone may hamper the rapport between interviewer and respondent since the interviewer cannot make judgments about accuracy and sincerity based on nonverbal cues. Nonetheless, telephone interviewing has become the first choice in the conduct of sample surveys.

Personal interviews remain an important, though expensive and time-consuming, survey method. The interviewer can make judgments based on the respondent's nonverbal as well as verbal cues, so no survey method is more accurate. Getting a good sample, however, is much more difficult than with the random digit dialing technique used for telephone interviews. Many people are reluctant to consent to a personal interview because of the time and inconvenience involved. As with mail questionnaires, personal interviews are most effective with respondents who are truly interested in the subject and willing to sacrifice their time.

With all their limitations, and with the onus of being considered "quick and dirty" by most social and behavioral scientists, surveys remain the most popular of quantitative research methods used in public relations.

Controlled experiments have been gaining in popularity in recent years, however. Conducted either in laboratory settings or in the field, experiments are the most accurate indicator of causality in the behavioral sciences. Experiments are often used in advertising or public relations to determine which forms of communication or messages may be most effective with selected audiences. In the experimental method, two groups of subjects are randomly chosen. One group is exposed to the communication media, and the other is not. Both groups are tested before and after the communication exposure. If the responses of the exposed group change significantly after the communication, then these responses can be attributed causally to the messages.

A third quantitative method of research often used in public relations is *content analysis*. This systematic procedure is used in analyzing themes or trends in the message content of selected media. Content analysis can be used to learn how the media are treating clients—their public image as reflected in the media, negative or positive coverage, and the like. This research procedure is also useful in issues management, in which practitioners identify and analyze the impact of public issues on a client's corporate or organizational interests. Thus, content analysis can be helpful in the evaluation of media treatment in the publicity process and in tracking social, economic, or political trends or issues that may affect clients.

Quantitative research should be conducted only by professional firms with good reputations in their field or by staff members who are trained and experienced researchers. Public relations staff members who have not received formal training in research techniques will waste the client's time and money. Worse, their work will probably be inaccurate and misleading.

With the public relations program's informational needs satisfied through nonquantitative or quantitative research methods, the practitioner is ready to attend to the second phase of the process—that of formulating objectives.

OBJECTIVES

Objectives are the single most important element in this public relations process. They represent the practitioner's desired outcomes in communicating with the targeted publics. They are the raison d'être for PR programs. Some writers draw a distinction between "goals" as more general outcomes and "objectives" as specific, immediate results. Here we avoid that confusion by consistently using one term to signify desired program outcomes, and that term is *objectives*. Whether they are to be broad or narrow, long-range or short-range, they should be stipulated in the statement of the objective itself. Before we discuss the types of objectives used in public relations, we should examine the method used in formulating such objectives.

Many organizations are now using management by objectives (MBO) to determine both general organizational objectives and those for individual work units, such as the public relations department. MBO is a well-established procedure that involves cooperative goal setting by groups of superiors and subordinates in the employee hierarchy. For example, the director of public relations and the assistant director may represent management, and various writers, graphics specialists, and other staff members may represent the "subordinates" in the MBO process. Together they devise short-term and long-range objectives and evaluation procedures for the work unit and for its particular programs. Then, using these procedures, both groups cooperatively evaluate their work at agreed-on times. They also periodically review and revise their objectives and evaluation procedures.

Our concern here is with objectives for individual PR programs. Regardless of whether such objectives are determined using MBO or more traditional authoritarian means, two criteria apply to all program objectives.

First, objectives should be stated in the form of infinitive phrases, each containing one infinitive and each being a specific and separately measurable desired outcome. An infinitive phrase consists of to plus a verb plus the complement, or receiver of the verb's action. For example, a practitioner may hope that, after the PR program is executed, the audience will be informed that a special event is taking place and will attend the event. The phrasing of the objectives in infinitive form could be:

- To publicize special event X
- To stimulate attendance at special event X

These objectives could be combined — to publicize and stimulate attendance at special event X — but this compound phrasing would complicate the measurement or evaluation of both objectives.

Second, public relations objectives should be verifiable. To be verifiable, the desired outcome should be stated in quantified, measurable terms, and a time frame or target date should be set for its accomplishment. Although the objectives just stated meet our infinitive test, they are not stated specifically in quantitative or chronological terms. Thus, they can be reworded:

- To publicize special event X through the community's daily newspaper, its TV station, and its three radio stations during the month of October
- To stimulate an attendance of at least 1,500 persons at special event X on May 15

We can measure the first objective by determining, through the use of a clipping service and a broadcast media monitoring service, how many media outlets actually used the announcement of the special event. We can measure the second objective by checking actual attendance figures or ticket sales at the event itself.

Two basic types of objectives are used in public relations programs: *impact objectives* and *output objectives*. Together, they can be viewed as a hierarchy in ascending order of importance (see Exhibit 2-b). Within each category, however, there is no performance hierarchy or order of importance. For example, informational objectives need not be completed before attitudinal or behavioral objectives, and the importance of each of these subsets of impact objectives is purely situational.

Output Objectives

Output objectives, the lower category in the hierarchy, represent the work to be produced, that is, the distribution or execution of program materials. Some writers refer to these activities as "process objectives," "support objectives," or "program effort." Whatever the terminology, these activities should not be confused with desired program impacts.

EXHIBIT 2-B	*A Hierarchy of Public Relations Objectives*

Impact Objectives

Informational objectives

Message exposure

Message comprehension

Message retention

Attitudinal objectives

Attitude creation

Attitude reinforcement

Attitude change

Behavioral objectives

Behavior creation

Behavior reinforcement

Behavior change

Output Objectives

Distribution of uncontrolled media

Distribution or execution of controlled media

Output objectives, as discussed here, refer to stated intentions regarding program production and effort (or output). They are classified as a form of objective because they describe a type of desired outcome often stated in public relations programs. In fact, the PRSA's Silver Anvil winners use a much higher percentage of output objectives than impact objectives. In the best of all possible worlds, PR directors would use only impact objectives. But here it seems appropriate to deal with PR objectives as they actually exist in the real world. Such objectives can easily be made specific and quantitative. For example:

- To send one news release to each of the community's major media outlets: its daily newspaper, its TV station, and its three radio stations by May 10

- To make an oral presentation to an important conference of security analysts in each of the following five cities: New York, Los Angeles, Chicago, Houston, and Denver, before December 15

These objectives can then be measured easily by counting the number of news releases actually sent to the media outlets and the number of oral presentations actually made to security analysts. Time frames can be added if desired.

Some practitioners use only output objectives in their public relations programs. The advantage of such usage is that output objectives set definite, specific, and attainable goals, which can be measured quantitatively. Once these goals have been met, the practitioner can claim success. Unfortunately, output objectives are unrelated to the actual impact the program may have on its intended audiences, and for this we must move to the top, and more significant, category in our hierarchy of public relations objectives.

Impact Objectives

There are three kinds of impact objectives: informational, attitudinal, and behavioral. These are called impact objectives because they represent specific intended effects of public relations programs on their audiences.

Informational Objectives. Informational objectives include message exposure to, message comprehension by, and/or message retention by the target public. Such objectives are appropriate when the practitioner wishes to publicize an action or event; seeks to communicate instructions, operating procedures, or other forms of information; or wants to educate an audience about a noncontroversial subject. Two examples of informational objectives are:

- To increase awareness of the company's open house (by 10 percent) among all segments of the community (during the month of May)
- To increase employee awareness of new plant safety procedures (by 50 percent during our three-month safety campaign)

Attitudinal Objectives. Attitudinal objectives aim at modifying the way an audience feels about the client or organization and its work, products, or services. Attitude modification may consist of forming new attitudes where none exist, reinforcing existing attitudes, or changing existing attitudes.

There will probably be no public attitudes toward a completely new organization. The task of public relations, then, will be the creation of favorable attitudes toward the organization. Two examples of such objectives are:

- To create favorable public attitudes toward a new department store (among 25 percent of mall shoppers during the grand opening celebration)
- To promote favorable attitudes toward a company's new retirement policy (among 80 percent of current employees during the current fiscal year)

It should be stressed that this type of attitudinal objective (forming new attitudes) applies only to organizations and actions that are not controversial and therefore have not generated prior audience attitudes. Some new organizations or actions immediately create reactions among affected groups. In these cases, objectives that seek to reinforce or change existing attitudes are more appropriate.

The second form of attitudinal objective has as its goal the reinforcement, enhancement, or intensification of existing attitudes. A given audience may have moderately favorable, but weak, attitudes toward an organization. In this case, public relations may seek to strengthen these attitudes through a variety of actions, events, or communications. An example of this might be:

- To reinforce favorable public opinion toward a nonprofit organization (among 80 percent of its past donors during March and April)

The final form of attitudinal objective is the changing, or reversing, of (usually negative) existing attitudes. In this case, the practitioner must be careful not to take on a "Mission Impossible." The reversal of attitudes is, of course, the most difficult of all tasks in public relations, so the old military adage "Don't fight a losing battle" may serve as a useful guideline here. Attitude or behavior reversal takes time and, as a rule, it cannot be accomplished with one short-range PR campaign. When Ivy Lee attempted to reverse the public image of John D. Rockefeller, Sr., the task took years. Little by little, Lee was successful in converting Rockefeller's image from that of the ogre responsible for the deaths of Colorado miners and their families to the image of a beloved philanthropist. Many practitioners would rightly have regarded such an enormous task as a "losing battle," given the resources of most individuals or organizations. But with unlimited Rockefeller money, the task was finally accomplished.

Sometimes the practitioner will seek to reverse existing positive attitudes. For example, some Republicans in Congress (and in the White House) have attempted to portray many of the government's social programs in a negative light, although most of these programs have enjoyed great popularity since their inception during President Franklin D. Roosevelt's New Deal era.

Two examples of objectives that seek attitude change are:

- To reverse (within a period of one year) the negative attitudes and ill will now being expressed toward the manufacturer of a defective product (among 20 percent of the manufacturer's former and current customers)
- To change the favorable attitudes that exist regarding the proposed program (among 10 percent of the members of the U.S. Congress before the vote on the bill)

Attitudinal objectives, then, may involve any of three goals: formation of new attitudes where none exist, reinforcement of existing attitudes, or change in existing attitudes.

Behavioral Objectives. Behavioral objectives involve the modification of behavior toward the client or organization. Like attitude modification, behavior modification may consist of the creation or stimulation of new behavior, the enhancement or intensification of existing favorable behavior, or the reversal of negative behavior on the part of an audience toward the practitioner's client or organization.

Examples of the creation of new behavior might include:

- To accomplish adoption of new safety procedures (among 75 percent of the organization's employees by September 15)
- To persuade (60 percent of) persons over the age of 50 to regularly take a colon cancer test (during the next two years)
- To stimulate new diet procedures (among 70 percent) of children in the city school system (during the current school year)

Enhancement or intensification of existing positive behaviors might involve such objectives as:

- To encourage (30 percent) greater usage of seat belts in automobiles (this year)
- To stimulate (50 percent) higher attendance at meetings by association members (during the next national convention)

The reversal of negative behaviors could include:

- To discourage defacement of public monuments (by 20 percent) in a city park (over a period of eight months)
- To discourage smoking (by 80 percent) in the east wing of the restaurant (during the next three months)

Objectives, as presented here, result from and are shaped by the findings revealed in the research phase. As mentioned earlier, research data should be sought in the area of audience information levels, attitudes, behaviors, and media habits. If information levels about the client or related matters are low, then informational objectives are called for in the public relations program. If audience attitudes toward the client are nonexistent, weak, or negative, then the practitioner will know the kinds of attitudinal objectives to formulate. Finally, if desired audience behaviors are nonexistent, weak, or negative, the practitioner will have a framework for developing appropriate behavioral objectives. Data regarding audience media habits may not contribute directly to the formulation of program objectives, but these findings are useful in determining appropriate media usage in the programming phase of the process.

In addition to impact objectives, the practitioner may devise output objectives for each PR program. These objectives are of less significance because they represent outcomes that have nothing to do with program effects on target audiences.

In the public relations process, objectives precede and govern programming decisions. The degree of influence these objectives exert can best be seen in the programming phase itself.

PROGRAMMING

Public relations programming, as presented in this process, includes the following elements of planning and execution:

1. Stating a theme, if applicable, and the messages to be communicated to the audiences
2. Planning the action or special event(s) sponsored by the client
3. Planning the use of the media, either uncontrolled or controlled
4. Effectively communicating the program

Theme and Messages

The first element of a program, its theme and messages, should encompass the program's entire scope and must be carefully planned in conjunction with the action or special event central to the program.

The program theme should be catchy and memorable. The best themes are in the form of short slogans consisting of no more than five words. Not all programs require themes or slogans, but a brief, creative theme can become the most memorable part of the entire public relations effort.

Most PR programs will have one central message epitomized in such a slogan or theme. In some cases, programs may have several messages, possibly one for each separate audience. The practitioner should work out as concisely as possible just what is to be communicated to each audience during the entire program.

Action[s] or Special Event[s]

A central action or a special event to be sponsored by the client should be considered along with the program's theme and message. The client's actions or events will usually be the focal point of the theme and messages, although some PR programs omit this element and concentrate on theme and messages alone. However, it is highly recommended that programs be action oriented. A central action or event can make most programs more newsworthy, interesting, and effective. To best advance the public image of the client, this action or event should be substantive, usually serious, and in the public interest. It will be most effective if the event involves large numbers of people and includes the presence of at least one celebrity. Shallow "pseudoevents" should be avoided; they sometimes do more harm than good by damaging the client's credibility. For the most part, gimmicks and stunts are best left to carnivals and circuses. There are exceptions, of course. Sometimes carnivals, circuses, beauty pageants, and similar activities can be presented as a means of raising funds for worthy causes. If these events can be seen as serving the public interest, they may enhance the client's credibility. Typical public relations actions and special events are included in Exhibit 2-c.

Uncontrolled and Controlled Media

The two forms of communication used in public relations are usually classified as *uncontrolled* and *controlled media.*

The use of uncontrolled media involves the communication of news about the client or organization to the mass media and to specialized media outlets. Specifically, the decision-making editors of these outlets become the target audiences for uncontrolled media. The objective of this form of communication is favorable news coverage of the client's actions and events. The standard formats used to communicate client news to the media include news releases, feature stories, captioned photographs or photo opportunities, and news conferences. A more complete listing of these formats can be found in Exhibit 2-d. They are called uncontrolled media because the practitioner loses control of these materials at the media outlet itself. An editor may choose to use the practitioner's release or feature story in its entirety, partially, or not at all; or editors may send reporters who will write or videotape their own stories about the client, ignoring the practitioner's efforts. Because the client or practitioner does not pay the media outlet to use the story as advertising, the use of the material is at the complete discretion of the media outlet.

The use of controlled media, on the other hand, involves communication about the client that is paid for by the client. The wording of the material, its format, and its placement in the media are all at the discretion of the client. The formats for controlled media include print materials such as brochures, newsletters, and reports; audiovisual materials such as films, slide shows, and PowerPoint (a program for providing a kind of slide show on a laptop computer); and interpersonal communication such as speeches, meetings, and interviews. Also included in controlled media are institutional advertising aimed at enhancing the client's image, advocacy advertising that communicates the client's stand on a controversial issue, and other forms of nonproduct advertising. Increasingly indispensable are the ubiquitous Web pages and websites, which can contain large amounts of information about the client. Exhibit 2-d includes a more detailed listing of the forms of controlled media.

EXHIBIT 2-C *Actions and Special Events*

Special days, nights, weeks, months

Displays and exhibits

Trade shows and exhibitions

Fairs, festivals, expositions

Meetings, conferences, conventions, congresses, rallies

Anniversaries, memorial events

Special awards, retirements, salutes

Open houses, plant tours

Town meetings, public debates, parties

Coffee hours, teas

Contests

Parades, pageants, beauty contests

Sponsoring community events

Sponsoring organizations (community youth organizations, Little League, Junior Achievement Organization)

Sponsoring scholarships, contributions

Creating charitable and educational foundations

Receptions

Concert tours, theatrical tours

Performing and graphic arts tours

Visits, pleasure tours for selected publics and groups

Picnics, outings, cookouts, barbecues

Nature trails, flower shows

Ground-breaking ceremonies, cornerstone layings, safety programs

Product demonstrations

Traveling demonstrations, home demonstrations

Visits by dignitaries, celebrities

Guest lectures, kickoffs, farewells, going-aways, welcome-backs, welcoming ceremonies

Elections of officers

Issuing reports or statistics

Announcing results of polls or surveys

Grand openings

Announcing an appointment

EXHIBIT 2-C   *Actions and Special Events (continued)*

Announcing a new policy or policy change

Announcing a new program, product, or service

Announcing important news about the client or organization

Public relations personalities (Miss America, Miss Universe, Maid of Cotton)

Dedications

School commencements, assemblies, events, convocations

Fetes, galas, proms, dances, balls, disco parties

Banquets, luncheons, breakfasts, dinners, buffets

Art shows, openings, exhibits

Concerts, plays, ballets

Film festivals, fashion shows

Animal shows (dogs, cats, birds)

Sporting events, ski trips, ocean cruises, pack trips, hikes, marathons, bike-a-thons, swim-a-thons, miscellaneous-a-thons, races

Celebrity sporting events, cruises

Museum tours, home tours

Embassy tours

Celebrity appearances, autograph-signing ceremonies

Car washes, neighborhood cleanups, services for the elderly

Health screening tests

Committee hearings

Training programs

Opinion-leader meetings and conferences

Special education programs: thrift education, health education, conservation education

Leadership programs

Participation in community events

Celebrations of national holidays

Theme events and celebrations: "Roaring Twenties," "Old New Orleans," "Colonial New England," "Ancient Greece"

Events honoring other nations or cultures

Events honoring the client or organization

EXHIBIT 2-D *Uncontrolled and Controlled Media*

Uncontrolled Media

News releases—print and video news releases (VNRs)

Feature stories

Photographs with cutlines (captions) or photo opportunities

News conferences

Media kits—paper or CD-ROM format

Radio/TV public service announcements (PSAs) (nonprofit organizations only)

Interviews

   Print media

   Broadcast media

Personal appearances on broadcast media

News tapes for radio

News slides and films for TV

Special programs for radio and TV

Recorded telephone news capsules and updates from an institution

Informing and influencing editors, broadcast news and public service directors, columnists, and reporters (phone calls, e-mail, tip sheets, newsletters with story leads, media advisories)

Business feature articles

Financial publicity

Product publicity

Pictorial publicity

Background editorial material (backgrounders and fact sheets)

Letters to the editor

Op-ed pieces

Controlled Media

Print communication methods

   House publications

   Brochures, information pieces

   Handbooks, manuals, books

   Letters, bulletins, memos

   Bulletin boards, posters, flyers

   Information racks

EXHIBIT 2-D *Uncontrolled and Controlled Media (continued)*

E-mail

External periodicals: opinion-leader periodicals, corporate general public periodicals, distributor-dealer periodicals, stockholder periodicals, supplier periodicals, periodicals for special publics

Annual reports

Commemorative stamps

Exhibits and displays

Mobile libraries, bookmobiles

Mobile displays

Attitude or information surveys

Suggestion boxes, systems

Instructions and orders

Pay inserts

Written reports

Billing inserts

Financial statement inserts

Training kits, aids, manuals

Consumer information kits

Legislative information kits

Teacher kits, student games

Teacher aids

Print window displays

Audiovisual communication methods

Institutional videos

Slide shows

Opaque projectors, flannel boards, easel pad presentations

Transparencies for overhead projectors

Telephone calls, phone banks, dial-a-somethings, recorded messages

Multimedia exhibits and displays

Audio tapes, CD-ROMs, and cassettes

Videotapes and DVDs

Visual and multimedia window displays

Oral presentations with visuals

Multimedia training aids

    PowerPoint (other software provides similar presentation capabilities such as UPresent and Medi@Show, multimedia managers, and iGrafx Designer and StarOffice-OpenOffice Impress)

    Teacher aids, student games

Specially equipped vans, trains, buses, boats, airplanes, blimps

Interpersonal communication methods

Formal speeches, lectures, seminars

Roundtable conferences

Panel discussions

Question-and-answer discussions

Oral testimony

Employee counseling

Legal, medical, birth-control, miscellaneous counseling

Committee meetings

Staff meetings

Informal conversations

Demonstrations

Speakers bureaus: recruiting and training speakers, speech preparation, clearance of materials with management, list of subjects, speakers' guide, engagements and bookings, visual aids, follow-up correspondence

Training programs

Interviews

Personal instructions

Social affairs

Face-to-face reports

Public relations advertising (not designed to stimulate product sales)

Print and broadcast advertising

Institutional advertising—image building

Public affairs (advocacy) advertising: institutional or organizational statements on controversial issues

Direct mail institutional advertising

Outdoor advertising: billboards, signs

Yellow Pages institutional advertising

Transit advertising, skywriting, fly-by advertising

Specialty items: calendars, ashtrays, pens, matchbooks, emery boards, memo pads

Websites

Effective Communication

The final aspect of programming is the effective communication of the program. Thus, the factors of source, message, channel, receivers, and feedback will be useful in our examination of communication principles. That is, effective communication depends on:

1. Source credibility
2. Salient information (message)
3. Effective nonverbal cues (message)
4. Effective verbal cues (message)
5. Two-way communication (channel and feedback)
6. Opinion leaders (receivers)
7. Group influence (receivers)
8. Selective exposure (receivers)
9. Audience participation (feedback)

Source Credibility.   The success or failure of the entire public relations transaction can hinge on how the *source* of communication, the spokesperson for the client or organization, is perceived by the intended audience. Credibility involves a set of perceptions about sources held by receivers or audiences. The personal characteristics of believable sources that continually appear in communication research are trustworthiness, expertise, dynamism, physical attractiveness, and perceived similarities between the source and receivers.[1] These characteristics should serve the PR practitioner as guidelines for selecting individuals to represent the client or organization. Communication coming from high-credibility sources will clearly be in the best interests of the PR program.

Salient Information.   A second principle of effective communication involves the use of salient information in the client's messages addressed to target audiences. Members of audiences can be viewed as information processors whose attitudes and behaviors are influenced by their integration of significant new information into their preexisting beliefs.[2] This is another way of saying that the message content must be motivational for the intended audiences—it must strike responsive chords in their minds. Information that is not salient to a given audience in a given context should be discarded.

Nonverbal Cues.   A third principle of effective communication involves the use of appropriate nonverbal cues in the PR program's messages. Countless volumes have been published on a variety of aspects of nonverbal communication. But for purposes of effective programming, the PR practitioner should closely examine the nature of the client's actions or special events that are to serve as a basis for the overall effort. Choosing appropriate symbols to represent the client or the cause can be the most important aspect of nonverbal communication. Questions involving the mood, or atmosphere, desired at the event, the personnel to be used, the guests to be invited, the setting, the forms of interpersonal interaction, and the scheduling should be raised. These are essential details that can make the difference between success and failure for the client. Exhibit 2-e provides more details useful in planning effective nonverbal communication for the client.

Verbal Cues.   The use of effective verbal message cues, or the actual wording of the client's messages, is the fourth principle of communication considered here. The two most important characteristics of effective language usage are *clarity* and *appropriateness*.

To be clear, language must be accurate. The forms of communication used in a PR program should use words precisely, so the practitioner may need to consult a dictionary or thesaurus. Messages should be tested with a small audience to eliminate ambiguity before their actual use in a PR program. In addition to accuracy, simplicity of word choice contributes to language clarity. Why use big words when simple ones will do? Audiences will relate to such words as *try* better than *endeavor, help* better than *facilitate, explain* better than *explicate, tell* better than *indicate*, and *learn* better than *ascertain*. Finally, coherence is an important factor in clear language. The words in a message should be logically connected — they should hang together well. The use of simple sentences rather than compound or complex ones contributes to coherence. Clear transitions and summaries in messages also aid coherence. Accuracy, simplicity, and coherence, then, are the major factors in constructing clear messages.

Messages should also be appropriate to the client, the audience, and the occasion. If the client is the city's leading bank, some levels of language may be inappropriate. Language used by a fast-food chain is different from that used in the messages of a funeral home. Similarly, language must be appropriate to the demographic level of the audience. Teenagers will obviously respond to a different use of language than senior citizens. The occasion for the use of the message also influences the level and type of language to be used. A diplomatic function held in a Washington embassy requires a different level of language from that used at a locker room gathering of an athletic team. Thus, appropriateness and clarity are the two major requisites for effectiveness in the use of verbal message cues.

Two-Way Communication.   The fifth principle of effective communication involves two-way interaction. Communication was once considered a linear process involving the transmission of a message from a source

---

EXHIBIT 2-E   *Nonverbal Communication*

Appropriate symbols

Mood or atmosphere desired: excitement, quiet dignity

Organizational personnel involved, including spokesperson(s) to be used

   Demographics of the audience: white/anglo, African American, Hispanic, Jewish, Asian, Arab (if applicable)

   Appearance, dress, actions/interactions expected

Guests: appearance and dress expected

Setting

   Buildings, rooms, or exterior environment desired

   Colors

   Background: banner, logo

   Lighting

   Sound system

   Nature and use of space

   Types and arrangement of furniture, seating arrangements

   Other artifacts to be used: paintings, wall tapestries, sports banners, colored balloons

   Nature of central presentation appropriate for setting (vice versa)

   Music: type, volume

   Entertainment (if any)

   Food, beverages, refreshments (if any)

Forms of interpersonal interaction: sit-down dinner, stand-up cocktail party, reception

Use of time: where will emphasis be placed; will activity build to climax?

---

through a channel to a receiver. On receipt of the message at its destination, the communication transaction was considered complete. Today, however, the PR practitioner must program two-way communication activities that permit audience response — or feedback — in brief, the interactive aspects discussed earlier.

A variety of print-oriented response mechanisms are available, such as the suggestion box for employee communication, response cards to be returned to the source of communication, and letters to the editors of publications. The most effective means of two-way interaction, however, is interpersonal communication activities: speeches with question-

and-answer sessions, small-group meetings, and one-on-one communication. It is usually possible to divide target audiences into small groups that provide excellent opportunities for interpersonal communication. This is the most effective form of persuasion because of the high level of source-receiver engagement.

Opinion Leaders. The sixth principle of effective communication involves the identification and targeting of opinion leaders as receivers of communication. Sometimes communication operates efficiently in a direct, one-step flow from source to receiver. On many occasions, however, communication is more effective when staged in a two-step or multiple-step flow. In these cases, the practitioner should seek opinion leaders, or "influentials," who in turn will communicate with their followers or cohorts. One simple way to identify opinion leaders is to catalog the leadership of all important groups in a given community or institution. These may include elected political leaders and others who hold formal positions in the community. In some cases, opinion leaders may hold no formal positions, but their advice is nonetheless sought and respected within given groups, institutions, or communities. Practitioners should create a list of opinion-leader contacts, much like their media contacts list, including all relevant data about the leaders, their positions, their availability, and their influence on other audiences.

Group Influence. A seventh effective communication principle involves the use of group influence. People belong to a variety of formal and informal groups. The most valued groups, which exert the greatest influence on their members, are known as *reference groups*. Members feel a sense of cohesiveness, of belonging together; have mutual, face-to-face interactions and influence each other; and share a set of norms and roles that structure and enforce a degree of conformity by each member.

The practitioner's task is to identify and target for communication key groups that can be most useful to the client or organization. Special effort should go into the preparation of a group contacts list, similar to the media and opinion-leader lists. Groups should be reached through interpersonal communication (speeches or presentations) as well as other appropriate methods. It is especially important to contact a formal group's program chairperson to schedule a speech or other presentation on behalf of the client. Acceptance of the client's message or position by key group leaders will then effectively engage the essential nature of group influence: acceptance by all members because of the group's operative cohesiveness and conformity.

Selective Exposure. An eighth principle of effective communication that should be observed by the public relations practitioner is selective exposure. Because the objectives of public relations include attitude and behavior modification, the temptation is always present to take on the most difficult of all tasks: changing existing attitudes or behaviors. Why is this the toughest task? The principle of selective exposure holds that people will accept and even seek out communication supporting their beliefs. However, communication researchers have also found that people will not necessarily avoid information incompatible with their views, as was once thought to be the case.[3] Moreover, other communication research indicates that when a persuasive message falls within the region (latitude) of personal acceptance, opinion or attitude will change in the direction of the advocated position. But when it falls within the region of rejection, attitudes will not change.[4] These communication research findings send a clear message to the PR practitioner— the easiest task in persuasion is reinforcement of existing attitudes or behaviors.

Clearly, trying to change attitudes or behavior is difficult and counterproductive, particularly in the face of strong resistance. Always avoid fighting a losing battle. When controversial messages are necessary, audiences or individual receivers should always be categorized on the basis of their agreement or disagreement with the message in question. Using terms that coincide with the Likert scale often used in attitude surveys, audiences can be categorized as "positive" (those who strongly agree with the message); "somewhat positive" (those who agree with the message); "undecided"; "somewhat negative" (those who disagree with the message); and "negative" (those who strongly disagree with the message).

The principle of selective exposure dictates that the practitioner first target the "positives," then the "somewhat positives," next the "undecideds," and last, if at all, the "somewhat negatives." The pure "negatives," those strongly opposed or in disagreement with the program's message, should usually be written off. If their attitudes are hardened, and especially if they have publicly expressed their disagreement, they are highly unlikely to change their minds. Given a long period of time, along with perhaps unlimited funds, the hard-core negatives may be slowly changed; but for most practical and immediate situations requiring persuasion, conversion of the negatives is not worth the time, effort, or money.

Audience Participation.   A final principle of effective communication, observed whenever possible, is the use of audience participation. This is the only means of communication that encourages audience self-persuasion through direct experience or involvement with the client's services or products. Communication researchers have found that self-persuasion is more effective, by far, than any other means of influence.[5] Therefore, the practitioner should constantly seek opportunities to include audience participation in PR programs.

In summary, public relations programming consists of planning, including attention to theme and message, the use of an action or special event, the use of uncontrolled and controlled media, and program execution following the principles of effective communication.

EVALUATION

Evaluation as discussed here is an ongoing process of monitoring and, when appropriate, final assessment of the stated objectives of the PR program. It is usually inadvisable to wait until the execution of the program has been completed to begin the evaluation process. Instead, the practices described here should be engaged in at stipulated intervals during the execution, with program adjustments made as deemed appropriate.

Evaluating Informational Objectives

The measurement of informational objectives includes three dimensions: message exposure, message comprehension, and message retention.

Message exposure is most commonly determined by publicity placement through national or local clipping and media monitoring services. It can also be measured through the circulation figures and audience-size data readily available for publications and broadcast media. Attendance figures for events or meetings also provide an index of message exposure. Finally, exposure is measured by computerized tracking systems that have been developed by some public relations firms for monitoring their effectiveness in delivering messages to audiences.

Message comprehension, or at least the potential for comprehension, is most frequently determined by the application of readability formulas to the messages used in PR programs. The most often used are the Flesch Reading Ease Formula, the Gunning Fog Index, the Dale-Chall Formula, the Fry Formula, and the Farr-Jenkins-Patterson Formula.[6] These predict ease of comprehension based on measuring the difficulty of the words and the length of the sentences used in messages, but surveys must be used to measure actual message comprehension.

Message retention is usually tested by asking appropriate questions designed to check target audiences' knowledge of the client's message. Although message retention can be measured by the nonquantitative research methods discussed earlier, retention questions are usually administered in the form of sample surveys.

Thus, the key to determining the effectiveness of informational objectives lies in the assessment of message exposure, comprehension, and retention. The more of these measurements used, the more accurate the evaluation of effectiveness is likely to be.

Evaluating Attitudinal Objectives

Attitudinal objectives can be measured by several well-established survey research instruments, the most frequently used being Likert scales and the Semantic Differential.[7] Both of these instruments measure attitude intensity and direction; thus, they are useful in assessing whether new attitudes have been formed or whether existing attitudes have been reinforced or changed. These measurements require both pretesting and posttesting of target audiences to determine the degree of influence on attitudes attributable to the PR program. To be of any value at all, attitude measurement must be done by competent professionals well-schooled and experienced in quantitative research methods.

Evaluating Behavioral Objectives

Finally, behavioral objectives can be measured in two ways. First, target audiences can be asked what their behaviors have been since exposure to the PR program. Like attitude measurement, assessment of audience behaviors requires testing before and after program exposure. However, the questions used will be different from those used in attitude research. Closed-end multiple-choice questions or checklists designed to determine audience behaviors are commonly used for this measurement.

A second means of assessing audience behavior is simply observing the behaviors of target audiences. In some cases, these can be counted, as in attendance at special events, numbers of telephone calls received, website "hits," or e-mail received. And in many situations, audiences may be small enough to observe before, during, and after exposure to the PR program.

Nonquantitative research methods can provide useful information both in asking audiences about their behaviors and in observing these behaviors. To obtain the most reliable evaluations of all three types of impact, however, competent professionals with established reputations in research should be retained.

Evaluating Output Objectives

In addition to measuring impact objectives, the PR practitioner must be concerned with assessing the effectiveness of output objectives, which involves the distribution of uncontrolled and controlled media. This effectiveness can be evaluated by keeping records of the number of news releases sent to publications and broadcast stations, the number of contacts made with journalists, the number of speeches given to targeted audiences, the number of publications distributed to each public, and the number of meetings held with key audiences. In the realm of output objectives, practitioners accomplish their goals by distributing appropriate quantities of media according to their original plans. Although these are easily achievable objectives, it should be reiterated that they have no bearing whatever on the PR program's priority goal—audience impact.

Evaluation of the two general forms of program objectives—impact and output—constitutes an ongoing dimension of this public relations process model. The process will not be completed, however, when the program objectives are evaluated. These evaluative data are recycled as part of a continuing procedure. They are useful in adjusting ongoing relations with various audiences, and they can be helpful when planning the client's next short-term PR program with similar audiences.

SUMMARY

The public relations problem-solving process includes four parts: research, determination of objectives, programming, and evaluation. The following outline provides a useful summary and review of the whole process.

Outline of the Public Relations Process

I. Research

    A. Client/organization: background data about your client or organization—its personnel, financial status, reputation, past and present PR practices, PR strengths and weaknesses, opportunities

    B. Opportunity/problem: proactive or reactive PR program; long-range or short-range campaign

    C. Audiences (publics): identification of key groups to be targeted for communication

        1. Desired research data: each targeted audience's level of information about your client/organization; image and other relevant attitudes held about your client/organization and its products or services; audience behaviors relevant to your client/organization; demographics, media habits, and media-use levels of each targeted audience

        2. Research procedures: nonquantitative and quantitative

II. Objectives

    A. Impact objectives

        1. Informational objectives: message exposure, comprehension, retention

        2. Attitudinal objectives: formation of new attitudes, reinforcement of existing attitudes, change in existing attitudes

        3. Behavioral objectives: creation of new behavior, reinforcement of existing behavior, change in existing behavior

B. Output objectives: distribution or execution of uncontrolled and controlled media

III. Programming — planning and execution of:

A. Theme (if applicable) and message(s)

B. Action or special event(s)

C. Uncontrolled media: news releases, feature stories, photos; controlled media: print, audiovisual, interpersonal communication, PR advertising

D. Effective communication using principles of: source credibility, salient information, effective nonverbal and verbal cues, two-way communication, opinion leaders, group influence, selective exposure, and audience participation

IV. Evaluation — ongoing monitoring and final assessment of:

A. Impact objectives

1. Informational objectives: measured by publicity placement, surveys

2. Attitudinal objectives: measured by attitude surveys

3. Behavioral objectives: measured by surveys and observation of behaviors

B. Output objectives: measured quantitatively by simply counting the actual output

NOTES

1.   For a summary of this research, see Daniel J. O'Keefe, *Persuasion: Theory and Research,* 2d ed. (Thousand Oaks, CA: Sage Publications, 2002), and Mary John Smith, *Persuasion and Human Action* (Belmont, CA: Wadsworth, 1982): 219ff, the latter a classic in its field.

2.   For a detailed discussion of the information integration approach to persuasion, see Smith, *Persuasion and Human Action,* pp. 243–261.

3.   The best discussion of selective exposure is David O. Sears and Jonathan L. Freedman, "Selective Exposure to Information: A Critical Review," *Public Opinion Quarterly* 31 (summer 1967): 194–213. Also a classic in the field.

4.   For a good explanation of this research, called *social judgment theory,* see Nan Lin, *The Study of Human Communication* (Indianapolis: Bobbs-Merrill, 1977), pp. 118–122. Also see Smith, *Persuasion and Human Action,* pp. 264–274.

5.   For a review of this research, see Smith, *Persuasion and Human Action,* pp. 191–207.

6.   For the Flesch Formula, see Rudolf Flesch, *How to Test Readability* (New York: Harper & Row, 1951); Gunning's Fog Index is found in Robert Gunning,

The Technique of Clear Writing, rev. ed. (New York: McGraw-Hill, 1968); for the Dale-Chall Formula, see Edgar Dale and Jeanne Chall, "A Formula for Predicting Readability," *Educational Research Bulletin* 27 (January and February 1948); the Fry Formula is found in Edward Fry, "A Readability Formula that Saves Time," *Journal of Reading* 11 (1968): 513–516, 575–578; for a review of readability research, see Werner J. Severin and James W. Tankard, Jr., *Communication Theories: Origins, Methods, Uses* (New York: Hastings House, 1979), Chap. 6.

7.   For a discussion of these and other research instruments used in attitude measurement, see O'Keefe, *Persuasion: Theory and Research.*

READINGS ON THE PUBLIC RELATIONS PROCESS

Research

Alreck, Pamela L., and Robert B. Settle. *The Survey Research Handbook,* 2d ed. Burr Ridge, IL: Irwin, 1994.

Beaulaurier, Bob. "Avoiding Pitfalls in Web-based Research," *Public Relations Tactics* 10 (November 2003): 17.

Broom, Glen M., and David M. Dozier. *Using Research in Public Relations: Applications to Program Management.* Englewood Cliffs, NJ: Prentice-Hall, 1996.

Buddenbaum, Judith M., and Katherine B. Novak. *Applied Communication Research.* Ames: Iowa State University Press, 2001.

Greely, Andrew. "In Defense of Surveys," *Transaction Social Science and Modern Society* 33 (May–June 1996): 26ff.

Hamelink, Cees J. *Mass Communication Research: Problems and Policies.* Norwood, NJ: Ablex, 1993.

Hocking, John E., Don W. Stacks, and Steven T. McDermott. *Communication Research,* 3d ed. Boston: Allyn & Bacon, 2003.

Johnson, James M., and H. S. Pennypacker. *Strategies and Tactics in Behavioral Research,* 2d ed. Hillsdale, NJ: Erlbaum, 1993.

Karlberg, Michael. "Remembering the Public in Public Relations Research: From Theoretical to Operational Symmetry," *Journal of Public Relations Research* 8 (fall 1996): 263–278.

Profolio: Research and Evaluation. New York: Public Relations Society of America, 1997.

Stacks, Don W. *Primer of Public Relations Research.* New York: Guilford Publications, 2002.

Stone, Gerald C. "Public Relations Telephone Surveys: Avoiding Methodological Debacles," *Public Relations Review* 2 (winter 1996): 327–339.

Objectives

Brock, Timothy C., and Melanie C. Green, eds. *Persuasion: Psychological Insights and Perspectives,* 2d ed. Thousand Oaks, CA: Sage Publications, 2005.

Broom, Glen M., and David M. Dozier. "Writing Program Goals and Objectives." In *Using Research in Public Relations: Applications to Program Management.* Englewood Cliffs, NJ: Prentice-Hall, 1996, pp. 39–44.

Cutlip, Scott M., Allen H. Center, and Glen M. Broom. *Effective Public Relations,* 9th ed. Englewood Cliffs, NJ: Prentice-Hall, 2006.

Frederico, Richard F. "What Are Your Core Communication Values?" *Communication World* 11 (October 1994): 14 ff.

Hauss, Deborah. "Setting Benchmarks Leads to Effective Programs," *Public Relations Journal* 49 (February 1993): 16–17.

Jaques, Tony. "Systematic Objective Setting for Effective Issue Management," *Journal of Public Affairs* 5 (February 2005): 33–42.

Shelby, Annette Neven. "Organization, Business, Management, Communication and Corporate Communication: An Analysis of Boundaries and Relationships," *Journal of Business Communication* 30 (July 1993): 241–268.

Winokur, Dena, and Robert W. Kinkead. "How Public Relations Fits into Corporate Strategy," *Public Relations Journal* 49 (May 1993): 16–23.

Programming

Cutlip, Scott M., Allen H. Center, and Glen M. Broom. *Effective Public Relations,* 9th ed. Englewood Cliffs, NJ: Prentice-Hall, 2006.

Grunig, James E., ed. *Excellence in Public Relations and Communication Management.* Hillsdale, NJ: Erlbaum, 1992.

Guth, David, and Charles Marsh. *Public Relations: A Values-Driven Approach,* 2d ed. Boston: Allyn & Bacon, 2003.

Hunt, Todd, and James E. Grunig. *Public Relations Techniques,* 2d ed. Fort Worth, TX: Harcourt Brace, 1997.

Lesly, Philip, ed. *Lesly's Handbook of Public Relations and Communications,* 7th ed. New York: AMACOM, 1998.

Newsom, Doug, Judy VanSlyke Turk, and Dean Kruckeberg. *This Is PR: The Realities of Public Relations,* 8th ed. Belmont, CA: Wadsworth, 2004.

Okigbo, Charles, and Sonya Nelson. "Precision Public Relations: Facing the Demographic Challenge," *Public Relations Quarterly* 48 (summer 2003): 29–35.

Pratt, Cornelius B. "Crafting Key Messages and Talking Points—or Grounding Them in What Research Tells Us," *Public Relations Quarterly* 49 (fall 2004): 15–21.

Seitel, Fraser P. *The Practice of Public Relations,* 8th ed. Englewood Cliffs, NJ: Prentice-Hall, 2001.

Smith, Ronald D. *Strategic Planning for Public Relations.* Mahwah, NJ: Erlbaum, 2002.

Wilcox, Dennis L., Glen T. Cameron, Philip H. Ault, and Warren K. Agee. *Public Relations: Strategies and Tactics,* 7th ed. Boston: Allyn & Bacon, 2003.

Evaluation

Broom, Glen M., and David M. Dozier. "Using Research to Evaluate Programs." In *Using Research in Public Relations: Applications to Program Management.* Englewood Cliffs, NJ: Prentice-Hall, 1996, pp. 71–88.

Charland, Bernie. "The Mantra of Metrics: A Realistic and Relevant Approach to Measuring the Impact of Employee Communications," *Public Relations Strategist* 10 (fall 2004): 30–32.

Cutlip, Scott M., Allen H. Center, and Glen M. Broom. "Step Four: Evaluating the Program." In *Effective Public Relations,* 9th ed. Englewood Cliffs, NJ: Prentice-Hall, 2006.

Freitag, Alan R. "How to Measure What We Do," *Public Relations Quarterly* 43 (summer 1998): 42–47.

González, Ana Rita. "Grassroots Approaches to Reach the Hispanic Audience: Nontraditional Approaches to Measure ROI," *Public Relations Tactics* 12 (July 2005): 24.

Hauss, Deborah. "Measuring the Impact of Public Relations: Electronic Techniques Improve Campaign Evaluation," *Public Relations Journal* 49 (February 1993): 14–21.

Holloway, Deborah. "How to Select a Measurement System That's Right for You," *Public Relations Quarterly* 37 (fall 1992): 15–19.

Lindemann, Walter K. "An 'Effectiveness Yardstick' to Measure Public Relations Success," *Public Relations Quarterly* 38 (spring 1993): 7–9.

Pilmer, John. "Small Business? Small Budget? How to Measure for Success," *Public Relations Tactics* 12 (July 2005): 23.

Richter, Lisa, and Steve Drake. "Apply Measurement Mindset to Programs," *Public Relations Journal* 49 (January 1993): 32.

Rossi, Peter H., and Howard E. Freeman. *Evaluation: A Systematic Approach,* 7th ed. Beverly Hills, CA: Russell Sage Foundation, 2003.

Stacks, Don W. *Primer of Public Relations Research*. New York: Guilford Publications, 2002.

Wiesendanger, Betsy. "Electronic Delivery and Feedback Systems Come of Age," *Public Relations Journal* 49 (January 1993): 10–14.

PART II

Reaching Major Audiences

CHAPTER 3   **Media Relations**

CHAPTER 4   **Internal Communications**

CHAPTER 5   **Community Relations**

CHAPTER 6   **Public Affairs and Government Relations**

CHAPTER 7   **Investor and Financial Relations**

CHAPTER 8   **Consumer Relations**

CHAPTER 9   **International Public Relations**

CHAPTER 10   **Relations with Special Publics**

Media Relations

Journalists representing the mass and specialized media usually make up the external audience of highest priority for public relations practitioners. Media relations consists essentially of obtaining appropriate publicity, or news coverage, for the activities of the practitioner's client or organization. The field of public relations began as publicity and for many years was called that. Indeed, this process remains the basis for the burgeoning disciplines of public relations, public affairs, and corporate communications.

Media relations involves targeting the "gatekeepers" of the mass and specialized media for communication about the client or organization. However, the media are actually intermediate audiences. The ultimate targeted audiences in media relations are the consumers of the media.

RESEARCH

The research process for media relations includes investigation of the practitioner's client or organization, of the opportunity or problem that accounts for communication with the media, and of the various audiences themselves to be targeted for the PR effort.

Client Research

First, the practitioner should be familiar with background data about the client or organization, including its personnel, financial status, and reputation. Special attention must be given to past and present relations with media representatives. Has the client had negative or positive news coverage in the past? Has there been little or no coverage? Does the client have any particular media coverage strengths, such as unusual or glamorous products or a newsworthy chief executive officer? On the other hand, what are the client's publicity "negatives"? In what areas is the client vulnerable? Finally, the practitioner should assess the client's publicity opportunities. What special events can be most profitably staged for the client? What can be done to tie the client in with ongoing community or national special events? With information of this kind, the practitioner will be better prepared to serve the client's publicity or media relations needs.

Opportunity or Problem Research

The second aspect of research in preparation for media relations involves determining the reason for the program. Is it because an opportunity has presented itself for good news coverage, or has some problem arisen that will bring media representatives to the client's doorstep? This chapter is concerned more with the former situation, the publicity *opportunity*. For information on managing the media when a problem or crisis develops, see Chapter 11, "Emergency Public Relations."

Audience Research

The final aspect of research for media relations is thought by most practitioners to be the most important—identifying the appropriate media and *their* audiences to target for communication. These media fall into two broad categories, mass and specialized, each of which can be further subdivided (see Exhibit 3-a).

With these media categories, the practitioner's task is to prepare a comprehensive list of media contacts. Appropriate *media directories,* such as those listed in the suggested readings in this chapter, should be consulted in preparing such a list. Practitioners may find that much of their work has already been done for them by these directories. The national, regional, state, and city directories are thorough, but in some cases more information must be gathered. To be of optimal use, the media contacts list should include:

1. The type and size of the audience reached by each media outlet

2. The type of material used by the media outlet—spot news, feature material, interviews, photos

3. The name and title of the appropriate editor, director, producer, reporter, or staff writer who handles news of organizations such as the client's

4. The deadlines for that media contact—monthly, weekly, daily, morning, afternoon, evening, date, day, or hour

The best advice for the practitioner in media relations is simply to *know the media outlet*. Each outlet has its own unique set of departments and editorial staffing, with particular requirements for submitting material. If in doubt, call the media outlet to obtain the necessary guidelines, along with the name and address of the person who holds the editorial position. It is usually best not to ask to speak with journalists themselves. They may be very busy and resent intrusions for routine information. As a rule, news releases for newspapers should be addressed to the city editor if general in nature or to the appropriate section editor if they are of special interest. For broadcast stations, news releases should usually be addressed to the news director or, in some cases, to the public service director.

Practitioners should never feel that their media contacts lists are complete when they have compiled necessary information about the mass media alone. Each client or organization will be operating in a special field. Automobile manufacturers, fashion designers, dentists, rock music groups—all have their own organizations or associations. And all are served by their own specialized publications. Public relations practitioners must be aware of all such publications that serve their client's field. The process of compiling a list of specialized media contacts begins with consulting a media directory. Among the best of such publications for comprehensive listings in a great variety of fields are Bacon's and Burrelle's media directories, both listed later in this chapter. Also listed are directories for medical, scientific, military, and minority media contacts.

Among the finished products of the practitioner's audience research, then, will be *two* media contacts lists: one for mass media and the other for specialized media. News releases, photos, and feature stories directed to and published in specialized publications can often be of greater value to the client than similar exposure in the mass media. It should be emphasized that the purpose of compiling these two media contacts lists is communication with the consumers of both the mass and specialized media—the client's ultimate intended audiences.

In the cases included later in this chapter, these audiences are sometimes specialized and sometimes mass in character.

EXHIBIT 3-A　　*Media Publics*

Mass media

Local
  Print publications
    Newspapers
    Magazines
  TV stations
  Radio stations
National
  Print publications
  Broadcast networks
  Wire services

Specialized media

Local
  Trade, industry, and association publications
  Organizational house and membership publications
  Ethnic publications
  Publications of special groups
  Specialized broadcast programs and stations
National
  General business publications
  National trade, industry, and association publications
  National organizational house and membership publications
  National ethnic publications
  Publications of national special groups
  National specialized broadcast programs and networks

Thus, the research process in media relations involves a thorough understanding of the practitioner's client or organization; the reason — opportunity or problem — for communicating with the media; and, most important, knowledge of the targeted media themselves — the nature of the media outlets, audiences reached, types of material used, specific names and titles of staff contacts, and their deadlines.

OBJECTIVES

Media relations uses both impact and output objectives. Some typical examples of both types are examined here, along with a sampling of the objectives used in the media relations cases included in this chapter.

Impact Objectives

Impact objectives represent the desired outcomes of modifying the attitudes and behaviors of target audiences. In media relations they usually include such statements as:

1. To increase knowledge of news about the client among community media representatives
2. To enhance the client's credibility among media people
3. To reinforce favorable attitudes toward the client on the part of media representatives
4. To increase favorable client news coverage

Note that in each of these statements, percentages and time frames can be added as desired. The first statement could be rephrased to read: to increase knowledge of news about the client by 30 percent among community media representatives during the period June 1–December 1. However, a majority of the award-winning cases in this book do *not* quantify their objectives or set time frames.

Almost invariably the objectives used in our sample cases targeted the client's ultimate audiences, rather than the media audiences, for desired impact. It is understood in each case, however, that the media must be the intermediate target audience. Perhaps the objectives would have been clearer and easier to measure if they had targeted *both* the desired media and the ultimate audiences.

Output Objectives

Output objectives in media relations refer to the efforts made by the practitioner on behalf of the client. These statements have nothing to do with the client's desired influence on audiences. Output objectives may include:

1. To be of service to the media — both proactively and reactively
   a. Proactively, to provide *newsworthy* stories about the client or organization
   b. Reactively, to be available for responses to media inquiries

2. To coordinate media interviews with client or organizational officers and personnel

3. To distribute feature story ideas to trade publications

PROGRAMMING

Programming for media relations includes the same planning and execution elements used in other forms of public relations: (1) theme and messages, (2) action or special event(s), (3) uncontrolled or controlled media, and (4) principles of effective communication.

Theme and Messages

Program themes, especially in connection with special events, should be included in the messages sent to media outlets. In media relations, the messages themselves should always be governed by the requirements for newsworthiness applicable to the targeted media outlets. Since media relations essentially involves the communication of client news to media outlets or the stimulation of news coverage of the client, the practitioner must understand the nature of news and the criteria for newsworthiness.

Some practitioners believe there are two kinds of news: "hard" and "soft." It is more accurate, however, to think of *spot news* and *feature material* as the two kinds of news.

Spot news is temporal, or time-bound, in nature. Within the rubric of spot news are two subcategories: hard and soft. *Hard spot news* is normally found on prominent pages of major metropolitan dailies. It affects large numbers of people and is of great and immediate interest to the audiences of most mass media outlets. Unfortunately, most hard spot news handled by PR practitioners is *bad news* about the client, such as disasters, plant closings, or layoffs. *Good* news about clients can usually be classified as *soft spot news*. It may not be of much interest outside the organization itself, in which case it should be printed in a house publication and not sent to a mass media outlet. A major challenge to the practitioner is to create special events or *make* good news about the client that will receive favorable coverage in the media.

Feature material, on the other hand, is not time-bound but may be used as "filler" for print and broadcast media. Feature stories for both kinds of media usually focus on human interest topics. Types of feature stories include "a day in the life of . . ."; profiles of personalities; interviews; descriptions of events that emphasize human interest factors and the personalities involved; and sidebars, or feature stories designed to accompany spot news stories in newspapers.

Keeping in mind the differences between spot news and feature material, the practitioner should also be sensitive to the general criteria used by journalists to determine what is newsworthy. The usual characteristics of news include what is new or novel, involves famous persons, is important to large numbers of people, involves conflict or mystery, may be considered confidential, will have significant consequences, is funny, is romantic, or involves sex.

News has also been defined as anything a media outlet chooses to print, broadcast, or film as "news." Since the selection is always the outlet's choice, the public relations practitioner must become familiar with the criteria used by that particular group of editors. This is simply another way of saying, *Know the media outlet.*

Like other aspects of programming, theme and messages should be governed by the practitioner's understanding of what is news and both the general and particular newsworthiness criteria in use at individual media outlets.

Action(s) or Special Event(s)

The use of actions on the part of the client and the staging of special events assume special importance in media relations. They provide the basis for news coverage. They *are* the news about the client. Thus, the PR practitioner should review the list of actions and special events included in Exhibit 2-c. These can serve as methods of *making* news for the client. Each action or special event should be carefully planned and orchestrated for its maximum news value. If possible, celebrities should be present, and as many other news criteria should be incorporated as is feasible.

The cases in this chapter illustrate a broad range of special events, including a grand opening ceremony and commemoration of a major disaster.

Uncontrolled Media

Uncontrolled media are the major vehicles for reporting client news to media representatives. The most commonly used forms are:

1. News releases—print and video
2. Photographs and photo opportunities
3. News conferences
4. Media interviews

News Releases—Print and Video. Of these four frequently used formats, news releases are the most popular with public relations practitioners. News releases provide a quick, economical means of communicating client spot news or feature material to appropriate media outlets. *Print news releases* are delivered by hand courier, mailed, faxed, or e-mailed. Corporations and other organizations often place current news releases on their websites.

Unfortunately, print news releases have become overused in major markets throughout the United States. Each morning, editors may be confronted with a stack of 70 to 100 or more releases from practitioners seeking news coverage for their clients or organizations. A prominent Washington bureau chief confided to one of my classes that, faced with his daily pile of news releases, he simply pulls a large, desktop-high wastebasket over to the edge of the desk and "files" most of the morning mail.

How, then, can practitioners expect to break through the blizzard of print news releases to call attention to their own client's news? The "secret" of successful news releases lies in the first word of the term itself—*news*. A really newsworthy story about a client can easily be telephoned to a city editor. The editor, if interested in the story, will assign a reporter to cover it. Major metropolitan editors or broadcast news directors rarely use news releases verbatim or even partially. If a story is there, the news release may alert them to it; but they invariably prefer to assign their own staff people to do the actual news gathering and writing. Be prepared to provide additional information and interviews to flesh out the story. Expect the reporter to contact both your friends and your critics.

Successful variations on the basic news release include the briefer *media alerts, media advisories,* and *fact sheets.* All media outlets, in markets large or small, depend on PR practitioners for *information* about news events in their market areas. Print news releases and their shorter variations, despite their overuse, remain the major method of transmitting information from the client to the journalist.

The *video news release (VNR)* became a popular form of client news in the past, but its popularity has waned because of the stigma broadcast journalists have attached to "fake news" designed to flatter a public relations client. Like its print counterpart, the successful VNR must focus on *news* rather than on promotional pap about the client. VNRs are most frequently used in medium or small markets rather than major metropolitan markets. They should be produced by a reputable firm specializing in VNRs, and, ideally, the firm should be equipped to handle the entire task, including scripting, production, and satellite distribution. Most VNRs today, if produced at all, include accompanying B-roll and sound bites[1] that might better be interspersed in television newscasts than the complete VNR.

Photographs and Photo Opportunities.   Photographs are a second widely used form of uncontrolled media. As with news releases, public relations photographs are seldom used by major metropolitan daily newspapers. But, like news releases, they may serve to attract the attention of major editors to client news that might otherwise be overlooked. Public relations photographs have a better chance of being used by smaller publications in smaller markets. They are important enough to warrant attention to the details of their proper composition and preparation for PR purposes.

Good public relations photographs should be creative and imaginative in composition, avoiding the clichés a client may request, such as a speaker standing at a podium, one person handing something to another, a group shot of ten or more people, or one person sitting at a desk. Photographs of this kind usually find their way into house publications. A good public relations photograph depicts something a newspaper photographer cannot duplicate or restage. Unique and interesting photographs may be used because of their creativity and news value.

A frequently used contemporary technique is the staging of a "photo opportunity," especially in markets where the major dailies or magazines are likely to assign their own photographers to a story. The photo opportunity should be carefully planned in advance and staged in a natural—not theatrical—way, so that it becomes an integral or necessary part of the news story and not something that can be missed by the assigned journalists and photographers.

News Conferences.   A third frequently used form of uncontrolled media is the news conference. News conferences should be used sparingly since they are usually inconvenient for journalists. If staged, the conference must live up to its descriptive adjective, *news*. Even on their very best days, metropolitan journalists are easily annoyed. They can resent being summoned to a news conference to hear a routine announcement that could have been faxed to the city desk or reported in a written release.

Many organizations use news conferences for significant announcements, such as major corporate changes, takeovers, mergers, introductions of new product lines, or responses to false accusations of wrongdoing. Other than for major government agencies, news conferences should never be routine. They should be reserved for truly newsworthy occasions that call for a personal presentation by the organization's chief executive officer or by a visiting celebrity or dignitary.

News conferences can be conducted profitably, but the practitioner should always keep the preceding reservations in mind and usually resist the urge to hold one.

Media Interviews.   Media interviews are a fourth frequently used form of uncontrolled media. Whether given to print or broadcast journalists, interviews provide the most direct contact between the client and the media. The practitioner's role in this situation is that of a link, or coordinator, and sometimes also that of a trainer or coach for the client.

The interview is not just to answer the reporter's questions, but to accent the themes and messages as outlined in the campaign.

In the case of print interviews, clients may have the options of declaring beforehand that their comments will be for background, not for attribution, or completely off the record. In these cases the client's name cannot be used; and in off-the-record interviews the content of the interview cannot be used in the media. Aside from interviews with high government officials in sensitive positions, however, most clients want to be both quoted and identified in the media as a means of promoting their organizations' interests.

Broadcast interviews do not permit the luxury of being off the record. If clients consent to broadcast interviews, they do so with the knowledge that while on camera (or microphone), they may be put through a "third degree" by an enterprising journalist. Moreover, the client loses control of the editing function. For this reason many organizations insist on bringing their own videotaping equipment and crew in order to have an independent record of the interview. Increasingly, organizations are paying specialized consultants for "media training" for their executives, who can then significantly influence favorable public opinion about their organizations.

Print and broadcast interviews, then, are one of the four most frequently used forms of uncontrolled media in the client's communication with journalists. In addition to news releases, photographs, news conferences, and interviews, the practitioner should consider the other communication vehicles listed in Exhibit 2-d.

Controlled Media

A variety of forms of controlled media can be used to provide journalists with background information. For example, practitioners usually prepare a media kit for news conferences. These kits include the opening statement made at the conference, a basic news release, backgrounder, fact sheet, photos with cutlines (captions), and such printed materials as brochures, folders, annual reports, speeches, and other information pieces. Increasingly, paper media kits are being supplemented or replaced by CD-ROMs, which can cover much more information, along with graphics, video, and sound. Additionally, media kit materials are now found on most corporate and organizational websites. In the true sense of the term, however, controlled media are not used in media relations. When journalists are given controlled communications, they make their own uses (or nonuses) of them. Thus, the client or practitioner has no control over how such materials will be used by journalists.

A case can be made that public relations advertising constitutes the use of controlled communications in media relations. The practitioner *does* deal with media outlets in such cases, but not with journalists. Advertising is purchased directly from the media outlet's advertising department.

The exhibits included with the cases in this chapter demonstrate the scope of both uncontrolled and controlled communications used in media relations.

Effective Communication

In media relations, the communication process can be aptly described as a two-step flow. The traditional two-stage model depicts a stream of messages from a mass media source to opinion leaders and then to the colleagues of the opinion leaders. In media relations, this process is partially reversed. Communication flows from the practitioner's client to the media and then in turn to the media audience.

Because of the special nature of media relations, not all of the nine principles of effective communication discussed in Chapter 2 apply.

Source credibility clearly *is* applicable in the case of media relations. Media representatives must perceive the client or organization and its spokesperson as trustworthy and reliable. Salient information, on the other hand, must be redefined for media relations. Information that meets the criteria of newsworthiness constitutes the salience for journalists. Both nonverbal and verbal cues contribute to communication effectiveness in media relations, just as they do in other forms of public relations. The use of two-way communication, however, plays a less important role in media relations than in other forms. Journalists generally resent inquiries from practitioners to see if a client's news releases are going to be used. The feedback that practitioners really want in media relations is the use of their materials in the media.

The use of opinion leaders in the usual sense is not a part of media relations. In media relations, practitioners communicate directly with journalists. In some instances, journalists are regarded as community opinion leaders, but this principle applies more directly to community relations. The selective exposure principle may apply in some cases to media relations but, in general, journalists are more openminded and often seek information that they may personally disagree with. Finally, the audience participation principle is valid and useful in media relations. When introducing new product lines, for example, many companies invite journalists to use the product on an introductory basis. Journalist participation at news conferences and other meetings arranged by PR practitioners provides other instances of effective audience participation in media relations.

Thus, most of the principles of effective communication apply to media relations to some degree. However, the group-influence principle is rarely used in media relations since journalists pride themselves on their independence of thought and action. But, on the whole, principles of effective communication should be a priority concern of the public relations practitioner in media relations.

EVALUATION

The evaluation process in all forms of public relations always refers to the program's stated objectives. In media relations, as in all of public relations, impact objectives are of the highest priority.

Evaluating Impact Objectives

The impact objective of informing the media about the client is generally measured by assessing the exposure of the message in the media, or publicity placement. National or local clipping and media monitoring services are usually retained to take this measure of effectiveness. Message exposure can also be measured by the circulation figures and audience-size data available from the publications and broadcast media themselves. Additionally, some public relations firms use sophisticated computerized tracking systems to evaluate effectiveness in delivering messages to audiences. Publicity placement, however, remains the predominant method for evaluating the success of message exposure.

Attitude objectives in most forms of public relations are measured by conducting sample surveys of the target audiences, but this may not be feasible with journalists targeted for communication. Some might react negatively to such an intrusion from a PR practitioner. Content analyses of media placement, however, can yield the desired measurements. A scientific assessment of attitudes is therefore possible and relatively easily obtained.

This same procedure is also useful in measuring favorable client news coverage. This objective is the ultimate goal of all media relations.

Evaluating Output Objectives

Along with the measurement of impact objectives, practitioners want to determine the effectiveness of their media relations output objectives. These consist essentially of distributing uncontrolled media to outlets, being responsive to media inquiries, and coordinating media interviews. They can be evaluated by keeping records of all such transactions. Although these objectives are easily accomplished, the practitioner should be reminded that these goals have no bearing on media relations impact.

Evaluation of media relations, then, is heavily concentrated on successful and favorable placement of the practitioner's uncontrolled media. Other objectives are useful, but successful media relations ultimately boils down to the matter of placement. This is clearly visible in the priority given to placement in the evaluations of the cases in this chapter.

SUMMARY

With some modifications, the four-stage process is as useful in media relations as it is in other forms of public relations. Essentially, media relations involves establishing a favorable working relationship between PR practitioners and journalists representing appropriate mass and specialized media.

The most important aspect of research for media relations is the preparation of up-to-date lists of media contacts for both mass and specialized outlets. Objectives in media relations usually emphasize the desired behavioral impact of obtaining favorable news coverage for the client. An absolute essential for media relations programming is an understanding of the particular media outlets' audiences and the media's definitions of news for those audiences. This information should provide criteria for the development of newsworthy, client-centered special events, news releases, photographs, news conferences, interviews, and/or other forms of uncontrolled media used in reaching journalists.

Evaluation of media relations always refers back to the program's stated objectives. Impact objectives are generally measured through publicity placement, circulation and audience data, computer tracking of messages, or content analysis. The accomplishment of output objectives can be simply determined by counting or otherwise observing the desired outputs as they are set in motion. In essence, however, the effectiveness of media relations always comes down to media placement, that is, obtaining the desired publicity for the client.

NOTE

1. The VNR itself is "A-roll." Most news directors prefer the unedited "B-roll" and sound bites to create their own news stories.

READINGS ON MEDIA RELATIONS

Alterman, Eric. "Better Red than Dead?" *Nation* 280 (February 2005): 11.

Beckman, Carol. "Nine Things to Remember When Talking to a Reporter," *Public Relations Tactics* 3 (September 1996): 13ff.

Beres, George. "A Major Distinction," *Editor & Publisher* 138 (July 2005): 70.

Bergman, Eric. "The Ethics of Not Answering," *Communication World* 22 (September–October 2005): 16–142.

Catuthers, Dewey. "Media Placement: An Art That Gets No Respect," *Public Relations Tactics* 5 (October 1998): 23ff.

Chermak, Steven, and Alexander Weiss. "Maintaining Legitimacy Using External Communication Strategies for Police-Media Relations," *Journal of Criminal Justice* 33 (September 2005): 501–512.

Collins, David. "Ten Rules of Editorial Etiquette," *Public Relations Quarterly* 39 (fall 1994): 8.

Detweiler, John S. "Source Power: New Leverage in Media Relations," *Public Relations Quarterly* 37 (summer 1992): 19ff.

Dilenschneider, Robert L. "Use Ingenuity in Media Relations," *Public Relations Quarterly* 37 (summer 1992): 13ff.

Erjavec, Karmen. "Hybrid Public Relations News Discourse," *European Journal of Communication* 20 (June 2005): 155–179.

Eveland, William P., and Douglas M. McLeod. "The Effect of Social Desirability on Perceived Media Impact: Implications for Third-Person Perceptions." *International Journal of Public Opinion Research* 11 (winter 1999): 315–333.

Feldman, Charles, and Suzanne Spurgeon. "After Deep Throat: How to Respond to Anonymously Sourced News Stories," *Public Relations Tactics* 12 (July 2005): 14.

Goldberg, Betsy. "That Other Broadcast Medium: Tuning in to the Power of Radio," *Public Relations Tactics* 12 (July 2005): 13–15.

Greve, Frank. "Journalism In the Age of Pseudoreporting," *Nieman Reports* 69 (summer 2005): 11–13.

Guiniven, John. "PR Professional, not Telemarketer: The Do's and Don'ts of Pitching," *Public Relations Tactics* 12 (July 2005): 6.

Howard, Carole M. "10 Media Lessons Learned the Hard Way," *Public Relations Strategist* 2 (summer 1996): 45ff.

Howard, Carole M., and Wilma K. Mathews. *On Deadline: Managing Media Relations*, 2d ed. Prospect Heights, IL: Waveland, 1998.

Levy, Ronald N. "Media Opportunity: Use your Head," *Public Relations Quarterly* 48 (summer 2003): 27–28.

Levy, Sue. "Media Expansion Tests PR Tracking," *Marketing* (February 24, 2000): 39ff.

Lubove, Seth. "Get Smart: A Reporter's Take on Good PR Practices," *Public Relations Tactics* 5 (October 1998): 20.

Macaluso, Susan. "The Media World in Transition: What is the VNR's Role in this New Landscape?" *Public Relations Tactics* 12 (June 2005): 21.

Marken, G. A. "Let's Do Away with Press Releases," *Public Relations Quarterly* 39 (spring 1994): 46ff.

———. "Press Releases: When Nothing Else Will Do," *Public Relations Quarterly* 39 (fall 1994): 9ff.

Martin, Aimee, and Carter H. Griffin. "Creatively Measuring Media Relations," *Public Relations Strategist* 4 (spring 1998): 36ff.

Miklya, Liz. "Making Your Message More Memorable for the Media — Plus, How to Bridge Difficult Questions," *Public Relations Tactics* 12 (May 2005): 21.

Morton, Linda P., and John Warren. "News Elements and Editors' Choices," *Public Relations Review* 18 (spring 1992): 47–53.

Murray, William P. "Running a Multifaceted Health Care Campaign During a Time of Increased Media Scrutiny," *Public Relations Tactics* 12 (July 2005): 10.

Owen, Anne R., and James A. Karrh. "Video News Releases: Effects on Viewer Recall and Attitudes," *Public Relations Review* 22 (winter 1996): 369ff.

Reese, Stephen D., Oscar H. Gandy, Jr., and August E. Grant. *Framing Public Life: Perspectives on Media and Our Understanding of the Social World*. Mahwah, NJ: Erlbaum, 2001.

Sallot, Lynne M., Thomas M. Steinfatt, and Michael B. Salwen. "Journalists' and Public Relations Practitioners' News Values: Perceptions and Cross Perceptions," *Journalism and Mass Communication Quarterly* 75 (summer 1998): 366ff.

Salzman, Jason. *Making the News*. New York: Perseus Books Group, 2003.

Sayres, Scott. "Reporters Do the Darnedest Things!: An Explanation of Some of Their Actions," *Public Relations Tactics* 12 (May 2005): 28.

Spaeth, Merrie. "Presidential Politics and Public Relations in 2004," *Journalism Studies* 6 (May 2005): 237–240.

Stoff, Rick. "Taking Back the Message," *St. Louis Journalism Review* 35 (April 2005): 6–7.

———. "Trust Us," *St. Louis Journalism Review* 35 (July–August 2005): 11–27.

Sweeney, Katie. "Fuzzy Picture for VNRs, SMTs — Both Vehicles Come under Scrutiny, and Congress Gets into the Act," *Public Relations Tactics* 12 (June 2005): 18.

Trufelman, Lloyd P. "Consumer-Generated Media — Challenges and Opportunities for Public Relations," *Public Relations Tactics* 12 (May 2005): 17–19.

Wallack, Lawrence M., et al. *News For a Change: An Advocate's Guide to Working with the Media*. Thousand Oaks, CA: Sage Publications, 1999.

Warneke, Kevin. "Keeping Tabs at the Ronald McDonald House in Omaha: How a Nonprofit Garnered Press Attention," *Public Relations Tactics* 12 (August 2005): 19.

Winter, Grant. "Improving Broadcast News Conferences," *Public Relations Journal* 46 (July 1990): 25–26.

Wright, Donald K. "We Have Rights Too: Examining the Existence of Professional Prejudice and Discrimination Against Public Relations," *Public Relations Review* 31 (March 2005): 101–119.

Media Directories

Bacon's Media Directories. Chicago: Bacon's.

Broadcasting/Cablecasting Yearbook. Washington, DC: Broadcasting Publications.

Burrelle's Media Directories. Livingston, NJ: Burrelle's.

Burrelle's Special Directories: Black Media /Hispanic Media/Women's Media. Livingston, NJ: Burrelle's.

Editor and Publisher International Yearbook. New York: Editor and Publisher.

Gale Directory of Publications. Detroit: Gale Research.

Gebbie Press. New Paltz, NY.

Guide to U.S. Business, Financial and Economic News Correspondents and Contacts. New York: Larriston Communications.

Guide to U.S. Medical and Science News Correspondents and Contacts. New York: Larriston Communications.

Harrison's Guide to the Top National TV Talk & Interview Shows. Lansdowne, PA: Bradley Communications.

Hudson's Washington News Media Contacts Directory. Rhinebeck, NY: Hudson's.

Military Publications. New York: Richard Weiner.

Media Services

Bacons' Information, Inc., Chicago.

BurrellesLuce, Livingston, NJ.

Business Wire, San Francisco.

Medialink, New York.

PRIMEZONE Media Network, Los Angeles.

PR News Wire, New York.

Vocus, Lanham, MD.

CASE 3-1

The long-awaited opening of the Smithsonian Institutions' Museum of the American Indian in 2004 had the potential for attracting extensive media coverage, but it took years of planning to make sure it materialized. To both celebrate the opening and attract visitors to the facility, the museum opening relied on an extensive media campaign to tell its story. Exhibit 3-1a is a photo of the opening ceremonies near the U.S. Capitol, and Exhibit 3-1b is the news release announcing the opening.

Promoting and Positioning the Grand Opening of the National Museum of the American Indian

Smithsonian Institution's National Museum of the American Indian with Hill & Knowlton

Overview

Millions of Americans claim Native American ancestry as part of their heritage, yet there has not been, until now, a national museum dedicated to Native cultures. The long overdue Smithsonian National Museum of the American Indian (NMAI) opened to the public on September 21, 2004.

Emotions were raw surrounding this new museum: Native peoples had waited centuries for cultural recognition in Washington while mainstream America continued to dismiss them as "relics of the past." Few knew the Museum was being built or that it would mark a long-overdue reconciliation for a culture still alive and thriving today. It would take a thoughtful and inclusive strategy to overcome these obstacles . . . and put the new Mall Museum on the global radar screen.

Could Hill & Knowlton pull it off?

Courtesy the National Museum of the American Indian, Smithsonian Institution

Research

Our task was clear: to let the world know the Museum was opening on the National Mall and to bring attention to the contributions Native Americans have made, and continue to make, on our society. With this in mind, we collaborated with the NMAI before embarking on other activities to set objectives for the communications campaign:

1. Jump start membership in the NMAI to allow for more Americans to begin a lifelong relationship.

2. Fuel early visitation and gift shop sales by generating buzz and highlighting unique aspects of the Museum tailored to specific audiences.

3. Increase awareness of the NMAI and its new Museum among a national/regional audience.

4. Help change long-held perceptions among youth (and their influencers) about Native Americans by influencing classroom teachings.

5. Generate hemispheric media attention to spread NMAI messages such as "We are still here," "Native peoples are a vibrant part of our culture," and "The history of the Americas begins here [at the NMAI]."

With goals and objectives formulated, our campaign began to take form. Step Two of formulating the communications strategy was to conduct thorough primary and secondary research to enable us to better assess the landscape.

Primary research included:

- A national Omnibus survey and regional poll that revealed 80 percent of regional audiences planned to visit D.C. in the next year and that 37 percent had not yet heard of the NMAI. This demonstrated to us the value in focusing most on those likely to visit (regional) while also reaching out to the national audience (49 percent of whom said they have visited a Smithsonian museum in the past and 79 percent had not heard of the NMAI).

- Interviews were conducted with NMAI leadership and stakeholders to gain perspectives on the Opening.

- H&K's proprietary online media analysis system (RADAR) was also activated to track volume and favorability of NMAI media coverage to enable us to see where coverage fell before, during, and after the Grand Opening campaign.

Additionally, secondary research was conducted by examining "lessons learned" from high-profile museum events (Holocaust Museum opening, Smithsonian 150th Anniversary, and the new Air and Space Museum annex, etc.).

Planning

Step Three of our precampaign due diligence included counseling the NMAI to embark on a formal planning process proprietary to H&K. This "Signature Event Planning Process" was new to the Smithsonian and played an important role in the concept, design, and tactical details of the Opening and led the NMAI to gain internal consensus on what would be a very complex and scrutinized event.

By utilizing this process, H&K was able to guide a very "silo-ed" NMAI staff through critical decisions over several months. A master event plan was then developed for the Opening and working committees were formed to oversee and manage all Opening events: Opening Ceremony, Native Nations Procession, First Americans Festival, and VIP Receptions.

Key audiences for the campaign were also defined through this process and included: Native Americans from the Western Hemisphere; potential visitors of all ages; donors; educators; elected officials; NMAI current and prospective members; Smithsonian stakeholders; and media.

Execution

With a two-year budget of approximately $1 million, the Grand Opening communications strategy internally dubbed "The NMAI Story: Five Chapters of the Grand Opening" was developed. Activities were prioritized into five distinct "chapters" beginning 15 months from the Opening. This approach enabled us to strategically build anticipation early while also forming a solid foundation of thoughtful media coverage around the world.

- **Chapter One:** "Getting Ready"—First, we navigated the NMAI through a series of "internal" foundation-building activities to jump-start a News Bureau operation. This included finalizing all outreach targets and pitches; working with a design firm to rejuvenate NMAI's graphic identity; developing a crisis/contingency plan in light of new terror threats; and lastly, partnering with Scholastic, Inc., to reach 250,000 students and 15,000 educators nationwide with NMAI-themed lesson plans emphasizing positive attributes of Native cultures.

- **Chapter Two:** "Building Relationships"—Next, H&K officially kicked off the "external" campaign with a series of events/activities. The goal was to beat the drum early and often about the Opening to trigger thoughtful and prolonged coverage all year. First, we held a national press conference to unveil Grand Opening plans, attended by 75 national/international press, generating 101 stories; distributed "Save the Date" cards to 6,000 media contacts and 25,000

NMAI supporters; reached out to long-lead media covering travel, arts, and architecture among other categories; began discussions with network morning and evening news programs; and conducted 50+ "hard hat" tours/photo opps and 40+ desk-side briefings.

- **Chapter Three:** "Setting the Stage"—Third, H&K worked with the NMAI to continue the dialogue with media in the months immediately preceding the Opening. This included facilitating prominent speaking opportunities for director Rick West (Chicago Historical Society, National Education Association, UNITY, and National Press Club); holding editorial board briefings with the *New York Times* and *Washington Post*; distributing a Latino B-roll package to extend reach into Central and South America; conducting 40+ media tours for top-tier reporters/producers, and producing a small-scale ($150K) regional print and radio ad campaign to enhance earned media efforts.

- **Chapter Four:** "Grand Opening Media Blitz"—September 2004 was "ground zero." This month H&K facilitated the Grand Opening on the National Mall. Strategically timed pre-Opening media events were held including a technical logistics briefing/walk-through for media; National Press Club address by Rick West; press junket for Rick West plus a satellite media tour and media teleconference; and a Media Open House & Briefing for 350+ media outlets to interview NMAI experts and tour the museum. Opening Day included coordinating 500+ media on the National Mall including 20+ broadcast crews, 10 satellite trucks, 60 photographers, and 2 satellite feeds (afternoon/evening).

- **Chapter Five:** "Sustaining Momentum"—Post-Opening, H&K worked with the NMAI to leverage the media spotlight to continue to tell the story. Specific activities included conducting post-Opening research and media analysis; placing limited "Now Open" billboard ads in 10 DC-area subway stations to drive post-Opening visitation and finalizing "round two" of Scholastic lesson plans to reach an audience of 42,000 teachers or 500,000 students.

Evaluation

The Grand Opening exceeded all expectations.
Objective 1: Thousands of new members flock to NMAI

- 25 percent increase in NMAI membership in 2004 (up 19,000 from 62,000 in January), exceeding goal of 10 percent.
- 3,700 new members joined in September alone.

Objective 2: Opening shatters Smithsonian sales record

- First-week gift shop sales exceeded $1 million, a Smithsonian record, as nine-day visitation exceeded 90,000.

- As of January 2005, more than 820,000 people have visited the Museum, with one million expected by mid-February.

Objective 3: Millions worldwide now aware of NMAI

- Benchmark research revealed a 28 percent increase nationally (from 21 percent to 49 percent) and a 23 percent increase in the Mid-Atlantic region (63 percent to 86 percent) in awareness.
- The percent of Americans who read/saw an article/ad about the NMAI jumped 10 percent nationally (13 percent to 23 percent); 33 percent of regional respondents said Opening media coverage inspired them to visit the National Mall in the next year.

Objective 4: Teachers and youth embrace Native educational materials and want more

- 100 percent of teachers recalling initial Scholastic materials had high praise for the NMAI program:
  1. 50 percent felt students would discuss the program with their parents;
  2. 97 percent felt it is important to teach students about Native Cultures and the NMAI; and
  3. 85 percent would find it helpful to have additional materials about Native American cultures.

Objective 5: NMAI messages span the globe

- H&K's RADAR (content analysis) tool found 92 percent of print media was favorable/neutral and that 45 percent of a representative sample of articles analyzed in the third quarter of 2004 included specific NMAI key messages.
- 25 percent of print coverage referenced the NMAI website, contributing to 1.2 million hits (17,025 visits) per day (prior average was 233,000 hits/4,298 visits per day).
- Global coverage resulting in circulation reach of 351 million in every state, Canada, Europe, Asia, and Central/South America. September coverage alone: 1,400 (TV), 900 (print). This equates to 1.1 billion impressions.
- Front-page coverage achieved in 14 of the top 25 papers. All network evening/morning news shows aired lengthy pieces and coverage was secured in all top newsweeklies.

"This is a project where the process was just as important as the result. It signals a new way to conceive, design, build and open a museum."
—**Lawrence Small**, *Secretary*, Smithsonian Institution.

EXHIBIT 3-1A   *Opening Ceremony*

Senator Ben Nighthorse Campbell addresses the crowd during the National Museum of the American Indian's opening ceremonies. Photo by Richard Strauss, Smithsonian Institution.
Courtesy the National Museum of the American Indian, Smithsonian Institution

EXHIBIT 3-1B   *News Release*

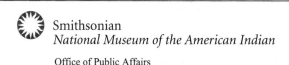

Smithsonian
National Museum of the American Indian

Office of Public Affairs

News

October 2004

Media only: Amy Drapeau   (202) 633-6614
                Thomas Sweeney   (202) 633-6611

National Museum of the American Indian Now Open at the Smithsonian

The Smithsonian's National Museum of the American Indian opened its doors to the public on Sept. 21. The museum, which was 15 years in the making, is the first national museum in the country dedicated exclusively to Native Americans, the first to present all exhibitions from a Native viewpoint and the first constructed on the National Mall since 1987.

"Visitors will leave this museum experience knowing that Indians are not just a part of history. We are still here and are making vital contributions to contemporary American culture and art," the museum's founding director, W. Richard West Jr. (Southern Cheyenne), said. "For example, one gallery is devoted solely to modern, groundbreaking Indian artwork, and we have a number of landmark pieces commissioned by the Smithsonian throughout the museum. In addition, we have thousands of priceless objects—from our collection of 800,000—in the three inaugural exhibitions and elsewhere in the museum."

The five-story, 250,000-square foot, curvilinear building was built on the last open space available on the National Mall, located between the Smithsonian's National Air and Space Museum and the U.S. Capitol. The textured golden-colored limestone exterior evokes natural rock formations shaped by wind and water over thousands of years. Set in a 4.25-acre landscaped site with wetlands and 40 boulders known as "grandfather rocks," the museum is a sharp contrast to neighboring Washington buildings. Its special features—an entrance facing east toward the rising sun, a prism window and a 120-foot-high atrium called the Potomac—were designed in consultation with many Native Americans over a four-year period.

A welcome wall of video screens at the museum's entrance greets visitors in 150 Native languages, conveying the significant presence and diversity of Native peoples throughout the Americas. This message is again reinforced in the Lelawi (leh-LAH-wee) Theater, a 120-seat circular theater located on the fourth floor offering a 13-minute multi-media experience, "Who We Are," that prepares museum-goers for their visit.

Courtesy the National Museum of the American Indian, Smithsonian Institution

EXHIBIT 3-1B   *News Release (continued)*

"The Smithsonian is honored to present this vital new museum, created by Native peoples from this hemisphere, to the American public and visitors from around the world," Smithsonian Institution Secretary Lawrence M. Small said. "Its importance can't be over estimated; it's a must-see for anyone visiting the nation's capital."

Opening Exhibitions

Approximately 8,000 objects from the museum's permanent collection are on display at the museum. Three major exhibitions are complemented by a contemporary art exhibit and landmark works of art—historic and contemporary—placed throughout the building.

"Our Universes: Traditional Knowledge Shapes Our World" focuses on Native cosmologies and the spiritual relationship between mankind and the natural world. It explores annual ceremonies of Native peoples as windows into ancestral Native teachings, featuring the annual Denver March Powwow, the North American Indigenous Games in Canada and the Day of the Dead in Mexico, as seasonal celebrations that unite different Native peoples.

"Our Peoples: Giving Voice to Our Histories" highlights historical events told from a Native point of view. The exhibition presents Native Americans' struggles to maintain traditions in the face of adversity. It includes a spectacular "wall of gold" featuring more than 400 figurines and gold objects dating back before 1491, European swords, coins and crosses made from melted gold, and a central area called "The Storm," with glass walls that change with shifting colors and video screens that present a narration of a vastly changed Native world.

"Our Lives: Contemporary Life and Identities" examines the identities of Native peoples in the 21st century and how those identities, both individual and communal, are shaped by deliberate choices made in challenging circumstances. Videos, wall labels, photographs and 300 objects work together to bring important Indian issues to the forefront. The exhibition also deals with the turbulent times of the 1960s and 1970s when the "Red Power" movement was born.

The museum's Changing Exhibitions Gallery features the works of Native artists George Morrison (Grand Portage Band of Chippewa, 1919-2000) and Allan Houser (Warm Springs Chiricahua Apache, 1914-1994). Through fall 2005, more than 200 works of art, including drawings, paintings and sculptures will be displayed.

Throughout the museum, the works of Native artists are on display as "landmark objects" in the public areas, including a 20-foot totem pole by carver Nathan Jackson (Tlingit) and a bronze sculpture by Roxanne Swentzell (Santa Clara Pueblo), as well as a carving of a Kwakiutl speaker and Navajo weavings from the museum's collections.

The "Window on the Collections: Many Hands, Many Voices" exhibition offers a view into the vast National Museum of the American Indian collections by showcasing 3,500 objects arranged in seven categories. Objects include animal-themed figurines and objects, beadwork, containers, dolls, peace medals, projectile points and qeros (cups for ritual drinking).

The demonstration program features Native boats, which will be under construction in the center of the Potomac over the course of the first year. The program begins with the construction of two boats, a Native Hawaiian canoe and an Inuit kayak.

Tickets for the museum

Timed free passes are required to visit the museum. Up to 10 advance passes are available at www.AmericanIndian.si.edu or at www.tickets.com or by calling 866-400-NMAI (6624) for a convenience fee of $1.75 per ticket plus a $1.50 service charge per order. A limited number of timed, same-day entry passes are available, starting at 10 a.m., at the museum's main entrance.

Background

Established in 1989, through an Act of Congress, the Smithsonian's National Museum of the American Indian is an institution of living cultures dedicated to the life, languages, literature, history and arts of the Native peoples of the Western Hemisphere. The museum includes the recently opened National Museum of the American Indian on the National Mall; the George Gustav Heye Center, a permanent museum in lower Manhattan; and the Cultural Resources Center, a research and collections facility in Suitland, Md. With the opening of the National Museum of the American Indian, the Smithsonian comprises 18 museums and galleries and the National Zoo.

# # #

SMITHSONIAN INSTITUTION 4th Street and Independence Avenue, SW, Washington DC 20560-0934
202.633.1000 Telephone 202.633.6920 Fax www.AmericanIndian.si.edu Web

A coalition of groups mobilized a strong media relations campaign to honor those who perished in the terrorist attacks on September 11, 2001. Exhibit 3-2a is a news release from the program, and Exhibit 3-2b is a portion of the promotional brochure.

How Will You Remember September 11?

One Day's Pay with PainePR, Magnet Communications, Peppercom, MediaLink, Winuk Communications, PR Newswire, Burrelles, Patrice Tanaka & Co., Carter Ryley Thomas, and Duffy Communications

Situation/Challenge

Soon after the terrorist attacks, a group of family members of 9/11 victims, public relations executives, and friends came together to create One Day's Pay ("one day's payment of service"), a nonprofit initiative to establish September 11 as a national day of voluntary service. The idea came from a desire to leave a lasting, positive legacy in honor of the victims of 9/11. Our goal was simple: to encourage individuals and organizations to set aside time on or around September 11 each year to help others in need, however they saw fit to do so, rekindling the spirit of unity that existed after the terrorist attacks. The challenge was to successfully launch the initiative, generating meaningful awareness and support with very limited cash resources (about $29,000 to start), no employees (everyone was a volunteer), and competition for "mind share" from other established "days of service," i.e., Martin Luther King Day (February), Make a Difference Day (October), and National Youth Service Day (April).

Research

2002 Pilot Program

We began researching the concept soon after the terrorist attacks, gathering information on other days of service and related initiatives. We found that while there were organizations already dedicated to days of service in general, no one was organizing or leading an effort to establish 9/11 as a day of service. In 2002, we launched a limited pilot test, creating a website and using an e-mail "chain letter" and limited PR (Newsday, CNN/fn, and other outlets) to encourage people (controlled awareness) to visit the site and register nonbinding "pledges" (and their plans)

Courtesy One Day's Pay

on the site to observe 9/11 through any form of service they desired. The pilot led to nearly 12,000 documented pledges on the website in 2002. Afterwards, we surveyed these individuals via an online questionnaire. Among the findings: (1) Strong qualitative support existed for observing 9/11 through service; (2) One Day's Pay attracted people who don't normally volunteer, with many saying they'd stay involved—vital information that helped us win support in 2003 from key influencers.

2002 National Survey

We also conducted a national telephone survey of adults, which revealed overwhelming support (79 percent) for observing 9/11 as a day of voluntary service.

Identifying Influencers

Securing the support and participation of key influencers was a key strategy to build credibility and reach. So, beginning in 2003, One Day's Pay spent initial months investigating potential supporters and influential groups using Internet searches, news coverage analysis, calls to selected groups, and review of websites. We produced a short list of key influencers including leaders of: (1) key 9/11 family organizations; (2) volunteer service and nonprofit sector; (3) government agencies; and (4) other "days of service" initiatives.

Planning

Objectives

- Establish a meaningful first-year foundation of public and nonprofit support for observing September 11 as a national day of voluntary service.

- Generate sufficient voluntary "participation pledges" in 2003 (50,000 to 100,000) on the One Day's Pay website, www.onedays pay.org, to demonstrate viability and provide local testimonials for the media.

- Secure significant national media attention in 2003 to build awareness, participation, and credibility.

- Solicit adequate in-kind and cash donations to support the 2003 launch.

Strategies

- Win endorsements by key partner organizations.

- Leverage resources of partner organizations to cost-effectively spread the word.

- Leverage the Internet and website to cost-effectively deliver information; help recruit partners interested in delivering their own messages; promote and measure participation; and document people's plans for 9/11.
- Actively involve founding relatives of 9/11 victims to help maintain the right tone and serve as spokespersons.
- Secure sufficient prelaunch participation commitments from volunteer centers and local nonprofits to establish a base of support (and media credibility) prior to announcing the initiative publicly.
- Leverage national and local publicity to generate broader public interest.

Audiences

- Local nonprofit organizations and volunteer centers
- Individuals, groups, and others interested in observing 9/11 as a voluntary day of service
- Vendors and other in-kind and cash donors

Budget Planning

Budget was $400,000 including services donated. Paine PR ($25,000), Peppercorn ($2,000), and Magnet ($2,000) made one-time cash donations. Strong commitments of in-kind support worth more than $350,000 were also secured from suppliers, including Medialink, Burrelle's, PR Newswire, VMS, and PR firms. Actual expenses were: $392,391, leaving a surplus of $860.

Execution/Tactics

Influencer Endorsements

From day one, we wanted the initiative to reflect the feelings of 9/11 family members and knew their support was critical. Led by family members on our Board, we first secured endorsements of key groups: Coalition of 9/11 Families, September Space, Families of 9/11, and Tuesday's Children. Then we approached and secured the endorsement of the Points of Light Foundation, which oversees 400 volunteer centers. That led to winning the support of Youth Service America, Citizen Corps (Department of Homeland Security), and USA Freedom Corps (White House Office of Volunteerism).

Website Enhancements/Collateral

We created a new website (www.onedayspay.org) to cost-effectively educate people/groups on the initiative; provide ideas, links, and resources to our partners (which helped to sign them up); and encourage visitors to participate by registering (optional) confidential good faith "pledges" to observe 9/11 as a day of service. We also invited people to share their plans, and we used many of these (with permission) to provide human interest/local angles necessary to generate substantial national and local market coverage. We included a link to ServeNET that allowed people to quickly and easily find volunteer opportunities in their communities.

Nonprofit Outreach

One Day's Pay secured exhibit space at the National Conference on Community Service, held on June 6–8, 2003. More than 4,000 leaders of nonprofit organizations attended. We distributed 2,500 brochures, then followed up by phone on the attendee list, securing advance commitments to participate by 48 nonprofits prior to a planned press launch in August 2003.

Media Launch

One Day's Pay launched officially on Tuesday, August 12, 2003, at the National Press Club in Washington, D.C., selected to capitalize on our strong Washington, D.C.–area support, and the slow news period when Congress is out of session. Board members Jay Winuk (who lost his brother, Glenn, at the WTC) and Alice Hoglan (mother of PR-exec Mark Bingham, passenger of Flight #93) served as principal spokespersons, along with President David Paine. Advance morning appearances were secured on NBC's *Today* and CNN's *American Morning* to prompt interest. All of the major networks and 35 national outlets attended the press event. Medialink also organized a Satellite Media Tour. Additionally, we lined up local PR resources to help in key cities. Follow-up pitching, including release of a new 2003 national survey showing continued support generated widespread coverage, including a second wave of coverage the week leading up to 9/11.

Evaluation

- Won significant high-profile support including Points of Light Foundation, Citizen Corps, Youth Service America, Coalition of 9/11 Families, Tuesday's Children, and USA Freedom Corps.
- Documented at least 100,000 registered participants in the first year on our website, including more than 300 nonprofit organizations, schools, and employers. Unofficial estimates taken from news articles and general reservations put undocumented participation at more than 1 million.
- Generated widespread national and local media coverage (promoting the 9/11 observance as a day of service), mentioning One Day's Pay, including 316 articles; 200+ national and local TV and radio

mentions; three AP features and stories in *USA Today* and other major outlets. Total media impressions over just 60 days exceeded 80 million.

- Raised $350,636 in in-kind services and $42,615 cash (in six months). Secured 501(c)(3) IRS status (tax-exempt nonprofit organization).

- Web tracking software consistently showed a direct correlation between media coverage and website traffic.

- Documented thousands of expressions of generosity and compassion inspired by One Day's Pay.

- Set the stage for continuation and growth of the initiative in 2004.

EXHIBIT 3-2A   *News Release*

 One Day's Pay

<u>**For More Information Contact**</u>:

Heather Bandura (For Print)   Susan Roth (For Broadcast)
Media Relations   Media Relations
One Day's Pay   One Day's Pay
212-613-4974   301-330-2587
949-305-1349 (alt #)

<u>**Family Members of 9/11 Victims, Leading Nonprofits Launch Major Initiative**</u>
<u>**Urging Americans to Observe September 11 as a National Day of Service**</u>

Goal is to Rekindle and Sustain Post-9/11 Spirit of Unity and Selflessness
While Honoring Victims;
More Than 100 Organizations Nationwide Already Committed

WASHINGTON, D.C., August 12, 2003 – Seeking to recapture the spirit of national unity following the September 11, 2001, terrorist attacks on America, relatives of 9/11 victims, business leaders and prominent nonprofit organizations have together launched a coast-to-coast initiative urging all Americans, businesses, schools and other groups to honor the victims of the terrorist attacks by permanently observing September 11 as a National Day of Voluntary Service, Charity and Compassion.

"Americans want to pay special tribute on that day, and we cannot think of a better expression than to rekindle and sustain the spirit of generosity, humanity and concern that turned strangers into neighbors and unified our entire nation during a very tragic time in our history," said David Paine, president of One Day's Pay (www.onedayspay.org), the New York-based nonprofit organization formed to lead the initiative. The goal of One Day's Pay, said Paine, is for more than 30 million people to actively participate annually by 2010, making September 11 one of the most widely observed days of service in American history.

<u>**Making A Pledge to Help Others**</u>

Organizations collaborating with One Day's Pay include the Coalition of 9-11 Families (www.memorialfor911.com); Families of September 11 (www.familiesofseptember11.org); Tuesday's Children (www.tuesdayschildren.com); the Points of Light Foundation & Volunteer Center National Network (www.1800volunteer.org);

Courtesy One Day's Pay

EXHIBIT 3-2A *News Release (continued)*

Youth Service America (www.ysa.org); and the Citizens Committee of New York; (www.citizensnyc.org).

Also, One Day's Pay is working with Citizen Corps (www.citizencorps.gov), an office within the Department of Homeland Security that promotes citizen preparedness programs through Citizen Corps Councils. "We encourage the Citizen Corps Councils around the country to work with their community leadership to promote volunteer service opportunities in support of first responders, disaster relief, community safety and health awareness. Our communities are more secure when neighbors help neighbors," said Michael D. Brown, Undersecretary Emergency Preparedness and Response, Department of Homeland Security. "Together we can make President Bush's vision a reality."

"One Day's Pay is an excellent way to demonstrate the power of healing through helping others," said Robert K. Goodwin, president and CEO of the Points of Light Foundation. "We are honored to be a part of this coalition to encourage people of all ages to share their time, talents, and resources to strengthen America's communities while paying tribute to those who perished as a result of the September 11 attacks."

One Day's Pay has set up a robust Web site (www.onedayspay.org) and is encouraging individuals, employers and organizations to go online and register non-binding, confidential pledges indicating their intention to engage in activities or make plans to help others in need on or around September 11, 2003. Already more than 100 organizations from across the country have pledged to participate in the initiative this year.

"A pledge is simply a good faith expression of intent to participate, and to help someone who needs it," said Paine. "A pledge isn't binding, the process is free, and the information people and organizations provide is completely confidential. Individuals and organizations that register pledges decide for themselves how they want to express their commitment to serving others, and when. They can give money to a charity they support, volunteer time at a soup kitchen, organize a used clothing or canned food drive at work, go grocery shopping for a neighbor who is homebound, become a Big Brother or Big Sister, or make an appointment to give blood – whatever matters most to them."

"We hope to establish a lasting legacy of selflessness and compassion, one that honors those lost and injured while permanently embracing the spirit of kindness and charity so meaningful and evident in the months following this national tragedy," said Jay S. Winuk, vice president of One Day's Pay and brother of Glenn J. Winuk, an attorney and volunteer fireman who lost his life trying to save those trapped in the World Trade Center's South Tower.

2

"Glenn was one of many heroes who put the interests of others ahead of his own that day," Winuk said. "In so many remarkable ways, that's how the entire nation responded, and with One Day's Pay we hope to keep that spirit alive and productive, for people in need every day, in every corner of this country."

Helpful Ideas

For those seeking suggestions on what they can do to assist others, the One Day's Pay Web site provides links that help people and organizations find local Volunteer Centers, join community-based Citizen Corps to assist in local disaster preparedness programs, or link to many other activities.

Visitors to the site can also search a nationwide database, set up by SERVEnet.org, which lists hundreds of thousands of community service opportunities, encourages nonprofits to register their volunteer or service needs, and even allows individuals to list special talents they want to offer to nonprofits. Other valuable resources include links to the American Red Cross, for those interested in giving blood, and to USA Freedom Corps, President Bush's volunteer service initiative, which has a database of local opportunities offered by more than 75,000 organizations.

"President Bush has called upon all Americans to answer the call to serve something greater than themselves," said John Bridgeland, Director of President George W. Bush's USA Freedom Corps. "We encourage all Americans to find ways like One Day's Pay to do more to help their neighbors and their nation by answering the President's call to service."

The name One Day's Pay refers to the idea of giving at least one day's payment of service to the community each year. The concept was originally inspired by the courage and heroism of Mark Bingham, Jeremy Glick, Todd Beamer and Thomas Burnett, passengers on United Airlines #93 who are believed to have confronted the terrorists and prevented them from striking their intended targets in the Washington D.C. area. During the struggle to gain control from the terrorists, Flight #93 crashed in the fields of Pennsylvania.

"So many people acted with courage, selflessness and generosity on that day, and in the days following the tragedy," said Alice Hoglan, Mark Bingham's mother. "It is very appropriate that we observe September 11 by rekindling and nurturing that spirit of unity and compassion."

Winuk and Hoglan are among five relatives of 9-11 victims who helped found One Day's Pay and who now participate as members of the group's Board of Directors. Others are Chris Burke, founder of the nonprofit organization Tuesday's Children and brother of Tom Burke, an employee of Cantor Fitzgerald; and Steve and Elizabeth Alderman, former members of the board of the Memorial Committee for Families of September 11 and parents of Pete Alderman, an employee at Bloomberg L.P. offices in the World Trade Center.

3

EXHIBIT 3-2A   *News Release (continued)*

A September 2002 survey conducted by Horizon Research on behalf of One Day's Pay found that 75 percent of the public supported the idea of establishing September 11 as a national day of community service. Nearly two-thirds thought their employers should do something to observe September 11, yet only 39 percent said their employers had something special planned in 2002, and that was most notably limited to a moment of silence. Seventy-six percent of those surveyed said they would participate in a community service activity if their employer organized one for them.

For more information, contact One Day's Pay at info@onedayspay.org, or at 212-613-4979.

#   #   #

EXHIBIT 3–2B *Brochure*

What is One Day's Pay?

One Day's Pay is a national nonprofit organization (501c3), working in partnership with 9/11 families, the Points of Light Foundation, Youth Service America, American Red Cross, Business Strengthening America, Citizen Corps, major employers and other leading groups to establish September 11 as a voluntarily observed national day of service. Visit our Web site at www.onedayspay.org.

How does One Day's Pay work? Are you asking people to donate one day's wages?

No we're not. The choice of what to do is entirely yours! We're simply asking individuals, employers and other organizations to observe September 11 by doing something good for someone else in need. That's it! In this way, we hope to forever keep alive the spirit of giving and service that unified our nation following the terrorist attacks. Donating money to a charity of your choice is just one option. Other ideas include arranging volunteer activities, participating in, or hosting a blood drive, helping an elderly neighbor buy groceries, or contacting a local Volunteer Center or United Way for other opportunities. Visit our Web site for other ideas. We offer toolkits, booklets, other resources and links to organizations that can provide help.

Do I select from a list of activities organized by One Day's Pay?

No. Individuals and organizations determine for themselves how they want to define service and what they want their "one day's pay" to be. We do not promote or favor any specific charity. Our mission is simply to encourage individuals and organizations to acknowledge the special significance of September 11 by planning activities that help others in the spirit of compassion and unity.

How do I participate?

It's easy. Simply visit the One Day's Pay Web site at www.onedayspay.org and register your good faith intention ("participation pledge") to observe September 11 by helping others in need. Making a participation pledge is free, non-binding and completely confidential. Your information will not be forwarded or revealed to anyone. Our goal is simply to track the total number of people participating. You also can request a manual registration form by e-mailing us at onedayspay@painepr.com or by calling 212-613-4979.

What if I'm not sure what to do?

You do not need to decide on your plans right now to register your intention to participate. You can decide that later. Plus, you can always come back to the Web site to update your information.

What about employers? Do they have to close? Can they do something on another day?

The spirit of One Day's Pay is to promote the concept of service and compassion on or around September 11. Companies need not close to live up to that. While a growing number of businesses today are providing employees with opportunities to volunteer during certain designated work days, there's a wealth of other things companies and employees can do on-site, as well as over the course of a number of days, weeks and even months. In fact, some employees may prefer not to take time off, but rather participate in activities planned over another weekend. Businesses may want to allow employees to make voluntary financial contributions to local charities. They may organize on-site blood, clothing or canned food drives, or sponsor other activities that do not involve employees leaving during the day. Lots of ideas, resources and links are available on our Web site at www.onedayspay.org.

Register your program at www.onedayspay.org

Courtesy One Day's Pay

Opening new exhibits at a museum is a way to attract media attention and a new Wild Reef at the Shedd Aquarium would also attract many new visitors to Chicago. Exhibit 3-3a is a scene from the Interactive Media Kit used in the campaign, and Exhibit 3-3b is the news release.

Shedd Sharks Go Wild

Shedd Aquarium with Public Communications, Inc.

Overview

With a limited budget and high expectations for opening its largest, most expensive exhibit ever, the Shedd Aquarium knew that its success would rely on effective public relations to build anticipation and excitement for the opening of Wild Reef in April 2003. The $48 million underground exhibit not only featured an eye-to-eye look at reef aquatic life, but it also brought to Chicago two dozen sharks.

Research

Communications planning began in early 2002 for Wild Reef and started with market research that identified five key audiences and the messages to which they would be likely to respond. For example, Young Urban Explorers would respond to messages that the exhibit was "the newest thing" and wasn't just for families or kids, while Fun-Loving Suburbanites want to get up close to the animals and need activities with kid-friendly features.

In addition, the Aquarium identified a sixth audience. Chicago has a vital Filipino community, which would take a keen interest in this exhibit, since it re-creates a Philippine island and the surrounding coral reefs. Through interviews and secondary research, team members learned about this community, especially its opinion leaders and media outlets, to build awareness about the opening of Wild Reef.

Planning

Using the marketing research, the communication team prepared a 12-month media plan starting in April 2002, culminating with the exhibit's opening on April 15, 2003, and continuing into the summer. Throughout the campaign, the communication team worked closely

Courtesy Shedd Aquarium

with the aquarium's animal care and facilities staffs to identify several key story opportunities in the year leading up to the exhibit opening.

The key objectives established for the campaign were (1) to increase the awareness among local residents and tourists by 20 percent that Wild Reef was opening in April, (2) to raise annual attendance by 10 percent, and (3) to expand annual membership revenue for 2003 by 8 percent and to garner a 1 percent return on direct mail. Because of limited advertising dollars, the public relations team was charged with generating a "buzz" about the exhibit to carrying the public awareness.

Although the exhibit featured a life around a coral reef, the communications strategy centered on featuring the sharks. Although nearly one million animals are in the exhibit (if you count the coral), the sharks were what captured people's imaginations and interest. Media materials and story pitches focused heavily on the sharks. To ensure as much favorable exposure as possible, the outreach started one year before the opening date with a tour of the empty shark tank that is three stories tall. Starting media outreach early helped position Wild Reef as the major "must-see" in Chicago.

Throughout the construction of the exhibit, Shedd and PCI worked with the animal care and facilities staffs at the aquarium and pitched an average of one story every month during the last six months before the exhibit opened. The resulting news stories served as periodic media previews to build excitement in prospective visitors for the opening.

In addition, to gauge the effect that the impending war in Iraq was having on national television news, Shedd and PCI made some initial "soft soundings" to producers with the national television networks to evaluate the chances of landing a feature story on Wild Reef. As a result of these calls, it was determined that the best strategy to deal with the impending war in Iraq was to minimize national TV public relations efforts early on. But to start targeting the national TV network morning shows after the war had been fought and the initial aftermath had subdued.

Execution

The communication team created a second, more elaborate media kit on CD-ROM, which was sent out to all target media three months before the opening.

By partnering with Borders bookstores, Wild Reef displays were featured in the front windows of Borders stores in Chicago. Closer to opening day, radio promotions were initiated, which included free Wild Reef tickets as part of the prize package.

In a unique promotional tactic, the aquarium created huge artificial shark fins and anchored them to the outside dome atop their building, which is visible from downtown Chicago. They also appeared at various locations in the aquarium. In addition, aquarium employees and volunteers wore a shark fin on the back of their uniforms. One employee even threw an honorary pitch at Wrigley Field with the shark fin on his back.

Opening day festivities included a performance by a dance troupe of Filipino children, who performed traditional Filipino dances. The mayor of Chicago and dozens of city and state dignitaries attended the opening ceremonies, along with 250 children from Chicago Public Schools. Guests received Wild Reef pins, which they enjoyed trading and collecting.

After the opening, when the media furor over the Iraq war had largely subsided, the communication team offered NBC's *Today* show an exclusive story on one of the signature animals featured in Wild Reef. The four-minute story aired on *Weekend Today* on September 13.

Evaluation

Shedd and PCI proved that no one could withstand the awesome power of sharks! Due to the early and widespread interest created by the aquarium's strategic communication plan, the aquarium surpassed each of its communications objectives:

1. To increase the awareness of local residents and tourists by 20 percent that Wild Reef was opening in April. In baseline research taken in January and February 2003, 35 percent of local residents and tourists surveyed knew that the new exhibit was opening later that year. When follow-up research was taken in April, 62 percent knew the exhibit was opening. This surpassed the aquarium's awareness objective by 27 percent.

2. To increase annual attendance by 10 percent. Through December 31, 2003, almost 2.1 million guests visited Shedd, exceeding actual attendance from the same time last year by 22 percent. To put this in context, Shedd's 2003 attendance is 400,000 people ahead of the second-place aquarium in the country and at least 600,000 people ahead of the second-place cultural institution in Chicago.

3. To increase annual membership revenue for 2003 by 8 percent and garner a 1 percent return on direct mail. To date, Shedd Aquarium's membership department reported that they nearly doubled the number of member households, have achieved a revenue increase of 66 percent (from $1.85 projected to $2.8 actual in hand), and have had a 2 percent response to direct mail. (National return average is between .4 and .6 percent.)

Shedd's communication department credits the aggressive public relations campaign with its success. Media relations secured more than 877 placements from April 2002 through August 2003, reaching an audience of more than 150 million. National, regional, and local placements were secured in all major media outlets, and the Wild Reef helped Shedd Aquarium set new attendance records in 2003, when it became the most visited cultural attraction in the Midwest and the best attended aquarium in the United States.

EXHIBIT 3-3A   *Interactive Media Kit*

Courtesy Shedd Aquarium

EXHIBIT 3-3B   *News Release*

Media Contact:
Roger Germann
312/692-3265

Tracy Boutelle
312/692-3330

For Immediate Release

Sharks at Shedd Aquarium Reveal Underwater Mysteries of One of the World's Preeminent Coral Reefs

New Wild Reef exhibit brings one of the largest shark collections in North America to Chicago

(Chicago, Ill.) – April 29, 2002 – The sharks are coming! One year from now, visitors will sink their teeth into a new underwater exhibit featuring sharks, sharks and more sharks as the Shedd Aquarium prepares to unveil one of the largest and most diverse shark exhibits in North America – the *Wild Reef*.

Several dozen of these mythic predators will descend into Shedd's new engaging and interactive shark attraction, as the *Wild Reef* is slated to open in April 2003.

Guests will experience the otherworldly mystery of diving the waters of a coral reef – in one of the world's largest displays – including face-to-face encounters with the most menacing undersea creatures: sharks. Faint-hearted guests are warned they may find themselves only inches away from more than 30 sharks in a curved-overhead 400,000-gallon habitat.

A re-creation of an Indo-Pacific island and the largest addition at Shedd since the Oceanarium, the new shark and coral reef exhibit will uncover the animals, biodiversity and cultural connection behind this unparalleled marine ecosystem.

A Daring Shark Experience

As home for some of the most mysterious and misunderstood animals of the sea, the *Wild Reef* will provide a "diver's eye" view of a Philippine coral reef and the menacing creatures that lurk in its fertile waters. Guests begin their journey at the surging shores of Apo Island and then "dive" 30 feet below the surface to one of the world's largest coral reefs, completing their trip by surfacing to the mangroves and beaches of this Philippine coast.

Designed for guests of all ages, the multi-sensory exhibit surrounds "divers"-for-a-day with an immersive underwater encounter: the smell of saltwater, the sound of waves, the feeling of sand and the sight of sharks swimming overhead and rays gliding under foot.

-more-

Courtesy Shedd Aquarium

What Lurks Beneath

"Sharks capture our dreams – and sometimes our nightmares. They are the product of millions of years of evolution, perfecting their predatory skills and creating the ocean's most efficient killer," said George Parsons, assistant curator of fishes at Shedd. "Sharks are a mystery and their secrets come to life on the coral reefs where they live, especially those surrounding Apo Island."

Eight years in the making, the *Wild Reef* – Shedd's new shark and coral reef exhibit – will feature 26 habitats with 540 species represented by 1 million animals – including sharks and coral and other fish – doubling the Aquarium's current number of species. Shedd's first new building in more than a decade, the exhibit will span 10 rooms, each ergonomically designed to truly immerse guests in an entertaining educational experience.

The 27,000-square-foot, $45 million exhibit will introduce, for the first time at Shedd, large sharks in a dedicated, state-of-the-art habitat. The exhibit requires 750,000 gallons of water, more than doubling the original aquarium's capacity to 1.2 million gallons.

"Our new shark exhibit is one of the most exciting things to ever come to Shedd and, more important, to Chicago," said Ted Beattie, president and CEO of Shedd Aquarium. "It furthers Shedd's prominent position as an innovator and leader among the country's aquariums."

Fins and Jaws and Teeth...Oh My!

Dubbed "devils from the sea," sharks have long conjured a mythic fear among landlubbers and seafarers alike. The *Wild Reef* will dispel the myths and explore how sharks fit into our imaginations and into our ecosystems.

The centerpiece of the exhibit will be the 400,000-gallon shark habitat – nearly five times the size of the Caribbean Reef exhibit – giving visitors the chance to experience – up close – the power and speed of "nature's eating machine." At least 30 sharks will reside in the new exhibit, including blacktip, whitetip, wobbegong and sand bar. Sharing the habitat will be other big reef fish that can hold their own or keep out of the way.

Diving in the Philippines

The *Wild Reef* exhibit brings to Chicago the coral reefs of the Philippines, the epicenter of the world's marine diversity and home to more than 40 species of sharks. The shark and coral exhibit will house eight distinct Indo-Pacific experiences, told by the seamless integration of live animals, authentic experiences and inspiring architecture.

-more-

EXHIBIT 3-3B   *News Release (continued)*

"The foundation of Shedd Aquarium is education and conservation. The coral reefs of Apo Island not only represent one of the sea's most distinct environments but also an ecosystem at risk due to human interference," said Bert Vescolani, vice president of aquarium collections and education at Shedd Aquarium. "Visitors will experience firsthand the awesome beauty of these endangered reefs and, we hope, be inspired to learn more about the world's ocean habitats."

The *Wild Reef* will also have one of the largest, most diverse public displays of live corals in North America.

The Master Plan

The *Wild Reef* exhibit is the cornerstone of Shedd's current exhibit master plan. This long-term exhibit plan focuses on bringing to Shedd six distinct regional aquatic ecosystems: The Pacific Northwest coast, Illinois waters, East African lakes and rivers, Florida Everglades and the Caribbean reefs, the Amazon River, and Indo-Pacific coral reefs. *Wild Reef* is the Shedd's Indo-Pacific coral reef exhibit.

Early in the planning stages for the exhibit, aquarium leaders formed an advisory group to solicit input from the Filipino community. The group's contributions are helping make the exhibit more interesting, relevant and authentic.

Sharks, Coral and Apo Island

The *Wild Reef* is scheduled to open in April 2003. The new exhibit explores Philippine coral reefs, which support an amazing abundance of life and anchor a delicate network of dependencies between animals, habitats and humans. The *Wild Reef* exhibit takes visitors down 25 feet below ground, at the same level as the surface of Lake Michigan. Construction of the underground addition began at the south side of the current Shedd structure in the fall of 1999.

#

Shedd Aquarium is supported by the people of Chicago through the Chicago Park District.
Chicago residents are eligible to receive discounted admission.

## Chapter 4

Internal Communications

Public relations conducted inside organizations falls into two general categories: employee relations and member relations. Employee relations includes all communications between the management of an organization and its personnel. Member relations refers to communications inside a membership organization between the officers and members.

EMPLOYEE RELATIONS

Research, objectives, programming, and evaluation are useful problem-solving tools in employee relations. Good management of an organization is often measured by the quality of communication within the organization. Senior leaders also understand that well-informed employees form the basis for many strategic communication initiatives with external publics.

RESEARCH

Research for employee relations concentrates on client research, studying the reason for communication, and identifying the employee audiences to be targeted for communication.

Client Research

Client research for employee relations focuses on *information* about the organization's personnel. What is the size and nature of the workforce? What reputation does the organization have with its workforce? How satisfied are the employees? What employee communications does the organization regularly use? Are any special forms of communication used? How credible and effective are the organization's internal communications? Has the organization conducted special employee relations programs in the past? If so, what were the results of such programs? What are the organization's strengths, weaknesses, and opportunities regarding its workforce? These questions might guide the initial research in preparation for an employee relations program.

Opportunity or Problem Research

A second focal point for research is the *reason* for conducting an employee relations program. Is a new program really necessary? Most organizations have regular and ongoing channels of internal communications that are used to convey management information, so this question should be answered with care because it justifies the necessary expenditure for a program. Would the program be reactive—in response to a problem that has arisen in employee relations, or would it be proactive—taking advantage of an opportunity to improve existing employee relations?

A survey of employee attitudes may reveal a variety of issues, including: low levels of satisfaction and morale, dislike of the physical surroundings, and/or frustration with internal policies. The survey results may thus demonstrate a strong need for a reactive employee relations program.

Audience Research

The final area of research involves precisely defining the *employee audiences* to be targeted for communication. These audiences can be identified using the following terms:

Management
  Upper-level administrators
  Midlevel administrators
  Lower-level administrators
Nonmanagement (staff)
  Specialists
  Clerical personnel
  Secretarial personnel
  Uniformed personnel
    Equipment operators
    Drivers
    Security personnel
    Other uniformed personnel
  Union representatives
  Other nonmanagement personnel

Effective research on employee relations is built on an understanding of the client's personnel, the opportunity or problem that serves as a reason for communication with the workforce, and the specific identification of the employee audiences to be targeted for communication.

OBJECTIVES

Objectives for employee relations include the two major categories of impact and output. Employee relations objectives may be specific and quantitative to facilitate accurate measurement. Optional percentages and time frames are included here in parentheses.

Impact Objectives

Impact objectives for employee relations include informing employees or modifying their attitudes or behaviors. Some typical impact objectives are:

1. To increase employee knowledge of significant organizational policies, activities, and developments (by 60 percent during March and April)

2. To enhance favorable employee attitudes toward the organization (by 40 percent during the current fiscal year)

3. To accomplish (50 percent) greater employee adoption of behaviors desired by management (in a three-month period)

4. To make (60 percent of) the employee force organizational spokespersons in the community (during the next two years)

5. To receive (50 percent) more employee feedback from organizational communications (during the coming year)

Behavioral, informational, and attitudinal impact objectives may be used in any combination in a public relations plan. The chosen objectives should be carefully determined so they demonstrate the program's goals.

Output Objectives

Output objectives in employee relations constitute the efforts made by the practitioner to accomplish such desired outcomes as employee recognition and regular employee communication. Some examples include:

1. To recognize employee accomplishments and contributions in (80 percent of) employee communications (during the current year)

2. To prepare and distribute employee communications on a weekly basis

3. To schedule interpersonal communication between management and a specific employee group each month (specify groups and months)

PROGRAMMING

Programming for employee relations should include the careful planning of theme and messages, action or special event(s), uncontrolled and controlled media, and execution, using the principles of effective communication.

Theme and Messages

The theme and messages for employee relations depend on the reason for conducting the campaign or program. Both of these elements should grow out of the opportunity or problem that accounts for the particular program. That is, themes and messages usually grow out of the problems faced by companies and the methods chosen to solve them. For example, a practitioner working for a company that is moving its facilities and offices to a new building could produce a brochure entitled "A Company on the Move."

Action(s) or Special Event(s)

Action and special events used in employee relations programs include:

1. Training seminars
2. Special programs on safety or new technology
3. An open house for employees and their families
4. Parties, receptions, and other social affairs
5. Other employee special events related to organizational developments

A bank, for example, could sponsor a surprise Dividend Day for participants in the employee stock program, and a company moving into a new facility could arrange an employee open house and party. The CEO (chief executive officer) can host a company-wide town meeting to signal an important announcement.

Uncontrolled and Controlled Media

The use of uncontrolled media in employee relations is usually limited to sending news releases or announcements about employees' accomplishments to outside mass and specialized media as warranted. Actually, this is media relations, not employee relations, but it is often considered part of the employee relations program, as a news report is often perceived by employees as a most credible source of information about the organization.

Controlled media, on the other hand, are used extensively in employee relations programs. The most frequently used controlled media are e-mail, voice mail, websites, and memoranda. Also often used are employee publications such as magazines, newspapers, and newsletters addressed to particular groups or levels of employees in larger organizations. These publications are often highly professional and creative, both in writing and design.

In addition to e-mail, voice mail, websites, and house publications, employee relations programs use a variety of other forms of controlled media, such as:

1. Bulletin boards
2. Displays and exhibits
3. Telephone hot lines or news lines
4. Inserts accompanying paychecks
5. Internal television
6. Videos
7. Meetings

8. Teleconferences
9. Audiovisual presentations
10. Booklets, pamphlets, brochures
11. Speakers' bureaus (employees address community groups)

The use of media in employee relations differs from that in other forms of public relations because of the heavy emphasis on controlled media.

Effective Communication

Principles of effective communication are virtually the same for employee relations as for most other forms of public relations, although two-way communication and audience participation should be stressed. Special events are an excellent way to use these elements in employee relations.

EVALUATION

Impact and output objectives in employee relations can be evaluated using the same tools of measurement as in other forms of public relations (see Chapter 2). In addition, a variety of research techniques have been developed to deal exclusively with internal organizational communication.

Follow-up surveys were used in most of the case studies in this chapter. These yield quantitative measures of the stated objectives. Objectives were also assessed through publicity placement and employee participation in the programs.

Again, remember that to be effective and useful to the organization, research—both initial and evaluative—should be conducted by trained, experienced professionals who work for reputable research firms.

SUMMARY

The ROPE process provides a useful approach to the planning and execution of employee relations programs.

Research for employee relations concentrates on demographic data about the organization's workforce, existing levels of employee satisfaction, the state of relations between management and employees, and the effectiveness of employee communication. The uniqueness of research in this form of PR is, of course, the focus on information gathering about the workforce itself.

Both impact and output objectives are generally used in employee relations programs. Impact objectives include such desired outcomes as increasing employee knowledge of organizational matters and eliciting favorable employee attitudes and behaviors toward the organization. Output objectives are the efforts of practitioners to recognize employee contributions, distribute employee communications effectively, and otherwise enhance the impact objectives.

Programming for employee relations may include catchy themes; special events such as training seminars, special employee campaigns or programs, or social events for employees; and controlled media such as e-mail, voice mail, websites, memoranda, house publications, bulletin boards, displays, meetings, and a variety of electronic means of communication.

Evaluation of employee communication should refer back to each stated objective. Follow-up surveys are a popular means of evaluating attitudinal and behavioral objectives.

Each element of the ROPE process should be tailored for the particular situation, as we will see in this chapter's cases.

READINGS ON EMPLOYEE RELATIONS

Barkow, Tim. "Blogging for Business," *Public Relations Strategist* 10 (fall 2004): 40–43.

Bishop, Larry A. "Merging with Employees in Mind," *The Public Relations Strategist* 4 (spring 1994): 46–48.

Buffington, Jody. "Can Human Resources and Internal Communications Peacefully Coexist?" *Public Relations Strategist* 10 (fall 2004): 33–36.

———. "A Tremendous Opportunity: Communicating During a Merger," *Public Relations Tactics* 11 (August 2004): 10.

Charland, Bernie. "The Mantra of Metrics: A Realistic and Relevant Approach to Measuring the Impact of Employee Communications," *Public Relations Strategist* 10 (fall 2004): 30–33.

Charles, Melissa. "Lessons from the Best in Fortune: Changing the Way You Look at Employee Publications," *Public Relations Tactics* 12 (January 2005): 21.

Corman, Steven R., and Marshall Scott Poole, eds. *Perspectives on Organizational Communication.* New York: Guilford Publications, 2001.

Crescenzo, Steve. "What Is the Role of the Corporate Editor?" *Communication World* 22 (September–October 2005): 12–142.

———. "Employees: PR Ambassadors, or Your Worst Nightmare?" *Communication World* 22 (May–June 2005): 10–11.

Cutlip, Scott M., Allen H. Center, and Glen M. Broom. "The Practice: Nonprofits, Trade Associations, and Nongovernmental Organizations." In *Effective Public Relations,* 9th ed. Englewood Cliffs, NJ: Prentice-Hall, 2006.

Deetz, Stanley A., Sarah J. Tracy, and Jennifer Lyn Simpson. *Leading Organizations Through Transition: Communication and Cultural Change.* Thousand Oaks, CA: Sage Publications, 2000.

Dixon, Tom. *Communication, Organization and Performance.* Norwood, NJ: Ablex Publishing, 1996.

Dowling, Michael J. "Adapting to Change: Creating a Learning Organization," *Public Relations Strategist* 10 (spring 2004): 10–14.

Downs, Cal W., and Allyson D. Adrian. *Assessing Organizational Communication: Strategic Communication Audits.* New York: Guilford Publications, 2004.

Ewing, Michelle E. "An Engaged Work Force—Selling the Value and Incorporating Best Practices of Employee Communications," *Public Relations Tactics* 12 (March 2005): 10–12.

Ferguson, Gary. "Give Your Employees the Business," *Public Relations Tactics* 6 (August 1998): 6.

Frey, Thomas. "Employee Relations: The Facade of Communication," *Public Relations Strategist* 10 (fall 2004): 22–24.

Gargiulo, Terrence L. *The Strategic Use of Stories in Organizational Communication and Learning.* Armonk, NY: M.E. Sharpe, 2005.

Grates, Gary F. "'Why Don't I Know?' The Strategic Role of Today's Internal Communications," *Public Relations Strategist* 10 (fall 2004): 14–18.

Green, Thad B., and Jay T. Krippen. *Breaking the Barrier to Upward Communication: Strategies and Skills for Employees, Managers and HR Specialists.* Westport, CT: Quorum Books, 1999.

Harris, John. "Employee Engagement: An Easy Investment with Large Returns," *Public Relations Tactics* 11 (January 2004): 13.

Harris, Thomas E. *Applied Organizational Communication: Principles and Pragmatics for Future Practice,* 2d ed. Mahwah, NJ: Erlbaum, 2002.

Hickman, Gill Robinson, ed. *Leading Organizations: Perspectives for a New Era.* Thousand Oaks, CA: Sage Publications, 1998.

Holtz, Shel. *Corporate Conversations—A Guide to Crafting Effective and Appropriate Internal Communications.* New York: AMACOM, 2003.

Howard, Carole M. "Are Your Employee Publications Truly Strategic Tools?" *Public Relations Quarterly* 41 (winter 1996–1997): 23–27.

Keyton, Joann. *Communication and Organizational Culture.* Thousand Oaks, CA: Sage Publications, 2004.

Khan, Julie. "Internal communications: Ensuring Strategy and Measurement Coexist," *Public Relations Tactics* 7 (February 2000): 20.

Klubnik, Joan P. *Rewarding and Recognizing Employees.* Burr Ridge, IL: Irwin Professional Publishing, 1994.

Larkin, T. J., and Sandar Larkin. *Communicating Change . . . Winning Employee Support for Business Goals.* New York: McGraw-Hill, 1994.

McNerney, Donald J. "Creating a Motivated Work Force," *HR Focus* 73 (August 1996): 1–4.

Milite, George. "Getting Staffers to Read Company Manuals," *Supervisory Management* 39 (April 1994).

Miller, Katherine. *Organizational Communication: Approaches and Processes.* Belmont, CA: Wadsworth, 1999.

Parker, Glenn. *Team Players and Teamwork.* San Francisco: Jossey-Bass, 1996.

Perkins, Lisa. "Inspiring Change and Driving Results: What Can your Employee Publication Do for You?" *Public Relations Tactics* 12 (May 2005): 10.

Peterson, Gary L. *Communicating in Organizations: A Casebook,* 2d ed. Needham Heights, MA: Allyn & Bacon, 2000.

Profolio: Internal Communications. New York: Public Relations Society of America, 1998.

Sanchez, Paul. "Defining Corporate Culture," *Communication World* 21 (November–December 2004): 18–21.

Selame, Elinor. "Public Relations' Role and Responsibility in Reflecting Changes in Companies' Culture, Structure, Products and Services," *Public Relations Quarterly* 42 (summer 1997): 12–17.

Thilmany, Jean. "Showing Up Happy," *Mechanical Engineering* 126 (November 2004): 3–5.

Tucker, Mary L., et al. "Organizational Communication: Development of Internal Strategic Competitive Advantage," *Journal of Business Communication* 33 (April 1996): 51ff.

Voeller, Greg, and Kelly Groehler. "Employees—Always the Primary Audience," *Public Relations Strategist* 10 (fall 2004): 27–30.

EMPLOYEE RELATIONS CASES

CASE 4-1

An insurance company with a long history of relationships with fire departments, took this natural affinity and turned it into an employee Bucket Brigade charity. In the process, employees connected more closely to the company and their local communities. Following its inaugural year (2004) described in this case study, the program began to take on a special life of its own. By the time Hurricane Katrina devastated the Mississippi coast and New Orleans in August 2005, the employees jumped in with grants to help area fire departments get back on their feet. Exhibit 4-1a is a brochure for employees and Exhibit 4-1b is a grant explanation and applications.

The Bucket Brigade: Creating Employee Loyalty through Corporate Philanthropy

Fireman's Fund Insurance Company with Ketchum

Summary

First on the scene of any emergency, firefighters respond to natural disasters, accidents, medical emergencies, and fires — despite having increasingly limited resources. Across the country, funding challenges have left many volunteer and paid fire departments without adequate resources to do their job. In 2004, Fireman's Fund Insurance Company (FFIC), a national property and casualty company, launched a multi-million dollar corporate philanthropy program, "Fireman's Fund Heritage," to provide grants to help fund equipment, firefighter training, and fire safety initiatives for fire departments in communities where its employees, agents, and policyholders live and work. More than a traditional corporate giving program, Fireman's Fund Heritage was designed

Courtesy Fireman's Fund Insurance Company

to build trust in the Fireman's Fund brand and create a more inspirational corporate culture. In year one, it would be critical to engage employees in the program and demonstrate its importance to the company's brand. The Fireman's Fund communications team and Ketchum created the Bucket Brigade—the employee involvement program for Fireman's Fund Heritage—to generate excitement in the new philanthropic mission and give employees a sense of pride in the company.

Research

Baseline Measurement

Before launching the program, the team added questions about Fireman's Fund's philanthropic involvement and its impact on employee morale to its yearly employee survey (conducted in December 2003/January 2004). Result: This gave the team a baseline understanding of how employees viewed the company before the launch of Fireman's Fund Heritage and the Bucket Brigade in 2004.

Pilot Program

Involving employees in the philanthropy program and sharing their stories through communications would be critical. To confirm assumptions, the team created a pilot in San Diego, California. This pilot not only tested the giving strategy to fire departments, but also allowed the team to assess different models for employee involvement and communications. Result: The team learned the power of involving employees directly by awarding grants to the fire service, organizing volunteer efforts at the local level, and capturing stories to share with employees throughout the company.

Historical Review

Fireman's Fund has a rich history of working with the fire service—it was founded in 1863 to give 10 percent of its profits to the widows and orphans of firefighters. Many of its founders were firefighters, and it was the only insurance company to survive and pay all claims for the 1906 San Francisco earthquake. The team captured unique aspects of this history that could be used to excite current employees about the new philanthropy program and build pride in the company. Results: The name of the employee program for Fireman's Fund Heritage would be called the "Bucket Brigade," to reflect both Fireman's Fund's and the fire service's unique histories, and much of the visual look of the program blended old and new pictures of the fire service from company archives.

Planning

Audience

All 4,400 Fireman's Fund employees.

Objectives

1. Create an attitude among 50 percent of employees that Fireman's Fund is a philanthropic company.
2. Create an attitude among 35 percent of employees that they'd rather work for Fireman's Fund than a competing company because of Fireman's Fund Heritage.
3. Create an understanding among 25 percent of employees that Fireman's Fund's philanthropic mission is good for business.

Strategies

- Brand the employee program for Fireman's Fund Heritage to create excitement, demonstrate a clear tie with the company's history, and give employees something they can own—the Bucket Brigade.
- Create an emotional tie to the program by communicating the stories of firefighters in need, as well as stories of employees who were involved in the pilot program.
- Communicate to employees the many opportunities they have to become personally involved with Fireman's Fund Heritage (volunteering, grant nomination, task forces, etc.).
- Emphasize that Fireman's Fund Heritage is good for the company's brand and good for the company's business.

Messages

1. Fireman's Fund has a philanthropic mission to support firefighters for safer communities through the Fireman's Fund Heritage program.
2. Through the Fireman's Fund Heritage program, Fireman's Fund and its network of agents provide grants and volunteer support for local fire departments, national firefighter organizations, and fire and burn prevention nonprofit organizations.
3. Fireman's Fund believes that when firefighters are supported, communities are better protected, making people safer.
4. The Bucket Brigade is designed to provide opportunities for employees to participate in the Fireman's Fund Heritage mission of supporting firefighters for safer communities in a meaningful way—right in their own communities. The Bucket Brigade provides

opportunities for all employees to get involved, not just those in markets the company has launched large-scale grants programs.

5. Currently, there are three ways for employees to become involved in the Bucket Brigade program: volunteering, employee-nominated grants, and serving on grant selection committees.

6. Fireman's Fund Heritage is good for business because it will build trust with policyholders and create a compelling branding advantage.

Execution

1. Tease the program with historical visuals to build excitement—The team created teaser posters and handouts of actual bucket brigade replicas to build excitement for the program and establish a historical link to the fire service for employees.

2. Enlist the support of local Bucket Brigade Captains and management to cascade message—The team selected Bucket Brigade captains in every major Fireman's Fund location and created a special communication program for this group to cascade messages to all employees. These captains would be responsible for organizing activities for employees at a local level. Managers were also given a thorough briefing on the program.

3. Create a unique training program for employees—The team created a Bucket Brigade certification course housed on the employee Intranet. The unique course teaches employees about the history of Fireman's Fund, the needs of the fire service, and how to nominate fire departments for grants.

4. Launch grant nomination program and volunteer opportunities on the company's Intranet—The team created visually appealing and thorough communication explaining how employees could easily get involved with the program.

5. Highlight employee stories about Fireman's Fund Heritage—Through the company's Intranet and at company meetings, employees' personal stories about helping the fire service were highlighted.

6. Give employees historical imagery to display at their desks—All employees received mouse pads and key chains that blended historical imagery of the fire service with the company's new philanthropy mission. Employees who complete the certification course receive special pins.

Evaluation

Objective 1: Create an attitude among 50 percent of employees that Fireman's Fund is a philanthropic company.

Result: From December 2003 to December 2004, the number of employees who said they agreed or highly agreed that Fireman's Fund is a philanthropic company rose 20 percent, from 41 percent of employees to 61 percent. Employees who agreed or highly agreed that Fireman's Fund is a contributor to the community rose 12 percent, from 33 percent of all employees to 45 percent.

Objective 2: Create an attitude among 35 percent (roughly 10 point increase) of employees that they'd rather work for Fireman' Fund than a competing company because of Fireman's Fund Heritage.

Result: From December 2003 to December 2004, the number of employees who said they agreed or highly agreed that they would rather work for Fireman's Fund because of the Fireman's Fund Heritage/philanthropy program rose 16 percent, from 24 percent to 40 percent.

Objective 3: Create an understanding among 25 percent of employees that Fireman's Fund's philanthropic mission is good for business.

Result: In the December 2004 employee survey, 82 percent of employees said they agreed or highly agreed that Fireman's Fund Heritage is "good for business and agency relations."

Additional note: these results were accomplished in a difficult year for Fireman's Fund employee relations. Major restructuring at Fireman's Fund, including many management changes and the departure of a CEO mid-year, occurred in 2004. Most other employee metrics not associated with Fireman's Fund Heritage were actually down for the year, demonstrating the positive power of the Bucket Brigade program even further.

EXHIBIT 4-1A   *Bucket Brigade Brochure*

Courtesy Fireman's Fund Insurance Company

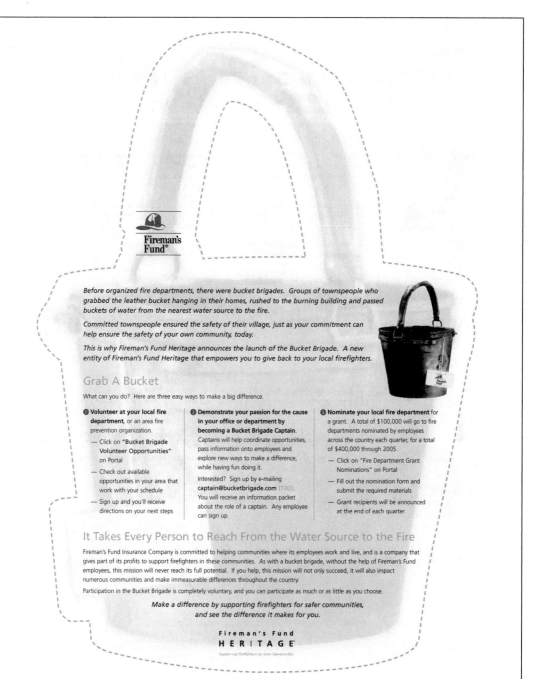

Fireman's Fund®

Before organized fire departments, there were bucket brigades. Groups of townspeople who grabbed the leather bucket hanging in their homes, rushed to the burning building and passed buckets of water from the nearest water source to the fire.

Committed townspeople ensured the safety of their village, just as your commitment can help ensure the safety of your own community, today.

This is why Fireman's Fund Heritage announces the launch of the Bucket Brigade. A new entity of Fireman's Fund Heritage that empowers you to give back to your local firefighters.

Grab A Bucket

What can you do? Here are three easy ways to make a big difference.

❶ **Volunteer at your local fire department**, or an area fire prevention organization.

— Click on "Bucket Brigade Volunteer Opportunities" on Portal

— Check out available opportunities in your area that work with your schedule

— Sign up and you'll receive directions on your next steps

❷ **Demonstrate your passion for the cause in your office or department by becoming a Bucket Brigade Captain**. Captains will help coordinate opportunities, pass information onto employees and explore new ways to make a difference, while having fun doing it.

Interested? Sign up by e-mailing **captain@bucketbrigade.com** (T&D). You will receive an information packet about the role of a captain. Any employee can sign up.

❸ **Nominate your local fire department** for a grant. A total of $100,000 will go to fire departments nominated by employees across the country each quarter, for a total of $400,000 through 2005.

— Click on "Fire Department Grant Nominations" on Portal

— Fill out the nomination form and submit the required materials

— Grant recipients will be announced at the end of each quarter

It Takes Every Person to Reach From the Water Source to the Fire

Fireman's Fund Insurance Company is committed to helping communities where its employees work and live, and is a company that gives part of its profits to support firefighters in these communities. As with a bucket brigade, without the help of Fireman's Fund employees, this mission will never reach its full potential. If you help, this mission will not only succeed, it will also impact numerous communities and make immeasurable differences throughout the country.

Participation in the Bucket Brigade is completely voluntary, and you can participate as much or as little as you choose.

Make a difference by supporting firefighters for safer communities, and see the difference it makes for you.

Fireman's Fund
HERITAGE
Supporting Firefighters for Safer Communities

EXHIBIT 4-1B   *Grant Information*

Fireman's Fund®

Heritage Bucket Brigade
Online Certification

Module Summary

What is Fireman's Fund Heritage?

Fireman's Fund Heritage is a national, community-based program dedicated to supporting firefighters for safer communities. The program awards grants and donations for firefighting equipment, fire protection tools, and firefighter training, as well as for community fire safety education.

The program has several components. The Bucket Brigade is geared toward offering Fireman's Fund Insurance Company (FFIC) employees and our agents the opportunity to get involved on a grassroots basis.

Fireman's Fund employees, agents, and agency employees are able to participate in the Bucket Brigade program.

Why Did We Launch Heritage?

We launched the program because:

- It relates to our philanthropic roots as a company.
- It reinforces our goals of innovation and community commitment.
- It helps us build relationships and trust within our local communities.

How is the program tied to FFIC's unique history?

FFIC was founded in 1863 in San Francisco with the mission to give 10 percent of profits to the widows and orphans of firefighters. Throughout its history, FFIC has carried on its rich heritage of innovation and community commitment by:

- being one of the few insurance companies to honor all claims following the 1871 Chicago fire and 1906 San Francisco earthquake
- a being a pioneer in insuring major civic infrastructure projects like the Golden Gate Bridge
- supporting volunteer programs and corporate giving.

Today, FFIC is carrying forward its heritage through its partnership with firefighters.

Courtesy Fireman's Fund Insurance Company

Fireman's
Fund®

Heritage Bucket Brigade
Online Certification

Module Summary

Why do firefighters need additional funding and support?

As demands for their services increase, firefighters and rescue workers around the country face serious funding challenges, leaving many volunteer and paid fire departments without adequate equipment or training. Here are some startling national statistics:

- 27 percent of fire department personnel involved in delivering emergency medical services lack formal training.
- 78 percent of fire departments must raise or seek funds to cover some or all of their expenses.
- One-third of firefighters on any given shift will not have access to a self-contained breathing apparatus, which is needed to enter smoke-filled buildings.
- An estimated 792,000 firefighters serve in fire departments without programs to maintain basic firefighter fitness and health.

How does the program support firefighters?

Fireman's Fund Heritage supports firefighters on many levels:

- **At the Local Community Level** – By creating local community programs to provide grants and donations in a concentrated geographic area with specific needs. FFIC awards grants and donations for firefighting equipment, fire prevention tools, firefighter training and community fire safety education. Communities are chosen based on firefighting needs as well as on where FFIC employees, agents and customers live and work. To date, community programs have been launched in San Diego, Atlanta and the San Francisco Bay Area.
- **By Creating Alliances with National Firefighting Organizations** – FFIC has created alliances with national firefighting organizations to support fire chiefs and firefighters around the country.
- **Through Employee Volunteerism** – FFIC employees volunteer at the community level and participate directly in the decisions to award local grants to fire departments and other agencies.
- **Through Agent Involvement** – FFIC agents may participate in Fireman's Fund Heritage programs at the local level.
- **By Raising Awareness** – Through Fireman's Fund Heritage, FFIC strives to draw attention to the resource challenges firefighters face.

113

EXHIBIT 4-1B   *Grant Information (continued)*

Fireman's Fund®

Heritage Bucket Brigade
Online Certification

Module Summary

How are FFIC and agency employees involved?

Both Fireman's Fund employees and agency employees can participate in grant nominations. Fireman's Fund employees can nominate a local fire department or fire prevention organization for a grant, and agency employees can support a grant nomination. In addition, both Fireman's Fund and agency employees can also volunteer for a fire department or fire prevention organization in their communities.

How are agents involved?

Agents can earn Heritage Rewards based on their overall relationship with Fireman's Fund. They can then use those rewards to nominate a local fire department for a grant. Agents can also volunteer for a fire department or fire prevention organization in their communities.

Grant Nomination Tasks

To submit a grant nomination, you need to do the following:

- Access the Grant Nomination Kit on Portal.
- Contact your local fire department's fire chief or public information officer to introduce the program and to gather information.
- Ask for agent support if you planned to do so.
- Complete and submit the online application.

For More Information

Contact your local brigade captains or send an email to:

bucketbrigade@ffic.com

Mergers often involve culture clashes between the cultures and values of the respective organizations. When two health systems consolidated, there were many vested interests that didn't like the new retirement system. A communication campaign with employees brought the employees together. Exhibit 4-2a is a "choice decision tree" fact sheet and Exhibit 4-2b is a script for a television news story for the internal network.

Trinity Health Retirement Redesign: Communicating Benefit Changes

Trinity Health with Watson Wyatt Worldwide

Overview

The consolidation of Holy Cross Health System and Mercy Health Services in May 2000 created the nation's fourth largest Catholic (eighth largest overall) health system, with revenues of $4.8 billion and more than 50,000 employees. Maintaining two separate retirement programs for the newly merged entity was cost prohibitive from an administrative standpoint. In addition, the disparity between the former organizations' programs (pension formula, savings plan vendors, savings plan match, retiree health, etc.) required resolution if Trinity Health was to create a single, common workforce with portable benefits between its 27 Member Organizations in seven states. The retirement program redesign was the first major collective initiative for the new organization. The integration came with a significant challenge: the new program was to be "budget neutral," and the former Holy Cross program was considered much more generous. To achieve system-wide equity, the scales would appear to be tipped away from former Holy Cross employees toward former Mercy employees. A combined team of Trinity Health and Watson Wyatt Worldwide began meeting in earnest in March 2001. The majority of planning and implementation took place in 2001, with a "go live" date of Jan. 1, 2002. Evaluation was completed in early 2002.

Courtesy Trinity Health, Novi, Michigan

Research

To gauge stakeholder opinion, 26 focus groups were conducted in November/December 2000 at seven locations, with a cross-section of employees and physicians participating. The feedback highlighted the monumental task ahead:

- Participants do not view the retirement program as an attraction and retention tool
- Participants do not view the current retirement program as adequate
- Retiree medical coverage is an important issue at all locations
- Participants are not adequately preparing for retirement
- Overall, retirement program communication is rated very low

In May 2001, the team also conducted three targeted focus groups with key spokespersons: chief HR and communications officers from the member organizations. Initial strategies and messaging were tested for credibility and clarity, and plans for field-level tactical support were reviewed and improved.

Planning

Goal: To completely and accurately communicate the benefits of the newly redesigned Trinity Health Retirement Program to ensure that all employees have a good understanding of and appreciation for each of the program's components, along with their roles and responsibilities in achieving their retirement income needs.

Attitudinal Objectives

- Retirement Program is perceived to be competitive within health care industry
- Comfort level with retirement planning falls into mid to high range, an understanding of how much income needed for retirement is recognized by employees, a frequency of communications is perceived as timely
- Satisfaction with retirement benefits increases from 28 percent
- Satisfaction with retirement information increases from 53 percent

Behavioral Objectives

- Participation in Savings Plan increases by 10 percent
- Voluntary contributions in the Savings Plan increases by 10 percent
- Increased participation/contributions in the Savings Plan for lower-paid employees

Strategies Derived from Our Objectives

- Develop overarching key messages about how and why the program was crafted; reinforce throughout
- Include mission-related rationale in the initial announcement of the new program
- Increase the credibility of communication through the use of local spokespersons to deliver key messages
- Provide spokespersons with the tools and resources they need to deliver clear and consistent messages
- Provide employees with the tools and resources they need to understand and accept the new program
- Include a long-term communication strategy, including ongoing feedback mechanisms
- Promote competitiveness of program through health care industry benefit research

The intended audiences were broken into four primary categories: (1) employees of the former Holy Cross entities, (2) employees of the former Mercy entities, (3) key HR personnel in the field, and (4) key communications staff in the field. Along with these four primary groups were several important subcategories, including key decision makers, local implementation team members, union leadership, local Catholic sponsoring organizations, and new hires/recruits.

Execution

The project forced a careful creative approach because Retirement Program tactics would serve as the first examples of how the new organization would communicate internally. Materials needed to reflect the organization's mission, values, diversity, and heritage in terms of art and language while matching the seriousness of the subject—retirement income—and the seriousness of the organization's business—patient care. Voice, written style, color selection, design, and scripture verses all reflected a warm, personal, and conservative approach. These themes were carried throughout all tactics, including print, telephone, presentation, sales collateral, Web, and meeting materials (one-on-one and group).

Additionally, the team employed a multimedia strategy to ensure each employee could learn in his/her preferred method. This included the use of personalized print media to help employees understand the program's overall value and the use of direct mail to ensure accurate and timely delivery. Finally, tactical deployment was timed over several weeks to manage the momentum of information, providing it in digestible "bites." This allowed the team to gradually develop awareness while preparing employees for upcoming triggering events that would result in the desired behavior.

Significant Challenges

Trinity Health had little credibility as an entity; it had yet to develop a relationship/identity with employees. Thus, the team's implementation strategy focused on local spokespersons who already had achieved a level of credibility among their employee groups. At the same time, convincing these sometimes "reluctant" spokespersons to carry the messages in a positive way proved to be a challenge, especially for members of the former Holy Cross hospitals who may have personally been adversely impacted by the change. Other key challenges included managing employee reactions and helping employees make an informed choice for retiree medical coverage.

Evaluation

In May 2002, 1,149 employees (random sample of 5,000) answered a voluntary telephone (IVR) survey regarding the recent retirement program rollout. Results overwhelmingly showed that the team succeeded in meeting its objectives.

Attitudinal Objectives

	Percent Agreed	Achievement
I appreciate the benefit offered by the Savings Plan	83.6	Very High
I appreciate the benefit offered by the Pension Plan	81.4	Very High
Frequency of communication is timely	77.8	High
I know how to obtain Retirement Program information	75.3	High
The amount of information I received was appropriate	73.5	High
Overall, I am satisfied with the retirement benefit	64.3	Good
Understand how much income needed to retire	61.7	Good
Perception of competitive retirement benefits program	61.1	Good
Comfort of retirement planning mid to high	55.1	Fair

Behavioral Objectives

	Percent Agreed	Achievement
Participation increases 10 percent	17.6	High
Contributions increase 10 percent	36.4	Very High
Participation increases for lower-paid employees	11.3	Good

The team also conducted an online survey of HR spokespersons in June 2002, with 29 staff responding (population of 89). Survey results showed that staff appreciated the training and that the training enabled them to adequately explain the Retirement Program and the changes to employees.

EXHIBIT 4-2A   *Choice Decision Tree*

YOUR RETIREE HEALTH CARE PLAN
Choice Decision Tree

As an employee of a former Holy Cross entity, you may choose to:

Option # 1: Receive the higher maximum employer matching contribution on your 403(b) Retirement Savings Plan contribution, in which case you will give up any potential eligibility for future benefits under the Retiree Health Care Plan and Retiree Life Insurance.

OR

Option # 2: Receive the lower maximum employer matching contribution on your 403(b) Retirement Savings Plan contribution and remain potentially eligible for the Retiree Health Care Plan and Retiree Life Insurance when you retire.

To give you an idea as to the types of issues you should consider in making your decision, a "Decision Tree" is provided below. This tool will help identify which option may be most advantageous. However, please keep in mind that the Decision Tree does not take into account all of your personal circumstances, such as your and your spouse's current health or financial resources. It also does not take into account any government or other health benefits you may receive. Therefore, before making this important decision, you should seek counsel from a trusted financial advisor. *If you do not make an election, you automatically will be defaulted to elect Option 2.*

QUESTIONS TO CONSIDER

1. One issue to think about is whether you plan to be working at Trinity Health until the time you retire. Consider the number of years you have until retirement: 5, 10, 20, 30 or 40.

> Based on this information, is it likely that you will retire from Trinity Health?

Not Likely	Likely
Consider waiving all eligibility for future Retiree Health Care Plan benefits and instead receive the higher employer matching contribution. (Option 1)	Consider retaining your potential eligibility for Retiree Health Care Plan benefits and receive the lower employer matching contribution. To further clarify if this option is right for you, continue to Question #2. (Option 2)

2. At the time you retire from Trinity Health, to receive benefits from the Retiree Health Care Plan, you must meet the Plan's eligibility requirements, which currently are:

- age 58 (or older) with 10 (or more) years of benefit service accrued after the age of 45, and

- 5 years of continuous coverage in a health care plan offered by your Trinity Health employer immediately prior to the date you retire. *(If you do not meet the eligibility requirements at the time of termination, you will not receive benefits even if you now choose to keep your eligibility for the Retiree Health Care Plan.)*

> At the time of your **retirement from Trinity Health**, what is the likelihood that you will meet the eligibility requirements?

Not Likely	Likely
Consider waiving all eligibility for future Retiree Health Care Plan benefits and instead receive the higher employer matching contribution. (Option 1)	Consider retaining your potential eligibility for Retiree Health Care Plan benefits and receive the lower employer matching contribution. To further clarify if this option is right for you, continue to Question #3. (Option 2)

3. When you think about retirement, you should consider any retiree health coverage to which your spouse may have access, as well as your own. Consider the level of benefits you would receive under each plan.

> Is it likely you will be eligible to participate in a retiree health plan available through your spouse's employer?

Likely	Not Likely
Consider waiving all eligibility for future Retiree Health Care Plan benefits and instead receive the higher employer matching contribution. (Option 1)	Consider retaining your potential eligibility for Retiree Health Care Plan benefits and receive the lower employer matching contribution. To further clarify if this option is right for you, continue to Question #4. (Option 2)

4. As you think about your future need for retiree health care, keep in mind that Trinity Health **cannot** guarantee future retiree health care coverage (either availability of the plan or the terms of the coverage) or the amount of the employer matching contribution.

> How confident are you in the future of employer-provided retiree health care benefits?

Not very	Very
Consider waiving all eligibility for future Retiree Health Care Plan benefits and instead receive the higher employer matching contribution. (Option 1)	Consider retaining your potential eligibility for Retiree Health Care Plan benefits and receive the lower employer matching contribution. (Option 2)

Remember, you should confirm your choice with your financial advisor.

TRINITY ✪ HEALTH

Courtesy Trinity Health, Novi, Michigan

EXHIBIT 4-2B   *Television Story Script*

News Story Script 1: To be released after October 1, 2001, but before Script 2.

VISUAL EFFECT	SCRIPT
Intro screen with Trinity Health logo and title of New Retirement Program	**Announcer: As Trinity Health introduces its new Retirement Program, which becomes effective on January 1, 2002, [Reporter's name] and [name of HR Manager/Representative] are here to discuss some of the reasons behind the changes.**
Footage of reporter introducing HR Manager/Representative	**Reporter:** We've heard that beginning January 1, 2002, Trinity Health will have a new Retirement Program. [Name], the [Title] from the Human Resources Department is here to explain the reasons for the change.
Footage of HR Manager/Representative	**HR Manager/Representative:** Trinity Health's leaders have been working for many months to create a Retirement Program that is competitive, helps attract and retain good employees, and is consistent with our mission and values. In addition, we want to provide fair and balanced benefits to our employees.
Footage of reporter and HR Manager/Representative	**Reporter:** Is Trinity Health reducing its level of financial commitment to the program?
Footage of HR Manager/Representative	**HR Manager/Representative:** No. In fact, Trinity Health's overall financial commitment ($27 Million in 2000) to providing retirement benefits to all employees is not changing. The primary objective of the change was to provide fair and balanced retirement plans across the organization that are consistent with our mission and values.
Footage of Reporter and HR Manager/Representative	**Reporter:** What has changed in the Retirement Program?

Courtesy Trinity Health, Novi, Michigan

EXHIBIT 4-2B   *Television Story Script (continued)*

Footage of HR Manager/Representative	**HR Manager/Representative:** Trinity Health evaluated the current retirement program to see how it helpedmeet our business objectives, within the context of our mission and values. This included criteria built around providing benefits that are fair to everyone, flexible for current employees, and attractive to new hires. The evaluation showed that Trinity Health needed to place a greater emphasis on the Retirement Savings Plan instead of the Pension Plan.
Footage of Reporter and HR Manager/Representative	**Reporter:** Will benefits be lower with the new Retirement Program?
Footage of HR Manager/Representative	**HR Manager/Representative:** Trinity Health's goal with the new program is to provide employees with a total benefit at normal retirement age (65) that is similar to the amount they would have received under the current plan. The main difference is that a greater portion of retirement income will be from the Retirement Savings Plan instead of the Pension Plan. This means that employees will need to participate in the Retirement Savings Plan in order to take full advantage of the employer matching contributions [localize percent match].
Footage of Reporter and HR Manager/Representative	**Reporter:** How does our new Retirement Program compare to our competitors?
Footage of HR Manager/Representative and then to comparison chart	**HR Manager/Representative:** That's a good question. When conducting a competitive analysis of the current Mercy and current Holy Cross plans, Trinity Health found that the former Holy Cross plan ranked at or near the top when compared to other similar health care organizations and the former Mercy program ranked just slightly above the average. To create a common plan for Trinity Health that was still competitive and comparable in our overall financial commitment, retirement resources were rebalanced to create a new program that continues to rank competitively when compared to other similar health care organizations.

Footage of Reporter and HR Manager/Representative	**Reporter:** [Name of HR Manager/Representative], thank you for taking time to explain the reasons for the changes to the Retirement Program.
Footage of Reporter and HR Manager/Representative	**HR Manager/Representative:** You're welcome.
Footage of Reporter	**Reporter:** [Name of HR Manager/Representative] will be with us again soon to continue our discussion about the new Retirement Program. Until then, be sure to attend an employee meeting on the new Retirement Program, and take advantage of the Retirement Program Hotline 1-800-700-4476 and the new Retirement Program Web site, Home: http://www.trinity-health.org Work: http://nexus.sb.trinity-health.org Thanks for joining us today.

Customer service complaints often relate to the quality of service provided by frontline employees, and this is often the case for customers wishing to install a cable television connection or to have service disruptions repaired. To meet aggressive corporate business goals, Cox Communications needed an aggressive internal communication campaign to gain the support of employees. Exhibit 4-3a is a company newsletter article about the campaign and Exhibit 4-3b is a poster.

Wheel of Fortune

Cox Communications

Need/Opportunity

Cox Communications, Inc., is the third largest cable company in the United States, offering analog and digital cable, high-speed Internet, and digital telephone to over 20 markets across the country. Cox Arizona is the company's largest cable system and serves over 700,000 customers in the greater Phoenix and Tucson metro markets. The company has nearly 2,500 employees combined in these Arizona markets. The Cox Arizona employee communications team consists of two members, a communications director and a senior communication specialist, and is responsible for all statewide internal communications.

In 2004, the Cox Arizona Senior Team established a set of critical goals for the year that would serve as the foundation of every initiative the system undertook. In addition, each of these goals contributed directly to our two core and critical metrics: revenue generating units (RGU)—an internal term for service subscriptions (if a customer subscribes to both our cable and Internet service, that is considered 2 RGUs)—and operating cash flow (OCF). These two measurements are also what drive our employee bonus program. It was determined that for the company to reach these very aggressive goals, it would require the full understanding, support, and effort of employees at every level.

To achieve our awareness objective and help drive the company to reach its goals, we determined that an in-depth and ongoing employee communications program was the most promising solution to reach employees across the system and earn buy-in, commitment, and action.

Courtesy Cox Communications

Because success in each of the areas covered by the goals would directly contribute to customer and cash growth, generating "fortune" for the company and its employees (via the bonus), the goals were branded as our "Wheel of Fortune." We built the communications program around this Wheel of Fortune branding.

Intended Audience

The audience for this effort was the 2,500 employees of the Cox Communications Arizona cable system. This is a diverse group of employees—from frontline field technicians and call center representatives to vice presidents and directors—spread over almost 20 facilities in greater Phoenix and Tucson. About a third of our workforce operates in the field without regular computer access to online communication tools. The remaining employees work in traditional office environments with dedicated computers at each desk.

Goals and Objectives

The Cox Communications Arizona Wheel of Fortune employee communications campaign was a creative and unique initiative designed to accomplish three key objectives:

- Educate employees on the company's goals in several key categories
- Provide regular updates on our progress toward those goals throughout the year and celebrate milestones along the journey
- Create a culture of engaged, empowered, and excited employees that would take this knowledge and transform the way they worked, the way they served our customers, and the way they represented their company—better positioning Cox Arizona against our competition

Measurement of success: 90 percent awareness of company goals determined through employee surveys.

We would also measure success by progress toward the Wheel of Fortune goals established by our Senior Team:

Employer of Choice—**Goal:** Voluntary employee retention of 90 percent

Dominant Digital Communications Provider—**Goal:** Market share per service: Video 72 percent; Internet 78.5 percent; Telephone 22 percent

Break Out System For Customer Service—**Goal:** 80 percent customer service score on quarterly survey

Improve Customer Loyalty—**Goal:** Save 14,000 customers contacting us to disconnect for controllable reasons between May and December (customer loyalty group was new in April 2004)

Improve Operational Efficiency—**Goal:** Labor dollars per RGU of $6.63

RGU Net Gain—**Goal:** RGU net gain of 351,008 (later adjusted to 334,292 due to changes in product rollout plans)

OCF Growth—**Goal:** 103.2 percent of budget

Solution Overview

We already had an array of communications tools in place that allowed us to reach our diverse employee base, both at home and at work. We decided to maximize these resources while introducing new tactics to help push this important information to every level and provide regular updates to keep employees energized, excited, and motivated.

The Wheel of Fortune employee communications program included the following tactics:

Launch video: We created a launch video and shared it with all leaders and provided copies so they could present the goals to their teams. We set a deadline for rollout and included a sign-off sheet.

Wheel Watching: Wheel Watching was a monthly update on our progress toward our goals that was e-mailed to all employees and posted in our offices.

Connexion newsletter: Our employee newsletter tied the majority of stories to the Wheel of Fortune goals so employees could see real-life examples of people and teams contributing. This was mailed monthly to the employee home.

e-Connexion electronic newsletter: Our weekly e-newsletter provided updates on our goals and provided links to our intranet. It also included a weekly Wheel of Fortune challenge, and all respondents received a Wheel of Fortune t-shirt to wear on Fridays.

Wheel on the Web: The online home of all Wheel of Fortune information that included explanations of the goals, updates, and contact information.

Cubicle/office placards: Each employee received a Wheel of Fortune 8.5″ × 11″ poster that provided a daily reminder of what we were all working towards.

Wheel prop/game: We had a real spinning wheel built and created a game-show-style competition to go with it. It was used at team and departmental meetings across the system throughout the year.

Wheel of Fortune recognition: We created on-the-spot recognition forms that allowed employees to recognize each other for contributions to the Wheel. Each month a few of these were drawn to win gift cards.

Posters: Wheel of Fortune posters were hung at all Cox facilities and included varying slogans encouraging employees to help keep the Wheel in motion.

Badge holders: Every employee received a badge holder that contained the Wheel of Fortune logo.

T-shirts: We created Wheel of Fortune t-shirts that we gave away as part of our weekly Wheel challenge in our e-newsletter. Employees wore these shirts on Friday so it created a competition, and we saw more and more shirts worn on Fridays as the year progressed.

RGU progress boards: To provide a continuous update on our RGU progress, tally boards were put up at our major facilities and updated daily.

Customer referral cards: To help give those employees not in sales positions a tool to help us with customer growth, we created the Wheel of Fortune customer referral card. Customers referred by employees earned a $25 credit on their new service while the employee's card was entered into a drawing to win prizes.

Implementation and Challenges

There were a couple of key challenges to achieving the desired objectives:

1. This would be the first time employees were to be substantially exposed to key company goals, measurements, and terms that often were only shared at the management level. Generating interest and educating employees on previously foreign concepts would be a key challenge.

2. These goals were aggressive so it was important the campaign was sustained throughout the year to ensure consistent employee commitment, attention, and action.

Our implementation plan was simple: regular and creative communications through a variety of channels; continuous recruitment of leadership to help drive down the messages and localize the information to their teams; and honest and open updates on how we were progressing, regardless of good or bad results. This built trust with our employees and motivated them to help the company reach its goals.

Measurement/Evaluation of Outcomes

The Wheel of Fortune campaign exceeded our expectations:

- We adjusted our RGU net gain goal mid-year due to changes in our product expansion plans. We finished the year with 346,921, easily surpassing our revised goal of 334,292 and coming just short of our original goal. We also exceeded our OCF goal, coming in 5 percent over a very aggressive budget target. Both results set company records and Arizona employees received their highest bonus ever.

- We finished the year at $7.02 labor costs per RGU. Considering that we started the year at $7.73, we are very satisfied with the status of our operational efficiency effort. This was intended to be a longer-term goal that would take more than 12 months to reach.

- We retained more than 15,000 customers attempting to disconnect, surpassing our goal of 14,000.

- While we continue to work toward an 80 percent quarterly customer satisfaction score, we trended positively toward that number with improvements each quarter and finishing at 79 percent. This is a long-term, ongoing objective.

We surpassed our market share goals, achieving: Video 73.8 percent (goal: 72 percent); Internet 80 percent (goal: 78.5 percent); Telephone 23.8 percent (goal: 22 percent).

We finished the year at 91.1 percent voluntary employee retention, surpassing our goal of 90 percent. This measures the percentage of employees that chose to stay with Cox in 2004.

Employees were surveyed in May and December to measure awareness of the Wheel of Fortune goals. In May, 90.3 percent of employees indicated they were familiar with the company's Wheel of Fortune goals and felt having this information changed their mindset and approach to their work. In December, this number increased to 97.3 percent.

Overall, the culture at the system has dramatically shifted this past year. The Wheel of Fortune campaign has been a key driver of this change and a significant reason the company was able to reach its goals. Employees made the Wheel of Fortune their own, creating team incentives and contests around the Wheel and using the tactics we provided to localize the goals for their teams. This energized and confident workforce has strengthened Cox's competitive position in this market because all 2,500 employees are focused on the same goals. Top leadership was so impressed that they requested the campaign continue in 2005.

EXHIBIT 4-3A Wheel of Fortune Newsletter Article

Wheel of Fortune News

The Wheel of Fortune News section highlights initiatives and activities that contribute to our company objectives. If you have any Wheel of Fortune stories to share with your fellow co-workers, please send them to the Employee Communications team at: **ARZ.EmployeeCommunications@cox.com**

We welcome any submissions whether they be industry information, customer tips, or stories of employees who have helped *"spin the wheel."* Send us your ideas...help us *keep the wheel in motion!*

How Can You Move The Wheel?
By Joe Ricciardi
Manager, Employee Communications

It's round with pretty colors and you see it everywhere. Is that how you view the Wheel of Fortune? While it is colorful, it has substance too. The wheel represents the goals your company is striving to achieve in 2004. To reach these goals, every employee must contribute even in the smallest way. If successful, Cox Arizona will again make great strides to become the top system in Cox Communications and the cable industry.

What's in it for you? A year-end bonus, job security, a sense of pride that you work for a leader and employer of choice, and the satisfaction that at the end of the day you are making a difference. So, when we ask "what have you done today to keep the wheel in motion", we are not just repeating a witty slogan. It serves as a reminder that every minute (OK, the majority of minutes) of your workday should be focused on activities that contribute to these goals. Listed below are just a few things that teams are doing to help make the wheel spin. You'll notice some are small, some are big but all are contributing to our goals:

✦ In **Sales Operations Support**, every request for office supplies is now reviewed before ordering to ensure a requested supply is not already available within the department or facility. In Tucson, administrative assistants check with each other before placing office supply orders.

✦ In **Human Resources**, the flower request process is being revamped to reduce monthly flower purchase expenses and HR leadership has encouraged its employees to bring other ideas forward.

✦ In **CRTV**, the TeleVideo team is increasing the number of marketing spots it will produce for Cox Arizona, reducing outside video production costs.

✦ In **Marketing**, completed campaigns are analyzed for efficiency to ensure the cost per lead for all of our products is as low as possible. Lessons learned from each campaign are analyzed and efficiencies added to the next campaign to lower costs and increase inbound sales calls.

✦ **Tucson Facilities** has completed its close out of the Columbia Training location that will save $5,730 per month or $45,838 for the remainder of the year.

✦ In **ITS**, the team was able to get a discount on an AutoCAD upgrade, saving over $90,000 on the latest CADMap software that enables our network operations team to improve operational efficiency.

✦ In the **Customer Care Center**, the technical team is partnering with the Technology Center and Training to train customer service representatives on tier 1 Test Desk support. This allows the representatives to immediately resolve customer issues in relation to voice mail, PIC/LPIC routing issues and other issues. They are also training all front line employees to recognize certain criteria within telephony troubleshooting that will allow them to stage a technician directly to the home and bypass routing through the Test Desk. This initiative will save time for the customer and manpower hours for both departments.

✦ The **Tempe ASC and Residential Sales** have developed a "special events" pool to create efficiencies in dispatching technicians. This allows the team to bulk work in one area (ie: ASU campus) reducing technician drive time and allowing for more jobs to be completed.

✦ In the **Tucson call center**, many employees use the backside of scrapped printed paper for taking notes while on calls, reducing overall paper usage.

✦ **Data Engineering** has developed an MTC rotation that is area-specific to employee residences, reducing mileage, drive time, and gas consumption on the company vehicles.

✦ In many areas, teams are not backfilling open positions and instead picking up the slack to help reduce labor expense through the remainder of the year.

So what is your team doing? If you haven't given it much thought, you've only got six months remaining in 2004 to do something! And many of the efforts listed above were suggested by employees without leadership titles. Regardless of your level, occupation or work location, you can contribute.

If you or your team are already making the wheel spin, send us an e-mail at **ARZ Employee Communications** or call **Joe Ricciardi** at **623-328-3253** and we'll share it with all employees. Remember, we all share in the fortune so we should all contribute in some way to the outcome.

Why Is Cox Arizona Your Employer of Choice?
By Libbie Grobmyer
Intern, Community Relations

Gene Marak Drives Better Business

Fifteen years ago **Gene Marak** came across an ad that read, *"Make what you are worth. Flexible hours, benefits, vacation, and quarterly contests."* That moment marked the beginning of a long and successful career with Cox Communications.

During the past fifteen years, Marak has held many titles including direct sales representative, MDU coordinator, commercial account executive, and senior account executive. He currently manages the Tucson Leasing Agent Program and serves as the account executive for Commercial Video Southeast Arizona and Hospitality Southeast Arizona.

> **"I have been blessed. I have worked and learned from many different leaders over the years."**

So much history and time spent with the company has created many memories for Marak. When asked to share his favorite time with the company, he said, *"The most memorable times were as an MDU coordinator with Steve Weber. Back in the day, we did everything from activating 1,000 drops in preparation for the UA Student Program to putting out newsletters."* He went on to say, *"It was really gratifying to run that business from A to Z."*

Besides having many fond memories, Marak has had extensive experiences, both with colleagues as well as different companies. Some of the various companies Marak has worked with through acquisitions include McCaw, Cook, Intermedia, TCI and Cox. When asked whom his most influential leader was he stated, *"I have been blessed. I have worked and learned from many different leaders over the years."* Unable to credit just one individual with his success, he stated, *"If you take the strengths of them all, you would have one great leader by the name of Joedainluciannecorkywueydedaansaudraginlisdontroy Janns."*

One reason Marak has experienced so much success with Cox can be credited to his work ethic and motivation. His motto is, *"What you drive is of the utmost importance! Focus on driving better business, not a better car! I drive a '90s Jeep, what do you expect me to say?"*

Congratulations to Marak for supporting the success of Cox over the last fifteen years. Here's to fifteen more!

Gene Marak, Southern Arizona Direct Sales

Courtesy Cox Communications

EXHIBIT 4-3B   *Poster*

Courtesy Cox Communications

MEMBER RELATIONS

Membership organizations include trade associations, professional associations, labor unions, interest groups, social and religious organizations, and thousands of other groups, large and small, which dot the societal landscape. Each has a need for communication between its officers and members. This process is called member relations.

RESEARCH

Research in member relations includes the client, the opportunity or problem, and the member audiences to be targeted for communication.

Client Research

As a prerequisite for the member relations program, the practitioner needs a thorough understanding of the membership organization conducting the program. The precise nature of the organization, its purpose, its headquarters organization and personnel, its financial status, its reputation with the general public and especially with its own members, its present and past public relations practices, and its public relations or image strengths and vulnerabilities will be part of the organizational profile the practitioner must construct.

Opportunity or Problem Research

As in all other forms of public relations, the second research objective of member relations is a determination of the reason for conducting the program. Will it be a long-range, proactive program, or will it address a particular problem? As membership is voluntary, major changes in programs or restructuring initiatives require the support and buy-in from the members or their elected representatives. It is crucial to gauge the level of commitment and support for new ideas. The expenditure necessary for the program should be thoroughly justified at this point.

Audience Research

Identification of audiences to be targeted for communication is the last of the three aspects of research in member relations. Member publics can be categorized into six groups:

> Organization employees
>> Headquarters management
>> Headquarters nonmanagement (staff)
>> Other headquarters personnel

Organization officers
  Elected officers
  Appointed officers
  Legislative groups
  Boards, committees
Organization members
  Regular members
  Members in special categories, such as sustaining, emeritus, students
  Honorary members or groups
  Prospective organization members
State or local chapters
  Organization employees
  Organization officers
  Organization members
Prospective organization members
Related or other allied organizations

Member relations research, then, consists of an examination of the client or organization conducting the program, the opportunity or problem that necessitates the program, and the member audiences targeted for communication.

OBJECTIVES

Impact and output objectives are used in member relations and, as in other forms of public relations, objectives should be specific and quantitative as far as possible.

Impact Objectives

For member relations, impact objectives consist of the desired outcomes of informing or modifying the attitudes and behaviors of the members of an organization. Some examples are:

1. To increase members' knowledge of organizational developments, policies, or activities (by 50 percent during the current year)

2. To engender (30 percent) more favorable member attitudes toward the organization (during the months of October and November)

3. To gain support (favorable vote) for a new programmatic initiative

4. To stimulate desired behavior modification among the organization's membership (by 30 percent during the next six months)

Impact objectives, in member relations, as in all types of communication, should be developed carefully for they are the standard against which the success of a program will be evaluated.

Output Objectives

Output objectives in member relations refer to the distribution or execution of essentially controlled forms of communication.

Some examples are:

1. To prepare and distribute three membership communications concerning the current initiative

2. To prepare and execute membership conventions, seminars, and other meetings on a timely basis

PROGRAMMING

Programming for member relations includes theme and messages, action or special event(s), controlled media, and the use of effective communication principles. These factors are the same for member relations as for employee relations except for the types of action or special event(s) and the types of communication used.

Actions or special events for member relations concentrate on conventions, seminars, conferences, and similar meetings. The headquarters management of an organization has an obligation to schedule and execute such gatherings for the membership.

Other actions on the part of the headquarters officials of an organization usually include the promotion of industry research, preparation of industry statistics and data, development of professional standards and ethical codes, development of in-service education and training for members, and promotion of standards of safety and efficiency among the members or in the industry.

Member communications are limited to controlled media. These usually consist of e-mail, websites, newsletters and other member publications, reports, industry brochures, pamphlets, and other printed materials, some of which can be distributed to the members' clients.

For example, the American Dental Association publishes dental care brochures for patients, and the American Heart Association prints materials for individuals who want to lower their levels of cholesterol.

Uncontrolled media in the form of news releases about employees or members are often considered part of the internal communication program. Strictly speaking, however, such communication falls into the category of external media relations.

Principles of effective communication are the same in member relations programs as in other forms of public relations.

Thus, programming for member relations shares many similarities with that for employee relations.

EVALUATION

Evaluation of member relations directs attention back to the objectives established for such programs.

Success for programs may be directly linked to the objectives — informational, behavioral, and/or attitudinal — stated at the outset of a program. Was there favorable reaction from the membership? Did the number of members increase or decrease? Have members actively supported a new initiative with their time and money? Have requests for membership information increased?

SUMMARY

Member relations is communication between the officers (management) of a membership organization and its members.

Research in member relations focuses on the demographics, information levels, attitudes, and behaviors of the organization's membership.

A complete member profile should be constructed through such research, with special attention to the typical member's attitudes and behaviors toward the organization itself.

Both impact and output objectives are used in member relations.

Impact objectives include the desired programmatic outcomes of favorable member attitudes and behaviors toward the organization.

Output objectives catalog desired PR practices, such as effective planning, preparation, and distribution of member communications.

Programming for member relations usually includes such events as conventions, conferences, seminars, and such actions as promotion of industry research, preparation of industry statistics and data, and general promotion and development of the industry or profession represented by the membership.

Common forms of communication are e-mail, websites, member publications, reports, printed materials, audiovisual materials, and meetings.

As in other forms of public relations, evaluation consists of measuring stated objectives through surveys, observation, or other appropriate means suggested by the objectives themselves.

READINGS ON MEMBER RELATIONS

"Association Public Relations" (special issue), *Public Relations Quarterly* 37 (spring 1992).

Cutlip, Scott M., Allen H. Center, and Glen M. Broom. "The Practice: Nonprofits, Trade Associations, and Nongovernmental Organizations." In *Effective Public Relations,* 9th ed. Englewood Cliffs, NJ: Prentice-Hall, 2006.

Dixon, Tom. *Communication, Organization and Performance.* Norwood, NJ: Ablex Publishing, 1996.

Encyclopedia of Associations. Detroit: Gale Research, published annually.

Miller, Katherine. *Organizational Communication: Approaches and Processes.* Belmont, CA: Wadsworth, 1999.

Tucker, Mary L., et al. "Organizational Communication: Development of Internal Strategic Competitive Advantage," *Journal of Business Communication* 33 (April 1996): 51ff.

CASE 4-4

Adjusting to changes in membership and business practices allows a large professional association to be flexible and better meet the needs of its members. The nursing society developed a member communication campaign when faced with a need to change operations. Exhibit 4-4a is a brochure used in the campaign, and Exhibit 4-4b is a fact sheet.

It's Up to Us. It's Up to You

Honor Society of Nursing, Sigma Theta Tau International

Situation Analysis

The Honor Society of Nursing, Sigma Theta Tau International, is a not-for-profit organization whose mission is to improve the health of people worldwide through leadership and scholarship in practice, education, and research. Founded in 1922, the honor society has inducted more than 340,000 practicing nurses, instructors, researchers, policymakers, entrepreneurs, and other nurse leaders in more than 85 countries. The honor society has 433 chapters worldwide. Biennially, Sigma Theta Tau International convenes a House of Delegates, at which each chapter is required to send two delegates. (If only one delegate can attend, that delegate can cast two votes for that chapter.) During this business meeting, delegates vote on proposed bylaws changes and elect a new slate of officers.

For the 2001–2003 biennium, delegates were asked to vote on several proposed changes that would significantly alter the structure and operations of the society. These changes revolved around the governance structure, membership eligibility, and fiscal authority. Specifically, the board of directors recommended:

- Streamlining the organizational structure to consist of three standing committees at the international level and two standing committees at the chapter level.

Courtesy Honor Society of Nursing Sigma Theta Tau International

- Adapting the honor society's membership eligibility language so that it was more applicable worldwide.
- Granting the board of directors authority to make incremental, restricted dues and fee adjustments, based on the rate of inflation, as needed in the future. (Previously, delegates had fiscal authority.)

Historically, proposed changes presented to the delegates do not have a good record of being passed, especially when related to the finances of the organization. In 1997, delegates voted down a proposed membership dues increase and in 2001 delegates again voted down a proposal to increase chapter assessment fees. With 62 percent of the society's revenues coming from membership dues and the society operating on a zero growth budget for more than five years, a dues increase was critical to the financial health of the organization.

Research

Secondary research on our past delegate databases told us that 75 percent were chapter leaders, most often the president or president-elect of one of the society's 433 chapters. We conducted benchmark and follow-up surveys to delegates, gauging their awareness and knowledge of the issues. A benchmark survey was sent August 19, 2003, almost three months prior to the House of Delegates, asking delegates if they were aware they would be voting on each of the three major proposed bylaws changes. It also asked them to indicate whether they had received enough information to make an informed decision on each of the changes. The same questions then were sent in a follow-up survey, one week prior to the convention.

Planning

Objective
- Receive the necessary three-fourths majority vote needed at the House to pass each proposed bylaws change

Strategies
- Educate delegates on proposed bylaws changes
- Use all available and appropriate society media to communicate audience-oriented messages

Audiences
Primary
- International-level board and committee chairs
- Chapter officers
- Appointed delegates

Secondary

- General membership of Sigma Theta Tau International

Based on the elective, strategies, and audiences, we knew the message must be simply stated, member focused and inclusive. Given this, the theme chosen for the campaign was "It's Up to Us. It's Up to You." The budget for this campaign was $25,000, which included a brochure, electronic newsletters, and surveys, among other existing society communication vehicles.

Execution

Banners: Based on the society's mission and vision—and the campaign's theme of "It's Up to Us. It's Up to You"—we identified six core values to communicate throughout the campaign; courage, honor, tradition, scholarship, excellence, and leadership. Banners that highlighted each of these attributes were hung in several places visible to our audiences: in the lobby of the society's headquarters, at Chapter Leader Academy (a workshop for chapter leaders in March 2003), and in the lobby of the hotel where the convention and House of Delegates took place.

Advertisements: A series of print ads used testimonials from society leaders and members, tying back to the key attributes. They appeared in society publications *Reflections on Nursing Leadership* and *Journal of Nursing Scholarship* and prompted members to visit the website for more information on the proposed bylaws changes.

Editorial: In the first-quarter issue of *Chapter Leader Emphasis* (a quarterly newsletter for chapter leaders), the CEO's column was dedicated to an overview and background of the proposed changes, and the circumstances that necessitated these changes. We also included an article highlighting the proposed changes in the *Delegate Newsletter* (mailed to each delegate 60 days prior to the House of Delegates). Finally, in the fourth-quarter issue of *Chapter Leader Emphasis,* we recapped the amendments that were passed and provided guidance for chapter leaders as to the transition of these changes.

Website: The "It's Up to Us. It's Up to You." pages were added to the society's website in the spring of 2003. Each of these Web pages contained a "Voice Your Opinion" button that allowed visitors to send an e-mail either requesting additional information or sharing their thoughts on any of the proposed changes.

Presentations: Several presentations helped educate the society's staff and board before branching out to educate our key audience, the delegates. First, presentations were made to staff, since any outcome, whether positive or negative, ultimately would affect all employees. Second, the society's board of directors was educated on the strategies and tactics of the communications plan. An oral presentation then was given at the Chapter Leader Academy.

Phone calls: Each board member held informal conversations with society committee chairs about the changes and reported concerns back to staff, which helped us evaluate the messages midstream and tweak them, when necessary. Board representatives also sat in on spring and fall conference calls between the regional coordinators and chapter presidents to review the proposed changes and answer questions.

Brochure: Chapter Leader Academy attendees were given a brochure when the board spoke to them about the proposed changes, and they were encouraged to take extra copies to their members. In May 2003, the brochure was inserted in *Reflections on Nursing Leadership*. Finally, in August it was mailed to all delegates as a quick reference guide for those still learning about the proposed changes.

Listserv: In September, all delegates automatically were subscribed to a listserv set up solely for the discussion of proposed bylaws changes. Delegates were encouraged to post questions or start a discussion to help prepare them for voting.

Electronic newsletters: For four weeks prior to the House of Delegates, a weekly electronic delegate newsletter addressed concerns and provided tips to help prepare delegates for the House.

Forums at convention: All delegates at convention could attend one of six forums during the convention to have questions answered or to comment on the proposed changes. A panel of board members addressed each forum, first giving a brief overview of the changes but allowing the majority of time for discussion and questions.

Evaluation

Most significant was the passage of all proposed bylaws amendments in the House of Delegates, with most proposed changes receiving a 99 percent or above for "yes" votes. Specifically, the campaign realized a significant return on investment when the delegates voted to grant the board fiscal authority, which allowed the board of directors to vote for a $10 dues increase, resulting in a $1.12 million annual increase in society revenue.

Other significant results:

Benchmark and follow-up surveys: The follow-up survey sent days before the House of Delegates showed that the majority of delegates felt they were educated on the issues and prepared to vote. Twenty-seven percent of delegates responded to the survey and more than 95 percent were aware of the three main issues on which they were going to vote. When asked whether they were confident they had enough information to make an informed decision on the issues, more than 60 percent were highly confident in each of the three issues, compared to only 40 percent in the benchmark survey.

Website: In the first three months (April–July 2003), the "It's Up to Us. It's Up to You." pages received more than 2,765 hits. From April until the House of Delegates session, these pages received a total of 4,230 hits.

Listserv: Seventy messages were posted to the listserv in the two months it was available.

Electronic newsletters: Based on the open rates, all four electronic newsletters were well read. More than 67 percent of delegates opened all issues of the newsletter.

EXHIBIT 4-4A   *It's Up to Us Brochure*

It's up to *us.*
It's up to *you.*

*Preparing for the 2003
House of Delegates*

The society's 37th Biennial Convention will be an exciting one. While this event is an opportunity to network with peers and continue our professional development, it's also the time to conduct society business during the House of Delegates, Nov. 4-5, 2003.

This biennium the house will vote on several important issues that directly affect the society's ability to continue providing high value to members while operating efficiently.

I'm excited about the direction the society is going. We continue to grow by chartering chapters and inducting members around the world. And we are building diverse relationships by partnering with organizations that have like missions, further expanding our ability to improve the health of the world's people.

Thank you for being an informed member by reading the information in this brochure. I encourage you to discuss this with your members and ask your chapter's delegate(s) to give careful attention to these issues.

All of these issues are vitally important to the success of the society. I hope that once you have had time to consider them, your delegate(s) will vote in favor of these proposed solutions.

It's up to us to ensure the future of Sigma Theta Tau International. **It's up to *you.***

May L. Wykle

President May L. Wykle
RN, PhD, FAAN

Courtesy Honor Society of Nursing Sigma Theta Tau International

EXHIBIT 4-4B   *Courage Fact Sheet*

Courage

It's up to *us* to embrace the future.

As you reflect on the history of nursing, courageous nurses stand out as influencing significant change. Icons include Florence Nightingale, for reforming nursing care in the mid-to-late 1800s; Clara Barton, founder of the American Red Cross; and our six founders, who had a vision for nursing knowledge, leadership and service.

While these characteristics have remained at the core of the society, the world around us is changing. Nurses have become an even more integral part of health care — serving in clinical, administrative and academic roles. As we look to the future, nursing and the society will continue to evolve.

As the society celebrates its 80-year anniversary, we must evaluate where we have been and where we want to go. Our founders established a strong base; it's up to *us* to build on their legacy. It's up to *you*, the member, to ensure the society's future by supporting changes that will create stronger networks, financial stability and membership growth.

It's up to *us*. It's up to *you*.

During the 37th Biennial Convention, the House of Delegates will vote on bylaws amendments that will have a positive impact on the society's future. Learn more about these proposed bylaws changes by visiting the society's Web site, and be sure to tell your chapter leadership how you want them to vote in November during the 2003 House of Delegates.

Visit **www.nursingsociety.org** and click "It's up to *us*" and let your voice be heard.

May L. Wykle, RN, PhD, FAAN
President

Sigma Theta Tau International
Honor Society of Nursing

Courtesy Honor Society of Nursing Sigma Theta Tau International

Member associations often attempt to influence public policy on behalf of its members. The most effective campaigns rely on the local grassroots efforts of its members throughout the country to bring their messages to Capitol Hill in Washington. The American Health Care Association crisscrossed the country with special events to let Congress know about a looming crisis. Exhibit 4-5a is a news release for a campaign event, Exhibit 4-5b is a media advisory, and Exhibit 4-5c is a photograph taken during the final event on Capitol Hill.

Driving for Quality Care

American Health Care Association with Edelman Worldwide

Alan DeFend

Background/Objectives

When you're a major, national trade association with members facing the financial crisis of their lives and those who can do something about it aren't getting the message, what do you do? You get creative, take the offensive, bypass national media, and institute a program of unprecedented member involvement and communications effectiveness.

In 2002, the American Health Care Association[1] (AHCA) and its more than 10,000 long-term care member-facilities nationwide were confronted with potentially catastrophic health care funding cuts. At a time when most of the nation was focused on the creation of a new Medicare benefit covering prescription drugs, an existing Medicare[2]

---

[1] The 55-year-old American Health Care Association is the nation's preeminent long-term care trade association, representing more than 10,000 long-term care facilities in 48 states and Washington, D.C. A federation, the vast majority of its member facilities are nursing homes, but a sizable percentage of assisted living residences are also represented through the affiliated National Center for Assisted Living.

[2] Medicare funds the care for approximately 10 percent of nursing home residents. It is the single most important category of funding for many nursing facilities as they take on patients with increasingly complex medical needs, who are being discharged earlier from acute care settings. Medicare payments have

---

Courtesy American Health Care Association

benefit for frail, elderly, and disabled people who require care in skilled nursing facilities faced a direct attack.

A strategic campaign was essential to create a national wake-up call concerning the looming cuts that would soon go into effect. The cuts would reduce federal nursing home funding by about $1.8 billion — or about $35 per patient, per day — funding critical for ensuring quality long-term care for millions of Americans. As the flagship long-term care association, AHCA took the leading role in a multipronged approach to call attention to the pending plight of nursing homes and their patients and residents.

Traditional methods of exerting influence were in place. Association regulatory experts kept in close touch with government specialists; lobbyists did likewise with members of Congress and their personal and committee staffs; news was regularly released, and trade and general circulation media were frequently "pitched"; and AHCA members were engaged in traditional grassroots activities. Persuasive and generally effective as these activities were, it soon became apparent that they would not be sufficient to trigger political involvement in time to avert rate reductions.

Major national media and health-focused trade publications would not provide sufficient or credible coverage of the situation to convince politicians of the need to act. Therefore, AHCA determined that only a combination of intensified grassroots activities, member involvement, and media coverage pinpointed to capitalize on the political pressure points would result in achieving the objective of preserving Medicare payments.

Programming

Consequently, the association undertook the most massive public relations effort in its history to act in virtually every state, reaching out to secondary media markets in decisive congressional districts where coverage was most likely. Because the program focused heavily on local awareness and action, the idea was to convey a sense of "a national tour visiting our community," and the efforts were dubbed the "Driving for Quality Care" campaign. The concept of "taking the cause to the people" was especially apt when the individuals who would be impacted by the pending Medicare cuts were among America's oldest, most frail, and least mobile citizens. The campaign vehicle was a modest motor home, shrink wrapped with custom art work featuring the name of the campaign and its major messages: "Save Our Seniors" and

---

seesawed in the past decade, and a major reduction in payments has been blamed for Chapter 11 filings in 1999 and 2000 that saw some 10 percent of the nation's nursing home beds operated by bankrupt companies.

"Stop Medicare Cuts." The RV also featured a roll-out petition affixed to its side that would ultimately be delivered to the nation's capital and presented to elected officials with tens of thousands of signatures at a Capitol Hill ceremonial event.

The first step in designing the "Driving for Quality Care Mobile Petition Tour" involved mapping a route based on congressional targeting: vulnerable incumbents, those holding key committee assignments, legislators heavily involved in health care issues, or those otherwise viewed as potential champions for the cause. Then communities in these key congressional districts were selected based upon demographic factors and the prospect for local media coverage. The tour was scheduled to run from March to September 2002 with 111 events and rallies in 45 states.

After the zig-zag nationwide course was plotted, the motor home was rented and wrapped, crews were chosen both to accompany the vehicle on the road and support its activities from a central command center. With these in place, the petition tour hit the road. A rotating staff of two kept the tour going seven days a week, and a team of four in Washington planned event details 4–10 days ahead.

The "Driving for Quality Care Mobile Petition Tour" held a daily media event/rally on the campus of a selected skilled nursing facility. The RV with the 120-foot petition scroll unfurled on its side formed the backdrop for the event. The typical crowd consisted of the nursing home residents, their caregivers, family members, concerned citizens from the community, and other invited guests, including elected officials. Everyone involved with the event wore specially designed t-shirts with "Save Our Seniors" on one side and "Stop Medicare Cuts" on the other. Handmade signs were distributed for residents to hold. The nursing home administrator opened the program by explaining the purpose of the event, which was to call attention to pending Medicare cuts and the need to stop them. The typical program also included remarks from a hands-on caregiver, a family member, a resident, and often elected officials including state, local, and federal legislators. The remarks were focused on the crux of the message: the direct impact the cut in Medicare funds would have on the quality of skilled nursing facility patient care. At the conclusion of the event, speakers and the entire crowd came forward to sign the petition, and media were encouraged to conduct individual interviews.

To maximize the grassroots benefit of each event, each facility administrator was asked to dedicate five to six phones for calls to be placed to the district offices of the U.S. Senators and Congressional Representatives through a toll free patch-through line (1-866-STOP-CUTS). Laptop computers were also set up to enable patients, family members, and caregivers to send personalized e-mails to their senators and representatives.

The more than 100 events were successful beyond imagination. Administrators loved the attention, and it provided a new and different activity to involve residents. In addition, it showed a tangible benefit of belonging to state and national trade associations. Media covered virtually every one of the dozens of press conferences, and the coverage was universally positive and reflected the simple, compelling messages.

The tour officially ended on the eve of the impending Medicare cuts on September 30 when AHCA drove the RV to Upper Senate Park on Capitol Hill for a major rally with hundreds of caregivers and residents and presentation of the signed scroll to political leaders. In advance of this visit, many of the more than 150,000 people who participated in grassroots efforts were energized to once again call or write their elected officials.

Evaluation

The campaign garnered media coverage nationwide, including articles or photos or both in more than 220 general circulation newspapers. There were frequent wire stories and more than 130 broadcast segments—among them live satellite feeds during newscasts. Newspaper editorials demanding the cuts be stopped appeared from Tulsa to Tampa; successful op-ed placements included the *Las Vegas Review Journal, Arkansas Democrat Gazette, Omaha World Herald, Kansas City Star, Des Moines Register, Indianapolis Star, Idaho Statesman,* and *Billings Gazette.* As well, the campaign collected thousands of petition signatures, and a database was created with the contact information for approximately 160,000 concerned citizens.

Focused around a national petition tour, AHCA's campaign rallied thousands of residents, caregivers, and family members against scheduled Medicare cuts. Through grassroots activities, coalition building, and special events, the campaign brought the issue to the forefront among key federal legislators, their constituents, and the local media. This program has been credited as decisive in the provision of Medicare funding that has allowed nursing facilities nationwide to again stave off bankruptcies.

Peer recognition in public relations provides an important gauge of program quality, and for 2002, the "Driving for Quality Care Mobile Petition Tour" received the prestigious Silver Sabre Award from The Holmes Group, a respected public relations trade organization. The Silver Sabre annually recognizes the best reputation or branding programs in specific industries.

EXHIBIT 4-5A   *News Release*

NEWS

American Health Care Association

FOR IMMEDIATE RELEASE
September 5, 2002

Contact: Maureen Knightly (202) 336-7963
On-site: Ellen Almond   (202) 365-1572

"Driving for Quality Care" National Petition Tour Comes To Alexandria to Help Stop Federal Medicare Cuts
Virginia Seniors Risk Losing $34.3 Million In Patient Care Resources
Congressman Moran Praised for Opposing Medicare Cuts Scheduled for October 1ˢᵗ 2002
Petition To President Bush, Congress Urges Rejection Of Medicare Cut

Alexandria, VA – While praising the recent effort of President Bush to cancel approximately $1 billion of a cumulative $3 billion federal Medicare cut scheduled to go into effect on October 1ˢᵗ, 2002, advocates of quality long term health care urged Congressman Tom Davis (R, VA-11) and Congressman James Moran (D, VA-8) to follow the President's lead by ensuring Congress cancels the remaining $2 billion in Medicare cuts, called the Medicare "cliff," that the advocates said, will put vulnerable Virginia seniors' access to quality patient care at severe risk.

"We thank President Bush for stepping in to stop approximately one-third of the Medicare cuts from going into effect, and now Virginia's vulnerable seniors are counting on Representatives Davis and Moran and the rest of Congress to stop the remainder of these deep, ill-considered reductions in patient care funding," said Steve Morrisette, Executive Director of the Virginia Health Care Association.

He explained that through executive branch action, President Bush was able to forestall approximately $1 billion of the proposed $3 billion, 17% cumulative cut to Medicare originally proposed in his federal budget, and that only Congress can overturn the remaining $2 billion in cuts.

Morrisette warned that the remaining Medicare cuts will slash approximately $34.3 million in patient care funding for Virginia's seniors, and, if implemented, will have "disastrous consequences for our most vulnerable Medicare beneficiaries."

According to new state-by-state data from Muse & Associates, an independent public policy research firm, the daily Medicare per patient reimbursement rate in Virginia for seniors, even after the positive action by President Bush -- will be reduced by more than *$33 per patient per day* between 2002 and 2003.

Today's event in Alexandria was lent the presence and support of Congressman James Moran. "We must prevent the October 1st proposed 10 percent cut in Medicare funding from happening," said Moran. "If these cuts go into effect many nursing homes will be forced to either shut down or lay off staff, jeopardizing the quality of care and the health and safety of our seniors. In Virginia alone, the consequence of the Medicare cliff will result in a loss of more than $34 million per year in patient reimbursements. The Republicans in Congress have passed massive tax cuts for the very wealthy but can't seem to find the money to help this country's most vulnerable seniors. This is unacceptable. Congress must act to prevent these cuts in Medicare spending immediately."

Stated Morrisette: "Those seniors who need around-the-clock skilled nursing care are clearly put in jeopardy by these proposed cuts because they will threaten the quality of patient care, limit beneficiary access to needed services, and perpetuate the nurse staffing crisis by eliminating important health care jobs. That clock is ticking now with less than 30 days left before access to quality care for our seniors is pushed into a freefall."

"Besides threatening the quality and availability of patient care, cuts this deep will result in a significant loss of jobs in a health care sector where there is a correlation between numbers of staff and level of care quality," continued Morrisette. "At a time when Congress and the public at large are demanding quality long term care, it's illogical to implement cuts that will eliminate key front line nursing staff jobs that boost the overall quality of care."

-more-

1201 L Street, NW • Washington, DC 20005 • (202) 842-4444

Courtesy American Health Care Association

EXHIBIT 4-5A *News Release (continued)*

Concluded Morrisette: "On behalf of Medicare beneficiaries throughout Virginia and the men and women who provide patient care, we are signing this petition to President Bush and the U.S. Congress urging them to reject the remainder of these cuts so we can protect seniors' access to quality long term patient care." He said that even though the President has now done his part to help stop the cuts, he could still use his power and influence to convince Congress to do its part by the October 1st deadline.

The residents and nursing staff of Woodbine Rehab and Healthcare Center in Alexandria, as well as concerned citizens in the area also signed the petition to President Bush and the U.S. Congress urging swift action on these matters. The petitions will be delivered to the President and the Congress upon the arrival of the tour in Washington in late September. Individuals can make their voices heard by calling toll-free **1-866-STOP-CUTS** or by visiting www.drivingforqualitycare.com.

Following the Alexandria event, the RV tour will continue into Pennsylvania as it continues its national drive through 45 states.

The American Health Care Association (AHCA) is a non-profit federation of affiliated state health organizations, together representing nearly 12,000 non-profit and for-profit assisted living, nursing facility, developmentally-disabled, and subacute care providers that care for more than 1.5 million elderly and disabled individuals nationally

####

EXHIBIT 4-5B   *Media Advisory*

MEDIA ADVISORY

National "Drive for Quality Care" Petition Tour To Stop in Spokane on Friday

Medicare Cuts Will Have a Long-term, Direct and Negative Impact on the Quality and Availability of Nursing Home Services for Medicare Patients across the Nation

What: The national mobile petition tour, *"Driving for Quality Care,"* is traveling from Texas to Washington, D.C. to build awareness and support among Congress and the Administration for addressing the impending Medicare cut. This 10% cut to the Medicare program for nursing home patients, estimated at $2 billion annually, will translate into $28.7 million for Washington alone. Failing to address these cuts could seriously affect access to quality care, and result in the loss of thousands of jobs.

A recently released study will be made available which shows the impact these Medicare cuts will have on Medicare beneficiaries in Washington who need skilled nursing care.

Skilled nursing residents, family members, staff and concerned citizens from the Spokane area will sign their names to a 4 ft. by 100 ft. petition calling on President Bush and Congress to take steps to address the looming Medicare cuts for skilled nursing care.

The mobile petition effort kicked off in Texas in March and will arrive on Capitol Hill in late September. Spokane is the 39th stop of the campaign, which will travel through more than 45 states.

Who: -   **U.S. Representative George Nethercutt, Jr. (R, WA-5),** *invited*
-    Administrator
-    Caregiver
-    Family member
-    Resident

When: Friday, May 31, 2002
11:00 a.m.

Where: **Royal Park Care Center**
7411 North Nevada
Spokane, WA 99208
509-489-2273

Contact: Neil Booth   Bree Flammini (On-site)
914-763-3381   202-365-1572

1-866-STOP-CUTS
www.drivingforqualitycare.com

Courtesy American Health Care Association

EXHIBIT 4-5C *Photograph of Capitol Hill Event*

The Driving for Quality Care RV arrives at Capitol Hill to deliver a national petition calling for Congress to support adequate funding for nursing home care.

Courtesy American Health Care Association

## Chapter 5

Community Relations

One of the most important audiences an organization has is its community, the home of its offices and operations. Maintaining good relations with the community usually entails management and employees becoming involved in and contributing to local organizations and activities. In addition, the organization may communicate with the community in other ways, such as distributing house publications or meeting with community leaders. Often community relations activities involve face-to-face interaction between an organization and a public, one of the most powerful forms of influencing attitudes.

Solving community relations problems may follow the usual sequence of research, objectives, programming, and evaluation.

RESEARCH

Research for community relations includes investigation to understand the client, the reason for the program, and the community audiences to be targeted for communication.

Client Research

Client research for community relations concentrates on the organization's role and reputation in the community. What is its level of credibility? Have there been significant community complaints in the past? What are the organization's present and past community relations practices? What changes in the community and political landscape are affecting relations with the organization? What are its major strengths and weaknesses in the community? What opportunities exist to enhance community relations? These questions provide a helpful framework for a community relations program.

Opportunity or Problem Research

Why have a community relations program in the first place? Considering the cost and benefits involved, this is a question worthy of detailed justification. The public relations practitioner should assess problems the organization may have had with community groups and make a searching analysis of community relations opportunities. Many organizations conduct ongoing proactive community relations as a form of insurance against any sudden problem requiring a reactive public relations solution. It is often easier to communicate with an organization's current community network than to build a new communication program from scratch.

Audience Research

The final aspect of community relations research consists of carefully identifying audiences to be targeted for communication and learning as much about each audience as possible. Community publics can be subdivided into three major groups: community media, community leaders, and community organizations. These categories can then be further subdivided as shown in Exhibit 5-a.

EXHIBIT 5-A   *Community Publics*

Community media
    Mass
    Specialized

Community leaders
   Public officials
   Educators
   Religious leaders
   Professionals
   Executives
   Bankers
   Union leaders
   Ethnic leaders
   Neighborhood leaders
Community organizations
   Civic
   Business
   Service
   Social
   Cultural
   Religious
   Youth
   Political
   Special interest groups
   Other

In conducting community relations programs, it is important for the practitioner to develop contact lists of journalists, community leaders, and organizations.

The media contacts list will be similar to those discussed in Chapter 3, on media relations. These lists should include the type and size of audience reached by each media outlet in the community, the type of material used by each outlet, the name and title of appropriate editors who handle organizational news, and deadlines.

The list of community and organization leaders should be equally thorough. It should include the name, title, affiliation, address, and telephone number of all important community leaders. These data should be categorized according to occupational fields, such as public officials, educators, media people, or religious leaders. In addition to a listing of leaders alone, there should be a list of organizations that includes frequently updated names of officers, their addresses, and telephone numbers. It is often a real challenge to identify the influentials or opinion leaders who have exceptional credibility with others in the community through reputation, expertise, economic clout, or political power. It is not always those individuals in "official positions of leadership." For example, the president of the local Parent Teacher Association (PTA) may be important, but the real power behind decisions about education may be a former school board member or a highly respected principal. When these people talk, others are careful to listen.

Research for community relations, then, consists of investigation of the client, the reason for the program, and the target audiences in the community.

OBJECTIVES

Impact and output objectives for community relations, like those for other forms of public relations, should be specific and quantitative.

Impact Objectives

Impact objectives for community relations involve informing the community audiences or modifying their attitudes or behaviors. Some examples are:

1. To increase (by 30 percent this year) community knowledge of the operations of the organization, including its products, services, employees, and support of community projects

2. To promote (20 percent) more favorable community opinion toward the organization (during a specified time period)

3. To gain (15 percent) greater organizational support from community leaders (during a particular campaign)

4. To encourage (20 percent) more feedback from community leaders (during the current year)

5. To increase the number of employees participating as leaders in local youth sport programs by 20 percent

Output Objectives

Output objectives consist of the efforts made by the practitioner to enhance the organization's community relations. Some illustrations are:

1. To prepare and distribute (15 percent) more community publications (than last year)

2. To be (10 percent) more responsive to community needs (during this year)

3. To create (five) new community projects involving organizational personnel and resources (during this calendar year)

4. To schedule (five) meetings with community leaders (this year)

Thus, both impact and output objectives are helpful in preparing community relations programs. They serve as useful and necessary precursors to programming.

PROGRAMMING

Programming for community relations includes planning the theme and messages, action or special event(s), uncontrolled and controlled media, and using effective communication principles.

Theme and Messages

The theme and messages for community relations are situational and grow out of research findings related to the organization, the reason for conducting the program, and the existing and past relationships with the targeted community audiences.

Action(s) or Special Event(s)

Actions and special events most often associated with community relations are:

1. An organizational open house and tour of facilities
2. Sponsorship of special community events or projects
3. Participation of management and other personnel in volunteer community activities
4. Purchase of advertising in local media
5. Contribution of funds to community organizations or causes
6. Meetings with community leaders
7. Membership of management and personnel in a variety of community organizations—civic, professional, religious
8. Participation of management and workers in the political affairs of the community—service in political office and on councils and boards

Involvement of the organization, its management, and its other personnel in the affairs of the community is the most significant aspect of a community relations program. With this kind of link to the community, there should be relatively smooth community relations, with few or no surprises.

Uncontrolled and Controlled Media

In the communications part of a community relations program, the practitioner should think first of servicing community media outlets with appropriate uncontrolled media, such as news releases, photographs or photo opportunities, and interviews of organizational officers with local reporters.

The use of controlled media, on the other hand, should include sending copies of house publications to a select list of community leaders. The practitioner should also help the organization develop a speakers' bureau, and publicize the availability of organizational management and expert personnel to address meetings of local clubs and organizations. It is also appropriate to target community leaders on a timely basis for selected direct mailings, such as important announcements or notices of organizational involvement in community affairs.

Above all, the organization must develop an informative and appropriate website. This can be used for both uncontrolled and controlled communication. Journalists should be able to obtain background information and up-to-date news about the organization on the website. This should include recent photographs of organizational leaders and facilities as well as other important and relevant data.

Both uncontrolled and controlled media in the community relations program should be focused on the eight types of community involvement listed earlier. These are the heart of the program.

Effective Communication

Three principles of effective communication deserve special attention in community relations programs.

First, the targeting of opinion leaders or community leaders for communication is crucial to the success of such a program. The leadership provides the structure and substance of the community itself.

Second, group influence plays a substantial role in effective community relations. Organizations exercise varying degrees of cohesiveness and member conformity. The community relations program must cultivate community groups, their leaders, and their memberships. The effective speakers bureau is a primary means for accomplishing this.

Finally, audience participation is highly significant. Targeted community media, leaders, and groups can be encouraged to participate in the client's organizational events. Most important, the client should reach out to the community by sponsoring attractive activities.

EVALUATION

If the objectives of the community relations program have been phrased specifically and quantitatively, their evaluation should be relatively easy. For example, it is simple to measure the number of presentations by the organization's speakers bureau or to measure the number of people attending special events sponsored by the organization. The success of a program should be directly linked to its attainment of the objectives stated at the program's outset.

SUMMARY

Research for community relations assesses the organization's reputation and its existing and potential problems with the community. Targeting audiences usually includes a detailed analysis of community media, leaders, and organizations.

Impact objectives for community relations are such desired outcomes as informing or influencing the attitudes and behaviors of the community. Output objectives consist of a listing of public relations efforts to enhance the organization's relations with the community.

Programming concentrates on organizational involvement with the community through sponsorship of events, employee participation in community activities, contributions to community causes, meetings, and the like. The uncontrolled media used in community relations are aimed at servicing local journalists with appropriate news releases, photographs, and interviews with organizational officers. Controlled media usually include house publications, speakers bureaus, and appropriate direct mailings to community leaders.

It is also important for the organization to develop an attractive and informative community-oriented website.

Evaluation of stated objectives uses methods appropriate to the type of objective. Impact objectives are usually measured by a survey or other appropriate quantitative methods, while output objectives may call for simple observation of whether the desired output was achieved.

READINGS ON COMMUNITY RELATIONS

Aldrich, Leigh Stephens. *Covering the Community: A Diversity Handbook for the Media.* Thousand Oaks, CA: Sage Publications, 1999.

Benedict, Arthur C. "After a Crisis: Restoring Community Relations," *Communications World* 11 (September 1994): 20ff.

Bete, Tim. "Eight Great Community Relations Ideas," *School Planning and Management* 37 (May 1998): 49ff.

Bruning, Stephen D. "Examining the Role That Personal, Professional, and Community Relationship Play in Respondent Relationship Recognition and Intended Behavior," *Communication Quarterly* 48 (fall 2000): 437–448.

Bruning, Stephen D., and Meghan Ralston. "Using a Relational Approach to Retaining Students and Building Mutually Beneficial

Student-University Relationships," *The Southern Communication Journal* 66 (summer 2001): 337ff.

Burke, Edmund M. *Corporate Community Relations: The Principle of the Neighbor of Choice.* Westport, CT: Quorum Books, 1999.

Cases in Community Relations. New York: Public Relations Society of America, 1998.

Center, Allen H., and Patrick Jackson. "Community Relations." In *Public Relations Practice: Managerial Case Studies and Practice,* 6th ed. Englewood Cliffs, NJ: Prentice-Hall, 2000.

Culbertson, Hugh M., and Ni Chen. "Communitarianism: A Foundation for Communication Symmetry," *Public Relations Quarterly* 42 (summer 1997): 36–41.

Dobmeyer, Doug. *Competing Successfully for Media Coverage: A Guide to Getting Media Coverage for Non-Profit and Community Organizations.* Chicago: Dobmeyer Communications, 1997.

Forrest, Carol J., and Mays, Renee Hix. "The Practical Guide to Environmental Community Relations," *Journal of Environmental Health* 67 (January–February 2005): 30ff.

Gaschen, Dennis John. "Play Ball: Community Relations and Professional Sports," *Public Relations Tactics* 7 (August 2000): 10.

Heath, Robert L., and Michael Palenchar. "Community Relations and Risk Communication: A Longitudinal Study of the Impact of Emergency Response Messages," *Journal of Public Relations Research* 12, no. 2 (2000): 131–161.

Holtzhausen, Derina R. "Public Relations Practice and Political Change in South Africa," *Public Relations Review* 31 (September 2005): 407–416.

Ledingham, John A., and Stephen D. Bruning. "Building Loyalty Through Community Relations," *Public Relations Strategist* 3 (summer 1997): 27–29.

Leeper, Kathie A. "Public Relations Ethics and Communitarianism: A Preliminary Investigation," *Public Relations Review* 22 (summer 1996): 163ff.

Lukaszewski, James E. *Building Quality Community Relationships: A Planning Model to Gain and Maintain Public Consent.* White Plains, NY: Lukaszewski Group, 1995.

———. "Getting to 51 Percent: Building Community Relationships That Gain and Maintain Public Consent," *Public Relations Tactics* 12 (May 2005): 11.

McDermott, David. "The 10 Commandments of Community Relations," *World Wastes* 36 (September 1993): 48ff.

Poston, Patty. "Grassroots Communications Reconsidered," *Public Relations Tactics* 9 (September 2002): 12–13.

Profolio: Community Relations. New York: Public Relations Society of America, 1998.

Reish, Marc S. "Chemical Industry Tries to Improve Its Community Relations," *Chemical and Engineering News* (February 1994): 8ff.

Sandman, Peter M. "Responding to Community Outrage: Strategies for Effective Risk Communication," *Journal of Environmental Health* 67 (January–February 2005): 30ff.

Schultz, David L. "Strategic Survival in the Face of Community Activism," *Public Relations Strategist* 7 (spring 2001): 36–38.

St. John, Burton. "Public Relations as Community-Building: Then and Now," *Public Relations Quarterly* 43 (spring 1998): 34ff.

CASE 5-1

Long-standing institutions in a community develop loyal follow-ings who want to be heard during a period of change. For the opening of a new library, Exhibit 5-1a is a news advisory for the event, Exhibit 5-1b is a news release, and Exhibit 5-1c is a poster for the campaign.

Dr. Martin Luther King, Jr. Library—Check It Out!

City of San Jose San Jose Public Library, San Jose State University, San Jose State University Library with Introducing: Dr. Martin Luther King, Jr. Library, McNutt & Company, Inc., Russell Leong Design, and Right Angle Design

Summary

Opening the Dr. Martin Luther King, Jr. Library, the first joint library in the United States between a major university and large city, posed unique PR challenges. Many diverse audiences needed to be reached with a limited budget. There was skepticism and confusion about how this first-of-its-kind library would operate. Nonacademic library patrons had to be enticed onto a campus that was not frequented by the public. This campaign leveraged its limited resources with innovative ideas, community collaborations, and media sponsorships. Attendance at the opening celebration was double the goal, and awareness and community support of the library were widespread.

Research

The concept of combining the Library of San Jose State University (SJSU) and the downtown main library of the San Jose Public Library required years of planning and community input. At every step, public opinion among the campus and city communities was gathered and became the research archives for creating an effective public relations campaign when the library opened. The concerns of the public were identified through a variety of activities including: Blue Ribbon Advisory Groups

---

Courtesy San Jose Public Library & San Jose State University Library

to both the University President and the San Jose Mayor: a series of public community meetings; a special hearing of the SJSU Academic Senate; and benchmark surveys conducted by Thomas A. Childers, Ph.D., from the Office of Institutional Research at Drexel University. All of this material was supplemented with informal interviews of representatives of the targeted audiences. Extensive research on approaches used by other libraries for grand opening activities was also conducted with the focus on budget, best practices, and lessons learned.

The **research phase** identified several challenges for the PR campaign:

- The innovative concept of a joint library raised many questions and generated skepticism about how the venture would work. Would these negative perceptions keep potential users away from the library?

- The library's large size (475,000 square feet, nine levels plus a mezzanine, covering 11 acres) and location on a corner of the SJSU campus could generate the perception that the library is intimidating and primarily for campus use. Although it has been located in the middle of downtown San Jose for 146 years, SJSU has remained separate from the city. Architects created a design that they hoped would be welcoming at both the public and campus entrances. Would the public be willing to cross the invisible wall around the campus to explore the library?

- Both the university and the city are diverse, attracting many ethnic groups. The public library also serves other diverse clientele, such as undocumented individuals, homeless, and others with extremely low incomes and limited education. Recent immigrants, especially those who speak Spanish and Vietnamese, with few English language skills are heavy users of the library. How could so many diverse audiences be reached with limited resources and be convinced that this library is for them?

- Resentment existed among users of public library branches that too many resources were being devoted to the main library, depleting resources available to the branches for collections, programs, and operations. Could these residents be persuaded that the investment in the King Library was a wise use of public funds?

Planning

The vision of the King Library is laudable—to create a world-class library that would serve the lifelong learning needs of both the university and the city. But explaining this innovative concept to multiple, diverse audiences and encouraging them to explore and embrace the King Library as a valuable asset for the community was not going to be an easy task. A thoughtful and comprehensive public relations plan for the library's opening was needed.

The PR plan identified 28 targeted audiences for the opening of the King Library and five overall goals:

1. Achieve public awareness of the location, concept, and content of the King Library among the general public and the university community

2. Encourage targeted audiences to explore, use, and feel welcome at the King Library

3. Highlight the innovative partnership among SJSU, the City of San Jose, and the San Jose Redevelopment Agency, as well as the unique features of the library

4. Instill pride in the community for the city, the university, and the King Library

5. Enhance the image of downtown San Jose as a center for creativity and knowledge

Quantifiable objectives included attracting 300–500 guests to a black tie gala and 10,000 to the dedication/community celebration. Ultimately, the PR campaign hoped to entice 700,000 visitors to the library by December 31, 2003—100,000 more than normal at the old libraries.

Communication efforts were incorporated into all phases of the development and construction of the King Library, but this campaign focused on the opening celebration as the most strategic opportunity to obtain widespread impact in introducing the new library building and concept to targeted audiences. Library staff wanted a "soft opening" on August 1 in order to smooth out operational issues. Moreover, faculty and students would not return to campus until later in the month, so the opening celebration was scheduled for August 15–16. A black tie gala would be held on Friday evening for donors and community leaders, and Saturday would be the day for the public dedication ceremony and community celebration.

A big library deserves a big introduction, but resources (both budget and people) were limited. The team included two library staff members who worked half-time on the opening PR effort and two consultants, with support from the public information offices of the library, the university, and the city. The King Library leveraged its resources with many community partnerships and media sponsorships.

Execution

The opening events for the Dr. Martin Luther King, Jr. Library included a black tie gala on the evening of Aug. 15 and a formal dedication ceremony on Saturday, Aug. 16. The community celebration following the dedication included 25 different exhibits, contests, performances, and other activities inside the library—19 free performances at two stages strategically placed outside the library appealing to varied ages, interests, and ethnic groups—and 45 activity/information booths outside the library. In order to emphasize the collaborative nature of the new university-city library, the celebration event was designed to involve participation by many campus and community organizations. These groups provided entertainment and family activities with reading and literacy themes at no cost to the library. The large size of the library and the adjacent campus plaza provided spacious areas so that multiple activities could be scheduled at one time, each appealing to a different target audience. At 1 p.m., for example, celebration attendees could choose from an autograph party with children's authors and illustrators, book bingo, a performance of Beethoven Bagatelles, Civil Rights Trivial Pursuit, multicultural storytelling, a talk by a local author, a tour of public art inside the library, Japanese animation, bookmark printing, and free copies of *Goodnight, Moon* in English, Spanish, and Vietnamese. Later in the day there was a mystery tea, Chinese ballroom dancing, operatic arias, puppet crafts, a Latin youth band, and dozens of other options.

Themes selected for events and promotional activities underscored key PR messages:

- Black Tie Gala—"The Magic of Dreams"
- Dedication Ceremony—"A Milestone in San Jose History"
- Community Celebration—"Dr. Martin Luther King, Jr. Library—Check It Out!"
- Tagline for Promotional Materials—"A world of ideas . . . a universe of possibilities"

Advance publicity for the opening celebration weekend was incorporated into media coverage of the closing of the old library, the move to the new library, and the library's first day of operation. Two special inserts were published in the *San Jose Mercury News*—a 24-page special section without ads describing the library and a 12-page advertorial promoting the dedication and celebration. In addition to the usual array of PR tools (see binder for information on news releases, PSAs, broadcast interviews on public affairs and news programs, media advisories, pre-opening background tours, direct media contact, street banners, bookmarks, movie theater slides, flyers, displays, etc.), the campaign used innovative and strategic tactics to accomplish its goals:

- Media Sponsors & Partnerships expanded promotional resources— Contracts were negotiated with the largest daily newspaper in Silicon Valley, two television stations (the NBC affiliate and a Spanish-language channel), and five radio stations (two Spanish-language, one popular music, one Asian-language, and the campus station) that resulted in more than $330,000 in free print and broadcast promotion.

- Read-aloud Marathon brought international attention—A team of six university and city library representatives was persuaded to launch a challenge to the Guinness Book of World Records for the longest continuous reading-aloud marathon during the second week the King Library was open. This not only built media buzz up to opening day, it added a unique and international interest to the community celebration, since the team timed its new world record, 74 hours, to coincide with the midpoint of the opening celebration.

Evaluation

The public relations campaign for the opening of the Dr. Martin Luther King, Jr. Library more than met its goals. Community support and involvement was achieved as evidenced by widespread participation in King Library opening celebration as sponsors or partners, adding $492,288 in cash and in-kind donations to the PR budget.

There were close to 500 guests at the black tie gala (at $125 per ticket). More than $110,000 in additional donations to the library was received after this event.

An estimated 21,000 people attended the dedication and community celebration on August 16—twice the number set as the objective. Public awareness of the location, concept, and content of the King Library among general public and the university community was widespread as a result of the promotion and media coverage (see binder), and key PR messages were reflected in media coverage such as these headlines:

- "Uniting Two Worlds: San Jose, university cover new ground with Dr. Martin Luther King, Jr. Library"
- "New Library Is Symbol Of Learning For Entire City"
- "Shared Goals. Shared Building: City, campus center is 'revolutionary' experiment"
- "Building Unites Campus, Downtown: New landmark at center of tidal wave of change"
- "Young Patrons Get Their Own Space: Rooms cater to different interests of children, teens"

Perhaps most important, the PR campaign was successful in encouraging targeted audiences to use and feel welcome at the King Library, as evidenced by visitor counts during the first four months of operation—one million people through the doors! Initial objective was to attract 700,000 visitors in five months, so the number of visitors was 45 percent higher than the original objective.

EXHIBIT 5-1A   *News Advisory*

DR. MARTIN LUTHER KING, JR. LIBRARY

Media Advisory

~ A collaboration between the City of San José and San José State University

<u>For Immediate Release</u>
Friday, August 15, 2003

<u>Contact:</u>
Lorraine Oback, 408-808-2176, lorraine.oback@sjlibrary.org
Nancy L. Stake, Ron Bottini at SJSU, 408-924-1166

Guinness Challenge for the World Record on Non-Stop Reading Aloud
To Conclude Saturday, August 16 at Noon

WHO: The six-member "King's Dream Team"

WHAT: Expect to exceed both the current official Guinness World Record (53 hours and 2 minutes) and the unofficial new record (61 hours and 16 minutes) for continuous, non-stop reading aloud by a handy margin of 12 hours and 44 minutes; 74 hours total.

WHERE: Dr. Martin Luther King, Jr. Library, 2nd floor
150 E. San Fernando St. at S. Fourth St., downtown San José

WHY: To commemorate the opening of the new King Library, kick off the activities of Literacy Classic Week and underscore the continuing importance of literacy in the Information Age.

During the entire period since the challenge began on Wednesday, August 13 at 10 a.m., the team has not been allowed to leave the reading area except for five-minute restroom breaks. They have been reading, sleeping, eating, and resting their vocal cords on the second floor of the King Library. The public is invited to stop by the challenge area during Saturday's grand opening festivities, following the dedication ceremony at 10 a.m., to cheer and encourage the team. They can also catch the final moments through a webcast link on the library's home page—www.sjlibrary.org

Courtesy San Jose Public Library & San Jose State University Library

EXHIBIT 5-1B   *News Release*

Dr. Martin Luther King, Jr. Library

News Release

~A collaboration between the City of San José and San José State University

<u>For Immediate Release</u>
Monday, July 28, 2003

<u>Contact:</u>
Nancy L. Stake, Ron Bottini at SJSU, 408-924-1166
Lorraine Oback at King Library, 408-808-2176

FIRST CO-MANAGED CITY/UNIVERSITY LIBRARY IN THE NATION OPENS ITS DOORS AUGUST 1

SAN JOSE, Calif., -- When the new 475,000 sq. ft. Dr. Martin Luther King, Jr. Library opens its doors to the public in downtown San José on Fri., Aug. 1, at 9 a.m., it will be the culmination of a seven-year, joint development effort between the City of San José, San José State University and the San José Redevelopment Agency. It is the first library in the nation to be funded, managed and operated by a city and a major university.

The new library is not only a model of creative partnerships and resource sharing, it is a model for libraries of the future. An expansive, lifelong learning center, the new King Library will serve as an information hub for the residents, students and faculty, employers and employees of Silicon Valley. It will offer access to the collections of a major university along with the resources of the city's main library and its 17 branches. The library will meet the learning needs of people of every age, culture, ability and income level.

Located close to San José's new Civic Center (now under construction), the King Library will play a significant role in the revitalization of downtown. Total project cost came in at $177.5 million.

The new library is on the SJSU campus at the corner of Fourth and San Fernando streets. Summer hours are: Mon.-Wed., 8 a.m. - 8 p.m., Thu.-Sat., 9 a.m.-6 p.m. and Sun., 1 -5 p.m. Parking at the new Fourth Street Garage is free after 6 p.m. on weekdays and all day on weekends. For more information on the library and the grand opening weekend celebration for the public on Sat., Aug. 16, call 408-808-2000.

####

150 E. SAN FERNANDO STREET I SAN JOSE, CALIFORNIA I TEL. 408.808.2355 I FAX 408.808.2133 I www.sjlibrary.org

Courtesy San Jose Public Library & San Jose State University Library

EXHIBIT 5-1C   *Poster*

Dr. Martin Luther King, Jr. Library –
Check It Out!

FREE

FREE

FREE

Grand Opening Celebration
Saturday, August 16
10 a.m. – 4 p.m.
4th & San Fernando, downtown San José

- *Entertainment on 2 stages for the whole family*
- *Games, crafts, children's activities, story times*
- *Book bingo*
- *Mystery tea*
- *Formal dedication ceremony at 10 a.m.*
- *Commemorative gifts*
- *Contests with prizes*
- *Tours and demonstrations*
- *A day of fun and surprises*

You've never seen a library like this one!

(408) 277-4000
www.newkinglibrary.org

*Lots of free parking in downtown City garages
Metered on-street parking is free on Saturday*

To arrange for an accommodation under the Americans with Disabilities Act, please call (408) 277-4000 or (408) 998-5299 (TTY) at least 48 hours prior to the event.

The Bay Area's **NBC11**

 FIRST 5 SANTA CLARA COUNTY

T48 TELEMUNDO

The Mercury News
The Newspaper of Silicon Valley
MercuryNews.com

 DR. MARTIN LUTHER KING, JR. LIBRARY

A collaboration between the City of San José and San José State University

Printing Donated to the King Library

Courtesy San Jose Public Library & San Jose State University Library

EXHIBIT 5-1C   *Poster (continued)*

Biblioteca Dr. Martín Luther King, Jr. - ¡Venga y Vea!

Celebración de la Gran Apertura
Sábado, 16 de agosto
10 a.m. – 4 p.m.
En el centro de San José entre la 4th y San Fernando

GRATIS

GRATIS

GRATIS

- Entretenimiento en 2 escenarios para toda la familia
- Juegos, trabajos manuales, actividades para los niños
- Bingo de libros
- Té con un escritor de libros de misterio
- Ceremonia de dedicación formal a las 10 a.m.
- Regalos conmemorativos
- Concursos con premios
- Demostraciones y recorridos
- Un día de diversión y sorpresas

Para acomodar personas con discapacidades de acuerdo a las normas de la Ley de Americanos con Discapacidades, por favor llame al (408) 277-4000 o al (408) 998-5299 por lo menos 48 horas antes del evento

¡Nunca ha visto una biblioteca como esta!

(408) 277-4000
www.newkinglibrary.org

DR. MARTIN LUTHER KING, JR. LIBRARY

Una colaboración entre la Universidad San José State y la Ciudad de San José

Habrá muchísimo estacionamiento gratuito en los garajes de la Ciudad Los medidores de tiempo en los estacionamientos de la calle serán gratuitos el sábado.

Thư Viện Dr. Martin Luther King, Jr. - Hãy Đến Coi Thử!

Lễ Kỷ Niệm Khai Trương Thư Viện
Thứ Bảy, Ngày 16 Tháng 8, 2003
Ngã tư đường số 4th và San Fernando,
khu phố San José

Có 2 sân khấu giải trí cho cả gia đình
Trò chơi, thủ công, sinh hoạt cho trẻ em
Chơi Bingo với giải thưởng sách đọc
Nói chuyện với các nhà văn
Lễ khai mạc vào lúc 10 giờ sáng
Tặng quà làm kỷ niệm
Thi đấu có giải thưởng
Triển lãm thư viện
Một ngày đầy sự ngạc nhiên và thích thú

Miễn Phí

Miễn Phí

Miễn Phí

Theo bộ luật của Hoa Kỳ dành cho những người bị khuyến tật, để cần được giúp đỡ về di chuyển, xin liên lạc số điện thoại (408) 277-4000 hoặc số (408) 998-5299 trước 48 tiếng.

Quí vị chưa từng thấy một thư viện nào như thư viện này!

Số điện thoại: (408) 277 - 4000
Mạng lưới: www.newkinglibrary.org

DR. MARTIN LUTHER KING, JR. LIBRARY

Được hợp tác giữa trường Đại Học San José State và Thành Phố San José

Đậu xe miễn phí trong khu đậu xe của thành phố. Thứ Bảy không cần bỏ tiền vào máy nếu đậu xe bên đường

Development issues quickly energize local activist groups, even when the organization involved is a hospital. When gaining community support and involvement in the development process, organizations rely on developing broad coalitions and extensive communication campaigns that involve personal contacts, media stories, and advertising. Exhibit 5-2a is an advertisement with "Ten Facts" about the initiative, and Exhibit 5-2b is a community guide.

Barberton Citizens Hospital: Keep Barberton Healthy

Barberton Citizens Hospital with Edward Howard & Company

Situation

Since 1915, Barberton Citizens Hospital (BCH) had served the small, blue-collar community of Barberton (population 27,899) just southwest of Akron, Ohio. Originally a city-owned hospital, BCH was purchased in 1996 by Quorum Health Group, Inc., and later by Triad Hospitals, Inc., of Plano, Texas, a for-profit hospital management corporation. BCH traditionally has served both the residents of Barberton and surrounding communities, many of them rural. In 2001, market research was conducted to help develop a branding strategy for BCH. The research showed that, among residents, BCH had only a 44 percent top-of-mind awareness among area hospitals. The research also showed a perception that BCH was "low tech" and that doctors referred patients to other area hospitals for specialty services. BCH launched a marketing campaign to address these concerns.

By the fall of 2002, BCH was ready to grow—to expand its facilities to provide additional services, improve some existing services, and improve parking by replacing an old, outdated parking deck and installing a new parking lot convenient to a new emergency room. Because the hospital was landlocked, the best option was to acquire eight acres

Courtesy Barberton Citizens Hospital, Edward Howard & Company, and ST&P Communications

of adjacent parkland for the expansion. However, the City Charter in Barberton requires approval by two-thirds vote—a super majority, not just a simple majority—to transfer parkland. Barberton City Council agreed to place the issue on the May 2003 ballot in a special election. This would be the only issue on the ballot. Edward Howard & Co. was retained to create significant interest, drive voters to the polls, and secure the issue's passage. In addition to the obstacle of a super majority, Tuscora Park was the largest park in Barberton, and it was expected that many residents would react negatively to losing any parkland at all. Also, the hospital's plans spanned a 10-year period, so the health care benefits to the community would not be immediate. BCH also had to overcome misperceptions about giving up parkland to increase profits for the corporate owner.

Research

We conducted both secondary and primary research to help shape tactics and messages throughout the campaign.

Secondary Research

Compile voting statistics—December

What we learned: Average turnout for special election 17 percent

Compile census data—December

What we learned: Average HH income $32,000; 12 percent beneath poverty level; manufacturing largest employer; median age 37

Lists of local officials—December

What we learned: Contact info, critical concerns

Lists of organizations—January

What we learned: Contact info, when they met, which would be most impacted

Primary Research

Benchmark analysis of registered voters—Early January
What we learned:

- 51 percent approval, 44 percent opposed, 6 percent undecided
- Strongly opposed (29 percent) outnumbered strongly in favor
- Older adults most likely to vote in favor
- Residents closest to park most likely to oppose

Focus groups to shape campaign messages—Three sessions; supporters, opponents, and "mixed"—February

We learned that it is important to:

- provide details about terms of sale
- show why expansion into park was best option
- position hospital as leading community institution
- capitalize on key endorsements

Planning

The objective was clear: Acquire a two-thirds majority vote approving the sale of eight acres of Tuscora Park to Barberton Citizens Hospital for expansion. We knew from our research that it would be difficult to change the minds of those strongly opposed, so we set out to win over those in the middle—the 27 percent somewhat supportive and 15 percent somewhat opposed—and motivate them to vote.

We determined that the best strategy was to frame the messages under the umbrella of the existing branding campaign, thereby strengthening the hospital's position within the community. Our overall plan was:

- Conduct research to help shape tactics and messages throughout the campaign.
- Identify allies, obstacles, and likely opponents early in the process.
- Whenever possible, use two-way dialogue to reach influencers directly.
- Stress community benefits (better healthcare, quality jobs, increased tax base, etc.).

Before we went public, we developed key messages:

- We believe in Barberton. We want Barberton to believe in us. (Demonstrate BCH commitment to community and intentions to stay and grow in Barberton.)
- Keep good health care close to home.
- BCH means good things for our town (good jobs, tax dollars, etc.).

We then trained presenters (hospital staff; credible community volunteers, e.g., retired OB/GYN) to deliver these messages, so they would be ready to make presentations as soon as the campaign went public.

Target Audience: registered voters within the City of Barberton. Because we needed a "super majority," we tried to strengthen support by focusing especially on "community elites" who would most appreciate the importance of the hospital to the community. These included civic leaders, emergency responders, teachers, and business owners.

Advertising for the campaign made up 22 percent of budget.

Execution

Our external campaign ran from February to May 8.
Tactics included:

- Reaching out to key audiences directly (personal meetings, phone calls). We included likely opponents (neighbors, community activists) and likely supporters (medical staff, employees, volunteers, political leaders, civic and business leaders, sports/recreation groups, labor unions, schools, churches).

- Establishing a "blue ribbon" committee of high-profile campaign leaders to lend their names, and a grassroots committee of volunteers to do "leg" work. We held weekly meetings/conference calls with leaders.

- Giving presentations to individuals, civic groups, and organizations (Rotary, downtown business owners, PTA, Chamber of Commerce, etc.) throughout the city. We invited residents to regular open meetings at the hospital to learn about the issue. During the campaign, more than 140 presentations were given.

- Obtaining endorsements from key groups—firefighters, unions, business owners, leaders in the community (political and otherwise)—and publicizing their support.

- Instituting an aggressive and proactive media relations campaign, including face-to-face meetings with reporters and editorial boards.

The opposition group's primary argument was that the hospital could expand without taking parkland; they even published drawings with other options. We countered by explaining healthcare design issues, e.g., cancer patients need nearby parking and expanded ER must be on ground level. Doctors and nurses explained why their patients needed these services. We carefully followed content on their website, corrected factual errors, and countered their arguments with letters to the editor and calls to Views Line in the local weekly paper. When a local radio talk show host cited misinformation on the air, we sent him information; he then challenged opponents who called in.

Tactics in the final weeks of the campaign included:

- Blanketing the community with yard and window signs with our message: "Keep Barberton Healthy."

- Distributing absentee ballots in nursing homes and senior centers.

- Organizing and implementing a "get out the vote" campaign, using door-to-door visits, reminder and personal postcards mailed by volunteers, and reminder phone calls the weekend before Election Day.

- Hosting special events, including a Saturday morning rally outside the hospital and a public debate. Additional polling conducted two weeks prior to the vote showed 67 percent in favor—a close margin!

Evaluation

Victory! The election attracted an unusually high turnout of 41 percent — more voters than had turned out for any election other than a general election in Barberton for at least five years, an extraordinary turnout for a single-issue election. An overwhelming 77 percent voted yes, approving sale of the parkland to the hospital — even more than the super majority we needed (4,525 yes, 1,329 no).

This project demonstrates the importance of establishing targeted and continuing connections with the local community — especially in a community where the bonds are long and emotional. This connection was crucial not only to the campaign's success but to the hospital's long-term success. The campaign united the community behind the hospital, demonstrated by the number of volunteers who actively participated (130 for the door-to-door campaign, for example — a healthy turnout in a community of 28,000 residents). The hospital's parent company, Triad, has since used this communication model with other hospitals planning expansions.

EXHIBIT 5-2A *"Ten Facts" Advertisement*

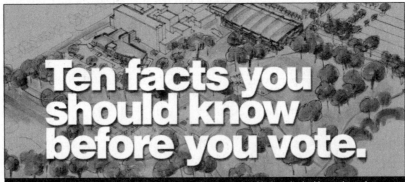

Ten facts you should know before you vote.

Please support the Hospital's purchase of eight acres of Tuscora Park and keep quality health care close to home.

Even with our purchase of eight acres from the City of Barberton, there will still be more than 20 acres of park land for recreation.

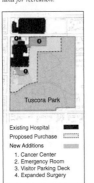

Tuscora Park

Existing Hospital
Proposed Purchase
New Additions
1. Cancer Center
2. Emergency Room
3. Visitor Parking Deck
4. Expanded Surgery

1. This ballot issue is not going to cost you a cent. The expansion will require no new taxes from the people of Barberton.

2. This is our best option. It's the only practical way to improve health care services without moving people out of their homes and routing truck traffic through residential neighborhoods.

3. The Hospital will pay the City of Barberton approximately $850,000 for the park land and facilities disrupted during expansion. A portion of this money will be used for improvements in Tuscora Park.

4. Even with the purchase of eight acres from the City of Barberton, there will still be more than 20 acres of Tuscora Park land for recreation. There are well over 300 acres of parks and green space in the city.

5. The Hospital has outgrown its existing facility.

6. The expansion will create a more comprehensive cancer treatment facility, including Radiation Oncology.

7. The expansion will also include an expanded, more accessible Emergency Room with better parking.

8. The Hospital's $41 million investment in Barberton's future is a sign of progress and commitment.

9. In its first phase alone, the expansion will create an estimated 100 union construction jobs and 60 Hospital jobs—and bring additional tax base to Barberton.

10. Our Hospital will be an even greater source of pride for everyone in the City of Barberton.

On May 6, Let's Build a Better Barberton Together.

Paid for by the Citizens for Barberton's Future. Dennis Liddle, Treasurer, 1096 South Azalea Blvd, Barberton, OH 44203

Courtesy Barberton Citizens Hospital, Edward Howard & Company, and ST&P Communications

EXHIBIT 5-2B *Community Guide*

Barberton Citizens Hospital: The Next Step

Barberton Citizens Hospital is ready to grow. An expansion of the Hospital's facilities and services is needed to help the Hospital meet the changing healthcare needs of the local community.

Barberton Citizens Hospital has been serving the healthcare needs of the local community in Barberton and southern Summit County since 1915. The current facility first opened in 1954. Times have changed and healthcare needs certainly have changed, with modern healthcare requiring more sophisticated technology and specialized treatments. To expand available services to patients and offer the most up-to-date technology, the Hospital needs to add capacity to the existing facility. This is important, to keep good healthcare close to home for the residents of Barberton.

GROWING TO SERVE COMMUNITY NEEDS

The Hospital leadership has proposed a concept that would expand its facilities to provide additional services and improve some existing services. These would include comprehensive services for cardiology care and cancer treatment facilities, and a more efficient and accessible emergency room. In addition, plans are underway to improve parking for visitors, staff and volunteers by replacing the outdated parking deck and installing new, more convenient parking facilities. This expansion plan will mean construction jobs, new tax money for the city and a minimum of 50-60 new professional, technical and support jobs at the Hospital.

Unfortunately, the Hospital is land-locked. It has already added as much as it can to the facility on the existing site and relocated some services to other sites in order to alleviate crowded conditions.

Now, in order to expand and meet demand, Barberton Citizens Hospital must acquire additional property. The Hospital is proposing to purchase eight acres of adjacent land from Tuscora Park. (Tuscora Park's total acreage is 28.7.)

Before making this request, the Hospital's leadership explored a number of expansion options to meet the community's changing healthcare needs. Each option had its disadvantages, such as moving people out of their homes or routing delivery traffic through residential neighborhoods. Overall, this clearly was the best long-term solution for the community and the Hospital.

THE NEED FOR CONSENSUS

Acquiring the proposed park property will require approval by the registered voters of Barberton on May 6, 2003. According to the City Charter, approval requires a two-thirds majority.

The Hospital would pay the City $75,000 an acre, a fair market price based upon a mutually agreed appraisal. In addition, the Hospital would also pay for park amenities and services interrupted during construction (replacement of trees, walking path, pavilions, etc.)

Barberton Citizens Hospital At a Glance

As a 311-bed, general acute care community hospital, Barberton Citizens provides inpatient services in the clinical areas of medicine, surgery, intensive care, intensive coronary care, extended care, psychiatry, rehabilitation and obstetrics. These services are supported by a Center for Emergency Services. BCH also provides many outpatient services and community outreach programs. The hospital offers a Family Practice Residency program and is a major teaching hospital with the Northeast Ohio Universities College of Medicine. Barberton Citizens Hospital is affiliated with Triad Hospitals, Inc. of Plano, Texas.

Year 2002
- Admitted 8,257 patients
- Delivered 731 babies
- Cared for 36,473 ER patients
- Performed 1,452 inpatient surgeries
- Performed 3,885 outpatient surgeries

ECONOMIC IMPACT

Total Employees	1,116
Salaries/Wages/Benefits	$48,605,577
Capital Funds Reinvested	$3,699,904
Local Vendor Purchases	$1,782,819
Total Economic Impact on Local Economy	$54,088,300

CHARITABLE CONTRIBUTIONS

Total Charitable Contributions/Public Service	$59,392

LOCAL TAXES PAID BY BARBERTON CITIZENS HOSPITAL AND ITS EMPLOYEES

Property Tax	$631,780
Sales Tax	$865,974
Income Tax	$806,316
Total Local Tax	$2,304,070

CHARITY AND UNCOLLECTED CARE

Charity Care for Patient Services	$2,713,932
Uncollected Care	$6,781,946
Total Charity and Uncollected Care	$9,495,878

VOLUNTEERS

Total Donated Hours	55,834

(Hours performed by 307 student and adult volunteers)

Courtesy Barberton Citizens Hospital, Edward Howard & Company, and ST&P Communications

CASE 5-3

Environmental problems may require broad community engagement. A network of community partners and clearly targeted audiences and behaviors can have significant improvements to air and water quality. Exhibit 5-3a is a campaign guide to recruiting sponsors, Exhibit 5-3b is a review of "Anti-Idling Taglines" considered for the campaign, and Exhibit 5-3c is a letter to bus drivers that elicits support for the campaign.

Dare to Care About the Air

Washington State Department of Ecology with PRR, Inc.

Situation Analysis

Vehicle exhaust is an easily avoidable source of hazardous air pollution in Washington State. One car dropping off one child at one school in one month generates three pounds of emissions. Children breathe 50 percent more air per pound than adults. Over the past decade, residents have increased their driving by more than 70 percent. The Washington State Department of Ecology—along with a regional consortium of air quality groups—decided to launch a pilot to decrease idling at elementary schools in urban, suburban, and rural settings. At the program's conclusion, data collected showed an overall decrease in idling time of 112 percent or 56.6 seconds.

Research

It is well known that idling is a serious, avoidable clement of poor air quality that is a significant contributor to poor health. Despite this, few formal campaigns in the United States have targeted idling behaviors, and no known formal campaigns have focused on cutting idling at schools. Because of this lack of pertinent information, our team needed to be more innovative than expected in the research phase. Our **secondary research** spanned the globe and included a literature review of more than 75 sources, gaining both general anti-idling knowledge and gleaning bits of information specifically applicable to our program. **Primary research** utilized several methodologies including executive phone interviews with environmental, transportation, and education authorities

Courtesy Washington State Department of Ecology

and focus groups of urban, suburban, and rural residents across the state. During the implementation, primary data were also gathered in the form of idling times at pilot and control schools and program participation at pilot schools.

Knowledge gathered during research directly informed the program plan in several ways. It gave us a target time for when people should shut off their engines. It gave us multiple copy points to motivate drivers to shut off their engines. We developed realistic classroom participation goals. And we were able to give program sponsors accurate projections of costs for participating.

Planning

The program's **goal** was to decrease idling times at schools. The **target audience** for behavior change included all drivers who are on school grounds during drop off and pick up times—parents, bus drivers, and delivery drivers, with primary emphasis on parents. Balancing our need for comparison data for evaluation with our concerns about weather conditions skewing data, our team chose to measure idling times at a pilot school (where the program was implemented) and a control school (similar in character to the pilot but no program influence) in each city—rather than measuring idling times at a single school pre- and post-implementation. Our team recruited one pilot and one control location at three different locations around the state—one urban, one suburban, and one rural—to fulfill DOE's desire for data from this diversity of community types.

Our strategies to decrease idling at schools were:

- Inform drivers of the environmental, health, and monetary effects of idling and benefits of shutting off engines
- Use a pledge card to garner commitment to immediate behavior change
- Provide incentives rewarding positive behavior

The program had several **objectives.**

- Objective 1: cut current idling times among drivers at pilot schools during pick up and drop off times by 50 percent during the one-week implementation period
- Objective 2: have at least 50 percent participation by parents across all schools during implementation
- Objective 3: distribute anti-idling information to 100 percent of the parents at all pilot locations during the week of implementation
- Objective 4: recruit at least one incentive sponsor in each town before the program was implemented

Execution

From initial research through final evaluation, the program ran from March through December 2003. As a result of valid information gathering and planning, the program was executed as expected. Local sponsors were recruited via telephone and e-mail with little difficulty. Materials were sorted and delivered in advance to faculty and staff who then distributed program materials by sending them home with students or through one-on-one contact with bus and delivery drivers. Signed pledge cards were then collected and returned for counting. In return, each pledging driver received discount pizza coupons and a free youth ticket to a local hockey team, both provided by program sponsors. One to two anti-idling signs were posted at pilot sites for program implementation. Two individuals measured idling times at each pilot and control school for five consecutive days. Since program implementation, the classrooms that met the 80 percent participation goal have received their pizza party from the local sponsor and teachers in these classrooms received their two free hockey tickets.

The most significant difficulty encountered occurred prior to implementation when it became clear that high school volunteers were not available to collect idling time information at all pilot and control locations. To deal with this, we hired temps to collect data in the two towns where high school students were not available to volunteer. Also, one pilot district chose to not participate due to a new principal at the proposed school. This was not a "make or break" for the study, so we contacted other surrounding districts—a move that developed interest for a second round of implementation. Another challenge was getting promotional pieces from sponsors in time for inclusion in program materials during the sorting and preparation process. To manage this challenge, we hired one temp to help with last-minute sorting. Our team recruited six individual businesses to sponsor the incentive portion of the program through in-kind support—one pizza restaurant and one hockey team in each pilot town.

Evaluation

In order to improve future generations of this program we kept track of "lessons learned" including: time of day seems to have greater influence than weather over idling time, with drivers idling longer in afternoons than mornings; districts can have different kindergarten schedules at each elementary; 80 percent classroom response is a realistic goal, 100 percent is not: and data collection sheets need as few open-ended responses as possible to made the job simple for individuals on site. To evaluate idling times vis-à-vis time of day, weather conditions, and other variables, the data collected at pilot and control schools were entered into a computer and analyzed using SPSS. To measure driver participation, returned pledge cards were tallied and compared to the total number of students in each classroom and school.

- Objective 1: Cut current idling times among drivers at pilot schools by 50 percent during the one-week implementation period

  Result: Overall, pilot school drivers idled 112 percent less (56.6 fewer seconds) than those at control schools

- Objective 2: 50 percent participation by parents across all schools during implementation

  Result: Overall participation was 66.8 percent, 16.8 percent beyond the objective

- Objective 3: Distribute anti-idling information to 100 percent of parents at all pilot locations during the one week of implementation

  Result: Evidence that this goal was accomplished came through returned, signed pledge forms and confirmation from pilot school principals that all faculty and staff distributed their materials as requested

- Objective 4: Recruit at least one incentive sponsor in each town before the program was implemented

  Result: Two sponsors—one hockey team and one pizza restaurant—were recruited as sponsors in each pilot town

EXHIBIT 5-3A   *Guide to Recruiting Sponsors*

Dare to Care About the Air

Guide to Recruiting Sponsors and Partners

There are many local businesses that want to help -- all you need to do is ask! The following outline shows the steps an organization should follow in recruiting a partner or sponsor.

Step 1

Define your goals – what is it you want to accomplish, have a start and end date & a way to measure the effectiveness, along with a measurable goal. Example – 100 parents signing "I Won't Idle" pledge forms.

Step 2

Know your numbers! Know how many people your program will potentially influence. Example – if you are a school, know how many students, how many teachers, how many classes, and how many volunteers can be reached. Do not inflate the numbers, keep them realistic.

Step 3

Look around the local community at who is already a "good community" partner-- sponsoring Little League teams, neighborhood events, etc. Give them the courtesy of being able to participate. Look to businesses that are new in town and want to make an impression. Evaluate local branches of major national companies as the store managers have some authority on local programs. Based on your numbers, think about which businesses can handle that type of volume. Consider companies who try to attract the same "customers" who you will be targeting.

Step 4

Be sure to look for companies/industries that are used to working with coupons or vouchers and can handle the numbers you are looking for. Also, look for companies with products that will be considered valuable to your audience.

Step 5

When developing your "offer" keep in mind what's in it for the partner besides being a good corporate citizen. Ask them what they want out of the relationship.

Step 6

Contact the businesses, lead with the facts, show them the difference they can make in their own backyard and give them a deadline for making a decision. A deadline will get them to say Yes or No.

Step 7

Before, during and after the event or campaign be sure to recognize, thank and include the partners in all correspondence, materials and with regular phone calls or in-person visits. Let them know the progress and the results. The more equity the partners have in the program, the better the chance for success.

Courtesy Washington State Department of Ecology

EXHIBIT 5-3B   *Anti-Idling Taglines*

Dare to Care About the Air

Anti-Idling Taglines
While it is desirable, and ultimately more effective, if messaging is consistently used and repeated frequently, it is understood that use of this theme may occasionally be problematic for many organizations that are collaborating in the initiative.

In order of preference, participating organizations would:
1. Use this theme as is
2. Use a variation of this theme
3. Use the theme in headlines or copy text

Guiding Principles for Tagline Development
- Must be transferable to other locations where drivers idle (other than schools)
- Desirable to be transferable to other air toxics behaviors
- Must motivate action
- Must inform that idling is a problem
- Health tested as a strong motivator for messaging

Recommendation

No Idle Zone: Dare to care about the air

Reasons for this recommendation
- Like the official sounding nature of "No Idle Zone"
- Like the challenge presented in "Dare to care about the air"—motivates individual action
- Line has good rhythm, will be memorable
- Serious, yet positive tone—not preachy
- Transferable to other idling locations
- Transferable to other air toxics behaviors (by just using "Dare to care about the air")
- Why not a more direct hit on the health message? We explored many tags (that you will see below) that attempted to directly make the connection with health. We found that these options tended to fall into the "scare tactic" category. We know that scare tactic messages don't work for these types of campaigns. Therefore our recommendation is to go for a tag that is motivating, yet less direct on the health message. The health message would be incorporated throughout the campaign in the text where there is more room to explain the health impacts of idling.

Secondary Recommendations
Please, No Idling: Because we all share the air
Please, No Idling: Because we all care, about the air
Please, No Idling: Together we can clear the air
Please, No Idling: Let's clear the air, together
No Idle Zone: Let's spare the air
No Idle Zone: You burn it, you breathe it
Please, No Idling: We'll all breathe easier

Courtesy Washington State Department of Ecology

EXHIBIT 5-3C   *Letter to Bus Drivers*

Dare to Care About the Air

Letter to Bus Drivers

(Date)

(Name of Bus Driver)
(School)
(Address 1)
(City, State, Zip)

Dear (Name of Bus Driver):

Parents and guardians trust you to transport their most prized possessions everyday to and from school. Riding a bus is one of the safest forms of transportation available. As a trusted member of the community, you have the ability to influence behavior of the students and their parents.

(Name of organization) has designed a program to reduce unnecessary vehicle idling, because it contributes to pollution in our state. We are asking you to set the example for the rest of the community by not idling at the schools and idling as little as possible whenever possible.

(Name of organization) also asks that you sign the enclosed "No Idling" pledge form. Please join us as an active participant in changing behaviors, which will drastically improve the air quality in our community. We have also sent a fact sheet to help illustrate just how important this issue is.

During the school year, students and parents will be part of a comprehensive "No idling" program and your involvement will help reinforce this messaging.

Thank you for your ongoing commitment to our children and the support of this program.

Courtesy Washington State Department of Ecology

## Chapter 6

Public Affairs and Government Relations

In the last decades, many U.S. corporations have subsumed what was formerly known as government relations within the broader enterprise now called public affairs. To add further semantic confusion, the U.S. government in the early 1980s decreed that the term public affairs would replace public information in all its departments and agencies.

Our principal concern here will be with how the enactment of legislation is influenced. This process includes the creation of political coalitions, direct and indirect lobbying, political action and political education activities, communication on political issues, and political support activities.

RESEARCH

The research process of public affairs includes investigation of the practitioner's client or organization, the opportunity or problem that accounts for the need for communication—including the important area of issues management—and the audiences to be targeted for public affairs programs.

Client Research

Client research for public affairs is similar to that for other forms of public relations. Background information about the client or organization should be obtained, including its personnel, financial status, and reputation, especially with government and community audiences. The practitioner should pay particular attention to past and present relations with the government and the community, along with any particular client strengths or weaknesses in these areas. Finally, the practitioner should catalog all opportunities for profitable communication with government or community audiences.

Opportunity or Problem Research

In public affairs programs, the process of issues management can make assessment of the client's opportunity or problem much easier. *Issues management* consists of listing and giving priority to all issues of interest to the client and then determining options and strategies for dealing with them. This process includes assessing political risks and monitoring social and political developments of concern to the client at the local, state, national, and international levels. An examination of each of these areas on a priority basis is a useful means of targeting the client's public affairs program.

Audience Research

The final aspect of research for public affairs consists of identifying target audiences, the necessary data regarding each one, and the methods of research necessary to obtain this information.

Public affairs programs target three audiences: community publics, government, and ancillary publics—this last group consisting of client allies, constituents of legislators, and media that reach both of them. Community publics were examined in the preceding chapter (see Exhibit 5-a). Government publics can be considered at the federal, state, county, or city level; they and the ancillary publics are listed in Exhibit 6-a.

Data necessary for understanding members of the legislative branches of government include officials' voting records on issues of concern to the client; their general attitudes or past and present reactions to the client; the size, location, and general demographics of their

EXHIBIT 6-A   *Government and Ancillary Publics*

Government Publics

Federal

    Legislative branch

        Representatives, staff, committee personnel

        Senators, staff, committee personnel

    Executive branch

        President

        White House staff, advisers, committees

        Cabinet officers, departments, agencies, commissions

State

    Legislative branch

        Representatives, delegates, staff, committee personnel

        Senators, staff, committee personnel

    Executive branch

        Governor

        Governor's staff, advisers, committees

        Cabinet officers, departments, agencies, commissions

County

    County executive

    Other county officials, commissioners, departments

City

    Mayor or city manager

    City council

    Other city officials, commissions, departments

Ancillary Publics

Allies

Constituents of legislators

Media

    Mass media

    Specialized media

        Trade

        Allied organizations' publications

    Constituent media

voting constituencies; their committee assignments; and their general interests and areas of expertise. Government officials in the executive branch may or may not hold elective office; this is their single most important characteristic. Beyond that, the nature and authority of the offices they hold, along with as much background about them as possible, should prove helpful. For officials in both legislative and executive positions, of course, the highest priority information about them is their degree of involvement with each issue or piece of legislation affecting the client, along with their stand and how they are expected to vote. Officials often rely on key staff and advice from leaders in organizations specializing in public policy issues. It is valuable to determine who has the ear of a representative or government official, to analyze what values underlie their advice.

Methods of gathering information about government officials are usually nonquantitative. Voting records or accomplishments are public knowledge and easily accessible. Beyond that, conducting surveys among officials is usually not feasible. Thus, the practitioner must rely on other sources of information, such as conversations with staff people, the officials' past behavior, and their public statements regarding issues of concern to the client.

Research on the ancillary publics listed in Exhibit 6-a is also of considerable value. Allies of the client must be identified and cultivated with the goal of building a coalition. The home districts, communities, and constituents of legislators must also be identified and studied. Old friends, business or professional partners, and local civic leaders are trusted sources of grassroots information for a legislator. Government leaders maintain close connections with their constituents to capture a sense of local concerns. They monitor local media in their district to gain a pulse on the body politic. Try to monitor these same sources. Finally, mass and specialized media for reaching constituents and client allies should be identified, and media contacts lists should be prepared, as discussed in Chapter 3.

OBJECTIVES

As in other forms of public relations, objectives for public affairs programs should be specific and quantitative.

Impact Objectives

A sampling of impact objectives for public affairs includes such statements as:

1. To increase knowledge of the client's current activities and field of operations among legislators (by 50 percent during the current year)

2. To create or enhance favorable attitudes toward the client's new initiative among officials (by 30 percent before the February vote)

3. To influence a favorable vote on a bill (by 30 members of the House of Representatives during the current session)

Output Objectives

Output objectives represent the effort of the practitioner without reference to potential audience impact. Such objectives might use such statements as:

1. To make oral presentations to 30 lawmakers
2. To distribute printed information to 45 lawmakers

PROGRAMMING

Public affairs programming includes the same four planning and execution elements used in other forms of public relations: (1) theme and messages, (2) action or special event(s), (3) uncontrolled and controlled media, and (4) principles of effective communication.

Theme and Messages

Always be aware that government audiences may be the most knowledgeable and sophisticated of all audiences for public relations communication. For this reason, the use of catchy themes or slogans may not be helpful; at times they can even be counterproductive. When addressing public affairs programming to ancillary audiences, however, more traditional use of themes or slogans may be appropriate. Messages, of course, should be carefully coordinated with the program objectives and actions or special events.

Action or Special Event(s)

Public affairs programming, like other forms of public relations, is structured around actions and special events. The practitioner should review the types found in Exhibit 2-c.

The actions unique to public affairs programming are:

1. Fact finding
2. Coalition building
3. Direct lobbying
4. Grassroots activities (indirect lobbying)
5. Political action committees

6. Political education activities
7. Communications on political issues
8. Political support activities

Fact Finding. Information gathering is an important aspect of public affairs. It includes attendance at openly conducted hearings, generally scheduled by both the legislative and executive branches of government when considering legislation or regulations. This monitoring function is indispensable for all public affairs programs.

In addition to monitoring hearings, fact finding often includes exchanging information with government officials, representatives of trade associations or interest groups, and other sources of reliable data. Fact finding may also include entertainment, since the relaxed atmosphere of most social gatherings can be conducive to exchanging information.

A final aspect of fact finding is the reporting of data and findings to the client, along with recommendations for appropriate responses.

Coalition Building. It is useful to organize groups or individuals with a common interest in the passage or defeat of legislation or regulations. Such coalitions can be much more effective in attaining goals than groups or individuals working alone. The power of a coalition is often based on the "perceived" cohesiveness and political clout of the group. Some coalitions will claim a large number of members to enhance the credibility of the organization, even though many members may actually be relatively small local activist organizations. Coalitions can pool such resources as staff time, legal help, and printing and mailing costs. Working together, they can set priorities and devise operational strategies more effectively. In brief, the building of coalitions is one of the most important and effective tactics in public affairs.

Direct Lobbying. The two "core" activities of public affairs are direct and indirect lobbying. In direct lobbying, the practitioner contacts legislators or officials who can influence the passage or defeat of a bill or proposed regulation. It is an overt advocacy process, although it takes the sometimes subtle forms of information exchange and hospitality.

Information exchange includes providing the lawmaker or official with data about the client's field of interest and the effect the proposed legislation or regulation would have on this field. The practitioner, or lobbyist, usually makes an authoritative oral presentation, including the publicity potential for the legislator or official and the potential interest or impact of the proposals on constituents. These two aspects—*publicity value* and *constituent interest*—strike the most responsive chords in the ears of legislators or officials. They should always be central to a public affairs presentation. In addition to presentations, the practitioner usually offers the official a sample draft of the proposed legislation or regulation that incorporates the views of the client. Position and background papers are a staple of information exchange.

Finally, information exchange may include providing authoritative testimony or offering witnesses for the hearings that are usually held in conjunction with proposed legislation or regulations. The practitioner often writes the testimony that is usually given by the client or the chief executive officer of the client's organization.

The second form of direct lobbying is still more subtle than information exchange. It involves offering *hospitality* to the legislator or agency official. The days of extravagant gifts, yachting trips, weekends in hunting lodges, and the like have passed. Legislators and agency officials are now very sensitive to the ubiquitous investigative journalist, constantly in search of untoward political influence by moneyed interests or wrongdoing in high places. Nonetheless, hospitality still plays an important role in public affairs, or, more particularly, in lobbying. Lawmakers and agency officials often accept invitations to social functions sponsored by influential associations or corporations. Personal relationships are still the realm of many political decisions and face-to-face exchanges work well in convincing an official of the merits of your initiative.

These social gatherings provide a relaxed and conducive atmosphere for the subtle conduct of the business of public affairs.

A more recent and widespread variety of hospitality has turned the tables. Now, more often than not, the legislator provides the hospitality in the form of thousand-dollar-a-plate breakfasts, lunches, dinners, or other special events at which the corporation, association, or union representatives pay or make large contributions to attend, and thus gain access to the lawmaker.

Access is a major goal of all lobbying, and to an increasing degree, hospitality events—usually linked to fund-raising for the legislator— have become the most used avenue for reaching this goal.

Grassroots Activities.   Indirect lobbying, or grassroots activities, is the second of the two core aspects of public affairs. This form of indirect lobbying involves mobilizing support for or opposition to proposed legislation or regulations at the state or local level, especially in the home districts of elected legislators. In the case of government departments or agencies, this grassroots level may be the location where a large agency is considering constructing or closing an installation that will profoundly affect the local economy.

Grassroots activities include working with national, state, or local mass media; the use of interpersonal communication; and the orchestration of campaigns to bring constituent pressure on legislators or officials.

The grassroots use of the mass media includes publicizing the client's position in national, state, or local media, demonstrating that this position will be beneficial to the media audience. This action is usually performed in cases where an elected official is in opposition to the client's position or is uncommitted. The practitioner, on behalf of the client, will use all feasible forms of media, including paid advertising, to generate news coverage about the situation. If the legislator has taken a stand contrary to that of the client's, the media messages will call attention to that, to voting records, and to the harm such a position will bring to the constituency. Care must be taken not to engage in overkill in this endeavor. In some cases, besieged legislators have also used the media, successfully portraying themselves as the victims of "fat-cat lobbyists." A second effective type of grassroots activity is the use of various forms of interpersonal communication at the national, state, or local level. This includes targeting key groups of opinion leaders in the home districts of legislators and getting expert and highly credible representatives of the client's viewpoint invited to their meetings, conferences, or conventions as guest speakers.

In addition to addressing important grassroots audiences, the client can meet with key executives at breakfast, with editorial staffs of newspapers, or with small groups of community leaders. Dyadic interactions may include interviews and meetings with key public officials, executives, and/or union leaders.

Interpersonal communication, then, in the form of speeches, small group meetings, or dyadic interactions can be a highly useful form of grassroots activity. When organizations host annual conventions in Washington, they arrange short meetings between legislators and association members who are constituents. The constituents arrive with specific talking points related to the organization's public policy agenda.

Finally, grassroots activities culminate in the orchestration of campaigns at the national, state, or local level designed to bring pressure from constituents directly on legislators or officials. These campaigns can be orchestrated by small or large membership groups, associations, or other affected groups. They may take the traditional form of organized letter writing to a legislator from home district constituents; or they may use more contemporary forms, such as e-mail, faxing, or the formation of "telephone trees." The "telephone tree" consists of groups of constituents who each may call five to ten friends, who in turn each call five to ten more friends, and so on, all of whom then call or otherwise communicate with the office of the lawmaker with a common request or purpose.

The National Rifle Association is a membership group that uses all of these forms of constituent communication effectively to influence the course of national legislation. The NRA boasts the ability to mobilize its membership within 24 hours to flood Congress with enough constituent communication to shape the course of gun legislation.

Of the two public affairs core methods, grassroots activities usually prove more effective. These actions—working with mass media, interpersonal communication, and constituent communication campaigns—can provide legislators and other officials with unmistakable evidence regarding the will of the electorate.

Political Action Committees. Political action committees (PACs) are an outgrowth of the reform in federal election campaign practices that followed the Watergate scandal. A PAC is a group established for the purpose of contributing an organization's money toward the election of political candidates. The Federal Election Commission (FEC) permits PACs to contribute a maximum of $5,000 per candidate per election. Thus, PACs may contribute a total of $10,000 to a candidate who is in both a primary contest and the general election. FEC limits are indexed for inflation and adjusted for every election cycle. Individuals may only contribute $2,100 per candidate/per election and $5,000 per year to a PAC.

Since their inception in the mid-1970s, PACs have enjoyed phenomenal growth. Each year PACs provide funds to several thousand candidates for federal office. Such money may be solicited (but not coerced) from an organization's employees. Large groups, such as the banking and finance industry, labor unions, and the insurance industry, have the resources of hundreds of PACs at their disposal. Of course, PAC money can be used collectively for candidates who support legislation favorable to an entire industry.

The use of such funds to support the campaigns of elected officials guarantees access to those officials. Thus, PACs have become a significant force in public affairs.

Political Education Activities. During the past 30 years, corporations have increasingly attempted to politicize their employees. They issue newsletters on the major political issues confronting given industries along with the company's positions on these issues. Employees are instructed in the methods of grassroots lobbying: writing letters to legislators, taking action through membership groups, or visiting legislators in their home district offices. Moreover, some large organizations provide their employees with political education seminars. Elected officials and candidates are invited to corporate facilities, where they make presentations and meet groups of employees. In return, the officials are often given honoraria, usually in accordance with legally allowable limitations. Political education activities, then, play an increasingly important role in the conduct of public affairs programs.

Communications on Political Issues. Corporations communicate on political issues chiefly through advocacy advertising and targeted communications, such as direct mail to community leaders or special audiences.

Advocacy advertising has become increasingly popular since the early 1970s, when Herbert Schmertz, vice president for public affairs of Mobil, decided that major media outlets seemed interested only in condemning large oil companies for their alleged role in the creation of the gasoline shortages of the day. Schmertz abandoned the use of news releases and other uncontrolled media to give the oil companies' side of the controversy. Instead he began to buy advocacy advertising space in the nation's most prestigious newspapers and later bought time on cooperative broadcast networks. Schmertz's success in calling attention to his corporation's political views gave rise to a boom in the corporate use of advocacy advertising. Expect to see advocacy ads not only in national newspapers such as the *Washington Post* with its political emphasis in the Capital, but in the local newspaper of a legislator who is the target of a campaign.

Their proliferation has probably diminished their effectiveness, but they remain a major vehicle for corporate communication on political issues.

Political communications can also be aimed at community leaders or occupational groups. Professors of communication, for example, are frequently the recipients of slick reprints of speeches by the chief executive officers of television networks and other corporations. These reprints are only one of many forms of mailings to community leaders and members of various professions.

Political Support Activities.   A final public affairs action is the support a corporation, association, or other organization offers an incumbent legislator or a candidate. Some organizations offer free media training, with expert consultants hired for the occasion. Guidance in effective public speaking, group communication management techniques, and other interpersonal communication skills are also offered. Some organizations provide volunteers to work on political campaigns. Additionally, political support can be offered in the form of expertise and other services needed for orchestrating election campaign events such as fund-raisers and testimonial dinners. Donations of facilities, recruiting celebrities to appear at the events, and any number of other services can be offered.

Like other forms of public affairs activities, political support can ensure access to the officeholder at a later time.

Another form of political support called "soft money" became the hottest — and most controversial — form of lobbying in the 1990s. Corporations and individuals were allowed to give unlimited amounts of money to national political parties for voter registration, television advertising, get-out-the-vote campaigns, and other party activities. This unlimited "soft money" could be contributed to support the party, but not specific candidates. Federal legislation passed in 2002, however, now prohibits corporations, unions, and individuals from giving unlimited contributions to national political parties. But this ban on "soft money" does not apply to independent groups or PACs. They are free to raise as much money as corporations, unions, or individuals will give them. They can spend unlimited sums of money to influence federal elections as long as they operate independently of election campaigns, stop short of calling for a specific candidate's election or defeat, and stop airing advertising within 30 days of a primary election and 60 days of a general election.

To counter the flow of this "soft money," the 2002 Bipartisan Campaign Reform Act limited the flow of large contributions to the political parties, but groups soon exploited Section 527 of the Internal Revenue Code, which had been added in 1974 to allow tax-exempt contributions for political activities, including voter mobilization efforts and issue advocacy. The 527 groups claimed to rely on grassroots efforts by small donors to encourage civic engagement, yet one study found the biggest 527s got 44 percent of their contributions from just 25 deep-pocket donors. During the 2004 political campaigns, MoveOn.org and the Swift Boat Veterans for Truth were some of the most visible and passionate in activating political engagement; however, neither was in the top 5 among all 527 groups that raised an estimated $550 million to influence the political process.

"Hard money" contributions to candidates for federal office continue to be strictly limited by the Federal Election Committee. However, with increasingly close relationships between candidates, especially incumbents, and PACs, it is likely that multimillion-dollar contributions of "soft money" to PACs will become the most certain of all paths to officeholder access.

Uncontrolled and Controlled Media

The practitioner's communication with public officials must largely be direct and interpersonal. The lobbyist or practitioner of public affairs uses uncontrolled media at the grassroots level. However, all forms of controlled media can be used both in direct contact with lawmakers and in grassroots communication with constituents. In general, then, the uniqueness of public affairs communication lies in the interaction that occurs directly with lawmakers and officials. To be effective, it should emphasize interpersonal, preferably one-on-one, communication.

Effective Communication

The communication flow in public affairs is best described as triangular (see Exhibit 6-b). The flow is targeted ultimately at lawmakers, in the legislative branch, or at regulation-makers, in the executive branch. Thus, communication is generally initiated from the private sector and flows appropriately toward those two targets. In many cases, however, communication is initiated in the executive branch. Presidents, governors,

---

EXHIBIT 6-B   *A Public Affairs Communication Model*

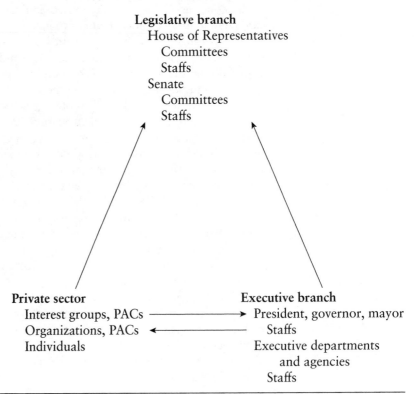

Legislative branch
House of Representatives
Committees
Staffs
Senate
Committees
Staffs

Private sector
Interest groups, PACs
Organizations, PACs
Individuals

Executive branch
President, governor, mayor
Staffs
Executive departments
and agencies
Staffs

---

and mayors may lobby their respective legislative branches for the passage or defeat of a law. Sometimes officials in the executive branch lobby a particular audience in the private sector to bring pressure on the legislative branch. Legislators often refer to this as "going over their heads to the people." Some U.S. presidents have been particularly fond of this form of lobbying.

The nine principles of effective communication discussed in Chapter 2 all apply in public affairs. Of special concern, however, is *selective exposure.* Public affairs, more than other forms of public relations, deals with legislation and regulations that are controversial. Therefore, it is important that the practitioner categorize the targeted receivers based on their agreement or disagreement with the public affairs messages. As suggested in Chapter 2, the terms that coincide with the Likert scale can be useful in this process. Thus, targeted legislators or other officials should be rated as "positives," "somewhat positives," "undecideds," "somewhat negatives," or "negatives." The selective exposure principle is applicable in this situation. The practitioner should thus begin persuasive efforts with the positives. Next to be targeted are the somewhat positives, then the undecideds, and last, if at all, the somewhat negatives. The pure negatives have hardened attitudes against the practitioner's cause and should not be targeted for communication. To communicate with those strongly opposed to the message is usually counterproductive; it simply makes them more determined and sometimes more active in their opposition.

Thus, the selective exposure principle of effective communication bears reiteration because of its special significance in public affairs. It is not necessary to convince everyone, just a few key votes that will swing the outcome. During the 2004 presidential election, selective exposure largely explained how some areas of the country seldom saw a political advertisement while other "swing states" were bombarded with thousands of ads and a flood of direct mail appeals.

All other principles of effective communication should also be observed. Each one can contribute to the success of public affairs programs.

EVALUATION

In public affairs, the measurement of impact and output objectives is somewhat different from the general methods of assessment presented in Chapter 2.

Evaluating Impact Objectives

There are two differences in the measurement of impact objectives for public affairs. First, message exposure, message comprehension, and message retention are not measured in the same way. The primary target audiences for public affairs are legislators and officials. The media, however, are used essentially to reach the *constituents* of these public officials. And though the officials themselves are usually media sensitive, message exposure in public affairs usually refers to *constituent* exposure.

The second difference in the measurement of impact objectives is that surveys or other quantitative methods of research cannot be used with the primary target audiences because legislators and officials will not usually take the time to respond to such PR surveys. Thus, nonquantitative measurements of message exposure and message retention are used in assessing the results of informational objectives.

Message comprehension, of course, can be measured, as usual, by the application of readability formulas. This will give the practitioner an indication of the *potential* for comprehension, not actual audience comprehension, which can be measured using nonquantitative research methods.

These same generalizations are applicable to attitude and behavioral objectives. Surveys among the primary audience are generally impossible, so the practitioner must rely on the nonquantitative research methods discussed earlier in this chapter—voting records or accomplishments, conversations, use of the practitioner's materials, and public statements by the targeted legislators or officials. At the grassroots level, of course, surveys are useful and should be employed to evaluate the impact objectives.

Evaluating Output Objectives

The practitioner needs to evaluate both forms of public affairs objectives. Output objectives can be measured through counting presentations and materials and through making qualitative value judgments. This is especially important in public affairs since surveys are impractical with the primary audiences. Evaluation of public affairs, then, ultimately focuses on observing the voting behavior or actions of legislators and other public officials. The practitioners in this chapter's cases accomplished all of their stated objectives remarkably well. In addition to informing their various targeted audiences, they also met their legislative or regulatory goals.

SUMMARY

Research for public affairs concentrates on problem assessment through issues management and on identifying and understanding target audiences. Audiences are usually in the legislative or executive branch of government, at various levels. Information about these officials consists of voting records, accomplishments, and public stands on issues.

Impact and output objectives are both useful in public affairs. Impact objectives consist of providing the target audience with information or influencing its attitudes or behavior, in this case, voting behavior. Output objectives catalog the practitioner's communication efforts without reference to the desired impact.

The most essential activities in public affairs programming are fact finding, coalition building, direct lobbying, grassroots (indirect) lobbying, the use of political action committees, political education, communications on political issues, and political support activities. Of special significance in lobbying is the principle of selective exposure. Lawmakers to be lobbied should be categorized as "positives," "somewhat positives," "undecideds," "somewhat negatives," or "negatives." The positives through the undecideds should be targeted for lobbying; the somewhat negatives should be targeted with caution, and the negatives, not at all.

Evaluation is not the same for public affairs as for other forms of public relations. Media exposure or placement does not ensure contact with legislators, and legislators and officials are often unresponsive to PR surveys. Nonquantitative measurements of impact objectives are thus more useful. Output objectives, of course, are measured by the same means as usual—observation and quantification. The ultimate means of evaluation in public affairs, however, is the voting behavior of the target audience.

READINGS ON PUBLIC AFFAIRS

"The Advocacy Book: Directory of Public Affairs & Grassroots Lobbying Firms," *Campaigns & Elections* 26 (2005): 84–95.

Alexander, Robert M. *Rolling the Dice with State Initiatives: Interest Group Involvement in Ballot Campaigns.* Westport, CT: Praeger, 2002.

Archer, Jules. *Special Interests: How Lobbyists Influence Our Legislation.* Highland Park, NJ: Mill Brook Press, 1997.

Beder, Sharon. "Public Relations' Role in Manufacturing Artificial Grass Roots Coalitions," *Public Relations Quarterly* 43 (summer 1998): 20–23.

Bodensteiner, Carol A. "Special Interest Group Coalitions: Ethical Standards for Broad-Based Support Efforts," *Public Relations Review* 23 (spring 1997): 31–46.

Brown, Clyde, and Herbert Waltzer. "Organized Interest Advertorials," *Harvard International Journal of Press/Politics* 9 (fall 2004): 25–48.

Cigler, Allan J., and Burdett A. Loomis. *Interest Group Politics,* 4th ed. Washington, DC: Congressional Quarterly, 1994.

Cook-Anderson, Gretchen. "Effectively Winning over Young Voters," *Public Relations Tactics* 11 (July 2004): 12.

Dennis, Lloyd B. *Practical Public Affairs in an Era of Change.* Lanham, MD: University Press of America, 1995.

Gabriel, Edward M. "The Changing Face of Public Affairs in Washington," *Public Relations Quarterly* 37 (Winter 1992): 24ff.

Goldstein, Kenneth M. *Interest Groups, Lobbying and Participation in America.* Port Chester, NY: Cambridge University Press, 1999.

Graziano, Luigi. *Lobbying, Pluralism, and Democracy.* New York: Palgrave, 2001.

Grefe, Edward A., and Martin Linsky. *The New Corporate Activism: Harnessing the Power of Grassroots Tactics for Your Organization.* New York: McGraw-Hill, 1996.

Grossman, Gene M., and Elhanan Helpman. *Special Interest Politics.* Cambridge, MA: MIT, 2001.

Guyer, Robert L. *Guide to State Legislative Lobbying.* Gainesville, FL: Engineering THE LAW, 2003.

Hallahn, Kirk. "Inactive Publics: The Forgotten Publics in Public Relations," *Public Relations Review* 26 (winter 2000): 499.

Heath, Robert L. *Strategic Issue Management: Organizations and Public Policy Challenges.* Thousand Oaks, CA: Sage Publications, 1997.

Jeffries, Leo W. *Urban Communication Systems: Neighborhoods and the Search for Community.* Cresskill, NJ: Hampton Press, 2001.

Johnson, Haynes, and David Broder. *The System: The American Way of Politics at the Breaking Point.* Boston: Little, Brown, 1997.

Kaid, Lynda Lee, ed. *Handbook of Political Communication Research.* Mahwah, NJ: Erlbaum, 2004.

Kerezy, John. "Rocking the Boat: What We Learned from the Swift Boat Campaign," *Public Relations Tactics* 11 (October 2004): 14–15.

Kramer, Tony, and Wes Pedersen, eds. *Winning at the Grassroots: A Comprehensive Manual for Corporations and Associations.* Washington, DC: Public Affairs Council, 2000.

Ledingham, John A. "Government-Community Relationships: Extending the Relational Theory of Public Relations," *Public Relations Review* 27 (fall 2001): 285.

Lerbinger, Otto. *Corporate Public Affairs: Interacting With Interest Groups, Media, and Government.* Mahwah, NJ: Erlbaum, 2005.

Levin, David. "Framing Peace Policies: The Competition for Resonant Themes," *Political Communication* 22 (January–March 2005): 83–108.

Lipsitz, Keena, Christine Trost, Matthew Grossmann, and John Sides. "What Voters Want From Political Campaign Communication," *Political Communication* 22 (July–September 2005): 337–354.

Long, Rich. "PR and GR: So Happy Together?" *Public Relations Strategist* 8 (summer 2002): 14–18.

Lordan, Edward J. "Trivial Pursuit in the '04 Campaign: Simple, Issue-free and Happy to Stay That Way," *Public Relations Quarterly* 49 (fall 2004): 27–29.

Mack, Charles S. *Business, Politics, and the Practice of Government Relations.* Westport, CT: Quorum Books, 1997.

Murray, Bobbi. "Money for Nothing," *The Nation* 277 (September 8, 2003): 25.

Mutz, Diana C., and Paul S. Martin. "Facilitating Communication across Lines of Political Difference: The Role of Mass Media," *The American Political Science Review* 95 (March 2001): 97ff.

Neptune, Torod B. "Five Lessons for Communicators from the 2004 Presidential Campaign," *Public Relations Strategist* 11 (winter 2005): 24–28.

Ortega, Felix. "Politics in the New Public Space," *International Review of Sociology* 14 (July 2004): 205–207.

Park, Hyun Soon, and Sejung Marina Choi. "Focus Group Interviews: The Internet as a Political Campaign Medium," *Public Relations Quarterly* 47 (winter 2002): 36.

Pinkham, Doug. "What it Takes to Work in Public Affairs and Public Relations," *Public Relations Quarterly* 49 (spring 2004): 15ff.

Poston, Patty. "Grassroots Communications Reconsidered," *Public Relations Tactics* 9 (September 2002): 12–13.

Richards, Barry. "The Emotional Deficit in Political Communication," *Political Communication* 21 (July–September 2004): 339–352.

Rose, Jonathan W. *Making "Pictures in Our Heads": Government Advertising in Canada.* Westport, CT: Praeger, 2000.

Smith, Hedrick. *The Power Game: How Washington Works.* New York: Random House, 1988.

Tate, Sheila. "Prescriptions to Avoid Disaster in Washington," *Public Relations Quarterly* 37 (spring 1992): 24ff.

Terry, Valerie. "Lobbying: Fantasy, Reality or Both? A Health Care Public Policy Case Study," *Journal of Public Affairs* 1 (August 2001): 266ff.

Trento, Susan. *Power House: Robert Keith Gray and the Selling of Access and Influence in Washington.* New York: St. Martins Press, 1992.

Ward, Hugh. "Pressure Politics: A Game-Theoretical Investigation of Lobbying and the Measurement of Power," *Journal of Theoretical Politics* 16 (January 2004): 31–52.

Wittenberg, Ernest, and Elizabeth Wittenberg. *How to Win in Washington: Very Practical Advice about Lobbying, the Grassroots and the Media.* Williston, VT: Blackwell, 1994.

Wolpe, Bruce C., and Bertram J. Levine. *Lobbying Congress: How the System Works.* Washington, DC: Congressional Quarterly, 1996.

Confronted with the good fortune of a sizable donation but the potential for that gift to cause complacency in the giving of others, National Public Radio relied on an extensive campaign to maintain listener support. Exhibit 6-1a is a news release, Exhibit 6-1b gives a statement of support from Congressman Earl Blumenauer, and Exhibit 6-1c is a fact sheet on the history of funding for NPR.

A Record Gift to NPR: Keeping Good News from Going Bad

NPR

Overview

In October 2003, National Public Radio (NPR) learned it had two weeks to plan a momentous announcement: that the network would receive a bequest of more than $200 million from the late philanthropist Joan Kroc—by far the largest gift in the network's history. Obviously, this was wonderful news. But it also presented challenges because of NPR's unique—and sometimes delicate—relationships with two key stakeholders:

- Congress, which through appropriations to the Corporation for Public Broadcasting (CPB) provides around 12 percent of annual revenue for local public radio stations. NPR feared that if the gift was perceived as a financial windfall for the network, congressional critics would try to reduce funding.

- NPR's 770-plus member stations, which pay the network for news and cultural programming (accounting for nearly 51 percent of NPR's revenues). Because the bequest would go into NPR's endowment fund, there would be no direct benefit to stations, which were already facing financial challenges. And local listeners might conclude that their station didn't need their contributions anymore.

The challenge was to announce the bequest in a way that would benefit NPR, without creating repercussions from member stations, lawmakers, or opinion leaders. A joint team from NPR and

Courtesy National Public Radio

Fleishman-Hillard (F-H) worked together to plan and execute the announcement.

Research

Because of the short lead time, no new research was possible. However, F-H and NPR reviewed relevant existing research. Among the findings:

- NPR had a strong track record not widely recognized outside broadcasting. While the audience for commercial radio had been shrinking, NPR's audience had doubled in 10 years, and it increased by a staggering 64 percent in the last five years. By spring 2003, an unprecedented 22 million people listened to NPR each week.

- The federal commitment to public broadcasting was weakening. The annual CPB contribution to public radio dropped in relative terms, from 13.5 percent of the total in 2001 to 12 percent in 2004, and a key congressional supporter declared last year that "the source of state support . . . is in jeopardy."

- An internal NPR memo from August 2003 warned, "As indicated in previous updates, action in the U.S. House of Representatives has been disappointing" regarding legislation funding CPB.

- NPR's annual survey of its member stations, completed September 26, 2003, identified several problem areas in the network's relationship with them, including, "Stations feel somewhat out of touch with NPR's fiscal plans and performance," and "many stations felt generally 'out of the loop' about NPR's future direction."

- A tracking study from summer 2003 found donors had greater loyalty to public radio than to their local station (57 percent vs. 43 percent), indicating the need for NPR to reinforce listener support for local stations.

- A February 2003 external study found that "only the collective local success of a wide range of stations" could propel NPR to its five-year audience goals. This indicated the importance of both the network's relationship with its members and the need for their continued financial success.

Planning

Objectives

Create greater recognition for NPR; ensure continued federal funding of public broadcasting/radio; prevent backlash against local stations from listeners, or against NPR from stations, Congress, or opinion leaders. Strategy: Use the intrinsic news value of the bequest ("NPR receives record gift") to deliver three key **messages**:

1. The size of the gift and Mrs. Kroc's careful research into NPR, along with record audience levels, validate the network's growing importance as a leading source or news and cultural programming.

2. The money will go into an endowment, and only its earnings will be spent. Therefore annual revenue from the gift can provide only a tiny percentage of the annual $720 million cost of public radio.

3. State and federal governments, sponsors, and listeners must continue their support of public radio stations, many of which still struggle financially.

Key Audiences

Members of Congress and the administration; state legislators who provide support for public broadcasting; opinion leaders, especially members of newspaper editorial boards; current and potential listeners to public radio, especially donors or sponsors; NPR member stations; and the NPR board and staff.

Execution

Because most key print and electronic media have reporters in Washington. D.C., F-H and NPR decided to hold a news conference at NPR headquarters on November 6, 2003. The primary target was Washington bureaus of key newspapers and wire services. We focused personal pitching on three newspapers especially — the *Washington Post,* the *New York Times,* and the *Washington Times,* along with several other important publications such as *National Journal* that are widely read among members of Congress. To boost interest, we issued an advisory the previous day saying NPR would announce a record bequest, but withholding the amount and the donor. This was a calculated risk that had the desired effect of piquing media attention.

Participants and statements in the news conference were carefully planned to reinforce our key messages with the media and member stations. NPR president Kevin Klose described the bequest's benefits to NPR and stressed it would not be a financial windfall, and emphasized its importance as a validator of NPR's achievements. Rep. Earl Blumenauer (D-Ore.), head of the Congressional Public Broadcasting Caucus, spoke of NPR's importance as an independent, reliable source of news, as well as the continued need for government funding of local public radio stations. A representative of San Diego public radio station KPBS described her relationship with Mrs. Kroc, providing a human-interest angle, and also publicly reinforcing NPR's partnership with its members. NPR special correspondent Susan Stamberg described the network's growth and the impact of the gift on the staff, providing an important internal message.

To encourage coverage by newspapers that lacked a Washington presence, we arranged a teleconference that allowed reporters to hear the speakers and actively participate in the Q & A. This was an unqualified success, with approximately 20 reporters calling in. Additionally, the entire conference was recorded on video, which was immediately up-linked to satellite, resulting in its use by 57 local and national television news programs. Before the news conference, NPR and F-H pitched reporters at more than 200 publications. We also arranged for Klose to make personal calls to newspaper publishers, paving the way for positive editorials. We also created a detailed rollout schedule and comprehensive press kit, drafted internal and external Q & As, and wrote messages and talking points for NPR leaders to inform network members, board, and staff. We assisted the Public Broadcasting Caucus in drafting its own news release, which was issued at our news conference. And we prepared a "toolkit" for local stations that included talking points, a draft letter/statement, and background information to assist general managers in dealing with local media and listeners. Finally, we tracked coverage and responded promptly with letters to the editor from NPR leaders or local public radio stations to rebut any criticisms.

Evaluation

At every level, the announcement of Mrs. Kroc's gift was an enormous success. Relating back to our original objectives:

- We significantly raised NPR's profile nationally, obtaining coverage in more than 230 media outlets in the United States and abroad.

- A media audit confirmed wide use of our key messages: validation of NPR's success; no "windfall" from the bequest; and a need for continued government support of public radio.

- At least 25 newspapers ran editorials, almost all positive, which confirmed that opinion leaders had seen and responded favorably to our messages.

- More than one dozen newspapers ran follow-up letters to the editor from NPR.

- After the bequest was announced, both the House and Senate approved CPB general funding of $400 million for 2006, an increase of $10 million from 2005. There was no attempt to reduce funding or to target NPR. In addition, new legislation reauthorizing the CPB for another five years remains on track.

- A January 2004 analysis showed that when critics were quoted, it generally was in response to NPR's messages, meaning opponents had to play defense, not offense.

- The same analysis found that news coverage of the gift "did not disrupt contributions to NPR's member stations" based on their initial feedback. Stations also cooperated with NPR on their local announcements—staying on message, being supportive of the bequest, and emphasizing the need for continued listener support. In summary, no "backlash" developed from either stations or listeners.

- Traffic to the NPR website increased in the first quarter of fiscal 2004, which included November and December of 2003.

- An external study, "NPR in 2004," found the NPR brand still "exudes credibility at an unsettled time."

- NPR audience levels remained strong. The November 6 news conference was held just past the halfway point of the fall 2003 Arbitron measuring period, which ended with an increase in NPR's ratings compared to the previous year—setting another record.

EXHIBIT 6-1A   *News Release*

National Public Radio®
635 Massachusetts Ave, NW
Washington, DC 20001-3753

Telephone: 202.513.2000
Facsimile: 202.513.3045
http://www.npr.org

 PRESS RELEASE

For Immediate Release
November 6, 2003

NPR: Jessamyn Sarmiento, 202-513-2307
Laura Gross, 202-513-2304
Jenny Lawhorn, 202-513-2754

NPR Receives a Record Bequest of More Than $200 Million
Gift Is From Philanthropist Joan Kroc, Longtime Supporter of Public Radio

Audio of the news conference will be archived at 800.252.6030 through midnight, Nov. 7th.

WASHINGTON – NPR has been honored with a bequest of more than $200 million from the estate of philanthropist Joan B. Kroc, believed to be the largest monetary gift ever received by an American cultural institution, NPR President Kevin Klose announced today.

"We are inspired and humbled by this magnificent gift," said Klose. "This remarkable act of generosity will help secure the future of NPR as a trusted and independent source of news, information and ideas for millions of listeners. Joan Kroc believed deeply in the power of public radio to serve the communities of America. She made this extraordinary gift from her steadfast conviction that NPR and our member stations provide a vital connection to millions of listeners. She wanted us to continue building a programming service marked by excellence to meet the challenges of this new century. This contribution reflects not only Mrs. Kroc's belief in the growing significance and enduring value of public radio, but her conviction that NPR will be a wise and responsible steward of her legacy."

NPR member station, KPBS in San Diego, also received a $5 million bequest from Mrs. Kroc, a long-time donor to the station. "Mrs. Kroc recognized the defining partnership of public radio: local stations working with national broadcasters to create this remarkable service. The relationship that Mrs. Kroc had with KPBS helped foster a deep understanding and appreciation of NPR and all of public radio," said Klose. "This exemplifies the close partnership that exists between NPR and local public radio stations."

Most of the gift to NPR will become part of the NPR Endowment Fund for Excellence. The fund was created in 1993 to provide a sustaining source of support for NPR activities that is independent of other revenue sources, which are affected by the economy and other factors beyond NPR's control.

"Public radio today is more important than ever," said Congressman Earl Blumenauer (D-Oregon), Chairman of the Congressional Public Broadcasting Caucus, who attended the Washington news conference at NPR headquarters. "NPR and its more than 750 member stations provide an invaluable and remarkable service to the American public. NPR and its members now reach more than 22 million listeners each week – an increase of more than 60 percent over the last five years. This is reflective of the need in this country for thoughtful and intelligent programming. But while this gift is a marvelous recognition of NPR's current achievement and future promise, it is also a reminder that we in Congress must continue to provide critical support for local publicly owned radio stations – the heart of public radio."

NPR Special Correspondent Susan Stamberg, whose voice has been heard on public radio since 1971, said she was "rendered almost speechless" by the magnitude of Mrs. Kroc's gift. "This was totally unexpected. Those of us who work for NPR are truly honored by this donation," said Stamberg.

Courtesy National Public Radio

The exact amount of the gift – more than $200 million – will depend on resolution of Mrs. Kroc's estate and the final value of her investments. Disbursement of trust funds will take a number of months, and there will be no immediate impact on NPR's budget. "We will use that time wisely to engage in a dialogue with our Board, with our staff at NPR, our member stations, our Foundation trustees, our supporters and our partners in public broadcasting to determine how best to translate this gift into an enduring legacy," said Klose.

John A. Herrmann Jr., chairman of the NPR foundation, said the contribution, combined with a generous flow of other donations to the Endowment Fund for Excellence, is a recognition that NPR has grown to be a linchpin of American news, information and culture. "This is an enormous act of faith by Mrs. Kroc and other donors," said Herrmann. "They are creating a legacy for the audiences of today and tomorrow."

Herrmann said the gift will increase the size of the endowment fund beyond $225 million. "Mrs. Kroc's generosity is an inspiring example for all of us who support NPR and public radio," he said. "She has given us the capacity to think big, both about the services of NPR and about further building the financial resources of this great institution"

"KPBS and National Public Radio are the beneficiaries of Joan Kroc's extraordinary generosity because she recognized that our programming provides vital public service to the American people" said Doug Myrland, general manager of KPBS. "Joan Kroc knew that the partnership between local stations like KPBS and national organizations like NPR is the key to maintaining and improving our programming, and she understood the special value of creating a vital mix of local and national news, information and cultural programming."

"It is no secret that these have been challenging economic times for public radio, a challenge that is still unmet," added Klose. "We hope this gift will inspire a broad conversation about the funding needs for public radio, particularly our member stations."

Klose remembered Mrs. Kroc as a "compassionate person who cared deeply about national and international issues, and especially in finding ways to help people and nations communicate better with one another. I believe those are among the reasons that she chose to leave a substantial gift to NPR."

Joan Kroc, who was nationally recognized for her philanthropy, died of cancer Oct. 12 at age 75. She was the widow of Ray A. Kroc, the founder of McDonald's Corp. In recent years, Mrs. Kroc had made many substantial gifts to organizations promoting world peace, including peace centers at the University of Notre Dame and the University of San Diego.

###

NPR is renowned for journalistic excellence and standard-setting news and entertainment programming. A privately supported, non-profit, membership organization, NPR serves a growing audience of more than 22 million Americans each week via more than 750 public radio stations. International partners in cable, satellite and short-wave services make NPR programming accessible anywhere in the world. With original online content and audio streaming, npr.org offers hourly newscasts, special features and seven years of archived audio and information.

EXHIBIT 6-1B   *Statement*

National Public Radio®
635 Massachusetts Ave, NW
Washington, DC 20001-3753

Telephone: 202.513.2000
Facsimile: 202.513.3045
http://www.npr.org

 STATEMENT

Congressman Earl Blumenauer, (D-Ore.)
Co-founder, Congressional Public Broadcasting Caucus

Good afternoon. It is a pleasure to be here.

On behalf of the Public Broadcasting Caucus, an organization supported by 100 Members of the U.S. House, I'm here today to congratulate NPR on this generous gift from the late Mrs. Kroc, and to emphasize that while this is a wonderful contribution, Congress needs to continue to provide adequate funding for public broadcasting.

We all need to do our part, especially in these difficult economic times with increased demands on budgets for programming and technology upgrades.

This is a remarkable gift, and it reflects the great value of NPR and public radio. Public radio provides careful, balanced, and thoughtful presentations of news and culture. NPR is a national treasure and this gift will help secure the future of this great institution. This gift is a reminder that public radio lives in every community in this country, with local stations providing irreplaceable local service.

NPR does not receive any direct federal funding. Funds appropriated by the Congress to the Corporation for Public Broadcasting, and other entities which support public radio, are directed to local stations. While the support from Congress is substantial, it provides only a fraction of the funds that public radio stations need for annual operations. Stations make up the difference through contributions from listeners, local businesses and underwriters.

America's *local, publicly owned, nonprofit* stations make up the heart of public radio, and we in the Congress need to make sure they have the resources to stay on the air and provide the news and information that is needed by local communities.

In fact, the hundreds of public radio stations located in every state and congressional district in America provide unique, balanced, in-depth local and national programming.
We hear a lot about how too much broadcasting is becoming little more than sound-bite news and standardized programming driven by focus groups. That I believe, is why NPR's audience has grown by two-thirds over the past five years; people across American thirst for thoughtful and intelligent programming. That is why in this town – Washington, D.C. – everybody listens to NPR, from Cabinet secretaries to cab drivers.

While this gift is a marvelous recognition of NPR's current achievement and future promise, it is also a reminder that we in Congress, as individuals and policy makers, must continue to provide critical support for local publicly owned radio stations – the heart of public radio.

This statement was prepared for delivery at NPR's news conference in Washington on Nov. 6, 2003

Courtesy National Public Radio

EXHIBIT 6-1C   *Fact Sheet*

National Public Radio®
635 Massachusetts Ave, NW
Washington, DC 20001-3753

Telephone: 202.513.2000
Facsimile: 202.513.3045
http://www.npr.org

 FACT SHEET

Funding Facts: NPR and Public Radio

NPR (National Public Radio) is a private, self-supporting nonprofit media company with hundreds of independent radio stations as members. NPR receives no direct federal funding for general support. NPR supports its operations through a combination of membership dues and programming fees from stations, contributions from private foundations and corporations, and revenue from the sales of transcripts, books, CDs, and merchandise. A very small percentage – between 1-2 percent of NPR's annual budget – comes from competitive grants sought by NPR from federally funded organizations, such as the Corporation for Public Broadcasting, National Science Foundation and the National Endowment for the Arts. At present, NPR's annual operating budget is approximately $100 million a year.

Published reports in *Worth Magazine* and *Consumers Digest* cited NPR as a leading U.S. nonprofit charity because of the company's program spending efficiency, high level of private support, and outstanding public service. NPR produces and distributes 32 programs weekly, including top-rated, award winning newsmagazines *Morning Edition* and *All Things Considered*. More than 22 million people listen to NPR programs each week.

The NPR membership in the U.S. includes more than 750 local, independent stations of varying formats, whose licenses are owned either by colleges and universities, community foundations, or other organizations. The strength of public radio's vital community service lies in its unique collaboration between local public radio stations and national program producers, such as NPR. NPR member stations are autonomous entities and are not owned or operated by NPR, nor does NPR fund member stations. Instead, station revenues come from a variety of other sources. In 2004, public radio stations and producers will receive $86 million from the Corporation for Public Broadcasting, which is funded by Congress (that amounts to only 30 cents per American to support local public radio stations). The appropriation from Congress accounts for only about 14 percent of the cost of operating local public radio stations, and the remaining 85 percent must be raised from a variety of sources, most importantly contributions from listeners.

Courtesy National Public Radio

Legislation in one state may have national implications for many large companies and organizations. Allstate responded to a challenge in California to minimize potential serious consequences for nationwide insurance companies and vehicle owners. Exhibit 6-2a is an advertisement, Exhibit 6-2b is a news release announcing the results of a survey, and Exhibit 6-2c is a news release with a corporate position paper.

Standing Up For Consumer Choice— The SB 1648 Battle

Allstate Insurance Company with Hill & Knowlton, Inc.

Summary

Hill & Knowlton's (H&K) work on behalf of Allstate Insurance Company helped defeat SB 1648 in the California Assembly, not once, but twice. Despite unanimous passage of the bill in the Senate, and acceptance by the Assembly Insurance Committee, Hill & Knowlton's clear messaging and successful media campaign swayed the opinion needle in the Assembly—ensuring defeat of a flawed piece of legislation that threatened consumer choice in the auto body repair industry.

Research

During an eight-week period in the summer of 2002, H&K developed and executed a public affairs campaign for Allstate that resulted in the defeat of California Senate Bill 1648 (SB 1648). Passage of the legislation would have negatively affected Allstate, both in California and throughout the nation, and jeopardized the company's multimillion-dollar investment in the Sterling Autobody Repair chain.

In 2002, Allstate began planning for the construction and operation of 20 Sterling Autobody Repair Centers in California, the wholly owned subsidiary's first entry into the California market. In response to this investment decision, State Senator Jackie Speier introduced SB 1648 to preclude any insurance company from owning or investing

Courtesy Allstate Insurance Company

in auto body repair shops in California. The auto body repair and auto dealer industries supported the legislation and anticipated a California victory would set the stage for similar legislation across the country.

Prior to engagement of H&K, the legislation moved swiftly, with unanimous passage in the State Senate and a significant majority vote in the Assembly Insurance Committee.

The main objective of the SB 1648 campaign, therefore, was to prevent the legislation from becoming law.

Hill & Knowlton began its work by conducting a statewide survey of Californians to determine and validate messages that Allstate hoped would resonate with its target audiences. The survey of 1,000 Californians verified that, with regard to auto body repairs, consumers were:

- concerned about the high rate of fraud in the industry
- wanted more choice in selecting auto body repair shops
- valued competition in this market

Additional research of existing third-party data revealed an auto body repair industry in California plagued by fraud and in dire need of reform. The state's Bureau of Automotive Repair published auto body repair fraud rates as high as 36 percent, costing California's consumers an estimated $1 billion annually.

Planning

Allstate contacted Hill & Knowlton on June 26, 2002. The following day, H&K presented Allstate with a preliminary communications plan that included program goals, anticipated target audiences, media and government relations strategies and tactics, and coalition/grassroots engagement suggestions. The plan was modified based on research findings, but the majority of the strategic and tactical suggestions were implemented and carried out through the eight-week campaign. On a daily basis, and in consultation with Allstate and its lobbying firm, Manatt, Phelps & Phillips (Manatt), we evaluated the progress of our game plan and adjusted our activities on an as-needed basis.

In consultation with Allstate and Manatt, we identified primary and secondary audiences for our campaign, namely the California Legislature and staff, the Governor's Office and key administration officials, and political, business, and trade media in California. Secondary audiences included Allstate employees and agents, Allstate customers, and California consumers in general.

With the likelihood of Assembly passage of the legislation, H&K, in collaboration with Allstate and Manatt, implemented an integrated public affairs communications program to defeat SB 1648. Recognizing the fluid nature of legislative action, H&K pursued the main objective through a three-tiered offensive approach. First, we worked to prevent or delay an Assembly floor vote. Second, we pursued every avenue to ensure defeat of the legislation on the Assembly floor. Third, we planned for the need to influence the governor and obtain a gubernatorial veto of the legislation should the bill pass in the Assembly. The strategy focused on repetitive communication of key messages to our target audiences through earned and paid media efforts, coalition development, and outreach and direct lobbying. We made it absolutely clear in our communications that SB 1648 limited competition, limited consumer choice, and perpetuated fraud.

Execution

Hill & Knowlton used the survey findings to develop key messages, fact sheets, media/information kits, press releases, and print advertisements to be used in the public affairs campaign.

Bilingual, paid advertisements were created by H&K's in-house graphics team and placed in the *Sacramento Bee* and *La Opinion* (California's oldest and most influential Spanish-language daily). We also worked to secure coalition members to oppose SB 1648.

Hill & Knowlton's media and coalition activity directly supported Manatt's simultaneous lobbying efforts.

Evaluation

The collaborative effort of Allstate, H&K, and Manatt resulted in a decisive victory. The team delayed an Assembly floor vote on SB 1648 for seven weeks and, when the Assembly did take up the measure, it was defeated on the floor, not once, but twice. This was an unlikely outcome, as the bill had passed the Senate 40–0 and had passed the Assembly Insurance Committee by a large majority. Success is attributable to the fact that key messages were validated and were found to be accurate and persuasive by our target audiences.

Although we had engaged the Governor's Office to lay the groundwork for a veto, defeat on the Assembly floor precluded the need to mount a risky and expensive veto campaign. Defeat of SB 1648 allowed Allstate to immediately begin construction of Sterling Autobody Repair Centers in California.

Our team succeeded in placing print stories in outlets such as the *Sacramento Bee, Bloomberg,* the *Orange County Register,* Associated Press, the *San Francisco Chronicle,* the *Stockton Record,* the *San Francisco Register,* the *San Jose Mercury News,* and the *Santa Cruz Sentinel.*

In addition, our team secured positive editorial coverage in the *Sacramento Bee,* the *Los Angeles Times,* the *Fresno Bee,* the *Modesto Bee,* and the *San Bernardino Sun.*

Broadcast coverage was secured on KNX radio (Los Angeles), KCRA-TV (Sacramento), Channel 31 (Sacramento), and NBC 3 (San Francisco).

We successfully engaged the California Chamber of Commerce, the California Business Roundtable, the Latino Coalition, the Latino Journal, the National Association of Independent Insurers, the American Insurance Association, CHARO Community Development Corporation, the William C. Valasquez Foundation, and the Environmental Hazards Management Institute.

In addition to the capital investment and jobs that will now be created, defeat of SB 1648 will help eliminate fraud in the auto body industry, increase competition among vendors, and enhance consumer choice. Ultimately, this important victory could preclude similar anti-competitive efforts from spreading to other states.

EXHIBIT 6-2A   *Advertisement*

PAID ADVERTISEMENT   PAID ADVERTISEMENT

The last time you took your car to an auto body repair shop, did you get what you paid for? Are you sure?

A preliminary study shows that over 40% of auto body repairs in California are performed fraudulently!

Allstate is committed to eliminating fraud in the collision repair process and providing California consumers with high quality auto body repairs and a positive experience when their cars are damaged in an accident.

That's why Allstate owns Sterling Auto Body Centers. Sterling currently operates in 7 states nationwide and in 8 large metropolitan areas.

On average, 95% of Sterling customers say they would recommend Sterling to their friends and family.

Senate Bill 1648 eliminates the Sterling option for California consumers.

SB 1648 perpetuates fraud, limits consumer choice, and eliminates jobs and investment in California.

Please join Allstate Insurance Company, the National Association of Independent Insurers, the Environmental Hazards Management Institute, the William C. Velasquez Institute, the Latino Journal, and CHARO Community Development Corporation in rejecting this anti-consumer legislation.

Contact your legislator at www.assembly.ca.gov or www.senate.ca.gov

SB 1648. Bad for consumers. Bad for business. Bad for California.

Paid for by Allstate Insurance Company, (916) 859-8847.

Courtesy Allstate Insurance Company

EXHIBIT 6-2B   *News Release on Survey*

Allstate.
You're in good hands.

NEWS

IMMEDIATE RELEASE

Contact: Bob Daniels
            Allstate Insurance Company
            916.859.8782

Survey Shows Californians Fed Up With Auto Repair Fraud
Pending Legislation Threatens to Block Reform and Restrict Competition

Sacramento, CA August 12, 2002 -- Poor quality work, cheating, and inflated pricing in auto body repair shops are big concerns among California consumers, according to a recent poll conducted by COMsciences, Inc. for Allstate Insurance Company.

Californians overwhelmingly support increased competition in auto repair as a way to stem widespread fraud, increase the quality of work, and lower prices.

Fully 85% of those polled believe that cheating is a major reason repair costs are so high in the state. In fact, an overwhelming majority (74%) feel they are often cheated by auto body repair shops that do poor quality work or charge for work that was never even done. Ninety percent said consumers should have more choices in where to bring their car for bodywork, including shops owned or associated with insurance companies. Eighty-seven percent believe that the insurance industry should play a leadership role in combating industry fraud.

"Allstate sees these numbers as a call to action. For Allstate, leadership means playing a more direct, hands on roll in the auto repair process," said Allstate Insurance Company Field Vice President for California Hank Barge.

California consumers agree. According to the survey, 87% of Californians feel that insurance company owned repair shops, which are now available in other states, should be available to California motorists.

The Allstate Corporation is proposing to invest tens of millions of dollars in California to build as many as 20 of its Sterling Autobody Repair Centers around the state.

-more-

Courtesy Allstate Insurance Company

EXHIBIT 6-2B   *News Release on Survey (continued)*

How bad is fraud in California? The California Bureau of Automotive Repair says there is a 43% incidence of fraud in California automotive repairs. Yet a bill currently before the California State Legislature seeks to ban insurance companies like Allstate from owning auto body shops in California.

"Senate Bill 1648 will deny California consumers the option of an additional, reliable, repair option. The bill is anti-consumer, anti-business, and perpetuates the existing fraud in the state's auto repair industry. California consumers should stand strong and voice their opposition to this measure." Barge said.

Again, Californians agree. Survey results show the majority (60%) of those surveyed are opposed to legislation preventing insurance companies from owning auto body repair facilities.

COMsciences polled a representative cross-section of Californians over the age of 18. About a third of the respondents were Hispanic, and approximately half were women. Almost half the survey sample (46%) report having been a driver involved in an auto accident. The survey had an error margin of ±3.1%.

<u>About Allstate</u>

Allstate (NYSE: ALL) is the nation's largest publicly held personal lines insurer. Widely known through the "You're In Good Hands With Allstate®" slogan, Allstate provides insurance products to more than 14 million households and has approximately 13,000 exclusive agents in the U.S. and Canada. Customers can access Allstate products and services through Allstate agents, or in select states at allstate.com and 1-800-Allstate[SM]. Encompass[SM] and Deerbrook[SM] Insurance brand property and casualty products are sold exclusively through independent agents. Allstate Financial Group includes the Allstate Bank and businesses that provide life insurance, retirement and investment products, through Allstate agents, workplace marketing, independent agents, banks and securities firms.

Allstate Non-Insurance Holdings, Inc., a subsidiary of The Allstate Corporation, acquired Sterling Collision Centers, Inc. in May 2001. Sterling Collision Centers, Inc. operates a network of more than 40 Sterling Autobody Centers in seven states and eight metropolitan markets. Allstate and Sterling share a common vision of providing a superior, seamless repair and claim handling experience. Sterling brings Allstate customers and claimants a fast, reliable, and honest repair option.

###

EXHIBIT 6-2C   *News Release on Corporate Position*

Allstate.
You're in good hands.

NEWS

FOR IMMEDIATE RELEASE

Contact: Lisa Wannamaker
            (916) 859-8611

Allstate Issues Statement Regarding Senate Bill 1648

Sacramento, CA – The Allstate Corporation issued the following statement today
regarding Senate Bill 1648 (Speier):

"Senate Bill 1648 is anti-consumer, anti-competitive and anti-investment in California.

"SB 1648 would prevent companies from investing in the health and development of an
industry that directly affects their customers – a precedent that could have a chilling
effect on corporate investment in California at a time that the state needs it most.

"By passing SB 1648, the legislature would limit competition by barring new autobody
shops from entering the California market. Reduced competition means higher costs,
which are ultimately passed onto the consumer in the form of higher premiums.

"SB 1648 would limit consumer choice not only by preventing new shops from entering
the California market, but also by denying consumers the option of choosing an insurer-
owned facility. Allstate does not require its customers to use Sterling facilities, but we
believe the consumers have a right to more choice. Based on customer satisfaction rates
in the upper ninety percent range, consumers in other states seem to appreciate the
insurer-owned alternative.

"SB 1648 would prohibit the introduction of a new business model in an industry that the
Bureau of Automotive Repair has indicated is plagued by fraud rates as high as 43
percent. By contrast, Sterling – Allstate's autobody subsidiary – has never had a fraud
allegation filed against any of its 40 shops in any of the seven states in which the
company currently operates.

"Allstate acquired Sterling Autobody Centers to give its customers a superior repair and
claim handling experience. Sterling, with Allstate's investment, can offer customers the
latest in auto body repair technology, experienced technicians, and expertise. The
Allstate-Sterling relationship streamlines the claim handling process, eliminates
redundancies and returns cars more quickly to owners. In fact, Sterling has an on-time

Courtesy Allstate Insurance Company

EXHIBIT 6-2C   *News Release on Corporate Position (continued)*

NEWS

Allstate Corporation, page 2

average of 94 percent, compared to an industry average of 30 percent. All work done by Sterling is guaranteed by Allstate for as long as the consumer owns the vehicle. These factors may help explain why Sterling enjoys a remarkable 96 percent customer satisfaction rate."

<u>About Allstate</u>

The Allstate Corporation (NYSE: ALL) is the nation's largest publicly held personal lines insurer. Widely known through the "You're In Good Hands With Allstate®" slogan, Allstate provides insurance products to more than 14 million households and has approximately 13,000 exclusive agents in the U.S. and Canada. Customers can access Allstate products and services through Allstate agents, or in select states at allstate.com and 1-800-Allstate[SM]. Encompass[SM] and Deerbrook[SM] Insurance brand property and casualty products are sold exclusively through independent agents.

# # #

The quality of health care is often linked to medical lawsuits and the cost of medical malpractice insurance. Framing the debate in terms of keeping good doctors in Maryland became the foundation of this campaign. Exhibit 6-3a shows a news release on campaign goals, Exhibit 6-3b is a brochure used in the campaign, and Exhibit 6-3c is a media advisory.

Save Our Doctors, Protect Our Patients: The Maryland Miracle

Potomac Incorporated

Situation Analysis

- From 2000 to 2004, medical malpractice awards more than doubled in Maryland, rising from $40.3 million to $93.2 million; the average payout per case rose from $234,000 to $410,000.

- Medical Mutual, the malpractice carrier for three-fourths of Maryland physicians, increased rates 28 percent in 2004.

- A malpractice reform bill introduced in the Maryland legislature was soundly defeated in March 2004. The forecast for major change was gloomy.

- A few months later, Medical Mutual received approval from the state insurance commission for a 33 percent increase in 2005.

- The governor traveled the state in the summer of '05 trying to rally support for major malpractice reform.

- Legislative hearings were held around the state; the governor appointed a malpractice task force.

- Going into the fall little progress had been made; the governor and legislative leaders were not seriously talking.

- In western Maryland, Washington County doctors were upset about this lack of progress; many were being forced to shut down their practices or move out of the area. They were also distressed by the ineffectiveness of the state medical society.

- They came to Potomac Incorporated to change the political dynamic in the state, and to help launch a grassroots public education campaign. Potomac began its consulting work in the first week of October.

Courtesy Potomac Unlimited

- With statewide elections looming around the corner and the national debate on malpractice becoming very partisan and ideological, it was imperative to build broad-based support across both political parties.

Research

- We started with a primary research benchmark from the yearly Maryland Poll conducted by the *Baltimore Sun.* In January 2004, this survey found that only 3 percent of respondents ranked health care as the most important statewide issue.

- As a first step in our secondary research, Potomac staff had to master the complexities of this issue, covering medical, insurance, and legal ramifications, with an eye toward its impact on Maryland's own circumstances.

- We performed an analysis of malpractice impacts on key medical professions, working with national and state associations to get updated data. We found best practices in California, Indiana, and Texas.

- We analyzed the legislative record from the prior session, examining testimony from key witnesses and the substance of main bills. We also conducted briefings with members of the key legislative committees.

- We examined media clips, both nationally and within the state, to dissect what the public was reading, seeing, and hearing on the eve of this campaign.

Planning

Strategic Considerations

- We needed to come across as a broad-based organization, not a group of self-interested, well-heeled physicians.

- We needed to make this a critical public issue, rather than a battle between lawyers and doctors.

- We needed to generate a large number of mass responses targeted to key members of the legislature, in order for them to believe this was an urgent problem that had to transcend typical Annapolis politics.

- We needed to forge alliances with other key groups on a community-by-community basis, especially those that had special clout with their legislators.

- Not wanting this effort to be identified as Washington County only, we brought together medical leaders from a half dozen major counties to forge greater political strength.

Goals

1. Passage of comprehensive legislation to lower premiums and reform the medical liability system so that doctors could afford to continue practicing in Maryland.

2. To pass a bill by the date the premium increase was due to take effect, the legislature would have to be called into Special Session by the governor.

Target Audiences

The Governor, his staff and task force, legislative leaders and members, legislative influencers (current and potential patients), doctors, allied medical professionals, and business/civic leaders.

Main Messages

Messaging stressed the impact of the crisis on patients rather than on doctors. We developed a five-part platform for comprehensive reform, modeled on the California MICRA (Medical Injury Compensation Reform Act of 1975) legislation, to serve as our messaging foundation. Media training sessions were held for members of the coalition's steering committee; speaking points were provided before media conferences. Constant direction was given to ensure quality and consistency of message. A grassroots tool kit was provided to all coalition members, including brochures to pass along to patients and staff plus instructions on how to contact local legislators. A series of high-profile media events was planned to create a "cyclone" of earned media coverage.

Execution

Implementation Challenges

- There wasn't time to build a statewide grassroots organization.
- We had to adjust our strategy on the spot, in order to respond to changing events on an almost daily basis.
- We had to fill the perceived void left by the state medical society and become the voice for doctors.
- The leaders of coalition were doctors who were expert on the subject but who were also being severely impacted by the crisis. We had to create credibility for them as spokespersons to be widely sought out for direct testimony and media commentary.

Branding

The theme "Save Our Doctors, Protect Our Patients" was graphically reinforced by a logo incorporating a red and white life preserver, with a red lifeline looping symbolically around the word "patients." This logo was dramatically brought to three-dimensional life by thousands of plastic red-and-white life preservers. Banners, handheld signs, T-shirts, and white lab coats further reinforced the coalition's "signature" life preservers.

Web Development/Coalition Building

Potomac developed a website (including content and programming) that became the engine of the campaign providing detailed information that included fact sheets, reform agenda, highlights of recent news coverage, and a public forum on the medical malpractice crisis. The site, www.saveourdoctors.org, gave coalition supporters the ability to send e-mails to state legislative leaders using specially designed templates. In addition, the site's broadcast e-mail capability enabled the coalition to send regular announcements to members, legislators, supporters, and the media. These daily Lifeline e-mail alerts provided updates on events and news conferences, recapped events of the special session, made direct appeals to legislators for reform, and requested that members and supporters continue to lobby their own legislators.

Media Launch and Follow-up

The main media launch took place on Wednesday, November 17 in Annapolis. This "Call to Action" event stressed that doctors in at least three Maryland counties had postponed elective surgeries that week to launch a statewide public education crusade on the need for medical liability reform. More than three dozen white-coated doctors converged on a plaza in front of the State House. This event produced blanket print and broadcast coverage across Maryland, with heaviest play in the Baltimore-Annapolis-Washington metroplex, along with stories picked up by affiliates across the country. After this initial attention-grabbing launch, we put individual doctors forward as experts for every conceivable media opportunity, including talk shows, op-ed pieces, quotable sources for news articles, feature articles, and special photo sessions. We held two more press conferences in the state capital, including a "Day of Reckoning" news conference on December 1 (payment due date for malpractice premiums) and a climactic gathering in the main lobby of the State House on December 28, moments before the legislative debate began in the House and Senate.

Evaluation

- No one would have predicted the ultimate turn of events in this campaign that lasted less than 100 days. The results were unprecedented in Maryland's modern political history.
- The coalition built such an intense media cyclone that the governor was moved to call a Special Session during the Christmas holidays.

The Maryland General Assembly had not been called into special session for more than a decade.

- With Save Our Doctors (SOD) leading the way, this Maryland legislative session became a national news story. Malpractice became the number one state news topic.

- We were able to get the legislature to deal with the malpractice issue more comprehensively than any of the political "experts" thought possible. Both houses passed malpractice reform legislation over a two-day special session. This legislation addressed three of the five planks in the SOD reform platform. Then, with SOD taking courageous leadership, we were able to withstand the governor's veto. By limiting malpractice increases to 5 percent instead of the 33 percent hike approved by the state insurance commission, the enacted legislation assures a total of $400 million in financial relief to doctors over four years.

Some Final Measures of Success

- The coalition website received 62,476 hits from December 10 through the end of January.

- Editorials supportive of the reform legislation ran in every major daily newspaper in the state.

- Dr. Riggle, named to the *Gazette's* list of "Who's News" for 2004, emerged as a major leader in the statewide fight for tort reform.

- More than 300 documented print and broadcast media placements reached a statewide and national audience approaching 10 million people. This earned media coverage is worth an estimated $2.5 million, a 25-to-1 return on the client's investment.

- The *Baltimore Sun's* January 2005 Maryland Poll found that health care is now the second most important issue overall, with 10 percent of respondents declaring it the most important issue. The same poll also showed that 83 percent of Maryland voters now consider the rising cost of medical malpractice liability insurance to be "a crisis that threatens the quality of health care."

EXHIBIT 6-3A   *News Release-Campaign Objectives*

News From...

SAVE *Our* DOCTORS
Protect Our Patients
w w w . s a v e o u r d o c t o r s . o r g

For Immediate Release	Contacts:	Heather Goethe	Bill Holleran
		Office: 301-656-7901	Cell: 301-996-9495
		Cell: 703-371-7470	

DOCTOR/PATIENT COALITION OFFERS PLATFORM FOR COMPREHENSIVE COMMON SENSE MEDICAL LIABILITY REFORM

The Save Our Doctors, Protect Our Patients Coalition believes that *FIVE LONG-TERM REFORMS* are essential to solve the medical liability crisis. Short-term solutions have been tried in other states, and they have not worked.

- *First, a new medical tort and liability insurance system modeled after the one enacted in California, which has stabilized that state's system and maintained open access to courts for all patients.*

    o Liability rates up 168 percent in California compared to national average of 420 percent.

    o Cost of settlements in California 53% lower than national average.

    o California cases settled in average of three years vs. national average of four.

    o Injured patients compensated more quickly in California than in any other state but Minnesota.

    o California reforms have lowered health care costs by estimated six percent – *saving patients $6 BILLION every year on health care.*

    o California now has a system working for benefit of patients – not trial lawyers.

- *Second, we need new rules for expert witness qualifications.*

    o Not fair for a doctor not in same specialty to be an expert witness in a malpractice case – just as it does not make sense for a plumber to evaluate the work of an electrician. Expert witnesses should be:

Courtesy Potomac Unlimited

- Practicing same specialty in Maryland;
- Board certified;
- Specially licensed by State;
- Subject to peer review *and* subject to sanctions in the event of false testimony.

  o Court brings witnesses to eliminate bias or incentives to give certain testimonies.

- *Third, stronger "Good Samaritan" protections are called for.*

  o Don't punish doctors for donating care to critically ill, often uninsured patients.

  o Make volunteer care economically feasible to keep retiring doctors practicing.

  o Establish immunity for ER/trauma care officials who cannot get patient consent.

- *Fourth, a Health Care Court can block frivolous lawsuits from making it to court and further cut down on legal costs.*

  o This reform is already working in Indiana.

  o System evaluates merits of malpractice claims before they go into the legal system.

  o One attorney and three health care professionals define standard of care and decide whether it has been violated.

- *Fifth, medical liability insurance reform* that includes accountability, transparency and a healthy respect for competition among providers of malpractice coverage to Maryland doctors.

  o Accountability means requiring Med Mutual to disclose its rate setting practices to doctors - because it's "doctor-owned."

  o Transparency means letting doctors know about Med Mutual's practices, full investigatory authority for the Maryland Insurance Commissioner and full disclosure to any legislative body that seeks oversight without throwing up protections that information is proprietary, etc.

  o Competition means looking into the potential or actual conflict of interest of MedChi and Med Mutual in allowing commissions to be paid to Med Mutual. Competition also means possible changes in the criteria at the Maryland Insurance Administration to allow more companies full access.

###

EXHIBIT 6-3B *"My Doctor Saved My Life" Brochure*

PLEASE HELP US NOW!

CONTACT KEY STATE LEGISLATORS: Maryland General Assembly leaders are the key to solving the medical liability crisis. Call them, or send them e-mail saying you want comprehensive common sense reform NOW!

SENATOR BRIAN E. FROSH
District 16, Montgomery County
Chair, Judicial Proceedings Committee
(410) 341-3124 or (301) 858-3124
e-mail:
brian_frosh@senate.state.md.us

SEN. THOMAS V. MIKE MILLER, JR.
District 27, Prince George's County
Senate President
1-800-492-7122, ext. 3700 (toll free)
e-mail:
thomas_v_mike_miller@senate.state.md.us

DELEGATE MICHAEL E. BUSCH
District 30, Anne Arundel County
Speaker of the House
(410) 841-3800 or (301) 858-3800
1-800-492-7122, ext. 3800 (toll free)
e-mail:
michael_busch@house.state.md.us

DELEGATE JOSEPH F. VALLARIO, JR.
District 27A, Calvert & Prince George's Counties
Chair, Judiciary Committee
(410) 841-3488 or (301) 858-3488
1-800-492-7122, ext. 3488 (toll free)
e-mail:
joseph_vallario@house.state.md.us

CONTACT YOUR LEGISLATOR: Find your own State Senator and Delegate at **WWW.MDELECT.NET**, and write or call them today. Tell them to support comprehensive reform. Consider paying them a visit individually or with a group of your friends or colleagues. They need to hear your voice!

CONTACT THE GOVERNOR: Call on Governor Robert Ehrlich to work with lawmakers to pass comprehensive common sense reform legislation now!

GOVERNOR ROBERT EHRLICH
Telephone: 1-800-811-8336
E-mail: governor@gov.state.md.us
Internet: http://www.gov.state.md.us/mail

MAKE TELEPHONE CALLS: Be active and get the word out. Call your doctor. Call family members, friends, and colleagues.

This crisis is about making sure our doctors are there when we need them. Unless we solve the crisis, your doctor may not be there the next time you need lifesaving medical care!

Log onto **WWW.SAVEOURDOCTORS.ORG** for more ways you can help.

www.saveourdoctors.org

My Doctor Saved My Life...

Dick & Sally Poole of Hagerstown, Maryland

www.saveourdoctors.org

Courtesy Potomac Unlimited

EXHIBIT 6-3C   *Media Advisory – Save Our Doctors*

News From...

SAVE *Our* **DOCTORS**
Protect Our Patients

www.saveourdoctors.org

For Immediate Release	**Contacts:**	**Heather Goethe**	**Bill Holleran**
		Office: 301-656-7901	Cell: 301-996-9495
		Cell: 703-371-7470	

MEDIA ALERT: *Crusade of Docs To Converge on State Capital*

WHO: Save Our Doctors, Protect Our Patients Coalition, a grassroots political action group made up of doctors, medical professionals and concerned citizens from across the state of Maryland. On November 15, the coalition launched a statewide "Call to Action" for comprehensive common-sense medical liability reform with coordinated activities in Washington and Prince George's Counties that received statewide print and broadcast media coverage.

WHAT: Continuing their crusade for preservation of patient access to medical care, dozens of doctors in white lab coats, supported by patients, will converge on Annapolis for a news conference urging state legislative leaders to convene a special session of the General Assembly to focus on comprehensive, common sense medical liability reforms. Without these reforms, more and more Maryland doctors will be forced to retire early, limit their practices or move out of state.

WHEN: Wednesday, November 17, 2004 at 10:30 a.m.

WHERE: Lawyer's Mall in downtown Annapolis.

WHY: Long-term medical liability reform is urgently needed to ensure that patients will have access to their doctors in the future. Consider these facts:
- Eighty-four percent of Americans are concerned that skyrocketing medical liability costs could limit their access to care.
- Fifty-six percent of Blue Cross/Blue Shield plans in 12 states are refusing high-risk procedures.
- Runaway malpractice premium hikes have driven the only thoracic surgeon in Washington County to retire 10 years ahead of schedule.
- Pediatric neurosurgery is no longer performed in Frederick County.
- Last year, not a single doctor graduating from the University of Maryland chose OB/GYN.

HOW: By encouraging an outpouring of public support for a special session of the state legislature to consider the following five-point platform of reforms:
- Adoption of California medical tort and liability insurance system that has brought stability to that state and maintained open access to courts for all patients;
- New rules for expert witness qualifications that require testifying doctors to be in same specialty;
- Stronger "Good Samaritan" protections that do not punish doctors for donating care to critically ill, often uninsured patients in emergency/crisis situations;
- Creation of a health care court, similar to one established in Indiana, that can block frivolous lawsuits from making it to court and further cut down on legal costs; and
- Medical liability insurance reform that includes accountability, transparency and competition among providers of malpractice coverage to Maryland doctors.

A detailed platform will be made available at the news conference.

###

Courtesy Potomac Unlimited

## Chapter 7

Investor and Financial Relations

Corporations that sell shares to the public must conduct a specialized form of public relations with the investment, or financial, community. Investor and other financial relations cannot be managed in the same aggressive manner that characterizes other forms of public relations. The U.S. Securities and Exchange Commission (SEC) prohibits the promotion of corporate stock under certain circumstances, and it has detailed regulations regarding the issuance of annual and quarterly reports and the timely disclosure of all information that will affect the value of publicly traded corporate shares. After a spate of scandals involving accounting irregularities by large corporations such as ENRON, Congress passed the Sarbanes Oxley Act in 2002 to set standards for corporate responsibility and internal audit practices. It included measures requiring chief executive officers (CEOs) and chief financial officers (CFOs) to certify financial and other information in their companies' quarterly and annual reports and to force disclosure of non-GAAP (Generally Accepted Accounting Practices) financial measures. Coupled with SEC policy changes making company information more transparent for the general investor, investor relations is a challenging communications field.

How, then, does our four-stage process apply to this highly specialized form of public relations?

RESEARCH

Investor relations research includes investigation of the client, the reason for the program, and the audiences to be targeted for communication.

Client Research

The public relations practitioner needs to focus first on the company's past and present financial status, its past and present investor relations practices, and its strengths, weaknesses, and opportunities specifically related to the financial community. Both internal management practices and external factors such as new pressures from competitors, changes in the cost of goods, and unfounded rumors may all affect decisions by the investment community and will need to be explored.

Opportunity or Problem Research

The second area of research involves assessing the need for a program of financial public relations. Most corporations engage in ongoing investor relations programs that may involve routine communication with the financial media, the annual report to shareowners, the annual meeting, as well as miscellaneous meetings with and tours for shareowners. When problems develop with particular publics, special programs may be devised reactively. Thus, the need for the program should be clearly justified and explained in this phase of research.

Audience Research

Finally, research for investor relations involves identification of key audiences or groups that make up the financial community:

Shareowners and potential shareowners

Security analysts and investment counselors

The financial media

   Major wire services: Dow Jones, Reuters Economic Service, AP, UPI, Bloomberg

   Major business magazines: *Business Week, Fortune*—mass circulation and specialized

   Major New York City newspapers: the *New York Times,* the *Wall Street Journal*

   Statistical services: Standard & Poor's, Moody's Investor Service

   Private wire services: PR News Wire, Business Wire, and PRIMEZONE

   Major broadcast networks: CNNfn, CNBC, Bloomberg TV

Securities and Exchange Commission

OBJECTIVES

Investor relations objectives, both impact and output, should be as specific and as quantifiable as possible.

Impact Objectives

Impact objectives for investor relations include informing investor publics and affecting their attitudes and behaviors. Some examples are:

1. To increase the investor public's knowledge of significant corporate developments (by 40 percent during the current year)
2. To enhance favorable attitudes toward the corporation (by 30 percent this year)
3. To create (40 percent) more interest in the corporation among potential investors (during this year)
4. To raise (20 percent) more capital through the investor relations program (by our deadline of December 1)
5. To receive (45 percent) greater responses from shareowners and other targeted investor publics (during the next fiscal year)

Output Objectives

In investor relations, output objectives constitute the distribution and execution of program materials and forms of communication. For example:

1. To distribute corporate news releases to 12 major outlets among the financial media
2. To make 18 presentations to security analysts during the months of March and April

Public relations directors often prefer to use output objectives exclusively. These clarify public relations actions and are much simpler to evaluate than impact objectives.

PROGRAMMING

As in other forms of public relations, the element of programming for investor relations includes planning the theme and messages, the action or special event(s), the uncontrolled and controlled media, and the use of effective principles of communication in program execution.

Theme and Messages

The theme and messages for an investor relations program will be entirely situational. Such programs usually provide assurances of credibility and attempt to enhance relations between the company and the financial community.

Action(s) or Special Event(s)

Actions and special events unique to investor relations include:

1. An annual shareowners' meeting
2. An open house for shareowners or analysts
3. Meetings with members of the financial community
4. Teleconference or Webcast with investors and analysts
5. Special seminars or other group meetings with analysts
6. Special visits to corporate headquarters or plant tours for analysts and shareowners
7. Presentations at meetings or conventions of analysts, in and outside of New York City
8. Promotional events designed to enhance the company's image in the financial community

Uncontrolled and Controlled Media

Uncontrolled media most frequently used in investor relations include:

1. News releases or feature stories targeted to the financial and mass media
2. CEO interviews with the financial and mass media
3. Media relations with key members of the financial press to stimulate positive news coverage of the company and its activities

Controlled media most often found in investor relations programs are:

1. Printed materials for shareowners, including the annual report, quarterly and other financial reports, newsletters, magazines, special letters, dividend stuffers, and announcements; much of this sent by e-mail and placed on the website
2. Company promotional films or videos
3. CEO and other corporate officers' speeches to key audiences in the financial community
4. Company financial fact books, biographies and photographs of corporate officers, special fact sheets, and news releases
5. Shareowner opinion surveys
6. Financial advertising
7. The company website, a repository for all of the above

Several examples of uncontrolled and controlled forms of communication are included with the cases in this chapter.

Effective Communication

The most relevant communication principles for investor and financial relations are source credibility and audience participation.

Much of the effort of the investor relations program is directed toward enhancing the credibility of the corporation inside the financial community. The financial media, security analysts, shareowners, and potential shareowners must have a favorable image of the corporation. To accomplish this, organizations have changed their stock offerings from regional exchanges to the NASDAQ, the American or the New York Stock Exchanges; have upgraded their printed materials, incorporating designs to convey a more "blue-chip" image; and have stepped up presentations to security analysts. Thus, corporate credibility must always be a paramount concern.

Audience participation is also a vital aspect of such programs. Prospective shareowners, financial media people, security analysts, and others targeted for communication are invited to as many corporate functions as possible. The ultimate form of "audience participation," of course, is the actual purchase of shares in the company.

EVALUATION

Evaluation of investor relations programs should be goal-oriented, with each objective reexamined and measured in turn. Although there is a great temptation to cite analyst reports about the company and the company's performance, especially its stock's price/earnings (P/E) ratio, these measures may not be related to investor relations programming, or there may be other intervening variables that overshadow the influence of such programming. Some firms use external measures of reputation to gauge success. These include such lists as the *Financial Times'* "World's Most Respected Companies," *Fortune*'s "100 Best places to work for," and *Washington Technology*'s "Fast 50" list of fastest growing technology firms.

SUMMARY

Research for investor relations aims at understanding the publicly owned company's status in the financial and investment community, the need for communicating with that community, and the makeup of that community as a target audience. The audience components are shareowners and potential shareowners, security analysts and investment counselors, the financial press, and the Securities and Exchange Commission.

Both impact and output objectives are used in investor relations. Impact objectives are oriented toward informing or influencing the attitudes and behaviors of the financial community, while output objectives cite distribution of materials and other forms of programming as desired outcomes.

Programming for investor relations usually consists of such actions and events as annual shareowners' meetings, an open house for shareowners, special meetings with analysts or other members of the financial community, and promotional events designed to enhance the company's image in the financial community. Uncontrolled and controlled media used in investor relations include news releases, interviews, printed literature, audiovisual materials, and/or speeches directed to targeted segments of the financial community.

Evaluation of investor relations should return to the program's specific, stated objectives and measure each one appropriately. Some practitioners attribute enhancement of the corporation's P/E ratio to the efforts of the investor relations program. However, the presence of intervening variables should always be suspected in such cases.

READINGS ON INVESTOR AND FINANCIAL RELATIONS

Adler, Rob. "Net Gain: An Effective Investor Relations Web Site Enhances Shareholder Communications," *Public Relations Tactics* 5 (November 1998): 19 ff.

Braznell, William. "A Guide to Investor Relations for Emerging Companies," *Public Relations Journal* 50 (July 1994): 26 ff.

Burns, Stuart. "Minority Rights (Voting Rights) of Minority Shareholders," *Accountancy* 125 (February 2000): 44 ff.

Casteel, Lynn. "Investing in an Effective Annual Report," *Public Relations Tactics* 9 (November 2002): 10.

Cole, Benjamin Mark. *The New Investor Relations—Expert Perspectives on the State of the Art.* Princeton, NJ: Bloomberg Press, 2003.

Corning, Beth. "Great Reputations: A PR Disaster Could Cost Your Corporation Dearly," *Accountancy* 123 (March 1999): 38 ff.

"Corporate Public Relations," *Public Relations Quarterly* 36 (fall 1991, special issue).

Easley, Lisa. "Using Media Relations (Instead of Investor Relations)," *Public Relations Quarterly* 43 (summer 1998): 39 ff.

Fernando, Angelo. "When Rumor Has It (or Not)," *Communication World* 22 (July–August 2005): 10–11.

Gaschen, Dennis John. "Restoring Public Confidence—The Challenges of Conducting Investor Relations in Today's Volatile Market," *Public Relations Tactics* 9 (November 2002): 8.

Gringsby, Ed, and Ted Blood. "Shareholders as Ultimate Customers," *Financial Management* 22 (spring 1993): 22 ff.

Higgins, Richard B. *Best Practices in Global Investor Relations.* Westport, CT: Greenwood Publishing Group, 2000.

Hooke, Jeffrey C. *Security Analysis on Wall Street.* Somerset, NJ: Wiley, 1999.

Johnson, Laura. "How to Succeed in a Close Proxy Vote," *Public Relations Quarterly* 39 (spring 1994): 35 ff.

Jones, Charles P. *Investments: Analysis and Management,* 6th ed. Somerset, NJ: Wiley, 1997.

Kanzler, Ford. "Poised for Public Offerings? Start Your Public Relations Efforts Now," *Public Relations Quarterly* 41 (summer 1996): 23 ff.

Macintosh, William. "Getting Focused—The Communicator's Role When a CEO Fails," *Public Relations Strategist* 9 (winter 2003): 16 ff.

Mahoney, William F. *Investor Relations: The Professional's Guide to Financial Marketing and Communications.* New York: New York Institute of Finance, a division of Simon & Schuster, 1991.

Marconi, Joe. "Taking Stock: Understanding Investor Relations," in *Public Relations: The Complete Guide.* Mason, OH: South-Western, 2004.

Merchant, Hemant, and Dan Schendel. "How Do International Joint Ventures Create Shareholder Value?" *Strategic Management Journal* 21 (July 2000): 723 ff.

Miles, Morgan P., and Jeffrey G. Covin. "Environmental Marketing: A Source of Reputational, Competitive, and Financial Advantage," *Journal of Business Ethics* 23 (February 1, 2001): 299 ff.

Nekvsil, Charles. "Getting the Most Out of Your Investor Relations Conference Calls," *Public Relations Tactics* 6 (August 1999): 10 ff.

Poe, Randall. "Can We Talk?" *Across the Board* (May 1994): 16 ff.

Radner, Greg. "The Promise of Web-based Disclosure," *Public Relations Tactics* 10 (November 2003): 13.

Roop, James J. "Investor Relations for Turnarounds," *Public Relations Quarterly* 40 (winter 1995–1996): 15 ff.

Savage, Michelle. "New Standards in Communicating to Financial Audiences—Why You Need to Understand XBRL," *Public Relations Strategist* 11 (winter 2005): 10–12.

Schneider, Carl W., Joseph M. Manko, and Robert S. Kant. *Going Public: Practice, Procedure and Consequences.* New York: Browne Publishing, 2002.

Seely, Michael W. "Hit the Financial Bull's Eye with Well-Aimed IR Programs," *Corporate Cashflow* (July 1993): 26 ff.

Silver, David. "Creating Transparency for Public Companies: The Convergence of PR and IR in the Post-Sarbanes-Oxley Marketplace," *Public Relations Strategist* 11 (winter 2005): 14–17.

Stapleton, Geof. *Institutional Shareholders and Corporate Governance.* New York: Oxford University Press, 1996.

Taggart, Philip W., and Roy Alexander, with Robert M. Arnold. *Taking Your Company Public: Red Lights and Green Lights for a Go/No-Go Decision.* New York: AMACOM, 1991.

Turner, Michael. "Surviving in the Era of Downsizing," *Public Relations Tactics* 4 (January 1997): 5 ff.

Turnock, Madeline. "IR and PR: Come Together," *Public Relations Strategist* 8 (spring 2002): 13–15.

INVESTOR RELATIONS CASES

CASE 7-1

Many factors directly influence the value of a company's equity such as accidents, lawsuits, and financial impropriety by the CEO. West Pharmaceutical suffered a serious accident at a facility and spent much communication capital to reclaim investor trust. Exhibit 7-1a is a news release.

New Beginnings: Recovering from Tragedy; Unlocking the Value

West Pharmaceutical Services with Financial Dynamics

Situation Analysis

West Pharmaceutical Services ("West" and "the Company") is one of the global market leaders in closure systems and syringe components for use with injectable drugs. In January 2003, one of West's major manufacturing facilities, located in Kinston, North Carolina, suffered a deadly explosion that claimed six lives. The Company spent most of 2003 handling the tragedy honorably and took care of the employees affected by the accident and the families of those who lost their lives. Amid these circumstances, the company managed to avoid major lawsuits, business interruptions, and customer losses. As the Company closed the saddest chapter in its history to embark upon a new beginning, the Company's money-losing drug delivery business, representing less than 2 percent of total sales, continued to dampen the valuation of its core pharmaceutical systems and its efforts to move the Company forward. Having always maintained good communications with West's investment constituents, Financial Dynamics (FD) communicated evidence to the Company that the investment community wanted to see West address the future of West's drug delivery business. FD's strategic input helped to validate and support West's own understanding of its investment sentiment and its decision to conduct a strategic review of its drug delivery business.

On June 30, 2004, West announced that it was reviewing strategic alternatives for its drug delivery business and said that it planned to an-

Courtesy West Pharmaceutical Services and Financial Dynamics

nounce a final decision by year-end 2004. On December 28, 2004, right on schedule, West announced that it had found a buyer for its drug delivery business. The Company had struck a deal with London-based private equity firm Warburg Pincus, which agreed to buy West's drug delivery business and gave West an equity interest in the new company. In the days surrounding this announcement, West's stock rose over 13 percent, as West had clearly responded to the investment community.

Research/Planning/Execution

In order to help West upgrade the communications of its valuation while transitioning the Company to be back on track after its own tragedy in 2003, Financial Dynamics conducted survey research, which entailed:

- conducting regular (unattributable) conversations and interviews with West's analysts and investors to gauge their perceptions about the Company, management, and what needed to be done to realize the value;

- analyzing the investor presentations of a collection of the Company's peers; and

- analyzing the investor presentations of other companies whose business models were similar to West's but who served different industries (i.e., not the pharmaceutical/healthcare sectors).

Based on this research, FD relayed to West that management was well respected, but needed to speak/meet with investors and analysts more frequently, now that Kinston is behind them; there was considerable confusion about West's investment story and the value of its pharmaceutical.

This comprehensive investor relations campaign entailed:

1. scheduling regular conference calls and meetings between West senior management and the Company's analysts and investors;

2. revising the Company's investor story and presentation to make the story more digestible and understandable for investors and highlight the strengths of its Pharmaceutical Systems business;

3. conducting extensive perception audits after the Company's earnings and material news announcements; and

4. reaching out to new investors.

To "unlock the value" of West shares, FD and West executed the following initiatives:

- Surveyed the investment community following the Company's earnings announcement, material news, and investor conference calls and meetings.

- Held several strategy meetings with West senior management and FD to relay the investment community's perceptions and FD's recommendations on the direction of the Company and communications strategy.

- Revamped the Company's investor presentation on multiple occasions to make it more digestible and understandable to investors, to ensure that it properly communicated the key strengths of West's pharmaceutical systems business and de-emphasized the Company's drug delivery business (especially when the business came up for strategic review in June 2004).

- Conducted proactive outreach to noncovering sell-side analysts and prospective institutional investors.

- Arranged for West to ring the closing bell on the New York Stock Exchange in conjunction with the official closing of the Kinston chapter in the Company's history and the reopening of the Company's Kinston manufacturing facility.

- Maximized coverage and publicity around West's ringing of the NYSE closing bell.

- Organized a major East Coast investor road show with one-on-one and group meetings in New York and Boston. Meetings included representatives from Hamilton Investment Management, RH Capital, Corsair Capital, Principled Capital Management, Thomas Weisel Asset Management, Lee Munder, and Cadence Capital Management.

- Held multiple strategy conference calls throughout the year with West senior management and the FD account team.

- Had in-depth involvement in drafting and revising of all business news releases and conference call scripts to ensure consistency of key messages and to keep on track with the communications strategy.

Evaluation

The West/Financial Dynamics 2004 investor relations campaign was a resounding success. FD's campaign helped West:

- Improve Stock Performance.
  West's stock price improved 53 percent to $24.92 on December 31, 2004, compared to $16.24 on December 31, 2003.

- Broaden Institutional and Research Coverage Support.
  Many of the institutional investors West met through FD have continued to follow the Company. There were about 54 institutional investors who own over 50,000 shares of West stock at the end of December 2004, representing an increase of approximately 60 percent from 34 institutional investors who own over 50,000 shares of

West stock at the end of the March 2003, the quarter when the accident occurred. Sell-side analyst, Arnold Ursaner at CJS Securities, launched coverage of West's stock in 2004.

- Increased Investor Participation on Conference Calls.
Furthermore, our outreach to the investment community generated a significant increase in investor and analyst interest, generating a 114 percent increase in conference call participation.

- Clear Communication of Company Value.
When West announced the sale of its drug delivery business to Warburg Pincus at the end of December 2004, the size of the deal was relatively small, but it captured the attention of the Associated Press, the *New York Times,* Dow Jones, Bloomberg, and *Medical Device Daily,* with many of the stories syndicated around the country. Media coverage was not an objective in this campaign. We view these results as a clear indication that the financial media understood the new value of the Company without the drug delivery business.

- Enhanced Credibility and Respect after a Tragedy.
Finally, the Company and management have strengthened their credibility with the investment community, solidified strong relationships with key members of their investment constituents, and are ideally positioned to enter 2005 as a Pharmaceutical Services company with a strong in investor and analyst following.

EXHIBIT 7-1A   *News Release*

WEST *Pharmaceutical* S E R V I C E S ®

GLOBAL HEADQUARTERS
101 Gordon Drive • Lionville, PA 19341
TEL 610-594-2900 • FAX 610-594-3000
www.westpharma.com

Contacts:
West Pharmaceutical Services, Inc.
Michael A. Anderson
Vice President and Treasurer
(610) 594-3345

Investors/Financial Media:
Financial Dynamics
Lanie Marcus/Julie Huang
(212) 850-5600
wst@fd-us.com

West Pharmaceutical Services to Explore Strategic Alternatives for Drug Delivery
- Affirms sales guidance and updates earnings guidance for quarter and year –
- Company will host investor conference call today at 4:15 pm Eastern Time -

LIONVILLE, Pa., June 30, 2004 -- West Pharmaceutical Services, Inc. (NYSE: WST), the global market leader in closure systems and syringe components for use with injectable drugs, today announced that it will explore strategic alternatives for its Drug Delivery Division and provided updates to its sales and earnings guidance for the 2004 second quarter and full year.

At its meeting yesterday, West's Board of Directors completed its periodic review of each of the Company's business units and, after careful consideration of timeline, priorities, and resources concluded that investments in the Company's Pharmaceutical Systems Division offer the best prospects for West's future growth and shareholder value. The Company's Pharmaceutical Systems Division accounted for approximately 98% of its $491 million revenue in 2003.

Donald E. Morel, PhD, West Chairman and CEO said "After much review and deliberation, we concluded that our core Pharmaceutical Systems business offers a broad range of exciting opportunities for the Company and as such deserves the full focus of the Company's resources. While the Board and management continue to believe that our drug delivery programs offer significant promise and potential, we do not believe the Company can continue to support that research effort while also pursuing our core business initiatives. We have therefore decided to initiate an evaluation of alternatives for the Drug Delivery Division that will provide for its near term needs and lead to its ultimate success."

For the quarter ending June 30, 2004, the Company expects *pro forma* earnings per share to be between $0.61 and $0.65, consistent with internal expectations, compared to $0.66 in the 2003 quarter. For the fiscal year 2004, the Company expects to generate year-over-year revenue growth of 5% to 7% and *pro forma* diluted earnings per share in the range of $2.00 to $2.10, an increase over the *pro forma* $1.88 generated in 2003. *Pro forma* diluted earnings per share for each reporting period of 2003 and 2004 exclude costs associated with the 2003 explosion and fire at the Company's Kinston, North

Courtesy West Pharmaceutical Services and Financial Dynamics

Carolina production facility and the planned closure of its UK medical device facility, which the Company now estimates will be between $0.52 and $0.65 per share for the fiscal year 2004, and 2004 annual guidance excludes a $0.04 per diluted share non-operating gain that was reported in the first quarter. Revenue and earnings expectations for the 2004 period reflect a higher effective tax rate, as a result of a change in Danish law, and changes to the Company's Drug Delivery operating plans, which no longer include license fees for a generic nasal product after the Company's development partner withdrew from its agreement when the product did not satisfy a regulatory milestone. This product does not involve any of West's proprietary drug delivery technologies.

Dr. Morel further commented, "The continued strong performance of our Pharmaceutical Systems Division at or above our expectations is reflected in our positive outlook for the remainder of 2004, despite the changes in drug delivery."

The Company seeks to reach a conclusion on the review of its drug delivery business by the end of the year and is being advised by Houlihan Lokey Howard & Zukin in connection with its strategic evaluation.

The Company will continue to plan for and carry out initial efficacy trials on three proprietary formulations: Nasal Fentanyl, for the treatment of episodic break through pain; Nasal Leuprolide, for the treatment of endometriosis; and an oral formulation of Budesonide which utilizes West's colonic delivery technology, for the treatment of inflammatory bowel disease. The Company expects preliminary efficacy data for its Fentanyl trial to be available in late 2004 and for its Leuprolide and Budesonide trials to be available in the first half of 2005. The Company will also continue to support its partnered development programs.

Management from West Pharmaceutical Services will host a conference call to discuss this announcement today at 4:15 pm (Eastern Time). To access the call, please dial either (800) 399-3081 or (706) 679-0718. In addition, the call will be broadcast live over the Internet and can be accessed at the Company's website, www.westpharma.com. A telephonic replay of the call will be available through July 13, 2004, and may be accessed by dialing (800) 642-1687 or (706) 645-9291 (access code: 8524733).

About West Pharmaceutical Services, Inc.
West is the world's premier provider of standard-setting systems and device components for parenterally administered medicines and an emerging leader in the development of drug formulation and delivery system technologies for the nasal and targeted oral delivery of drugs. Internationally headquartered in Lionville, Pennsylvania, West supports its partners and customers from 50 locations throughout North America, South America, Europe, Mexico, Japan, Asia and Australia. For more information, visit West at www.westpharma.com

Problems with one company in a business segment may quickly ripple throughout the entire industry. Utility companies that had expanded their scope of operations following government deregulation, found themselves under the investor microscope following revelations about Enron's business practices. Aquila had a change in leadership, adding another layer of uncertainty for edgy investors. Exhibit 7-2a is a fact sheet, and Exhibit 7-2b is a list of "key messages" used in the campaign.

Navigating Through a Current of Uncertainty: Getting Aquila Back on Solid Ground

Aquila with Edelman

Situation Analysis

The collapse of Enron fundamentally changed the energy utility landscape. It placed the entire sector under a cloud of uncertainty and intense scrutiny, raising the bar on management credibility. With the resulting collapse of merchant energy trading markets, utilities were forced to post massive amounts of capital to cover open positions at a time when credit markets had tightened. Many companies had to either exit the merchant trading business at significant losses or risk bankruptcy.

Kansas City–based Aquila was among the U.S. utilities facing such difficult choices. Over 17 years, Aquila had become a diversified utility company with energy trading and international operations. After analyzing the severe deterioration in the operating environment, Aquila decided to return to its roots as a regulated utility, liquidating its positions, posting needed collateral, and refinancing its debt. Because of the complexity and uncertainty of these actions, the company entered a "quiet mode" until it could communicate specifics and a timeline for success.

Absent any information, stakeholders and the media began to paint Aquila with the same brush as scandal-ridden energy companies such as Enron and El Paso, although there was no evidence of fraud at the company. Investors began to sell their holdings and creditors began to reconsider their loans. Some questioned the continued involvement of

Courtesy Aquila

Chairman/CEO Rick Green, whose family had founded/directed the firm for more than 80 years. Aquila's stock price fell, hovering around the $1 delisting mark.

Research

Aquila asked Edelman to help it create and implement a communications strategy that would manage perceptions of its diverse stakeholders to help buy the necessary time to complete its restructuring.

The Aquila/Edelman team identified key audiences as equity and debt holders, creditors, regulators, employees, and the media. Realizing each audience required different messages, the team initiated significant research. Research centered around a two-phased framework marking key milestones: Phase 1: Communication CPR (cardio pulmonary resuscitation) and Overcoming Financial Hurdles, and Phase 2: Re-energizing the Aquila Story.

Phase 1: To evaluate stakeholders' mindsets, the team conducted a perception audit. The study found confusion among some shareholders. Several investors and analysts did not realize that Rick Green had succeeded his brother as CEO and had developed a detailed strategic plan to confront Aquila's problems. Next, the team conducted an extensive media analysis to analyze reporters' perceptions of Aquila's situation. The team also researched communications best practices of companies that had undergone restructurings. Once Phase I was underway, the team conducted a second perception audit to gauge progress and redirect efforts.

Phase 2: Prior to the annual meeting, the Aquila/Edelman team initiated extensive research and analysis to assess the shareholder landscape on "hot topics," such as ISS voting recommendations (Institutional Shareholder Services provides proxy voting and corporate governance services), shareholder proxy battles, executive compensation, and options expensing. The team also researched Aquila's largest shareholders to determine the best approach to communicating with them.

During this time, the Federal Energy Regulatory Commission (FERC is an independent agency that regulates the interstate transmission of electricity, natural gas, and oil) was conducting analysis into the collapse of the wholesale energy trading market. Aquila would be named in its report (they had one incident of irregular pricing). To understand the situation better, the team conducted a number of soft-soundings with local, state, and federal government officials.

Planning

The Aquila/Edelman team provided communications support as CEO Green and his management navigated through a number of intricately connected milestones:

Phase 1: Communication CPR and Overcoming Financial Hurdles

a. Renewing a revolving line of credit.

b. Defending the stock price when announcing Aquila's 2002 year-end and Fourth Quarter earnings.

Phase 2: Reenergizing the Aquila Story

a. Successfully executing Aquila's annual meeting, in which CEO/Chairman Rick Green would stand for re-election.

b. Managing potential outcomes of a national regulatory inquiry on fraudulent transactions known as "wash trades."

As it was almost impossible to determine when potential outcomes might occur, each milestone required its own strategic plan built off the preceding one's resolution. The Aquila/Edelman team's research led to this approach:

Phase 1:

a. Make every effort to demonstrate open communications, giving stakeholders confidence they were receiving timely, complete information.

b. Balance news about difficult near-term actions with information on Aquila management's longer-term strategy for restoring the company's financial health.

Phase 2:

a. Increase management's contacts with key stakeholders as a means to build credibility.

b. Mitigate any information that associated Aquila with the wash trade scandal.

Phase 1: As part of the strategy, the team worked with management to strengthen information sharing among key players at Aquila. The Aquila/Edelman team arranged an info-summit of key corporate-level executives and staff from investor relations (IR), government affairs, and media relations. Result: An agreement on objectives, messaging, and clearer understanding of the audience needs and upcoming milestones. With the earnings announcement held hostage to renewing a revolving line of credit, Aquila needed to decide whether to delay the earnings announcement in advance or wait in hopes that the credit would be approved on time. If it wasn't, Aquila would announce late earnings. Aquila would also receive a Letter of Going Concern from auditors if the financing package was not approved. As a result, the team created strategic communications plans for each scenario to evaluate the best course of action.

Phase 2: With CEO Green personally committed to rebuilding the company's credibility, the team implemented plans to make shareholder communications more direct and targeted. The Aquila/Edelman team conducted research on concentrations of shareholders and, in advance of the annual meeting, helped plan and conduct road shows in which Mr. Green responded to their questions in direct, candid terms. For the FERC report, the team created press releases and scenario plans evaluating when and how Aquila should respond to the expected report.

Execution

Phase 1: Since the Aquila/Edelman strategy was to resume more active communication, the team leveraged a small regulatory announcement to begin the communications initiative. First, the Aquila/Edelman team helped create a presentation that explained Aquila's entire restructuring and business plan, to be posted on the company's website. The team distributed a release about the regulatory decision, directing all audiences to the website PowerPoint document for complete information. The team also resolved the earnings announcement dilemma by noting in the release that the revolving credit was on track and that earnings would be announced once it was completed, thereby setting expectations of late reporting within a positive context. For the annual report, the chairman's letter was direct and forthright about past problems while emphasizing his plan for securing the company's future. The team then created an integrated employee communications protocol to brief the top 20–30 senior managers one day prior to any external communications effort. The team also briefed key reporters in advance, especially the local *Kansas City Star,* which had been exceptionally critical.

Phase 2: Road shows were organized in a Town Hall format. Meetings began with Mr. Green promising to answer every question. Once their issues were on the table, shareholders were willing to listen as Mr. Green addressed time frames for the restructuring. The Aquila/Edelman team created messaging documents, presentations, and a Q&A to prepare for each meeting, and Mr. Green also received message training and a briefing session with a conflict resolution consultant. As the annual meeting approached, shareholders demonstrated growing confidence in Aquila's business plan and Mr. Green's ability to implement it. Finally, as the FERC Report was issued, the Aquila/Edelman team issued the company's response simultaneously with the FERC announcement to minimize misunderstanding or damage to Aquila's reputation.

Evaluation

Phase 1: Aquila's management team successfully renegotiated the company's line of credit, avoiding a Letter of Going Concern (goal 1a). The company also avoided negative response (widespread equity sell-off) to announcing late earnings (goal 1b). Following the announcement the stock rose 13 percent. A second perception study showed the opening of communications and issuance of the strategic business plan were well received by stakeholders. While stakeholders were not always happy with business decisions, communications helped mitigate negative reactions and even won supporters. Key messages were included in media coverage (the *Kansas City Star* even began to paint Aquila in a more positive light) and analyst reports.

Phase 2: The chairman won strong endorsements and support for his openness and directness with stakeholders. He was reelected as chairman of the board at the company's annual meeting with a more than 95 percent affirmative vote (goal 2a), and Aquila was rarely mentioned in media coverage on the FERC inquiry (goal 2b). Ultimately, this vote of confidence in Aquila's plan earned the company the needed time to execute on strategy and return the company to its roots. Aquila's stock price has risen from a 52-week low of $1.07 on March 12, 2003, to attain recently a 52-week high of $4.50.

EXHIBIT 7-2A   *Fact Sheet*

Fact Sheet

(Background information for use in discussion with audience.)

Prepaid natural gas supply contracts termination:

*BACKGROUND: In 1999 and 2000 the company's unregulated business, Aquila Merchant Services (AMS), entered into six prepaid natural gas supply contracts. These prepaid natural gas supply contracts were with public agencies that had the ability to borrow money at low interest rates to purchase natural gas for resale to communities and towns in their service area, generally limited to a few states. AMS was paid in advance (prepaid) for the full term of these natural gas supply contracts, which generally expire in 2010-2012. To protect themselves, these public agencies required AMS to purchase an insurance or surety bond that provides for a termination payment by the sureties to the public agencies in the event of default by AMS. AMS is also required to repay or indemnify the surety in the event of default and payment by the surety as described above. In the contracts now being terminated, **Chubb Group of Insurance Companies and St. Paul Travelers** are the sureties that provided the insurance bond.*

- The company is taking two separate actions:

  1. It is settling with the Chubb Group of Insurance Companies and St. Paul Travelers on **four** prepaid natural gas supply contracts. These four contracts represent 92 percent of Aquila's prepaid natural gas obligations.

  2. It is initiating the process to terminate **three** prepaid natural gas supply contracts; two with APEA (American Public Energy Agency) and one with MGAM (Municipal Gas Authority of Mississippi).

- The settlement agreements include the following:

  * Aquila will provide $485 million to Chubb in support of the surety bonds for two contracts with APEA.

  * This is not a new payment. This amount is already escrowed as a result of the court ruling in the Chubb litigation. The proceeds will be placed into a new escrow facility and will be released to APEA upon conclusion of the termination process of the two contracts between AMS and APEA.

  * Aquila and Chubb jointly filed with the U.S. District Court for the Western District of Missouri to dismiss the current litigation between the two companies.

Courtesy Aquila

EXHIBIT 7-2A   *Fact Sheet (continued)*

* Aquila will provide $90 million to St. Paul Travelers in support of the surety bonds on the MGAM contract. This settlement further requires that Aquila will immediately provide $25 million in support of the surety bond held by St. Paul Travelers on another APEA contract and take additional actions in the coming months to support the remaining position under this bond.

- Aquila has offered to arrange for an alternate natural gas supplier to APEA and MGAM, and is prepared to assist with an orderly transition to a new supplier.

- The three prepaid natural gas supply contracts represent 75 percent of Aquila's prepaid natural gas contract obligations.

- There are three remaining long-term prepaid natural gas supply contracts. Two are with APEA and the third is with MGAG (Municipal Gas Authority of Georgia). Aquila will continue to perform under these contracts and will continue to analyze future options.

Financing/Capital Markets:

- The company is updating its SEC shelf registration statement and will make similar filings with the FERC and with state regulatory agencies.

- The shelf registration statement with the SEC gives the company standby authority to issue up to $712.5 million in securities.

- Accessing the capital markets has always been a part of the company's repositioning plan. However, it is difficult to judge the timing of regulatory approval. In the past, it has taken from 30 days to eleven months.

- When approved, these applications will ensure access to the capital market over the next two years.

EXHIBIT 7-2B   *Key Messages*

Key Messages

<u>Key Messages</u>

(For use in framing discussions with key audiences)

Key Audiences:
- Media
- Financial Analysts
- Employees
- Customers
- Suppliers/Vendors
- Regulators
- Key legislators
- Key State Officials

1. The actions the company is taking are all **part of its financial repositioning plan that has been underway since 2002.**

2. The long-term goal of the repositioning plan is to return Aquila to an investment grade rating. That plan remains balanced with the **continued focus on providing safe and reliable service to our customers.**

3. The settlement with Chubb Group of Insurance Companies and St. Paul Travelers **allows the company to move forward** with its plan to terminate prepaid natural gas supply contracts with American Public Energy Agency (APEA) and Municipal Gas Authority of Mississippi (MGAM).

4. **Aquila is using a win-win approach** to settle three prepaid natural gas supply contracts. The company is offering to arrange for an alternate gas supplier to APEA and MGAM.

5. The beginning of the process to terminate the prepaid natural gas supply contracts and the settlements with Chubb and St. Paul Travelers are clear examples that Aquila is continuing to execute on its repositioning plan. **It is a company that does what it says it will do.**

6. These efforts also further strengthen Aquila's financial resources as the company continues to provide reliable, customer-focused energy service. The **actions being taken require no changes in current operations or workforce levels.**

7. Beginning the process to terminate the contracts with Lincoln, Neb.-based APEA will **not affect the service** the company's Nebraska-based utility provides to its 190,000 natural gas customers in the state.

Courtesy Aquila

## Chapter 8

Consumer Relations

A development almost as significant to business as the Industrial Revolution has been the "Age of the Consumer." This emphasis on consumerism began with the establishment of the National Consumers League in 1899. It received added impetus with the establishment of the Consumers Union and the publication of *Consumer Reports* in 1936. The creation of government regulatory agencies such as the Food and Drug Administration (FDA) and the Federal Trade Commission (FTC) added to the movement's impact, and consumerism finally came of age with the installation of a consumer affairs adviser in the White House during the presidency of John F. Kennedy.

Today, no corporation can ignore the need for a fully functioning program in consumer relations, or, as it is often known, consumer affairs. The ROPE process model is a useful means of preparing and executing a consumer relations program.

RESEARCH

Research for consumer relations includes investigation of the client, the reason for the program, and the consumer audiences to be targeted for communication.

Client Research

In the case of consumer relations, client research will be centered on the organization's reputation in its dealings with consumers. How credible is the organization with activist consumer groups? Has it been a frequent target of their attacks? What are its past and present consumer relations practices? Does it have a viable program in place? What are its major strengths and weaknesses in this area? What opportunities exist to enhance the organization's reputation and credibility in consumer affairs? The answers to these questions will provide a reasonably complete background for further development of a consumer relations program.

Opportunity or Problem Research

Explanation and justification of the need for a consumer relations program is part of the research process. The need grows out of the client research phase in determining past and present dealings with consumers. If problems already exist, a reactive program will be necessary. If there are no problems with consumers at the moment, the practitioner should consider preparing a proactive program. The organization's "wellness" in its relations with consumers should be made a matter of priority concern to management. Also, opportunities and challenges are often connected to the competition faced by the organization. For example, other companies are vying for the same audience by capturing market share or consumer loyalty.

Audience Research

The final aspect of research consists of identifying and examining audiences to be targeted in a consumer relations program. These audiences usually include:

Company employees
Customers
   Professionals
   Middle class
     Working class
     Minorities
     Other

Activist consumer groups

Consumer publications

Community media — mass and specialized

Community leaders and organizations

Information about the customer groups and activist consumer groups should be of particular interest. Their attitudes and behaviors toward the company and their media habits are especially important.

OBJECTIVES

Consumer relations programs may use both impact and output objectives.

Impact Objectives

Some likely examples of impact objectives are:

1. To increase consumers' knowledge about the company's products, services, and policies (by 30 percent during the current year)
2. To promote (30 percent) more favorable consumer opinion toward the company (before December 1)
3. To stimulate (15 percent) greater participation in the company's consumer relations programs (this year)
4. To encourage more positive feedback (20 percent) from consumer groups to the company's programs (in the coming year)

Output Objectives

Output objectives for consumer relations involve the practitioner's measurable communication efforts with targeted audiences:

1. To distribute (10 percent) more consumer publications during the period June 1–August 31
2. To develop three employee consumer seminars for this fiscal year
3. To meet with five important consumer groups during the next six months
4. To prepare and distribute recipes for using the product to 12 major food editors in the state during the campaign

PROGRAMMING

Programming for consumer relations includes planning the theme and messages, action or special event(s), uncontrolled and controlled media, and effective communication principles to execute the program.

Theme and Messages

The theme and messages will grow out of the consumer relations situation and will reflect research findings and objectives for the program.

Action(s) or Special Event(s)

Organizational actions and special events in a consumer relations program generally include:

1. Advising management and all employees about consumer issues

2. Developing an efficient consumer response system

3. Handling specific consumer complaints through a customer relations office

4. Creating a company ombudsman, whose role is the investigation and resolution of complaints

5. Maintaining liaison with external activist consumer groups

6. Monitoring federal and state regulatory agencies and consumer legislation that might affect the company

7. Developing emergency plans for a product recall

8. Establishing a consumer education program, including meetings, information racks with printed materials on product uses, training tapes on product uses, celebrity endorsements and tours, and paid advertising on consumer topics

9. Holding employee consumerism conferences, seminars, and/or field training.

These actions and events form the basis of a thorough consumer relations program.

Uncontrolled and Controlled Media

Community, and sometimes state or national, media should be targeted for appropriate news releases, photo opportunities or photographs, interviews, and other forms of uncontrolled materials reporting the company's actions or events in consumer affairs.

Controlled media for a consumer relations program usually include printed materials on the effective use of the company's products or on health, safety, or other consumer-oriented topics. In addition, specific printed materials are developed for meetings, conferences, and other special events. Audiovisual materials such as training videos and DVDs are often used as vehicles for consumer education. One of the most important mechanisms for effective consumer communication is the company website. This can contain virtually unlimited amounts of information useful to consumers. The cases included in this chapter illustrate a variety of forms of both uncontrolled and controlled media.

Finally, interpersonal communication should play a significant role in any consumer relations program. Ideally, the company can employ a consumer affairs spokesperson whose tasks may include conferring with consumer groups, addressing community organizations, or even representing the company in mass media appearances, including paid consumer advertising. Interpersonal communications should also be used generously in the company's consumer response system, its customer relations office, and other meetings and conferences in the consumer relations program.

Effective Communication

The principles of special interest for effective communication in consumer relations are source credibility, two-way communication, and audience participation.

A major purpose of consumer relations programs is credibility enhancement. For example, Giant grocery chain employs a consumer adviser who produces a "weekly column" for radio stations and listens to customers. One woman held the position for more than 25 years and captured considerable name recognition and credibility for her nutritional and shopping information.

Consumers are increasingly quality conscious in their purchases of goods and services. To cite another prominent example, U.S. automobile manufacturers have suffered a loss of public confidence and credibility in comparison with the high-quality standards of their Japanese competitors. Because of this stiff overseas competition, the U.S. companies have been forced to improve their quality controls, their warranties, and their treatment of consumers in general. Once lost, corporate credibility is difficult to rebuild, but effective programs in consumer relations can be a decisive factor in that rebuilding process.

Two-way communication and audience participation go hand in hand in consumer relations. There can be no substitute for direct, interpersonal communication in some situations. The proper treatment of consumers demands that their grievances be heard and, in most cases, personally resolved. The most effective consumer education programs are those that go beyond mere distribution of literature on store information racks. The best programs involve the consumer personally in meetings, interviews, conferences, and/or other interpersonal presentations that allow audience feedback and participation.

EVALUATION

There are no surprises and nothing out of the ordinary in the evaluation of consumer relations programs. The practitioner uses the previously discussed methods to evaluate the program's stated objectives.

Measures of reputation and sales are frequent mainstays of evaluating successful programs.

SUMMARY

Research for consumer relations concentrates on an organization's reputation with its consumers and on the reason for conducting a program of this kind. In some instances, the consumer publics are segmented, with different messages and media designed for communication with each group.

Consumer relations uses both impact and output objectives. Impact objectives propose outcomes that increase consumers' knowledge or influence their attitudes and behaviors. Output objectives propose outcomes in terms of measurable practitioner efforts without regard to impact.

Programming involves organizational actions such as advising management about consumer affairs, developing consumer-oriented programs, and/or holding meetings or conferences about consumerism. Communication for consumer relations includes uncontrolled, controlled, and interpersonal formats, although the use of controlled printed materials is often emphasized. But interpersonal communication is increasingly being used.

Evaluation, as in other forms of public relations, consists of discovering appropriate measurements for the program's stated objectives.

READINGS ON CONSUMER RELATIONS

Abboud, Leila. "Stung by Public Distrust, Drug Makers Seek to Heal Image," *Wall Street Journal* 40 (August 26, 2005): sec. B.

Baher, Connie. "Keeping Your Customers Satisfied," *Small Business Reports* (February 1992): 16 ff.

Beaupre, Andre. "Getting Your Customers to Help with Public Relations," *Public Relations Tactics* 10 (October 2003): 9.

Bell, Chip R. *Customers as Partners: Building Relationships That Last.* San Francisco: Berrett-Koehler, 1994.

"Best Practices in Customer Service Communications," *Public Relations Tactics* 5 (July 1998): 10.

Colgate, Mark R., and Peter J. Danaher. "Implementing a Customer Relationship Strategy: The Asymmetric Impact of Poor Versus Excellent Execution," *Journal of the Academy of Marketing Science* 28 (Summer 2000): 375 ff.

Crawford, Alan Pell. "Why We Need to Begin Our Work With a Customer-First Approach," *Public Relations Tactics* 7 (April 2000): 12.

DeVries, Dave. "Oprah's Car Giveaway: Marketing or Public Relations? A PR Pro Decides," *Public Relations Tactics* 11 (December 2004): 9.

"Eat Me, I'm Safe," *Onearth: Environmental Politics People* 27 (fall 2005): 9.

Falbo, Bridget. "Wow Customers with Service to Build Positive PR," *Hotel and Motel Management* 213 (May 4, 1998): 45.

Fornell, Claes. "A Method for Improving Customer Satisfaction and Measuring Its Impact on Profitability," *International Public Relations Review* 15 (1992): 6 ff.

Greene, Richard. "Two Steps to New Product Success," *Public Relations Tactics* 11 (December 2004): 17.

Holtz, Shel. "Establishing Connections," *Communication World* 22 (May–June 2005): 9 ff.

Lesly, Philip. "Consumer Relations." In *Lesly's Handbook of Public Relations and Communications,* 5th ed. New York: AMACOM, 1998.

Pare, Terrence P. "Finding Out What They Want," *Fortune* 128 (1993): 39 ff.

Quick, John, and Anna Dé. "Update to the Direct-to-Consumer Debate: The Risks and Benefits of Pharmaceutical Promotion Across the Atlantic," *Public Relations Strategist* 10 (spring 2004): 29–31.

Rappleye, Willard C., Jr. "Customer Relationship Management," *Across the Board* 37 (July 2000): 47 ff.

Rhea, Darrel. "Understanding Why People Buy," *Business Week Online* (August 15, 2005), http://www.businessweek.com/innovate/content/aug2005/id20050809_077337.htm.

Schneider, Joan. "Countdown To Launch: 10 Lessons Learned About Publicizing New Products," *Public Relations Tactics* 8 (May 2001): 24.

Scott, David Meerman. "The New News Cycle," *EContent* 28 (July–August 2005): 48.

Sjoberg, Goran. "Customer Satisfaction and Quality Control: What's in It for Public Relations Professionals?" *International Public Relations Review* 15 (1992): 5 ff.

Snider, James H. "Consumers in the Information Age," *Futurist* 27 (January–February 1993): 23 ff.

"Target Practice," *Economist* (April 2, 2005): 13 ff.

Thompson, Gary W. "Consumer PR Techniques in the High Tech Arena," *Public Relations Quarterly* 37 (winter 1992): 21–22.

Trudel, Mary R. "Consumer Marketing Synergy: PR Comes of Age," *Public Relations Quarterly* 36 (spring 1991): 26 ff.

Walther, George R. *Upside-Down Marketing.* New York: McGraw-Hill, 1994.

Whitely, Richard. "How to Push Customers Away," *Sales and Marketing Management* (February 1994): 29 ff.

Willing, Paul. "Paul Willing Says . . . Be a Partner with Your Community" *Nursing Homes: Long Term Care Management* 54 (August 2005): 14–16.

Zoda, Suzanne M. "Rebuilding Credibility with a Hostile Public," *Communication World* 10 (October 1993): 17 ff.

CONSUMER RELATIONS CASES

CASE 8-1

Jenn-Air looked for ways to differentiate their brand of kitchen appliances from a crowded list of competitors by partnering with a nonprofit organization. Exhibit 8-1a is a fact sheet on the Share Our Strength partnership, and Exhibit 8-1b is an internal planning memorandum.

A Stronger Way to Sell Appliances

Maytag Jenn-Air with Carmichael Lynch Spong

Situation Analysis

Jenn-Air makes high-performance, beautifully designed kitchen appliances. Just like Wolf, Sub-Zero, Kitchen Aid, and Thermador, the list goes on and on. In late 2002 and 2003, Jenn-Air and its agency of record, Carmichael Lynch Spong (CLS), sought a new way to differentiate the brand's line of top-notch kitchen appliances from the competition. That search led to the doorstep of Share Our Strength (SOS), a national anti-hunger organization that taps top chefs to cater high-ticket charity benefits. In SOS, Jenn-Air saw an opportunity to enhance its brand while turning SOS's stable of top chefs into Jenn-Air ambassadors who would help sell appliances. In late 2002, Jenn-Air signed on as the presenting sponsor of Share Our Strength's Taste of the Nation (TOTN) and asked CLS to help accomplish two tasks: create a point of differentiation by publicizing the sponsorship and help use this sponsorship to sell appliances.

Research

Jenn-Air conducted a segmentation study to analyze market share, target audience, and consumer trends.

Key Findings

- The target responds well to experiential sales initiatives, such as cooking demonstrations and events.
- Charity affiliations are well received among high-end consumers.

Courtesy Jenn-Air

Audience Analysis Consumers

- Adults 25–54, $100,000+ HHI (Household Income)
- Skews female

Influencers

- Appliance dealers
- Top chefs
- Designers

Media

- Home/shelter magazines
- Epicurean magazines
- Consumer print and broadcast media
- Design and building trade magazines

Planning

Positioning

Jenn-Air enhances the style and performance of your kitchen.

Objectives

1. Generate 100 media placements about the Jenn-Air partnership to help build loyalty, goodwill, and point of differentiation among target audience.
2. Turn cause initiative into a 5 percent increase in appliance sales.

Strategies

1. Create a splash for the Jenn-Air Taste of the Nation sponsorship through a high-profile charity auction.
2. Generate media and attendee attention at Share Our Strength's Taste of the Nation events.
3. Bring the benefits of the partnership to retail.

Execution

Strategy 1

Create a high-profile, initial splash for the Jenn-Air Taste of the Nation sponsorship.

The Charity Auction

- Announced the sponsorship by holding a charity auction for a one-of-a-kind Jenn-Air Luxury Series refrigerator designed by fashion designer Nicole Miller.

- Hired Miller to create the one-of-a-kind product. Miller developed a stained-glass refrigerator modeled after the windows of a church near her New York cottage.
- Provided national visibility and opened up access to the product to people throughout the country by hosting the auction online on eBay.
- Drafted and distributed a news release to magazines and daily newspapers announcing the auction and encouraging people to log on and bid on the product.
- Launched the auction by hosting a reception for kitchen designers in Nicole Miller's Los Angeles store.
- Created a broadcast story by developing and distributing a VNR package.

Strategy 2

Generate media and attendee attention at Taste of the Nation events.

Taste of the Nation Launch Event

- Provided live cooking equipment for the 2003 Taste of the Nation media launch event, in which chefs from across the country come and sample regional cuisine.
- Cooking stations included Jenn-Air-branded kiosks highlighting the brand's role as presenting sponsor and developing implied endorsement from chefs.
- Developed PSA to announce the 2003 Taste of the Nation season and Jenn-Air's role as presenting sponsor.

TOTN Cooking Demonstrations

- Hosted cooking demonstrations at Taste of the Nation events in 10 key markets: Atlanta, Boston, Chicago, Denver, Stamford, Conn., Los Angeles, New York, Phoenix, San Francisco, and Washington, D.C.
- Created a traveling kitchen that housed the Jenn-Air products used in the demonstrations.
- Earned implied endorsements by having well-known local chefs prepare food on Jenn-Air appliances.
- Hired moderator to provide product mentions and benefits while chefs conducted demonstrations.
- Created collateral materials to communicate the sponsorship.

Appliance Auction and Donation

- Created goodwill among Taste of the Nation attendees by auctioning the appliances used in the demo at the end of the night. Donated the money raised to local anti-hunger programs.

- Donated appliances to local charities in each of the top 10 markets. Jenn-Air and Share Our Strength publicized these donations in Taste of the Nation event programs and on event signage.
- Distributed news releases announcing donation and how much money was raised through appliance auction.

Strategy 3

Bring the benefits of the partnership to retail.

TOTN Dealer Involvement

- Created a retail aspect to the charity event by involving one local dealer at each event.
- Offered small giveaway items to all attendees. Items, such as stainless steel measuring spoons, featured the Jenn-Air logo as well as name and phone number of local dealer.
- Distributed coupons in attendee goodie bags. Coupons ranged from free financing to thousands of dollars off on full appliance suites.

Dealer Events

- Hosted influencer/consumer events at local appliance dealerships.
- Tapped Taste of the Nation chefs to give cooking demonstrations at the events.
- Arranged for dealers to provide Jenn-Air discounts and Share Our Strength contributions with all appliance purchases.

Charlie Trotter SMT/Dealer Event

- Used SOS tie to secure world-renowned chef Charlie Trotter's presence at a Phoenix dealer event. Had Trotter conduct cooking courses and hold a satellite media tour.

Evaluation

All objectives were exceeded.

Objective 1

Generate 109 media placements to help build loyalty, goodwill, and point of differentiation.

- Result: Secured more than 165 media placements throughout the course of the program, resulting in 66 million gross impressions.
- The Nicole Miller–designed refrigerator auction generated more than 100 media placements and 60 million gross impressions.
- High-profile auction coverage included the *Washington Post,* the *Los Angeles Times,* and a Gannett Newswire story.

- The Luxury Series auction VNR generated more than 250,000 gross impressions, including multiple usages in Los Angeles.
- Sponsorship announcement and postevent news releases resulted in 53 media placements and 6 million impressions.
- PSA generated 100 million gross impressions. Publicity efforts with Chef Trotter delivered 15 broadcast placements and a major print article in the *Arizona Republic*.
- Nicole Miller–designed Luxury Series refrigerator attracted hundreds of page views on eBay. Bids for the refrigerator exceeded $6,500.
- Appliance auction raised more than $30,000 for anti-hunger charities in the top 10 markets.
- Donated an additional $25,000 in product to local grant recipients.

Objective 2

Turn cause initiative into a 5 percent increase in appliance sales.

- Result: Helped increase unit sales by 7 percent, more than doubling the appliance industry's 3.2 percent unit sales growth. In addition, Jenn-Air revenue increased by 15 percent.
- Reached over 50,000 consumers at 2003 Taste of the Nation events.
- Distributed 36,215 coupons at Taste of the Nation events.
- Return on dealer coupons reached $50,900 within a month after Taste events ended. Given a 12-month appliance purchase cycle, Jenn-Air expects that number to at least triple.

EXHIBIT 8-1A *Share Our Strength Fact Sheet*

June 24, 2003

Jenn-Air®/Share Our Strength Team Up to Fight Hunger

FACT SHEET

Overview:

In 2003, Jenn-Air® is partnering with Share Our Strength, one of the country's leading anti-hunger organizations, to fight hunger in North America. As a co-presenting sponsor of Taste of the Nation, Jenn-Air joins American Express to host a large-scale culinary benefit in major cities throughout the country. Each event will raise money for anti-hunger and anti-poverty programs.

Key Elements:

Taste of the Nation rallies chefs and community leaders to put their talents to work at more than 100 culinary events in 65 cities across the United States. The event has raised nearly $70 million since its inception 15 years ago, and all proceeds support projects that work to end hunger.

In the partnership with Share Our Strength, Jenn-Air saw a unique opportunity to raise awareness of an important cause that resonates with its core consumers. Jenn-Air's sponsorship will include appliance auctions and donations at events throughout the country. In addition, chefs will use Jenn-Air appliances during cooking demonstrations at select Taste of the Nation events.

A brand in the family of Maytag Appliances, Jenn-Air produces a full line of high-end kitchen appliances, including refrigerators, ranges, cooktops, dishwashers and wall ovens. For more information on Jenn-Air's kitchen products, call 1-800-JENN-AIR or visit jennair.com.

source:
Maytag Corporation
403 W. 4th St. N.
Newton, Iowa 50208 USA
http://www.maytagcorp.com

contact:
Jill Spiekerman
Jenn-Air
641-787-6886
jspiek@maytag.com

David Kargas
Carmichael Lynch Spong
720-946-6342
dkargas@clynch.com

From downdraft cooktops, wall ovens and Pro-Style ® ranges to dishwashers, refrigerators and entertaining essentials, Jenn-Air offers a full line of built-in kitchen appliances. Consumers interested in more information on Jenn-Air kitchen products, a part of the complete collection of brands offered by Maytag headquartered in Newton, Iowa, should visit www.jennair.com or call 1-800-JENN-AIR.

Courtesy Jenn-Air

EXHIBIT 8-1B *Planning Memo*

Share Our Strength PR ideas for 2004

<u>Media Relations Ideas</u>

The Local Tastes Campaign

- Conduct regional searches for the best recipe from a home cook that uses local ingredients and conveys a local flavor
    - o Tap top chefs or food network personalities to serve as judges
    - o Have local winner conduct one of the market's cooking demonstrations
    - o Consider awarding local winner a Jenn-Air-branded table at Taste of the Nation where they can serve the award-winning recipe
    - o Publicize the contest through local market media relations

Taste of Your Neighborhood

- Offer Taste of the Nation attendees the opportunity to bid on an outdoor dinner party/picnic catered by a Taste chef
    - o Bring the Jenn-Air truck to the winner's neighborhood or a public place that is convenient for the auction winner
    - o Have chef cook a special dinner for winner's family and friends from the Jenn-Air truck
    - o Pitch photo-op to dailies and broadcast outlets

The Ultimate Remodel Auction Package

- Create an auction package that combines a full suite of Jenn-Air products along with the services of a top local designer
    - o Provide winning bidder with choice of up to $10,000 in Jenn-Air products along with $10,000 in designer's time
    - o Shoot before and after photography at the home
    - o Encourage bidding by promoting auction prior to Taste of the Nation through inserts in invitations and media relations
    - o Pitch transformed home to national shelter magazines, local newspapers and city books

Courtesy Carmichael Lynch Spong

The Celebrity Chef "Kitchen Warming" Campaign

- Remodel the home kitchens of well known Taste of the Nation chefs with Jenn-Air products, using the remodels as a way to reach shelter publications
  - Work with Share Our Strength to identify chefs who may be interested in remodeling their kitchen
  - Offer chefs free Jenn-Air products in exchange for right to pitch kitchens to national shelter publications
  - Create local news and culinary media story by having chefs host charity dinner party at their redesigned place

The Art of Fighting Hunger Campaign

- Have three celebrity chefs develop limited-edition bowls and pitchers for the new Jenn-Air Attrezzi Small Appliance
  - Shoot for top-name chefs such as Wolfgang Puck, Charlie Trotter or Stephen Pyles
  - Enlist one or two retail partners to be exclusive sellers of special product
  - Donate portion of sales to fight against hunger
  - Auction personally autographed originals at key market Taste of the Nation events
  - Introduce custom product with media relations

Jenn-Air Lifetime Achievement Award

- Honor one longtime volunteer with the Jenn-Air Anti-Hunger Lifetime Achievement Award
  - Seek secret nominations from local grant recipients
  - Bring local finalists to each Taste of the Nation event
  - Surprise one winner during that Taste's formal program (when applicable)
  - Offer winner choice of Jenn-Air products and gift certificate for dinner at top local restaurants
  - Pitch story to local newspapers

Dealer Event Ideas

Follow That Food Events

- Partner with the Food Network's Gordon Elliott to host version of his Follow that Food at dealers prior to Taste events
- Pair Elliott with local chef to give cooking demonstration and explain key local ingredients
- Consider hosting events in parking lot of dealership, using Jenn-Air truck as forum
- Sell tickets to Taste of the Nation and new Jenn-Air branded Taste of the Nation cookbooks
- Conduct events in each of the top 10 markets

EXHIBIT 8-1B *Planning Memo (continued)*

Jenn-Air Wine Tastings

- Host pre-Taste wine tastings at high-end wine stores
    - Partner with well regarded local wine shops
    - Raffle or auction stocked Jenn-Air Wine Chiller, with proceeds benefiting Share Our Strength
    - Invite interior designers and architects
    - Set-up kitchen vignette for designers to see new Jenn-Air products

Grocery Store Demos

- Bring the Jenn-Air truck to parking lots of gourmet grocery stores
    - Offer cooking demonstrations from known local chefs
    - Give away or sell tickets to Taste of the Nation
    - Pitch truck presence to local broadcast outlets

Frito-Lay developed a novel approach to introduce a new product when the market was dominated by a long-term rival. Exhibit 8-2a is a news release and Exhibit 8-2b is a photo of the Stax Challenge.

Lay's Stax Challenge

Frito-Lay with Ketchum Entertainment Marketing

Situation Analysis

Following a sizable corporate investment, Frito-Lay was ready to introduce its much-anticipated new Lay's Stax—stacked potato crisps in a portable, resealable, crush-resistant container—to consumers nationwide. The challenge?

How do you break into a completely new product category (stackable chips) and go head-to-head with a formidable competitor (P&G's Pringles) that has long dominated the market? Even more challenging, public relations rather than advertising was chosen to introduce the product to consumers during the first two weeks of launch. The solution? Knowing that it would be a tall order to secure verbal "Lay's Stax" messages via editorial media coverage, Ketchum Entertainment Marketing (KEM) staged a larger-than-life, visually branded media launch event that would make it hard for consumers and the media to ignore Lay's Stax's entry into the stackable chip marketplace. In addition, rather than taking its cue from Pringle's marketing playbook, KEM provided a fresh and innovative platform for Lay's Stax by negotiating a partnership with the Speed Stacks organization and the hot new sport of cup stacking. Taking place in the center of New York City's Times Square, the Lay's Stax launch event brought kids "with the fastest hands" together to attempt to set the sport's first-ever Guinness World Records™ and set up a visually branded event that communicated Lay's Stax "stackable chip" message to the public. The end result was an "over-the-top" launch event that: (1) generated "full court" media attention, (2) met objectives via a built-in branded imagery strategy, (3) allowed public relations to take the place of advertising, and (4) positioned Lay's Stax as a formidable new competitor.

Research

Consumer Target Research: Mediamark Research (MRI) confirmed that significant percentages of the "married with children" target, broken down by personal and "youngest child" age range, indicated that they attended "any sporting event at least once a month": 28 percent ages 35–49, married, youngest child is between 12 and 17; 24 percent ages 35–49, married, youngest child is between 6 and 11; 19 percent ages 18–34, married, youngest child is between 6 and 17.

The findings against the Frito-Lay consumer target suggested a strong interest in "all family," sport-related activities.

Partner Research

Based on the MRI data against the consumer target, KEM researched youth-oriented sports and family activities to uncover a fresh platform that would reach the target and reinforce the product's "stacked" messaging. Based on that research, KEM selected the Speed Stacks organization, the founding organization of the new sport of cup stacking, as the launch partner. The sport's family focus and the fact that cup stacking was an exciting individual and team sport where participants stack and unstack 12 specially designed plastic cups (Speed Stacks) at lightning speeds, provided KEM with the insight to use it as a platform to launch Lay's Stax. KEM also learned that cup stacking had generated international interest and was poised to do the same in the United States. Finally, cup stacking, unlike soccer or other standard youth sports, was not saturated with corporate brand tie-ins. The end result was a groundbreaking brand partnership that celebrated the product's family target.

Competitive Research

In order to gauge the competitive landscape, KEM researched the media coverage for rival brand Pringles. The insight? Pringles marketing was primarily focused on targeting teens. Teen-focused advertising and promotional partnerships with New Line's *Lord of the Rings* film series confirmed this research. Based on the information, the team concluded that in order to launch Lay's Stax effectively, the brand would have to directly appeal to the consumer target in a unique and innovative way to differentiate itself from Pringles.

Spokesperson Research

Understanding the need for a celebrity personality to both host the New York launch event and provide an added media draw, KEM conducted research to secure a celebrity that would: (1) resonate with the consumer and (2) make a logical companion to the Speed Stacking organization.

Based on this research, KEM approached television personality and comedienne Caroline Rhea to host the event: Rhea became a household name due to her daily talk show targeted to moms, *The Caroline Rhea Show*. Rhea was also familiar with the sport because several cup stackers had previously been guests on her show. Ultimately, the choice of working with Rhea provided the brand with a family-friendly association with a talent who appealed to the target demographic and made logical sense to deliver key messages at the event.

Planning

Objectives

1. Generate more than 20 million media impressions for the launch of new Lay's Stax (with a broadcast media focus) during the first two weeks of launch.
2. During the first two weeks of launch, secure a minimum of $2 million in PR-generated advertising equivalency.
3. Drive Lay's Stax sales to meet company projections at launch.
4. Deliver Lay's Stax branded imagery in at least 75 percent of launch media coverage.

Audiences

1. Established by Frito-Lay and the Lay's brand team, the primary target was adults 25–54, with children
2. The secondary audience was national/major-market broadcast/print consumer media

Strategies

1. Create a visual launch event to generate branded media coverage for the product launch prior to the start of national advertising
2. Partner with an up-and-coming youth/family–targeted organization that would reinforce the "stacked" product message
3. Secure a family friendly celebrity to add credibility and enhance the event's news appeal

Execution

To ensure the success of the Lay's Stax launch, KEM worked with the Speed Stacks organization, the city of New York, the NASDAQ Tower, and the Guinness Book of World Records™ to create an event that would make the brand's market introduction hard to ignore.

Event Visual Branding/Backdrop

To celebrate the launch of Lay's Stax, the brand brought the fastest hands together in New York City's Times Square to set the first-ever Guinness World Records™ in the new sport of cup stacking. KEM transformed the event into a visually branded powerhouse by creating a stage setting that reinforced the product/brand message via compelling backdrops, branded T-shirts, and oversized pyramids made entirely of Lay's Stax containers. To make the launch event "bigger," Lay's Stax created a seven-story-high Lay's Stax canister with the help of the NASDAQ Tower in Times Square. The 120-foot-tall, 84-foot-wide Lay's Stax canister caught the attention of New Yorkers as well as the snack food world. Lay's Stax also took the city of New York by storm with a Lay's Stax street team distributing thousands of product samples in high-traffic locations. The team gave away more than 5,000 canisters of Lay's Stax and helped get the word out to the public.

Event Partnerships

By creating a Lay's Stax partnership with the Speed Stacks organization, the brand was able to communicate a "stack" message that was synonymous with the product. The partnership also provided access to a previously untapped family-oriented youth sport and provided a platform for a media event that reinforced the product's "stacked" messaging. The team also negotiated the participation of celebrity host Caroline Rhea (*The Caroline Rhea Show*) and aligned the event with Guinness World Records™ for added media value.

Launch/Event Media

The team outreached to media with Lay's Stax product deliveries and information inviting them to witness the record-breaking attempt. The morning of the event, Speed Stacking World Record holder Emily Fox appeared on CBS's *The Early Show* to demonstrate her skills. With the help of Lay's Stax, the local outreach attracted New Yorkers and media alike to Times Square (five out of six local stations in New York attended the event, which is a rarity) where 16-year-old Emily Fox set the first-ever Guinness World Records™ in the sport of cup stacking. B-roll video and wire photos were created and distributed to make the Lay's Stax launch a national event.

Evaluation

Objective 1

Generate more than 20 million media impressions (broadcast focused) for the launch of new Lay's Stax during the first two weeks of launch: The event generated 36,063,732+ media impressions—an important task, since the brand's advertising was not yet in rotation. Broadcast-focused media hits included CBS's *The Early Show, ABC World News Now, The O'Reilly Factor, FOX News Live, FOX & Friends First, Up to the Minute, FOX Report,* and more than 100 major market broadcast hits.

Objective 2

During first two weeks of launch, secure a minimum of $2 million in PR-generated advertising equivalency: The launch of Lay's Stax generated a media equivalency of approximately $4,400,319, more than double the original goal and a 1 in 12 return on investment.

Objective 3

Drive Lay's Stax sales to meet company projections at launch: With public relations serving as the primary brand sales driver (since national advertising began rotation two weeks after the event), sales of Lay's Stax met projections during the first two weeks of launch. This was confirmed by the product's mention as a growth driver in PepsiCo's 2003 third-quarter earnings report. In addition, just two weeks after launch, Lay's Stax pound share of the market increased from 1.1 percent to 8.4 percent.

Objective 4

Deliver Lay's Stax branded imagery in at least 75 percent of launch media coverage: Lay's Stax branded messaging was visually present in 100 percent of the placements related to the program—exceeding the message delivery goal by 25 percent.

EXHIBIT 8-2A   *News Release*

Frito-Lay Introduces New Lay's Stax Potato Crisps

Plano, TX (August 14, 2003) – Starting next week, Frito-Lay begins rolling out Lay's Stax, potato crisps stacked in a portable, resealable, crush-resistant container with an irresistible taste people have come to expect from the Lay's brand. Full nationwide distribution expected by the end of August.

"Lay's Stax potato crisps offer the great taste that consumers expect from Lay's, America's favorite potato chip," says Stephen Quinn, chief marketing officer, Frito-Lay. "Its convenient packaging also expands the Lay's brand's already broad appeal to a new audience."

Lay's Stax crisps are a fun, neat-to-eat snack that is convenient to throw in your bag when on the go or to enjoy at home – and their unique shape makes them great for dipping. The crunchy crisps in the easy to grip upright canister combines innovative packaging, the powerful appeal of the Lay's brand and Frito-Lay's powerful DSD system.

"Our superior frontline sales force will be placing Lay's Stax potato crisps on store shelves across the nation," said Tom Greco, senior vice president, sales, Frito-Lay North America. "This means consumers will have an unmatched snack experience available on a daily basis."

Lay's Stax crisps will be available on store shelves nationwide in four flavors Original, Sour Cream & Onion, Barbecue and Cheddar, with Original in 6 oz. and the flavors in 5 3/4 oz. canisters. Lay's Stax potato crisps is another Frito-Lay offering with zero grams of trans fat.

"Lay's Stax proprietary package provides better breakage protection," said Rocco Papalia, senior vice president, Research & Development, Frito-Lay North America. "By offering a brand new snack experience from Frito-Lay -- great tasting crisps in a uniquely convenient canister – we've given consumers more reasons to enjoy our snacks."

Lay's Stax crisps will be supported by a fully integrated launch program including print and television advertising as well as coupon inserts, product sampling and in-store merchandising. The television advertising will feature Dana Carvey as different characters in an entertaining commercial showing how creative you can get with a "deck" of Lay's Stax potato crisps. The :30 spot, created by longtime ad agency BBDO New York, is set to break on September 21, 2003 during the Emmy Awards.
Frito-Lay is the convenient fun foods division of PepsiCo, Inc., which is headquartered in Purchase, NY. Frito-Lay makes and sells some of America's favorite snack brands including Lay's potato chips, Ruffles potato chips, Doritos tortilla chips, Tostitos tortilla chips and Cheetos cheese-flavored snacks. The company also offers a wide variety of low-fat, reduced fat and no-fat snacks like Baked Doritos, Baked Lay's, Baked Ruffles, Baked Tostitos, Ruffles Reduced Fat and its Natural line, WOW! line, and Rold Gold pretzels. The company also makes and sells Cracker Jack snacks, Quaker Chewy granola bars, Quaker Fruit and Oatmeal bars, Gatorade energy bars and Quakes rice snacks.

Courtesy Frito-Lay

EXHIBIT 8-2B *Photograph of Stax Challenge*

Children compete in the first-ever Guinness World Records™ sport of cup stacking in New York City's Times Square.

Courtesy Frito-Lay

## Chapter 9

International Public Relations

During the past several decades, international public relations has become a major concern of practitioners. The two principal aspects of this field are counseling domestic clients in their programs to reach markets or audiences in other countries and counseling foreign clients, both corporate and governmental, in their efforts to communicate with American audiences.

International public relations problems should be approached using the ROPE process.

RESEARCH

The research process for international public relations includes understanding the client, the opportunity or problem involved, and the audiences to be reached.

Client Research

A thorough investigation of the client will begin with background information on their nationality or home country. The next need will be for knowledge of the client's reputation and status in the country of its target audiences, along with past and present public relations practices in that country. Finally, the client's public relations strengths and weaknesses in the host country should be assessed.

Opportunity or Problem Research

In this phase of research, the practitioner should determine why and to what extent the client needs an international public relations program. The program may be either reactive, in response to a problem experienced in the host country, or proactive in the interest of establishing a presence and creating goodwill in the host country.

Audience Research

Whether domestic or foreign, the client—and, more important, the practitioner representing the client—must understand various aspects of the target audience, including the language and its centrality to the culture of the host country, its cultural values, patterns of thought, customs, communication styles—both verbal and nonverbal, and the target audience's cultural norms. In addition, the public relations practitioner must become acquainted with the host country's various systems: legal, educational, political, and economic. Moreover, knowledge of the host country's social structure, heritage, and, particularly, its business practices will greatly benefit communicating with target audiences. Finally, audience information levels regarding the client and its products or services, audience attitudes and behaviors relevant to the client, and specific audience demographics and media use levels should be gathered as part of the research for an international public relations program.

As in audience research for community relations, international practitioners will need to investigate and understand the media, leaders, and major organizations of the host country. Collectively or singularly, they will often provide the key to success in communicating with a target international audience. Thus, audiences for international public relations will include those listed in Exhibit 9-a.

EXHIBIT 9-A *International Publics*

Host Country Media

Mass

Specialized

Host Country Leaders

Public officials

Educators

Social leaders

Cultural leaders

Religious leaders

Political leaders

Professionals

Executives

Host Country Organizations

Business

Service

Social

Cultural

Religious

Political

Special interests

OBJECTIVES

International public relations programs may employ both impact and output objectives. They should be both specific and quantitative.

Impact Objectives

Impact objectives for international public relations involve informing target audiences or modifying their attitudes or behaviors. Some possible examples are:

1. To increase (by 20 percent) the international audience's knowledge of the client, its operations, products, or services (during a specific time period)

2. To enhance the client's image (by 15 percent during the current year) with the target international audience

3. To encourage (20 percent) more audience participation in the client's international events (during a particular program)

Output Objectives

Output objectives for international public relations consist of the practitioner's measurable efforts on behalf of the client. They may include such operations as:

1. Preparing and distributing (20 percent) more international publications (than last season)

2. Creating (five) new international projects (during the current calendar year)

3. Scheduling (eight) meetings with international leaders (during a specified time period)

4. Developing (three) special events for the public

PROGRAMMING

Programming for international public relations includes planning a theme and messages, actions or special events, uncontrolled and controlled media, and effective use of communication principles.

Theme and Messages

The nature of the opportunity or problem and the research findings in the situation will govern the messages and theme, if any, to be communicated in the international public relations program. Subtle differences in themes in countries may be required due to translation and cultural factors.

Action(s) or Special Event(s)

Client actions and special events for international programs often include:

1. Sponsorship of cultural exchange programs between the host and the client's countries

2. Establishment of institutes in the host country to teach the language and culture of the client's country

3. Meetings with leaders of the host country

4. Seminars or training programs held in schools, businesses, or institutions in the host country

5. Awards programs honoring leaders and other celebrities of the host country

6. Festivals in the host country celebrating the foods, dress, dance, art, or other aspects of the culture of the client's country. These may coincide with such holidays as creation of the client's country, its independence, victory in key battles or wars, birthdays of its founding fathers or heroes, and so on.

7. Participation of the client organization, its management, and its personnel in the special holidays and events of the host country

A major key to successful international public relations is the client involvement and interaction that actions and special events in the host country can provide.

Uncontrolled and Controlled Media

In international public relations, the practitioner should service the media of the host country with such appropriate uncontrolled media as news releases, interviews with officers of the client organization, and photo opportunities, all centered around the actions or special events composing the program itself.

Controlled media may also use the client's actions and special events as a major focus, with related print materials mailed to a select list of leaders and a speakers bureau created to provide important organizations in the host country with oral presentations from officers of the client organization. Both uncontrolled and controlled media should be centered on the client's involvement with, participation in, and contributions to the interests of the host country.

The client's website may play a significant role in the program. It may provide a wealth of information available in the language of the host country and reflect the client's interest in the host country.

Effective Communication

The most important communication principles involved in the programming of international public relations are source credibility, nonverbal and verbal cues, two-way communication, the use of opinion leaders, group influence, and audience participation.

Nothing is of greater importance in international public relations than the perceived credibility of the client organization in the host country. Target audiences must believe that the practitioner's client has *their* best interests at heart and is not simply operating in the host country for purposes of exploitation of cheap labor, low production costs, lax environmental standards, and similar factors. In such situations, credibility enhancement requires tangible and visible contributions to the host country on the part of the client organization, its management, and its personnel. These organizational representatives simply *cannot* set themselves apart as an elitist enclave or separate community in the host country and expect to maintain their credibility. They must become active and constructive *participants* in the life and culture of the host country. This will be best reflected in constructive actions and special events as part of the organization's public relations programming.

Effective use of verbal and nonverbal cues in the programming will include an understanding not only of the official language of the host country but of that country's special applications or dialectical usage of the language. Although French is the official language of France, Canada's province of Quebec, and Haiti, its usage varies as widely among these countries as does Spanish usage from Madrid to Santo Domingo. The astute practitioner will understand such verbal nuances, as well as the many nonverbal cultural differences in the uses of time, spatial relationships, and visual and vocal cues. Failure to take these verbal and nonverbal distinctions into account can spell doom for international public relations programming.

Two-way, or interpersonal, communication is especially important in an international context. This presupposes the use of native speakers and writers in the public relations programming. The deadly public relations sin of overreliance on the mass media or other forms of one-way communication (mainly print) can take a serious toll on the effectiveness of international public relations efforts.

The inclusion of opinion leaders and groups is another indispensable element in international public relations programming. While important in most American contexts, attention to and communication with important leaders and groups can become magnified in the international context. This requires a thorough understanding of the complexities of the social and political context in the host country. It may require the employment of authoritative consultants in the host country. Though the cost of getting this right may be high, the cost of getting it wrong will, in the long term, be unbearable if not disastrous.

Finally, there can be no substitute in any public relations program for *audience participation*. If interactive programming is the norm for American public relations, it should be an absolute requisite of international public relations. This principle again underlines the significance of participative actions and special events as the core of effective programs.

Effective use of these communication principles cannot be overemphasized. They serve to heighten the practitioner's sensitivity to and awareness of the interactive and participative nature of public relations, especially in the international context.

EVALUATION

The evaluation of an international public relations program should be driven by the monitoring and final assessment of its stated objectives. Both impact and output objectives can be evaluated using the same measurement tools as in other forms of public relations (see Chapter 2). A significant difference may lie in the necessity to use research firms with credible reputations in the host country. It could be a serious mistake to bring in firms and employees from the client's country to conduct surveys, focus groups, and the like in the host country.

SUMMARY

The ROPE process is a useful format for the conduct of international public relations. In all aspects of the process, unusual precautions must be taken to observe the social, political, and cultural norms of the host country of the program's target audience. Not only must successful practitioners understand effective public relations principles, they must also become working cultural anthropologists and sociologists versed in the host country's history and politics.

READINGS ON INTERNATIONAL PUBLIC RELATIONS

"An International Sensibility," *Public Relations Tactics* 6 (February 1999): 31.

Arfield, George. "As the World Changes, So Must Communicators," *Communication World* 10 (June–July 1993): 33–34.

Bates, Don. "Update on Japan: Tips on Dealing with the Press," *Public Relations Journal* 50 (October–November 1994): 14.

"Best Practices in Global Communications," *Public Relations Tactics* 5 (June 1998): 10.

Botan, C. "International Public Relations: Critique and Reformulation," *Public Relations Review* 18 (summer 1992): 149–159.

Busch, Per-Olof, and Jörgens Helge. "The International Sources of Policy Convergence: Explaining the Spread of Environmental Policy Innovations," *Journal of European Public Policy* 12 (October 2005): 860–884.

Chen, Ni, and Hugh M. Culbertson. "Two Contrasting Approaches of Government Public Relations in Mainland China," *Public Relations Quarterly* 37 (fall 1992): 36–41.

Clarke, Terence M. "An Inside Look at Russian Public Relations," *Public Relations Quarterly* 45 (spring 2000): 18 ff.

Creedon, Pam, and Mai Al-Khaja. "Public Relations and Globalization: Building a Case for Cultural Competency in Public Relations Education," *Public Relations Review* 31 (September 2005): 344–354.

Culbertson, Hugh M., and Ni Chen, eds. *International Public Relations: A Comparative Analysis.* Mahwah, NJ: Erlbaum, 1996.

Curtin, Patricia A., and T. Kenn Gaither. "Privileging Identity, Difference, and Power: The Circuit of Culture as a Basis for Public Relations Theory," *Journal of Public Relations Research,* 17, no. 2 (2005): 91–115.

de Souza, Cerena, et al. "Navigating New Seas: Advice on Communicating Internationally," *Communication World* 11 (June–July 1994): 33.

Drobis, David R. "The New Global Imperative for Public Relations: Building Confidence to Save Globalization," *Public Relations Strategist* 8 (spring 2002): 36–38.

Fawcett, Karen. "An Embassy Can Be a Communicator's Ally," *Communication World* 10 (May 1993): 24–27.

Fortner, Robert S. *International Communication: History, Conflict, and Control of the Global Metropolis.* Belmont, CA: Wadsworth, 1993.

Greenberg, Keith Elliot. "Indian PR Business Discovers Its Purpose," *Public Relations Tactics* 3 (April 1996): 15 ff.

Guth, David. "The Emergence of Public Relations in the Russian Federation," *Public Relations Review* 26 (summer 2000): 191 ff.

He, Mike H. "Working with High-Tech Media in China," *Public Relations Tactics* 10 (May 2003): 23.

Huang, Yi-hui. "The Personal Influence Model and *Gao Guanxi* in Taiwan Chinese Public Relations," *Public Relations Review* 26 (summer 2000): 219 ff.

Josephs, Ray, and Juanita W. Josephs. "Public Relations in France," *Public Relations Journal* 49 (July 1993): 20–26.

———. "Public Relations the U.K. Way," *Public Relations Journal* 50 (April 1994): 14 ff.

Katz, Michael E. "A PR Market Grows in Central America," *Public Relations Tactics* 5 (August 1998): 24.

Kobayashi, Sanae. "Characteristics of Japanese Communication," *Communication World* 14 (December 1996–January 1997): 14–16.

Kotcher, Raymond L. "The Changing Role of PR in Latin America," *Public Relations Tactics* 5 (March 1998): 26 ff.

Kunczik, Michael. *Images of Nations and International Public Relations.* Mahwah, NJ: Erlbaum, 1996.

Leaper, Norm. "Ahh . . . the Pitfalls of International Communication," *Communication World* 13 (June–July 1996): 58 ff.

Moore, Tom. "A World of Differences Faces the International Communicator," *Communication World* 11 (October 1994): 7 ff.

Morley, Michael. *How to Manage Your Global Reputation: A Guide to the Dynamics of International Public Relations.* New York: New York University Press, 1998.

Newsom, Doug, and Bob Carrell. "Professional Public Relations in India: Need Outstrips Supply," *Public Relations Review* 20 (summer 1994): 183 ff.

Panol, Zenaida Sarabia. "Philippine Public Relations: An Industry and Practitioner Profile," *Public Relations Review* 26 (summer 2000): 237 ff.

"PR Evaluation Goes Global," *Marketing News* 30 (July 15, 1996): 16 ff.

Reaves, Lynne. "One Country, Two Systems: PR in the New Hong Kong," *Public Relations Tactics* 4 (September 1997): 12 ff.

Reitman, Valerie. "Enticed by Visions of Enormous Numbers, More Western Marketers Move into China," *Wall Street Journal* (July 12, 1993): B1, B12.

Rieff, David. "Their Hearts and Minds?" *New York Times Magazine* 154 (April 9, 2005): 11–12.

Ritchey, David. "Mastering the Fundamentals: PR in China," *Public Relations Tactics* 4 (September 1997): 16 ff.

Robles, Jennifer De, Carolyn Munckton, and Brian Everett. "Global Perspectives," *Communication World* 22 (September–October 2005): 138 ff.

Sharlach, Jeffrey R. "A New Era in Latin America: Free Markets Force Changes in Five Key Nations," *Public Relations Journal* 49 (September 1993): 26 –28.

Sharpe, Melvin L., ed. "International Public Relations," *Public Relations Review* 18 (summer 1992): 103–221.

Singh, Raveena, and Rosaleen Smyth. "Australian Public Relations: Status at the Turn of the 21st Century," *Public Relations Review* 26 (winter 2000): 387 ff.

Stevens, Art. "Emergence of Global Public Relations Networks," *Public Relations Strategist* 4 (spring 1998): 18 ff.

Strenski, James B. "The Evolving Practice of Public Relations in North and South America," *Public Relations Quarterly* 41 (spring 1996): 27 ff.

Sturaitis, Laura. "What's the Big Idea?" *Public Relations Tactics* 11 (December 2004): 11.

Taylor, Maureen. "Toward a Public Relations Approach to Nation Building," *Journal of Public Relations Research* 12, no. 2 (2000): 179 ff.

Taylor, Maureen, and Michael L. Kent. "Challenging Assumptions of International Public Relations: When Government Is the Most Important Public," *Public Relations Review* 25 (summer 1999): 131 ff.

Ting-Toomey, Stella. *Communicating Across Cultures.* New York: Guilford Publications, 1999.

van Ham, Peter. "The Rise of the Brand State: The Postmodern Politics of Image and Reputation," *Foreign Affairs* 80 (September–October 2001): 2 ff.

Van Ruler, Betteke. "Communication Management in the Netherlands," *Public Relations Review* 26 (winter 2000): 403 ff.

Wilcox, Dennis L., Philip H. Ault, and Warren K. Agee. "International Public Relations." In *Public Relations Strategies and Tactics,* 8th ed. New York: HarperCollins, 2006.

Wouters, Joyce. *International Public Relations.* New York: AMACOM, 1991.

Zaharna, R. S. "Intercultural Communication and International Public Relations: Exploring Parallels," *Communication Quarterly* 48 (winter 2000): 85–100.

———. "'In-awareness' Approach to International Public Relations," *Public Relations Review* 27 (summer 2001): 135–148.

CASE 9-1

Looking at future business opportunities with digital photography, Eastman Kodak Company rolled out integrated communication campaigns about the company's premium photo processing, "Kodak Perfect Touch," in the Midwest USA market and in Austria. Charles S. Smith, director of Market Transformation Communication for Kodak, said the name was changed slightly to "Picture Perfect" in Europe due to translation issues, but that overall the same message resonated with both audiences. The research pointed to the importance of targeting the female head of household as "memory keepers." Exhibit 9-1a provides a news release for the Indianapolis event, Exhibit 9-1b is the news release in Cologne, Exhibit 9-1c is a radio spot, and Exhibit 9-1d is the event plan for Indianapolis.

Convincing the World That Film Processing Matters—The Launch of Kodak Perfect Touch Processing

Eastman Kodak Company with Ketchum

Situation

Overnight film processing is big business to Eastman Kodak Company—more than a half billion rolls of film are processed overnight worldwide each year. But this service was headed toward commodity status as more consumers shopped on price, thinking all processing services were equal. Such a threat had to be met head on. Kodak reasoned it could convert consumers to its brand by applying breakthrough digital technology to make its premium processing service compellingly better. Kodak Perfect Touch (KPT) processing, the company's digital processing innovation, would deliver dramatically better pictures and differentiate Kodak's pro-

Courtesy Eastman Kodak Company

cessing from that of its rivals. Shifting consumers to KPT would translate to higher revenues and profits for Kodak and its retailers, and better pictures for consumers.

To sell KPT, Kodak needed to convince consumers that processing matters. Most don't realize how important film processing is in producing quality photos. They usually blame themselves or their camera for a bad picture. Showing consumers that their real nemesis is poor processing—and that Kodak's KPT processing is the solution—was critical for public relations success. Proving KPT's superiority was equally critical for building credibility within the business community.

One hitch—Kodak couldn't launch KPT with one big bang, since more than 40 Kodak labs in the United States alone had to be upgraded with KPT, requiring tens of millions of dollars and years to complete. Therefore, a staggered strategy was employed, piloting a "KPT Challenge" in four U.S. test markets and then Austria, and following great success there, moving forward on a regional basis throughout the United States, and later Europe, to persuade the consumer and business community that KPT would revolutionize photo processing forever.

Research

Business Case

KPT could generate millions of dollars in incremental revenue and improve margins because U.S. and European consumers who upgraded to KPT would pay an additional $1 per roll processed—Kodak learned consumers would pay more to get better pictures. Conclusion: If consumers ask for premium more often, retailers will more likely offer KPT. This research validated the potential market size for Kodak.

Consumer Satisfaction/Purchase Intent (based on market tests prior to rollout)

Seventy-four percent of U.S. consumers noted a dramatic difference in their pictures—eight out of ten indicated they would buy the service again and pay more for it. The majority would switch retailers to buy KPT. Similar findings in Austria with 74 percent being completely satisfied with their pictures and 64 percent saying they would buy again.

Conclusion

Communications plan should allow consumers to see the KPT difference firsthand. This research demonstrated consumer intent to purchase.

U.S. Consumer Omnibus Survey: Commissioned solely for developing the public relations strategy, surveys in the test markets and U.S. Midwest region indicated that 60 percent of consumers blamed themselves when their pictures didn't meet their expectations. Top challenges included dark shadows and lack of detail. Conclusion: Convince consumers that processing matters through side-by-side comparison prints.

This research revealed the consumer attitude change required by public relations.

Planning

Target Audiences

1. Photography influentials, including media and industry analysts;
2. Consumers who process film, primarily women gatekeepers;
3. Investors and financial analysts

Communications Objectives

1. Create perception among photo influencers that KPT is the best way to get dramatically better pictures;
2. Drive KPT trial and sales among consumers in test and regional rollout markets; and
3. Increase credibility of Kodak's digital strategy within investment community (via KPT)

Key Strategies

1. Drive media and business influencers to take the KPT Challenge and see (and report) the difference for themselves;
2. Customize media events and outreach for each test market and rollout region, paving a course for the national rollout

Execution

Strategy 1

Drive media and business influencers to take the KPT Challenge and see and report the difference

KPT Challenge—The "KPT Challenge" invited journalists and analysts to experience the KPT difference by snapping a roll of film and letting Kodak develop it twice using both standard (optical) and the KPT (digital) processing service. The "KPT Challenge" was executed by:

- Sending creative mailers to all "Challenge" participants—trade/channel media, consumer media, and industry and financial analysts in test and rollout markets.

- Beginning with trade/channel media and analysts at the Photo Marketing Association trade show—the industry's largest—in February 2002, followed by the test markets and the Midwest rollout. National media influencers also received the "Challenge" to condition them for the national launch in 2003.

This tactic was a success in the four initial KPT U.S. test markets and the European test in Austria, which produced highly positive coverage in consumer and trade media, which ultimately reached photo enthusiasts and film processing gatekeepers.

Strategy 2

Customize media events and outreach for each rollout market and region

U.S. Test Events—In U.S. test markets, Lisa Bearnson, a scrapbooking expert and author, was added to the KPT activities to give retail media events an additional hook. In addition to conducting media interviews, Bearnson conducted live scrapbooking demos at important Kodak retailers, featuring before-and-after shots dramatizing the advantages of using KPT in preserving cherished moments. In addition to her media draw, Bearnson drove store traffic and resulting sales.

European Test Event—Kodak adopted a "Universe of Kodak" theme to add local flavor to the test market event in Austria. A before-and-after KPT photo gallery of European photography was displayed for media, while Kodak's senior management appeared to deliver the KPT innovation message to a wide audience.

Midwest Region Rollout: Chicago Launch Event—The "Changing the Face of Chicago" press launch event featured Kodak CEO Dan Carp, who unveiled a before-and-after photo gallery of pictures taken of the city of Chicago using standard photo processing and KPT. As an added hook, local children took the photos. Access to Kodak senior management stirred media attention and generated significant business coverage.

Midwest Region Launch Activities—The initial regional rollout, timed to the availability of KPT in the Midwest, utilized Lisa Bearnson via a B-roll video package, along with regionalized survey findings that revealed consumer attitudes toward photo processing. This customized the media hook for the ten Midwest markets. The regional rollout plan continued throughout 2003 as KPT's availability expanded nationally.

Evaluation

Objective

Create perception that RPT is the best way to get dramatically better pictures among photo influencers

Influencer Outreach: Convinced 130 influencers (media and analysts) in U.S. and European test/launch markets to take the KPT Challenge.

Positive Message Delivery

90 percent of the resulting coverage delivered three or more key messages.

"Prints processed in an optical mini-lab were under-exposed and had dust marks and scratches. Prints processed using Kodak's Perfect Touch system were perfectly exposed and free of blemishes." *Popular Photography,* September 2002

"Moments are about to become more special with the new film developing process using Kodak's Perfect Touch. It's aimed at eliminating shadows, over- and under-exposure and other faults in snapshots." CNN, *The Money Gang,* October 7, 2002

"Just as compact discs banished the scratchy sounds common to vinyl records, [Kodak's] new digital film processing promises to do away with washed-out faces, dark backgrounds, other snapshot shortcomings." *Chicago Tribune,* October 7, 2002

Mix of Media

Nearly 40 million television, radio, and print impressions were generated in the United States/Austria

- Covered by all significant print and electronic media during U.S. and Austrian Test
- Delivered mix of business and consumer media during Chicago launch event, driving 30 million impressions
- Covered by all top ten dailies and at least one television/radio station per market in U.S. Midwest region

Objective

Drive trial and sales of KPT among consumers in rollout markets

Purchase of KPT premium processing compared with standard in the U.S. Midwest climbed 25 percent from October through year-end 2002, exceeding Kodak and retailers' expectations; Europe increased by 6 percent with the acquisition of ten new accounts from competitors.

More than 6,000 retailers invested in the KPT processing service in the U.S. Midwest, partially in response to positive press and consumer reaction.

Objective

Increase credibility of Kodak's digital strategy within investment community (via KPT)

EK stock upgraded to BUY from HOLD by a Deutsche Bank analyst Peter Ausnit after trying KPT: "Based on improving analog to digital strategy . . . KPT adds credibility to consumer digital strategy."

Generated favorable national business media coverage featuring CEO Dan Carp highlighting KPT as a positive feature of Kodak's digital strategy. Coverage reached investors via Bloomberg TV and radio, CNBC, CNN, and FOX News.

EXHIBIT 9-1A   *News Release — Indianapolis*

For Immediate Release

Media Contacts:

Sha'Nia Dickerson	Deisha Galberth
Eastman Kodak Company	Ketchum
770-522-2764	404-879-9159
shania.dickerson@kodak.com	**deisha.galberth@ketchum.com**

KODAK TESTS REVOLUTIONARY PHOTOPROCESSING, NEW TECHNOLOGY WITH INDIANAPOLIS CONSUMERS

Kodak, CVS/pharmacy partner to bring Indianapolis consumers new *Kodak Perfect Touch* processing which dramatically improves photo quality to reveal more detail in pictures

ROCHESTER, NY, February 14, 2002 — Eastman Kodak Company's new *Kodak Perfect Touch* processing represents a revolutionary leap in photofinishing from traditional 'optical' processing technology to new 'digital' processing technology. *Kodak Perfect Touch* processing launches today in a test at participating CVS/pharmacy stores in Indianapolis, which is among the first four cities in the U.S. to benefit from this historic innovation.

Kodak Perfect Touch processing individually inspects each picture to improve the color and contrast in every photo, revealing more detail and better quality.

"Think of that special moment. You thought you took the perfect picture. Got it processed. Opened the envelope and … the picture didn't reflect the moment as vividly as you remembered it," says Scott Auer, general manager and vice president, Photofinishing, Consumer Imaging, Eastman Kodak Company. "By simply checking the box for new *Kodak Perfect Touch* processing when you drop off your film, your treasured photographs will look amazingly true to life."

For most people, the picture-taking process stops at the point the film is dropped off, not realizing the important role processing plays in capturing the detail of a moment as perfectly as they remember it. In fact, according to a recent survey conducted to determine what many Indianapolis picture-takers perceive as major obstacles in obtaining high quality photos, only **13 percent** attributed imperfections to processing. Moreover, more than **56 percent of respondents blamed the problem on themselves** *(for more on survey, see snapshot included in press kit).*

-more-

Courtesy Eastman Kodak Company

EXHIBIT 9-1A   *News Release—Indianapolis (continued)*

KPT Processing Revolution in Indianapolis, page 2

With *Kodak Perfect Touch* processing, however, anyone can get better pictures without having to change their normal routine. Here's how the process works: take pictures as usual, drop off the film at your favorite Indianapolis CVS/pharmacy store, and check the box on your film processing envelope for *Kodak Perfect Touch* processing. From there, each of your pictures will be digitally scanned and individually examined for color, lighting and detail that traditional 'optical' processing cannot provide.

"As an industry leader in photo processing, we are excited about *Kodak Perfect Touch* processing, and glad to be Kodak's exclusive partner in providing Indianapolis residents with this revolutionary technology," says Judy Strauss-Sansone, vice president, Merchandising, CVS/pharmacy. "Now, CVS customers are able to get even more great shots that truly reflect how they remember the moment."

Some specific benefits of *Kodak Perfect Touch* processing include:

- Removes dark shadows
- Reveals richer detail in pictures
- Improves sharpness and contrast
- Reveals more vibrant colors

Other highlights include:

- Improved *Kodak Duralife* paper that provides whiter whites, darker darks and improved flesh tones
- Index print that allows easy roll identification for ordering reprints and enlargements
- Sleeved negatives for protection
- Back printing reminder of when the picture was taken
- Suggested price point $9.99 for single prints and $11.99 for double prints

As the latest breakthrough in photofinishing, *Kodak Perfect Touch* processing has arrived just in time to help Indianapolis snap shooters get quality photos with richer detail than traditional processing offers.

Survey Methodology

Kodak's "Processing I.Q." survey was conducted by ICR, an independent research company. Two hundred telephone interviews were completed among men and women between the ages of 18-54 in Indianapolis. In addition, a nationwide poll of 500 adult men and women was conducted via telephone.

-more-

About Eastman Kodak Company & Infoimaging

Kodak is the leader in helping people take, share, enhance, preserve, print and enjoy pictures -- for memories, for information, for entertainment. The company is a major participant in "infoimaging" -- a $225 billion industry composed of devices (digital cameras and PDAs), infrastructure (online networks and delivery systems for images) and services & media (the software, film and paper that enable people to access and print images). Kodak harnesses its technology, market reach and a host of industry partnerships to provide innovative products and services for customers who need the information-rich content that images contain, such as *Kodak Perfect Touch* processing. The company, with sales last year of almost $14 billion, is organized into five major businesses: Photography, providing consumers and professionals with digital and traditional products and services; Commercial Imaging, offering image capture, output and storage products and services to businesses and government; Components, delivering flat-panel displays, optics and sensors to original equipment manufacturers; Health, supplying the healthcare industry with traditional and digital image capture and output products and services; and Entertainment, providing Hollywood with motion picture film, post-production services and digital cinema systems.

About CVS

CVS is America's #1 pharmacy, dispensing prescriptions in more stores than any other retailer. With annual revenues that exceed $22 billion, CVS has created innovative approaches to serve the healthcare needs of all of its customers through more than 4,100 CVS/pharmacy stores; CVS ProCare, its specialty pharmacy business; CVS.com, its online pharmacy; and PharmaCare, its pharmacy benefit management company. General information about CVS is available through the Investor Relations portion of the Company's website, at http://www.CVS.com.

# # #

(*Kodak, Perfect Touch* and *Duralife* are trademarks of Eastman Kodak Company.)

Editor's Note: For additional information about *Kodak Perfect Touch* processing and other *Kodak* products and services, please call 1-800-242-2424.
2002

EXHIBIT 9-1B   *News Release — Germany*

Media Contact:

Brian Bottomley   Mark Jackson
Eastman Kodak-Kodak LTD   Ketchum
011-44-2845-978   44-207-611-3858

Editor contacts only. Please see last paragraph for reader contact information.

Test market results highlight Kodak's superior new processing service

Initial results from Austria confirm benefits of *Kodak Photo Perfect* Service

COLOGNE, Germany, September 24, 2002 — Eastman Kodak Company today announced initial consumer feedback from the launch of its *Kodak Photo Perfect* Service which shows consumers consider their pictures to be "significantly better" compared to other digital processing solutions.

The results come as part of the company's roll-out of the *Kodak Photo Perfect* Service across Europe and were implemented to ensure the Service more than met the needs of consumers across the region. Initial results show:

- 74% of consumers surveyed were "completely satisfied" with their digitally processed pictures.
- 58% of those interviewed considered the digital pictures to be "better" or "much better" than those processed optically, which shows that consumers find a dramatic difference in their pictures with the new service.
- 64% of those interviewed said they would choose digital processing from the *Kodak Photo Perfect* Service next time.

Courtesy Eastman Kodak Company

"A significant number of consumers declared themselves completely satisfied with the service and thought it 'significantly better' than our competitors' digital solutions. Why? Well *Kodak Photo Perfect* Service improves the colours, shadow details and contrast in people's photos," said Pierre Cohade, chairman of Kodak Europe. "In addition, it helps lighten dark subjects, brightens hazy photos and reduces extreme flashes. And all of this is done digitally by our labs. It goes to prove that we can help our consumers take visibly better pictures more of the time – and will help our retail customers offer a superior service to their customers."

The *Photo Perfect* Service is an example of how Kodak is using digital technology to expand the benefits of film for consumers and give consumers visually better pictures from film, increasing their enjoyment and satisfaction with photography. By giving consumers better pictures, Kodak also hopes to increase consumer demand for premium photo processing services.

Kodak Photo Perfect Service

By individually scanning and digitally processing each picture, Kodak Photo Perfect Service:

- Removes dark shadows
- Reveals richer detail
- Improves contrast
- Reveals more vibrant colour in pictures

Other highlights include:

- Each order printed on *Kodak Duralife* Paper that provides whiter whites, darker darks, and improved flesh tones
- Index print that allows easy roll identification for ordering reprints and enlargements
- Sleeved negatives for protection
- Back printing reminder of when the picture was taken

EXHIBIT 9-1B   *News Release — Germany (continued)*

Kodak Introduces New *Photo Perfect Service* / Page 3

Market Availability

The initial launch was carried out in Austrian because it offers a unique opportunity to test the service in a market that makes comparisons with the rest of Europe relatively easy. The launch came as part of the existing 'Kodak Pictures' brand and was supported by one of Kodak's largest marketing campaigns.

The knowledge gained from the launch in Austria will be applied to other markets the service is rolled out across the European region in 2003. Target markets will include France, UK and Benelux. More details will be made available closer to the launch of the service in each market.

Consumer Education

Many consumers remain unaware of the role processing plays in achieving quality pictures. Kodak plans to support the Kodak Photo Perfect Service with an aggressive, integrated communications program that includes advertising, compelling in-store merchandizing and public relations to educate consumers on the digital processing difference. Highlights of this education programme include:

- **Aggressive advertising campaign**. *Kodak Photo Perfect* will become a central focus of Kodak's multi-million dollar, "Share Moments. Share Life" campaign.
- **Simplified merchandising packages.** All in-store merchandising packages will incorporate clear options communicating benefits of each service.
- **Side-by-side comparisons**. Consumers will see the difference first-hand through visual demonstrations that compare an optically processed image with the same image processed digitally, highlighting the dramatic improvements. This tool will be used prominently in all advertising and in-store displays.

Eastman Kodak Company and infoimaging
Kodak is the leader in helping people take, share, enhance, preserve, print and enjoy pictures -- for memories, for information, for entertainment. The company is a major participant in "infoimaging" -- a $385 billion industry composed of devices (digital cameras and PDAs), infrastructure (online networks and delivery systems for images) and services & media (software, film and paper enabling people to access, analyze and print images). Kodak harnesses its technology, market reach and a host of industry partnerships to provide innovative products and services for customers who need the information-rich content that images contain, such as **Kodak Photo Perfect**. The company, with sales last year of $13.2 billion, is organized into four major businesses: Photography, providing consumers, professionals and cinematographers with digital and traditional products and services; Commercial Imaging, offering image capture, output and storage products and services to businesses and government; Components, delivering flat-panel displays, optics and sensors to original equipment manufacturers; and Health, supplying the healthcare industry with traditional and digital image capture and output products and services.

#

(Kodak is a trademark of Eastman Kodak Company.)

Editor's Note: For additional information about Kodak, visit our web site on the Internet at:

www.kodak.com.

2002

EXHIBIT 9-1C   *Radio Spot*

KPT/INDY RADIO SPOTS

60-second spot for WYXB (W/O FREE PROCESSING)
Air Dates: 3/11 – 3/13

Ever get your pictures back, and they didn't capture the moment as you remembered it? Want to find out how your pictures can be more true to life?

Now, there is a revolutionary new service called Kodak Perfect Touch Processing that gives you dramatically better pictures. This Friday, take the Kodak Perfect Touch Challenge and see the difference for yourself.

Simply, stop by **CVS at 1299 West 86th Street** on Friday and drop off your roll of film from 9 a.m. to 4 p.m. You'll get incredibly sharp pictures that reveal more vibrant colors, richer detail, plus fewer dark shadows and improved contrast.

You'll be so proud of your pictures developed with Kodak Perfect Touch Processing that you'll want to share them with family and friends. Scrapbooking expert and author, Lisa Bearnson, will be on hand to provide quick and easy tips to make sharing your pictures and memories more fun and exciting.

So, don't forget… this Friday, stop by **CVS at 1299 West 86th Street**, from 9 a.m. to 4 p.m., bring in your roll of film for Kodak Perfect Touch Processing and discover how good your pictures can be.

Please limit one roll of film per household.

60-second spot for WYXB (FREE PROCESSING)
Air Dates: 3/14 – 3/15

Ever get your pictures back, and they didn't capture the moment as you remembered it? Want to find out how your pictures can be more true to life?

Now, there is a revolutionary new service called Kodak Perfect Touch Processing that gives you dramatically better pictures. This Friday, take the Kodak Perfect Touch Challenge **– for free** -- and see the difference for yourself.   Yes, **that's right, FREE FILM PROCESSING!**

Simply, stop by **CVS at 1299 West 86th Street** on Friday and drop off your roll of film from 9 to noon. You'll get incredibly sharp pictures that reveal more vibrant colors, richer detail, plus fewer dark shadows and improved contrast.

You'll be so proud of your pictures developed with Kodak Perfect Touch Processing that you'll want to share them with family and friends. Scrapbooking expert and author, Lisa Bearnson, will be on hand to provide quick and easy tips to make sharing your pictures and memories more fun and exciting.

So, don't forget… this Friday, stop by **CVS at 1299 West 86th Street** from 9 to noon and bring in your roll of film for free Kodak Perfect Touch Processing and discover how good your pictures can be.

Please limit one roll of film per household

Indy Radio Spot Scripts
Page 1 of 4

Courtesy Eastman Kodak Company

EXHIBIT 9-1D   *Event Plan*

DETAILED INDIANAPOLIS EVENT RUN OF SHOW
3/14/02 – 3/15/02

THURSDAY, 3/14/02:

TBD a.m.	RES set up at both CVS locations *** tent, flooring only.*
11:00 a.m.	Ketchum/Kodak arrive in-market
2:30 p.m.	Ketchum/Kodak to meet with CVS/Indy store manager – site checks *** determine ideal areas for film drop-off; Kodak Photo Gallery, etc.*
4:30 p.m.	Ketchum/Kodak to meet with CVS/Greenwood store manager – site checks *** determine ideal areas for film drop-off; Kodak Photo Gallery, etc.*
6:30 p.m.	Ketchum/Kodak to meet with L. Bearnson in hotel (location TBD) ***review key messages, event details, etc.*

FRIDAY, 3/15/02:

TBD a.m.	RES set up at CVS *** photo gallery, counter, etc.*
6:00 a.m.	Ketchum/L. Bearnson arrive at NBC station for interview
7:30 a.m.	Ketchum/Kodak to arrive at CVS store for event set up
8:00 a.m.	Radio crew to arrive (WYXB-FM/B105.7 – on-air talent Jim Cerone)
8:30 a.m.	L. Bearnson to arrive for set up
9:00 a.m.	**LIVE radio remote AND mini workshops with L Bearnson begin** ***media will be invited to come out anytime during the event*
11:00 a.m.	LIVE radio remote ends ***mini workshops with L. Bearnson and photo gallery display continue*
4:00 p.m.	**Event ends** *** pack up for Saturday event*
5:00 p.m.	Event wrap up/RES break down ** *determine number of participants, send film to Rochester, etc.*
6:30 p.m.	Ketchum/Kodak/Spokesperson head to dinner (location TBD) ***key learning discussion held at this time*

KPT Event Detailed ROS Page 1 of 2

Courtesy Eastman Kodak Company

EXHIBIT 9-1D   *Event Plan (continued)*

SATURDAY, 3/16/02:

TBD a.m.	RES set up at CVS *** photo gallery, counter, etc.*
7:30 a.m.	Ketchum/Kodak to arrive at CVS store for event set up
9:00 a.m.	Radio crew to arrive 9 (WENS-FM/97.1 – on air talent Chris Ott)
9:30 a.m.	L. Bearnson to arrive for set up
10:00 a.m.	**LIVE radio remote AND mini workshops with L. Bearnson begin** **media will be invited to come out anytime during the event*
12:00 a.m.	LIVE radio remote ends **mini workshops with L. Bearnson and photo gallery display continue*
4:00 p.m.	**Event ends**/L. Bearnson heads to airport
5:00 p.m.	Event wrap up/RES break down ** determine number of participants, send film to Rochester, etc.*
6:30 p.m.	Ketchum/Kodak head to airport

CVS LOCATIONS:
3/15/02: 1299 West 86th Street, Indianapolis, IN
3/16/02: 655 SW Highway 31, Greenwood, IN

ON SITE KETCHUM CONTACTS:
Deisha Galberth
Office: 404/879-9159
Mobile: 404/431-4399

ON SITE KODAK CONTACTS:
Sha'Nia Dickerson
Office: 770/522-2764
Mobile: 404/452-8770

Jeff Wagner
Office: 770-777-2858
Mobile: 404-452-9491

KPT SPOKESPERSON:
Lisa Bearnson
Office: 801-796-5520
Mobile: 801-209-2878

KPT Event Detailed ROS Page 2 of 2

With a global economy comes global communication challenges when setting new international standards for commerce. The radio frequency identification (RFID) system is quickly becoming a global standard for "scanning" products instead of the older bar code system, but it took considerable communication initiatives to make it happen. Exhibit 9-2a is a news release in Belgium, Exhibit 9-2b provides a video news release advisory, Exhibit 9-2c is an audio script, and Exhibit 9-2d is a "messaging" presentation.

The Electronic Product Code: From Concept to Commercialization in One Year

Creating the EPCglobal Brand—Real value. Right partner. Right now

Uniform Code Council, Inc., with Fleishman-Hillard, Inc.

Situation Analysis

The bar code. Most of us only think of it in the supermarket checkout lane. But this technology—developed and commercialized by the Uniform Code Council (UCC)—is scanned 10 billion times every day. Now, the growing complexity of global commerce and the growing demand for more sophisticated and effective supply chain management has given the UCC the opportunity to bring to the marketplace the next generation of the bar code—the Electronic Product Code (EPC). This exciting new technology harnesses radio frequency identification (RFID) to give companies the expanded ability to track products as they move from point to point, anywhere in the world. But in the fall of 2003, as the UCC began the commercialization efforts for EPC technology, it faced some real challenges. Some of the world's largest organizations, such as Wal-Mart, P&G, Gillette, Marks & Spencer, Tesco, and even the United States Dept. of Defense were clamoring to implement the technology. Their support created relentless demand for standardized products, which awaited guidance from the UCC and its soon-to-be-created affiliate, EPCglobal, Inc. Simultaneously, consumer privacy groups, fearful of the technology's capabilities, had organized an all-out misinformation campaign. Industry proponents were stunned into silence as state legislators and federal officials began considering regulation of the technology. The

Courtesy GS1 US

media and analyst communities, woefully underinformed about EPC, played into the hands of its opponents. Within this environment, the UCC and Fleishman-Hillard, Inc. (FH), launched EPCglobal to focus and drive the commercialization of the technology forward. To date, the efforts are succeeding beyond expectations; with membership in EPC-global soaring by more than 200 percent, and share of voice in the media reaching a height of 35 percent, up from 5 percent at the start of the program.

Research/Planning

To ascertain what brand recognition the UCC had in the marketplace, assess the key opinions of target audiences, and uncover obstacles, FH conducted primary and secondary research. The research can be clustered in three categories:

C-level and supply chain executives. FH conducted interviews with senior-level corporate executives across target industries. Findings uncovered high confidence in the UCC, high awareness of RFID, but low awareness of the EPC. Results also indicated business-driven messages were important and prioritized. As a result, the brand architecture, "Real value. Right partner. Right now" reflected the essence of each message.

Consumers. FH conducted a global audit of all existing information on consumer concerns around RFID. The firm was able to tap into additional research conducted by the client. It was discovered that consumers, when presented with the facts about EPC in the supply chain, overwhelmingly supported its use. As a result, EPC-global's privacy platform is consumer benefits focused.

Member Organizations (MO). Based on survey data from 103 MOs, FH created tools to help push the commercialization effort forward within their respective countries. Results included the creation of a global news summary and newsletter.

Strategy

Based on the research, FH and the client determined that efforts should focus on the following areas:

Gain momentum in the United States and then expand globally. With the majority of early adopter companies in the United States the campaign first focused efforts domestically. Traction in the United States would then entice others to join in other regions.

Articulate the value of the organization to drive membership. The new standards body required membership fees to feed standards development efforts and push adoption quickly.

Simplify the technology to focus on real benefits for business. Key audiences simply wanted to hear the value proposition and how it could improve their business and the lives of their customers.

Seed the marketplace with factual information about the technology. Communicate developments through business, trade and vertical media, analyst reports, and the organization's website. Counteract negative coverage with aggressive response tactics to keep positive messages in front of key audiences.

Objectives

Establish credibility. Develop a brand that would effectively communicate the value and vision of the organization.

Gain subscribers. EPCglobal is supported by membership fees. To create a sustainable business model, EPCglobal needed subscribers fast.

Gain industry support. Although some of the world's largest organizations supported the technology, few had embraced its value proposition.

Audience

EPC technology is a global supply chain tool, but at launch, many early adopter companies were in the United States. To focus resources, tactics were first executed domestically, and additional elements were added to fuel adoption in the rest of the world.

Primary—U.S.-based C-suite executives, IT leaders and supply chain and logistics managers in the aerospace/aviation, automotive, consumer packaged goods, healthcare/pharmaceutical, and retail industries

Secondary—More than 100 MOs representing individual countries from around the world

Execution

Phase I (September 2003 to present)

Brand identity. FH developed the core brand and brand positioning for the new organization. The selected name, EPCglobal, underwent a global name screen and was selected because of its connection to the technology and its emphasis on the global nature of the technology. The tag line emphasized "Real value. Right partner. Right now" to communicate the value of the technology, the viability of the organization, and the sense of urgency to begin implementing the EPC today. The brand mark was leveraged across multiple vehicles with the media launch conducted at a high-profile, industry trade show.

Steady drumbeat of information to key audiences through media relations. FH executed ongoing proactive and reactive media relations efforts throughout the year. To maximize exposure, FH planned significant events around the following:

Making the Technology Real, the Selection of VeriSign to Operate the EPCglobal Network—A key challenge was the natural tendency of companies to "put off" investing in the technology. By announcing a key contract with VeriSign, FH was able to reposition the conversation to begin tracking the buildup of the EPCglobal Network.

Hearing Consumer Concerns and Taking Steps to Address Them—To take a proactive stance on the issue of consumer privacy, EPCglobal formed a collaborative Public Policy Steering Committee (PPSC). Made up of experts from various industries, the PPSC published guidelines for the responsible deployment of EPC. At this time, EPCglobal also began proactively responding to media queries, balancing the conversation.

Wal-Mart Launches First Commercial Trials of EPC—To further highlight the rapid deployment of EPC in the marketplace, EPCglobal, in conjunction with Wal-Mart, opened the first commercial tests to the media. Though prepared for potential picketing from privacy advocates, the event coverage and customer feedback were positive.

Happy Birthday to the Bar Code—On June 26, the ubiquitous U.P.C. (Universal Product Code) turned 30 and offered an opportunity to reframe the conversation for the transition from the world of U.P.C. to EPC. Media coverage relentlessly connected the U.P.C. to the EPC, the next generation bar code.

EPCglobal US Fall Conference. Culminating a year's worth of effort, the conference provided a platform to update the industry on the incredible progress. Featuring high-level media secured by FH, including David Kirkpatrick of *FORTUNE,* Ron Insana of CNBC, and Mark Roberti of *RFID Journal,* attendance rocketed past projections and dwarfed a competitive show held weeks before.

Gen 2 Ratification—Built upon the excitement that occurred at the EPCglobal US Fall Conference, Generation 2 (Gen 2) Ratification marked the culmination of a year's worth of standards development efforts. Reported by major business publications, trade journals, and key verticals, the ratification was the landmark news event for the RFID industry in 2004.

Phase II (August 2004 to present)

Global Member Communications. As U.S. efforts took off, interest grew around the world. To capitalize on the growing interest, FH created an online newsletter that allowed each MO to brand the piece with their respective country. In addition, FH also distributes a weekly news roundup of international coverage to help keep interest high.

Evaluation

Created a unified, global brand. Since the launch in September, 103 UCC Member Organizations have adopted the EPCglobal brand in their markets.

Created a sustainable organization and increased industry support. At the brand launch in September there were no members of EPCglobal. Today, after one year, there are nearly 400 subscribers worldwide with more than 200 headquartered domestically, including companies like Wal-Mart, Target, Johnson & Johnson, Abbott, Pfizer, Sun, HP, Boeing, and Michelin.

The EPCglobal US Fall Conference, the first one held, hosted nearly 2,000 attendees, with more than 70 media in attendance, successfully dwarfing a competing show held just weeks earlier.

Added EPC into the conversation. At the start of the campaign, the mentions of RFID significantly outweighed those of EPC. Through aggressive media relations, share of voice and inclusion of EPC in stories reached a high of 35 percent, climbing from less than 5 percent. The VeriSign partnership announcement achieved more than 20 million impressions. The bar code birthday celebration generated more than 17 million media impressions.

Aggressively addressed misinformation regarding privacy. Less than a year ago, consumer privacy groups owned the conversation and did not focus on consumer benefits. EPC is now consistently included in more than half of privacy coverage. Overall tone has shifted from predominantly negative to neutral, and in many cases positive with inclusion of key consumer benefits.

EXHIBIT 9-2A   *News Release*

FOR IMMEDIATE RELEASE

For More Information Contact:
Audrey Ni Cheallaigh, 011.32.2.227.10.25
audrey.nicheallaigh@gs1.org

EPCglobal Ratifies Royalty-Free UHF Generation 2 Standard

Announcement Marks Culmination of Collaborative Process; Opens Door for Proliferation of Standards-Based Hardware to Drive EPC Implementations Worldwide

BRUSSELS, Belgium – December 16, 2004 – EPCglobal Inc™, a subsidiary of GS1 a not-for-profit standards organization entrusted with driving global adoption of Electronic Product Code (EPC) technology, today announced the ratification of the royalty-free EPCglobal UHF Generation 2 candidate specification. Today's announcement marks the much anticipated completion of the UHF Generation 2 air interface protocol as an EPCglobal standard. With the Generation 2 standard now in place, technology providers will create products that will meet the requirements of suppliers, manufacturers, and end users; and industries as a whole can drive EPC implementation with standards-based equipment.

Today's announcement follows successful testing of prototypes from several technology providers, which illustrated that the ratified standard can meet the EPCglobal community end user requirements, as well as final determination that all intellectual property presented on a licensed basis during the standards development process was not necessary to the standard. Commercially available products are expected the first half of 2005.

"Today marks both an exciting culmination and a much anticipated beginning in the commercialization of RFID and EPC technology," said Chris Adcock, president, EPCglobal Inc. "Many of the world's leading technology companies collaborated to develop the UHF Generation 2 specification, and we celebrate and applaud their efforts as we launch the royalty-free UHF Generation 2 standard. With this standard in place, technology manufacturers and end users alike can begin exploring how to deploy the technology in such a way to make a significant impact in improving their own business."

- more -

Courtesy GS1 US

The EPCglobal UHF Generation 2 protocol, a consensus standard built by more than 60 of the world's leading technology companies, describes the core capabilities required to meet the performance needs set by the end user community. The UHF Generation 2 standard will be used as a base platform upon which standards-based products and future improvements will be built. An EPCglobal standard ensures interoperability and sets minimum operational expectations for various components in the EPCglobal Network™, including hardware components. While EPCglobal oversees interoperability and conformance testing of standards-based products, the actual development of these products comes from leading solution providers around the globe.

During 2004, EPCglobal has worked with the global community of end-users and solution providers to complete a number of activities aimed at building out the EPCglobal Network. The UHF Generation 2 standard is a foundational element in the continued build-out of the EPCglobal Network, a network that combines RFID technology, the Internet and the EPC to provide accurate, cost-efficient visibility of information throughout supply chains.

Concurrent with the ratification of UHF Generation 2, EPCglobal has set up a special committee to consider whether additional numbering features are necessary to the EPCglobal standard. Following the outcome of this work group, EPCglobal plans to submit the Generation 2 standard to the International Organization for Standardization (ISO).

About EPCglobal Inc. EPCglobal Inc™, a subsidiary of GS1, is a not-for-profit organization entrusted by industry to establish and support the EPCglobal Network™ as the global standard for real-time, automatic identification of information in the supply chain of any company, anywhere in the world.

The EPCglobal Network combines radio frequency identification (RFID) technology, existing communications network infrastructure, and the Electronic Product Code™ (a number for uniquely identifying an item) to enable accurate, cost-efficient visibility of information in the supply chain. The end result helps organizations be more efficient, flexible, and responsive to customer needs. EPCglobal US is an affiliate of EPCglobal Inc, serving subscribers in the United States to help foster the adoption of the EPCglobal Network and related technology. For more information about EPCglobal visit: www.EPCglobalinc.org.

About GS1. GS1 is the global not-for-profit organisation that creates, develops and manages the EAN•UCC standards jointly with the Uniform Code Council, one of its Member Organisations. These are open, global, multisectoral information standards, based on best business practices. By driving their implementation, GS1 and its Member Organisations play a leading role in supply and demand chain management improvement worldwide. For more information on EAN International, please visit: www.GS1.org.

#

EXHIBIT 9-2B   *VNR Advisory*

* * * ATTN: NEWS / FEATURE / CONSUMER & FINANCIAL EDITORS * * *

U.P.C. BAR CODE CELEBRATES
30th BIRTHDAY ON JUNE 25TH

Uniform Code Council Returns to the Site of the History-Making First Scan; First Product Scanned Was a Pack of Wrigley's Gum

VIDEO FEEDS FRIDAY, JUNE 25, 1:15 – 1:30 PM ET
PATHFIRE Story # NBN 23393

Lawrenceville, NJ/Troy, OH -- The Uniform Code Council (UCC) is celebrating the 30th anniversary of the Universal Product Code, or U.P.C., by returning to Marsh Supermarket in Troy, Ohio, the store that hosted the world's first live scan on June 26th, 1974. The original cashier, Sharon Buchanan, who scanned the first product – a pack of Wrigley's Gum – will join others in commemorating the occasion.

The U.P.C. was the outgrowth of meetings that took place in the late 1960's by leaders of the U.S. grocery industry, who were hoping to reduce food costs and congestion at the checkout line.

The U.P.C. is composed of a row of 59 black and white bars that vary in length and are read by a scanner. Beneath the bars is a series of 12 human-readable numbers, which together identify the manufacturer and the specific product.

Today, the U.P.C. is used by 23 major industry sectors, including retail, healthcare, government, foodservice, transportation and high-tech. **The UCC estimates that bar codes are scanned over 10 billion times a day in over 140 nations around the world**. The UCC is now standardizing its newest innovation, a "wireless bar code" called the Electronic Product Code.

The original pack of Wrigley's gum and the checkout scanning unit from the Marsh store are housed at the Smithsonian Institution's National Museum of American History in Washington, DC.

WHAT YOU'LL GET: B-roll and soundbites package
FOOTAGE of the first item scanned, a pack of Wrigley's chewing gum; Marsh Supermarket of Troy, OH, the first store to use the U.P.C. system; the U.P.C. on various products; new bar code technology
SOUNDBITES include Michael Di Yeso, President of the Uniform Code Council (UCC) and Sharon Buchanan, cashier who scanned first U.P.C

VIA SATELLITE, C-BAND FEED:
FRIDAY, JUNE 25   1:15 – 1:30 PM ET   IA 5, Tr. 14, DL 3980
                    ** *IA 5 Formerly known as Telstar 5* **

Technical Info DURING FEED ONLY, NBN TOC, 212 – 684 - 8910 x 221

VIA PATHFIRE:
On the left panel of Pathfire, double click on News Broadcast Network, Story # NBN 23393.

FREE FROM NEWS BROADCAST NETWORK, 212 – 684 – 8910
Hard Copy Requests: Shannon Speck, 800 – 920 – 6397
shannon@newsbroadcastnetwork.com
Editorial Contact: Laura Ojile, 314 – 982 - 1740

w w w . n e w s b r o a d c a s t n e t w o r k . c o m

Courtesy GS1 US

EXHIBIT 9-2C   *Audio News Release*

6.18.04

UNIFORM CODE COUNCIL
30TH BIRTHDAY ANR

ANNOUNCER:

MICHAEL DELL...BILL GATES. MANY OF US THINK OF THESE INDIVIDUALS AS BUSINESS ICONS. SATURDAY, JUNE 26TH ANOTHER BUSINESS ICON IS TURNING 30 – THE U.P.C. BARCODE. THIS SATURDAY AT THE MARSH GROCERY STORE IN THE SMALL TOWN OF TROY, OHIO – WHERE THE WORLD'S FIRST SCAN OCCURRED – A CELEBRATION IS TAKING PLACE TO MARK THE OCCASION. THE ORIGINAL CASHIER, SHARON BUCHANAN, WHO SCANNED THE FIRST BARCODED PRODUCT – A PACK OF WRIGLEY GUM – WILL JOIN OTHERS IN COMMEMORATING THE OCCASION. JACK GRASSO, FROM THE UNIFORM CODE COUNCIL, THE GROUP THAT BROUGHT THE BAR CODE TO LIFE WAS THERE.

SOUNDBITE:

"THE UNIFORM CODE COUNCIL IS THRILLED TO CELEBRATE THE 30TH YEAR OF THE REVOLUTIONARY UPC, WHICH PROVIDES TREMENDOUS COST-SAVINGS AND IMPROVED INVENTORY TRACKING FOR BUSINESSES AND CONSUMERS. THE UPC HAS PAVED THE WAY FOR TECHNOLOGIES IN DEVELOPMENT TODAY, LIKE THE ELECTRONIC PRODUCT CODE, OR EPC. EPC WILL HAVE AS REMARKABLE AN IMPACT ON THE FUTURE OF THE SUPPLY CHAIN AS THE UPC DID THREE DECADES AGO."

ANNOUNCER:

TODAY, THE UNIVERSAL PRODUCT CODE IS NOW USED BY 23 MAJOR INDUSTRY SECTORS, INCLUDING RETAIL, HEALTHCARE, GOVERNMENT, FOODSERVICE, TRANSPORTATION, AND HIGH-TECH. THE ORGANIZATION ESTIMATES THAT THESE BAR CODES ARE SCANNED MORE THAN 10 BILLION TIMES A DAY IN OVER 140 NATIONS AROUND THE WORLD.

#

Courtesy GS1 US

EXHIBIT 9-2D   *Message Training Presentation*

PRIVACY IS AS IMPORTANT AS ANYTHING ELSE WE ARE DOING.

COMMITMENT	BENEFITS	TECHNOLOGY
We are committed to understanding and addressing the complex questions that surround consumer privacy.	Consumers and businesses will reap benefits through the use of EPC technologies.	The technology creates data about products not people.

EPC subscribers adhere to published public policy guidelines relating to consumer privacy. These guidelines provide that consumers should be given: - **notice** when EPC technology is in use, - **choice** over using or disposing of the tag after purchase, - **education** about EPC technology and its uses and - **control** of information retained through the use of EPC technologies. • We established a multi-industry, global public policy steering committee (PPSC) to provide education and outreach to key stakeholders in the public and private sectors. **The PPSC has and will continue to:** • Reviewed all relevant, recent and future studies on consumer privacy to inform and guide our discussions. • Study consumer perceptions and opinions regarding privacy and EPC. • Provide various state and federal bodies information that includes, relevant facts on EPC and its benefits to consumers and business.	• Consumers will have access to the right products at the right time. • Consumers believe in the benefits of the technology. • No longer will consumers receive expired or short-dated products. • EPCs will help speed product recalls and aid in the recovery of stolen property, and reduce the opportunity for counterfeit items; especially in the pharmaceutical and electronics industry. • Business can improve efficiency in their business processes through RFID in the supply chain. • Retail theft costs retailers, and ultimately consumers, $50 billion per year. EPC will help retailers keep better track of items in the supply chain to reduce theft. • Counterfeiting is a $500 billion problem. EPC technologies will help lessen counterfeiting.	• The EPC is merely a license plate for a product. It creates data about products not people • Current applications help companies see how, when and where their products move within the supply chain helping them create new efficiencies in their business. • The licensing arrangements for EPC specifically prohibit their use for tracking or identifying people. • EPC tags are passive, they have no power of their own, transmitting data only when prompted by a signal emitted from a reader that is in close proximity. • The technology currently has limitations: — EPC tags cannot be read at great distances. They have an average read range of less than five feet. — Radio waves cannot penetrate some materials; particularly dense materials such as frozen foods, foils and liquids.

Courtesy GS1 US

Mergers by international organizations provide special commu-

nication challenges ranging from reaching diverse internal audi-

ences to establishing a recognizable international brand. Exhibit

9-3a is a news release announcing a new international board,

and Exhibit 9-3b is a news release on an event in the United

Kingdom.

IDRC Merges with NACORE: The Launch of CoreNet Global

CoreNet Global with Imre Communications, LLC

Overview

In 2002, the world's two largest associations serving the corporate real estate profession became one. Moreover, due to a successful communications program, the successor association was launched amid great excitement and without alienating or losing members, or upsetting constituencies.

For decades, the International Development Research Council (IDRC) and the International Association of Corporate Real Estate Executives (NACORE) were competing professional associations, each with a distinct mission, personality, and culture. The membership of each (both had roughly 3,500 members) primarily served real estate asset managers at large corporations and industry service providers. In early 2000, the leaders of each group decided to merge the associations for economic reasons.

However, several obstacles remained to successfully communicate the reasons for, and the logistics of, the merger. Each organization still had members set in traditional ways with loyalties to their particular association and its respective culture. Each association treated similar functions differently, most notably the number of conferences held each year, the name given to the professional certification program, the financial structure for regional and global chapters, and the treatment of practitioner members versus industry service providers. Yet another potential obstacle was the threat of a fledgling competing organization that was attracting a significant portion of CoreNet Global's membership.

As the new board of CoreNet Global worked to resolve each of these issues, Imre Communications partnered with the organization to communicate these changes and launch the association's new brand. This official launch took place on May 1, 2002.

Courtesy CoreNet Global

Research

IDRC and NACORE conducted research via a joint e-mail to their memberships to measure acceptance of the proposal. While prior to the survey there had been a few outspoken individuals and anecdotal evidence that the merger would not be universally accepted, the poll results were conclusive and, once established, drove the entire effort. The poll indicated that more than 80 percent of the total membership supported the merger and would continue to remain members.

Board members from each predecessor organization were deployed to speak around the United States and global regions at chapter meetings and relayed feedback from "the front lines."

Individual members with long histories of loyalties to their organization were interviewed informally and their concerns about merging vetted. Research was also conducted along a parallel track on what the new name of the association should be, and how the logo and messaging statement would position it. Finally, a survey was designed to measure satisfaction following the launch.

Planning

Target Audiences

Existing IORC and NACORE memberships, potential members, corporate real estate community

Fueled by research that the membership would support the merger, key decisions were made. Adopting the name CoreNet Global, and an informal tag line of "the best of IORC and NACORE," the board developed a program module for national and international conferences, a name and structure for industry certification, and financial frameworks for individual chapters. CoreNet Global created a special communications budget of $250,000 to formally launch the brand and establish the identity of CoreNet Global.

CoreNet Global identified the following objectives, which were to be met through communications tactics:

- Maintain a membership retention rate of better than 80 percent through fall 2002, the first key turnover period for many members.

- Achieve a satisfaction rate of better than 75 percent to be measured by an internal survey.

- Achieve attendance of greater than 3,000 and sponsorship revenues of greater than $1.2 million at the Global Summit in November 2002 (San Diego), the first U.S. conference to follow the merger announcement.

- Generate six to ten mainstream media placements in both general business press and the real estate trade media to establish the

CoreNet Global brand and its image as a corporate real estate thought leader and create a tool that would allow individual chapters to generate grassroots public relations.

- Reposition the website as an information center for the corporate real estate industry and increase Web traffic by 50 percent.

Execution

The program was executed with much buildup and excitement, designed to win over members who may have been skeptical. Member enthusiasm was ensured when, with great fanfare, including confetti cannons and pyrotechnics displays, the two leaders of each organization met onstage to shake hands and ceremoniously launch the organization before the joint membership at the inaugural Global Summit in Salt Lake City. Similar events were held at inaugural events in Melbourne, Australia, and Cannes, France.

To meet the program objectives, CoreNet Global/Imre Communications developed a multifaceted communications plan that included the following additional tactics:

- Established a media presence by:
  1. Creating the "CoreNet Global Quarterly Corporate Real Estate Benchmark," an online survey of members that would primarily function as a media relations device. The survey is recognized by the media as a valuable tool and has been quoted in *Business Week,* the *Wall Street Journal,* and *CFO Magazine,* among numerous other general interest and trade publications.
  2. Positioning CoreNet Global board members as sources for expert commentary in news articles.
- Developed a "branding kit" for regional chapter presidents and public relations committee chairs. The kit included a (electronic and paper copy) sample press release, chapter announcement, style guide, CD-ROM with electronic letterhead, media lists, tips on generating positive public relations, and media talking points on the new association. (Conference calls were held with chapter leaders to explain how to use the book, and a special orientation session was held at the Global Summit in November.)
- Created CoreNet Global identity by designing logo and incorporating into overall identity suite.
- Conducted media training briefings for individual chapters at the Global Summit in fall 2002.
- Created an internal newsletter and weekly e-mail industry and association briefings to keep members up to date.

- Launched a new industry trade magazine, *Corporate Real Estate Leader,* and newsletter, *CoreNet Global News.*
- Held a media tour in which the chairman and president of the association met with reporters from the *Wall Street Journal, FORTUNE,* and *Business Week.*
- Conducted an extensive and statistically significant member survey to measure overall satisfaction.

Evaluation

The communications program established the brand and identity of CoreNet Global to the membership, the general public, and the media, was completed on budget, and met key objectives:

- In the follow-up members survey, 87 percent indicated their intent to remain with the association.
- In addition, satisfaction with the overall association was rated at 78 percent.
- Attendance at the San Diego Global Summit was 3,100, and the sponsorship budget of $1.2 million was exceeded by $51,729.
- Mainstream media and trade publication placements numbered more than ten and included multiple articles in the *Wall Street Journal,* the *Wall Street Journal Europe, FORTUNE, Bloomberg, Commercial Property News, and Real Estate Forum.*
- Chapters have generated calendar listings, articles, and bylines through the use of the branding kits.
- Web traffic of 40,000 visits each month.

EXHIBIT 9-3A   *News Release—Atlanta*

CONTACTS
Richard Kadzis, CoreNet Global
404-589-3201
Rkadzis@corenetglobal.org

Ashby McIntire, Imre Communications
410-821-8220
ashbym@imrecommunicatio ns.com

New Directors Elected to CoreNet Global Board
2003 – 2004 Leadership Slate Announced

ATLANTA, GA (May 27, 2003) -- CoreNet Global, the world's leading professional association for corporate real estate executives, has announced the election of its 2003 – 2004 Board of Directors, which members elected via electronic balloting May 9 - 16.

Effective May 2003, the newly-elected Board members that will fill four open positions for three-year terms are:

- **Mary Manning**, Senior Vice President, SBC Communications, Dallas, TX
- **John Igoe**, BCCR, Vice President of Real Estate and Site Services, Palm Solutions Group, Milpitas, CA
- **Klaus Ansmann**, MCR, Managing Director, Deutsche Post, Bonn, Germany
- **Simon O'Reilly**, European Region Representative to the Global Board; Partner, Global Corporate Services, Cushman & Wakefield Healy & Baker, London, UK

Directors who will continue their current terms on the Board are:

- Chairman **Sean B. McCourt**, Chairman, Ford Land, Dearborn, MI *
- Chair-elect **Leslie Whatley**, MCR, Senior VP Real Estate, JP Morgan Chase, New York *
- Treasurer **John F. Igoe**, BCCR, VP Real Estate, Palm Solutions Group *
- Past Chairman **Matthew P. Cullen, MCR.h**, Detroit, MI *
- **William F. Concannon**, President /CEO, Trammell Crow Co., Dallas, TX
- **Jeffrey L. Elie,** Vice President Real Estate & Facilities, Kaplan Inc., New York
- **Alex Dominguez, MCR**, Senior Director of Real Estate, Chick-fil-A Inc., Atlanta, GA
- **Del Boyette**, Southeast Practice Leader, Deloitte & Touche, Atlanta, GA
- **John W. Davis, MCR,** Executive Managing Director, CB Richard Ellis Inc., Los Angeles, CA
- **Parkash P. Ahuja**, San Francisco, CA
- Associate Board Member **Peter Van Sickle**, Bank of Montreal, Canada

-more-

Courtesy CoreNet Global

EXHIBIT 9-3A *News Release—Atlanta (continued)*

2003-2004 CoreNet Global Board of Directors – Page 2 of 2

- Associate Board Member **Richard Watton**, MRICS, JP Morgan Chase & Co., Hong Kong
- Associate Board Member **Warrick Hobart**, Caltex Australia, Sydney

CoreNet Global also recognizes **Linda E. Rains, CCIM, MCR**, for her service on the Board of Directors. Ms. Rains, Field Real Estate Director, Metromedia Restaurant Group, completed her term on the CoreNet Global Board of Directors in May 2003.

CoreNet Global serves as the corporate real estate industry's thought and opinion leader, offering the MCR (Master of Corporate Real Estate) professional designation across a comprehensive platform of professional development and knowledge-sharing programs and services. Its 7,500 members are located in 25 countries worldwide and manage $1.2 trillion in real estate and workplace assets globally.

For more information, please visit www.corenetglobal.org

* The CoreNet Global leadership team also includes the officers of the association, who were elected May 5, 2003, by the Board of Directors.

###

EXHIBIT 9-3B   *News Release—United Kingdom*

Corenet Global UK - Sir Stuart Lipton Addresses the Thames Valley Branch at Chiswick Park

October 18, 2002 - A strong turn-out to the CoreNet Global UK Chapter Thames Valley Branch autumn forum at Chiswick Park heard Sir Stuart Lipton, chief executive of Stanhope plc, explain the design concept behind his latest development.

Describing the development of thinking from Stockley Park, 'buildings on their own, an 80's icon for freedom', to Broadgate, 'moving on to an interesting urban scheme', to Chiswick Park, 'a 33 acre suburban site with a five acre park'. He drew a parallel with the surrounding area: "We wanted to maintain a relationship," he said, "and we looked at developing villas in Chiswick, identical buildings, not different as in Stockley Park, and we set our architect, Richard Rogers, a target to recreate the Georgian villa in a modern vernacular. This is what we have recreated, with six identical buildings in a street and six more to follow. They are ultimately simple buildings, designed to encourage interaction and reaction, to create a feeling of space and energy."

To provide strong branding for the site, Stanhope turned to Wolff Olins. Explaining the process, Robert Jones, a director of Wolff Olins who led the team charged with the task, outlined the initial workshops which examined the reasons for the success of a series of leading developments. "We wanted to create a sense of liberation" he said. "Liberation from pressure, which would help to keep talented people, where work would be seen to be exciting and enjoyable." Onsite the occupants, described as 'guests', are now 'living the brand'. "We aimed to create two key elements" he continued, "thoughtfulness (removing hassles) and surprise (providing stimulation), so everyday services can be delivered via an intranet all supported by a programme of events and activities centred on an arena in the middle of the park."

The site is not as yet fully developed and during the debate which followed questions were raised as to the types of businesses targeted as occupants, plans for future buildings, the types of activities catered for 'after hours' and how brand value and brand performance would be measured.

Thanking the speakers, Thames Valley Branch chairman Tim Caiger of Oracle, who chaired the debate, remarked that while most sites eventually acquired their own brand the idea of creating a brand in advance was novel and definitely worth considering for all future developments.

Courtesy CoreNet Global

EXHIBIT 9-3B   *News Release—United Kingdom (continued)*

Notes to Editors
CoreNet Global UK , the result of the integration of IDRC and NACORE completed on 1st May this year, currently has a total membership of around 560 property profesionals.

CoreNet Global is the leading corporate real estate association worldwide. The association has a worldwide membership of approaching 7,000 across all five continents. There are currently around 1,000 members in 11 countries across Europe of which approximately 560 members, spread across five branches, are based in the UK.

CoreNet Global UK holds Chapter Meetings six times a year on a bi-monthly basis, and six joint meetings are held with SPROG (Society of Property Researchers Occupier Group) throughout the year, there is an annual dinner in February and an annual UK summit in November.

The Northern regional Branch was launched in February 1998, the Thames Valley Branch in November 1998, the Midlands Branch in May 1999 and the Scottish Branch in April 2000. A fifth regional Branch covering the West and Wales is shortly to be launched.

In the UK there are current plans for meetings as follows:

- A UK Summit, Queen Elizabeth II Conference Centre (8th November).
- A Northern Branch meeting at Manchester Stadium (13th November)
- A Thames Valley Branch meeting at Axis Park (20th November)
- A Midlands Branch meeting at Capital One, Nottingham (21st November)

For further information
Contact: Alison Sutherland at AVS Publicity on 020 7373 4427   alison@avsp.fsnet.co.uk

## Chapter 10

Relations with Special Publics

Special publics are defined as those unique or distinctive groups with which an organization needs to communicate. These groups may be minority publics, such as African Americans, Hispanics, or Asian Americans. Practitioners should be aware of the extensive national, geographic, and ethnic subsets that exist within each of these broadly defined minority groups in the United States. For instance, practitioners might mistakenly lump all Hispanics together under the Mexican umbrella. For a Hispanic special event, they could employ a mariachi band and serve Mexican dishes. However, such treatment would easily offend Spaniards, Argentines, or Dominicans, all of whose home cultures differ sharply from one another and from that of Mexico, although all share Spanish as a common language. A similar mistake would be to treat Asian Americans as a singular group or, worse, to refer to them as Orientals. These Asian groups share neither common languages nor common cultural heritages. Many of them, in fact, have been enemies for centuries.

When dealing with a minority group with national origins outside the United States, practitioners would be well advised to consult in advance the embassy or consulate of that group's homeland and certainly the group's local leaders as well.

In addition to ethnic or national minority publics, practitioners may target for special communication such groups as women, students, educators, environmentalists, school-age children, the business community, municipal officials, or community physicians. The list of potential special publics can actually be extended to include all the segments of society.

The fastest growing and most significant of these special groups in the United States is the "senior citizen" segment of the population, a segment expected to double in size by the mid-twenty-first century. Age groupings, such as 50–64 for the "active" seniors, 65–74 for the "less active," and 75-plus for the "elderly," are often used to describe subsegments of the senior citizen audience. These age groupings alone, though, are usually less useful in targeting senior audiences than are their organizational affiliations. Organizations such as AARP (formerly the American Association of Retired Persons), the National Council on the Aging (NCOA), the National Hispanic Council on Aging, the National Council of Senior Citizens, the National Senior Sports Association, and the Gray Panthers have chapter networks and affiliate organizations that can be used to reach their members. Thus, the key to reaching a senior audience lies in cosponsorship of an event or project with an organization such as AARP or the NCOA.

As with other forms of public relations, the four-part ROPE process model is a helpful format for preparing and executing programs that target special publics.

RESEARCH

Research for special programs includes investigation of the client, the reason for the program, and, most important, the distinctive audience to be targeted.

Client Research

Client research for an organization's relations with a special public should focus on the client's role and reputation with the particular audience. How credible is the organization with this public? Have there been significant complaints against it from this public in the past? What are its past and present communication practices toward this audience? What are its major strengths and weaknesses relative to this public? What opportunities exist to enhance its relations with this public?

Opportunity or Problem Research

Should a proactive public relations program be devised for this particular audience? Or has some problem arisen that must be addressed with a reactive program? Why should the organization communicate with this audience at all? Detailed answers to these questions will provide the necessary justification for the outlay of funds required for relations with a given special public.

Audience Research

Obviously, the practitioner should learn as much as possible about a special public. One way to do this is to regard such publics as differentiated communities. In community relations, practitioners address community media, community leaders, and community organizations. These same audience subsets may also be applicable in defining a special public:

> Media utilized by this public
>> Mass
>> Specialized
> Leaders of this public
>> Public officials
>> Professional leaders
>> Ethnic leaders
>> Neighborhood leaders
>> Others

Organizations composing this public

    Civic

    Political

    Service

    Business

    Cultural

    Religious

    Youth

    Other

As in community relations, practitioners should develop special contact lists for the appropriate media and for the special public's leaders and organizations. These materials are indispensable in relations with a special public. Remember, some audience segments are more actively engaged in an issue than others.

OBJECTIVES

Programs that target special publics can use both impact and output objectives; and, as in all other types of public relations, the objectives should be specific and quantitative.

Impact Objectives

Impact objectives represent the desired outcomes of informing or modifying the attitudes or behaviors of the special audience. Some examples include:

1. To increase the knowledge of the organization's minority-benefits program among members of this special public (by 50 percent before January 1)

2. To promote more favorable opinion (30 percent) toward the organization on the part of this special public (during the current year)

3. To stimulate greater participation (15 percent) in the organization's programs by this special public (during the summer months)

Output Objectives

Output objectives comprise the specific efforts to enhance relations with special publics. For example:

1. To prepare and distribute materials to (30 percent of) the Hispanic community in Washington (during the coming year)

2. To schedule four meetings each year with leaders of the Chinese community in Houston

3. To develop five new projects for African American instructors' use in their classrooms (during the current school year)

PROGRAMMING

Programming for relations with special publics includes planning the theme and messages, action or special event(s), uncontrolled and controlled media, and effective communication principles in the program's execution.

Theme and Messages

Both the theme and messages should reflect the desired relationship between the organization and the targeted special public. They will also be an indicator of past and present relationships that exist between the organization and this public. Cultural, ethnic, and gender values will likely affect the themes and messages used in a campaign so look for messages that will resonate with your public.

Action(s) or Special Event(s)

Actions and special events should concentrate on the major interests of the targeted audience. The most successful actions and special events address the interests, needs, and problems of the particular target group. The special events in the cases in this chapter clearly meet this criterion. For example, if the target audience is very attuned to "family and community," think in terms of family-oriented events.

Uncontrolled and Controlled Media

As mentioned earlier, representatives of both the mass and specialized media aimed at the special audience are an important segment of the audience itself. Uncontrolled media in the form of news releases, photo opportunities or photographs, feature stories, and/or interviews should be prepared in the language of the designated media; they should be directed to media outlets known to be used by this special public.

Controlled media should be prepared with all the cultural, language, ethnic, age, or other demographic specifications of the target public in mind. Obviously, the organization's website will play a crucial role in the program. The website can include a great body of information of interest to the target public. As with other publics, there can be no substitute for personal interaction in the effective execution of programs.

Effective Communication

Principles of effective communication are the same for special audiences as they are for most others. Extra care should be taken, however, in the matter of source credibility, which can be enhanced by the selection of a spokesperson from the same demographic group as the targeted audience.

In addition to source credibility, two-way communication and audience participation should also be given extra emphasis in relations with special publics.

Finally, the use of opinion leaders may be highly significant in relations with special publics, especially when the public is an organized ethnic or demographic group. In sum, all aspects of programming for relations with special publics are similar to those of community relations. The special public, in fact, can often be thought of as a community with its own media, leaders, and organizations.

EVALUATION

The process of evaluating communications aimed at special audiences must take into account the program's objectives. Each one should be measured using previously discussed standards and methods.

Evaluation of special publics cases rely generally on the degree of participation by the target audiences and, in most instances, the amount of publicity generated by the program.

SUMMARY

Research for programs that target special audiences focuses on the credibility of the client with a particular special public, along with the need or justification for the program. The audience itself can be analyzed using the same categories applicable to community relations—media, leaders, and organizations. Special audiences can usually be treated as communities, or sub-communities, in their own right.

Objectives for relations with special publics may be impact or output in nature. Impact objectives express desired outcomes, such as augmenting the public's knowledge or influencing its attitudes or behaviors. Without reference to impact, output objectives consist of practitioner efforts to execute the program.

Programming for special publics often uses the significant events of the public's ethnic or cultural past. Along with this, of course, the programming must also address the problems or potential problems of the special group. Although standard controlled and uncontrolled media are used in this form of public relations, there can be no substitute for two-way communication with such audiences. More than others, they need to know that the organization cares enough about them to include a personal touch.

As with other forms of public relations, the special program's stated objectives must be evaluated appropriately. In general, the level of participation by the targeted group and the publicity generated by the program are used as benchmarks of success.

READINGS ON SPECIAL PUBLICS

Bouttilier, Robert. *Targeting Families: Marketing to and Through the New Family*. Ithaca, NY: American Marketing Tools, 1993.

Crispell, Diane. "The Real Middle Americans," *American Demographics* 16 (October 1994): 28 ff.

Daddario, Gina. *Women's Sports and Spectacle: Gendered Television Coverage and the Olympic Games*. Westport, CT: Praeger, 1998.

Edmondson, Brad. "The Minority Majority in 2001," *American Demographics* 18 (October 1996): 16 ff.

Ferguson, Robert. *Representing "Race": Ideology, Identity and the Media*. London: Oxford University Press, 1998.

Gandy, Oscar H. *Communication and Race: A Structural Perspective*. London: Oxford University Press, 1998.

Gardner, Susan, and Susanna Eng. "What Students Want: Generation Y and the Changing Function of the Academic Library," *Portal: Libraries and the Academy* 15 (July 2005): 405 ff.

Giles, Jeff. "Generation X," *Newsweek* (June 6, 1994): 62 ff.

Gothard, Ann Marie. "Black Newspapers: An Overlooked PR Opportunity," *Public Relations Tactics* 5 (October 1998): 24.

Grunig, Larissa A., Elizabeth Lance Toth, and Linda Childers Hon. *Women in Public Relations: How Gender Influences Practice*. New York: Guilford Publications, 2001.

Jackson, Ronald L. *African American Communication and Identities*. Thousand Oaks, CA: Sage Publications, 2004.

Jandt, Fred E. *Intercultural Communication*. Thousand Oaks, CA: Sage Publications, 2001.

Jones, Mathew, Debra Salmon, and Judy Orme. "Young People's Involvement in a Substance Misuse Communications Campaign," *Drugs: Education, Prevention & Policy* 11 (October 2004): 391–405.

Lazer, William. *Handbook of Demographics for Marketing and Advertising*. New York: Lexington Books, 1994.

Levine, Joshua. "Generation X," *Forbes* (July 18, 1994): 293 ff.

Longino, Charles E., Jr. "Myths of an Aging Population," *American Demographics* 16 (August 1994): 36 ff.

McGee, Tom. "Getting Inside Kids' Heads," *American Demographics* 19 (January 1997): 53–55.

Milhouse, Virginia H., Molefi Kete Asante, and Peter O. Nwosu. *Transcultural Realities*. Thousand Oaks, CA: Sage Publications, 2001.

Mitchell, Susan. *Generation X: The Young Adult Market*. Ithaca, NY: New Strategist Publications, 1997.

Morgan, Carol M., and Doran J. Levy. *Segmenting the Mature Market*. New York: Probus, 1994.

Morton, Linda P. "Targeting Hispanic Americans," *Public Relations Quarterly* 47 (fall 2002): 46–48.

Palen, J. John. *The Suburbs*. New York: McGraw-Hill, 1994.

Peterson, Peter G. "Will America Grow Up Before It Grows Old?" *The Atlantic Monthly* 277 (May 1996): 5 ff.

Price, Vincent, Lilach Nir, and Joseph N. Cappella. "Framing Public Discussion of Gay Civil Unions," *Public Opinion Quarterly* 69 (summer 2005): 179–212.

Rabin, Steve. "How to Sell Across Cultures," *American Demographics* 16 (March 1994): 56 ff.

Romaine, Suzanne. *Communicating Gender*. Mahwah, NJ: Erlbaum, 1998.

Saindor, Gabrielle, et al. "The Other Americans," *American Demographics* 16 (June 1994): 36 ff.

Spethmann, Betsy. "Speaking to the Sisterhood," *Promo* (October 1998): 50 ff.

Stanfield, John H., II. "Multiethnic Societies and Regions," *American Behavioral Scientist* 40 (September 1996): 8 ff.

Svoboda, Sandra A. "Promoting Detroit's African-American Cultural Sites," *Public Relations Tactics* 5 (April 1998): 21.

Thau, Richard. "So-called Generation X: How Do You Target a Market That Wants to Be Left Alone?" *Vital Speeches of the Day* 62 (August 15, 1996): 664 ff.

Ting-Toomey, Stella. *Communicating Across Cultures*. New York: Guilford Publications, 1999.

Tully, Shawn. "Teens: The Most Global Market of All," *Fortune* (May 16, 1994): 82 ff.

Underhill, Paco. "Kids in Stores," *American Demographics* 16 (June 1994): 22 ff.

Vahouny, Karen. "Opportunities for Improvement," *Communication World* 21 (May–June 2004): 32–38.

Wolfe, David B. "Targeting the Mature Mind," *American Demographics* 16 (March 1994): 32 ff.

Yun Kim, Young. *Becoming Intercultural.* Thousand Oaks, CA: Sage Publications, 2001.

Ziegler, Dyhana, ed. *Diversity.* Mahwah, NJ: Erlbaum, 1996.

Zinn, Laura, et al. "Teen," *Business Week* (April 11, 1994): 76 ff.

SPECIAL PUBLICS CASES

CASE 10-1

Women have a tendency to dismiss heart attacks as a man's problem. Changing their attitudes and changing behavior to reduce health risks required a major campaign to convince them that women also were at risk. The "Heart Truth Campaign" started with a fashion week event in 2003 and has blossomed into a multifaceted series of activities that has captured broad national exposure each year since the inaugural campaign. Exhibit 10-1a is the 2003 Red Dress Project announcement, Exhibit 10-1b is an infographic fact sheet, Exhibit 10-1c is an "action plan" target to African American women, and Exhibit 10-1d is a pitch letter to the media.

A Fashionable Red Alert Warns Women of The Heart Truth

National Heart, Lung, and Blood Institute, with Ogilvy Public Relations Worldwide

Summary

In 2000, only 34 percent of women knew that their #1 killer is heart disease. Yet, one in three women dies of heart disease, eight times more than breast cancer, and misperceptions about the disease abound—including the belief that it's only a man's disease. This crisis demanded action. *The Heart Truth* campaign and its Red Dress symbol, created by the National Heart, Lung, and Blood Institute (NHLBI) and Ogilvy Public Relations Worldwide, have sparked a powerful awareness movement within the national women's health community, the media, and corporate America—reaching women nationwide.

Courtesy The National Heart, Lung, and Blood Institute

Research

The Heart Truth evolved through extensive primary and secondary formative research:

- A comprehensive analysis of mid-life women: demographics, psychographics, geographic and socioeconomic factors, cardiovascular health knowledge, attitudes and behaviors, media preferences;
- An NHLBI-conducted literature review of 200+ research articles on cardiovascular health and women;
- Eight focus groups in four cities across the country to test creative concepts and messages; and Materials review by the campaign's core government and community organization partners.

This research informed a range of elements in the planning process, including target audience selection, message and materials development, channel and activity selection, and partner recruitment.

Planning

Objectives

Since its launch, *The Heart Truth* has continually aimed to:

- Increase awareness that heart disease is the #1 killer of women;
- Increase awareness of the risk factors that can lead to heart disease, disability, and death; and
- Encourage women to talk to their doctors and take action to control these risk factors.

Strategic Approach

The Heart Truth primarily targets women ages 40–60 (an age when risk increases), with a secondary target of women ages 18–39. *The Heart Truth* team prepared an extensive national marketing, media relations, and public service campaign, building relationships with partners who could help reinforce messages at all levels of society. Beyond the communications impact these proven strategies would deliver, we knew that women needed a striking wake-up call to change their thinking—and perhaps even save their lives. *The Heart Truth* triumphed with its centerpiece creative element, the Red Dress, paired with the tagline: "Heart Disease Doesn't Care What You Wear—It's the #1 Killer of Women." Why a Red Dress? It was proven in focus groups with women to forge a strong emotional link between a woman's focus on her outer self and the need to focus on her inner self—specifically her heart health. Like the pink ribbon for breast cancer, the Red Dress icon gives the cause an unforgettable identity and has proven to be a rallying symbol for partners, media, and women with heart disease.

Execution

To reach women, *The Heart Truth* campaign has delivered messages through:

- Creative design using compelling photos and stories of real women's struggles with heart disease, which put a face on women's heart disease and provided consistent branding across materials;

- Educational and marketing materials—including a 100-page *Healthy Heart Handbook for Women* and a Speaker's Kit (with a 10-minute video and PowerPoint presentation)—to promote heart health;

- A website with ideas and materials to help audiences plan *Heart Truth* events (www.hearttruth.gov);

- National public service advertising (print, radio, and television);

- Partnerships with national nonprofit organizations reinforced at the local level, including WomenHeart, the American Heart Association (AHA), American College of Cardiology, Association of Black Cardiologists, Hadassah, National Black Nurses Association, General Federation of Women's Clubs, the National Association of Latina Leaders, and The Links, Inc.; and

- Corporate and media partnerships with Mercedes-Benz Fashion Week, IMG Models, Time Inc. Women's Group, *GLAMOUR,* Wal-Mart, RadioShack, California Pistachio Commission, Swarovski, Inc., Olympus Fashion Week, Johnson & Johnson, Albertsons, Smart Ones, General Mills (Berry Burst Cheerios and 8th Continent Soy Milk brands), Celestial Seasonings, and Minute Maid.

Seeking to mobilize an industry intrinsically tied to the target audience, *The Heart Truth* team forged a groundbreaking collaboration between the federal government and the fashion industry to launch the Red Dress as the national symbol for women and heart disease awareness. The value of the fashion-based partnerships alone—to launch the Red Dress in 2003 and expand campaign messaging through Fashion Week activities during American Heart Month in 2004 and 2005—is conservatively valued at more than $6 million. Programming to advance the Red Dress and campaign messages from February 2003 through March 2005 included:

- A partnership with 7th on Sixth (producers of Fashion Week), IMG and IMG Models, and title sponsor Mercedes-Benz to name women and heart disease awareness as the "cause" for Mercedes-Benz Fashion Week in February 2003 in New York. Nineteen top fashion designers—from Vera Wang and Donna Karan to Oscar de la Renta and Ralph Lauren—contributed red dresses to a weeklong launch exhibit, and acclaimed jewelry designer Angela Cummings created a Red Dress Pin to launch the symbol;

- The participation of one of the most recognizable women in the world—First Lady Laura Bush—to champion the cause and introduce the government's campaign and its symbol under the Bryant Park tents at Fashion Week, including appearances on all of the network morning shows on February 14, 2003, and again in February 2004 and 2005;

- Corporate and media partnerships secured by Ogilvy PR subsequent to the February 2003 launch of the Red Dress Project, including Time Inc. Women's Group, *GLAMOUR*, Wal-Mart, RadioShack, California Pistachio Commission, Swarovski, Inc., Johnson & Johnson, Albertsons, General Mills, and Smart Ones, among others;

- A press conference in Washington, D.C., hosted by U.S. Department of Health and Human Services secretary Tommy Thompson, who issued a proclamation declaring "Women's Heart Day";

- Production, placement, and sales of the Red Dress Pin at Wal-Mart in time for Mother's Day 2003 resulting in mainstream media coverage of the pin (*Parade* and *USA Today*);

- *GLAMOUR* magazine's partnership debut in a 15-page cover-story spread in October 2003, featuring Shania Twain on the cover, an exclusive interview with the First Lady, a foldout of 24 celebrities in red dresses, and a three-year editorial commitment about the issue;

- Launch of the *LifeWise Heart Truth Pledge* program with RadioShack's *LifeWise* brand of wellness products, encouraging women to make one small change every month to improve their heart health;

- Placement of oversized store banners and end cap displays in Albertsons stores nationwide that highlighted the campaign's real women in red and sale of Red Dress Pins and *The Heart Truth* T-shirts, along with free distribution of 250,000 copies of *The Healthy Heart Handbook for Women;*

- More than 100 local *Heart Truth* events spearheaded by partners (e.g., health fairs, dances, walks, rallies, celebrity teas, power breakfasts, red dress fashion shows), including 31 *Heart Truth* Single City Stops across the country; with five community hospital events hosted by Mrs. Bush featuring local heart patients and presentation of campaign messaging to community leaders, local media, and local heart health organizations;

- A *Heart Truth* campaign press event at The White House featuring President and Mrs. Bush declaring February 2004 as American Heart Month and announcing upcoming *Heart Truth* campaign efforts;

- *Woman's Day* magazine's recognition of the NHLBI/Ogilvy PR *Heart Truth* team as innovators in women's heart health awareness with an inaugural Red Dress Award presented in February 2004;

- The creation of the first annual National Wear Red Day (February 6, 2004) and the same-day debut of the Red Dress Collection 2004 at Olympus Fashion Week with a star-studded fashion show featuring 26 new designs worn by top fashion models and celebrities such as Vanessa Williams and Beverly Johnson, hosted by Patti Hansen;

- Implementation of *The Heart Truth* Road Show in five U.S. cities from March to May 2004 reaching more than 86,000 consumers, exhibiting designer red dresses (including Mrs. Bush's own red Oscar de la Renta suit) and offering free heart health screenings to more than 4,000 individuals;

- Adoption of the Red Dress symbol by a full range of campaign partners, including the American Heart Association's introduction of its complementary campaign in February 2004, *Go Red for Women;*

- WomenHeart's expanded cause-marketing program with companies such as CIGNA to launch its Red Bag of Courage in early 2005 with information for patients with heart disease;

- Launch of *The Heart Truth*'s Communities of Color initiative at a February 4, 2005, press event in New York featuring First Lady Laura Bush, Duchess of York Sarah Ferguson, Dr. Anne Taylor of the Association of Black Cardiologists, and Dr. Elizabeth G. Nabel, director of NHLBI;

- Ongoing development of corporate partner programs to utilize distribution and promotional channels reaching tens of millions of women, including a J&J-sponsored retail FSI (Free-Standing Newspaper Insert) in November 2004, the debut of the first-ever on-pack promotion with 8th Continent in the fall of 2004, the launch of the Berry Burst Cheerios box featuring the Red Dress in February 2005, and Minute Maid packaging featuring the Red Dress symbol through a partnership with WomenHeart; and

- Debut of the Red Dress Collection 2005 on the second annual National Wear Red Day — February 4, 2005 — featuring 26 new designs showcased by celebrities from the arts, sports, and entertainment industries, such as Vanessa Williams, Venus Williams, Paula Abdul, Sheryl Crow, Rosanna Arquette, Phylicia Rashad, Sarah Ferguson, Christie Brinkley, Carly Patterson, and Carmen Dell'Orefice.

Evaluation

The most significant outcome of *The Heart Truth* is the number of women who are now aware that heart disease is their #1 health threat. An encouraging and steady rise in awareness of heart disease as the leading killer of U.S. women has occurred in recent years. In AHA's 2000 survey, only 34 percent of women spontaneously listed heart disease as women's leading cause of death, a figure that jumped to 57 percent in 2004 — less than two years following *The Heart Truth* launch. As well, 18 months after the Red Dress launch, 25 percent of American women identified the Red Dress as the national symbol for women and heart disease awareness, according to a national survey commissioned in Fall 2004 by Ogilvy PR. This heightened awareness was confirmed again in January 2005 in a survey commissioned by WomenHeart, a founding partner of *The Heart Truth*.

In addition, *The Heart Truth* and its Red Dress have amassed impressive process evaluation results:

- Women-targeted and health-focused coverage in major national and local media totals 1,089,242,427 audience impressions (does not include multipliers or pass along rates): Television PSAs garnered nearly 206 million impressions (January–December 2003), radio PSAs gained close to 187 million impressions during their first two months, and airport dioramas currently appear in approximately 22 major airports — often in multiple locations — representing an advertising equivalent of approximately $7 million;

- Color PSA placements in *Essence, Parenting, Health, Heart & Soul, BabyTalk, People en Español,* and *Balance,* representing an advertising value close to $500,000 and total impressions of more than 25 million;

- 795,000 Red Dress pins, more than 300,000 copies of the *Healthy Heart Handbook* and more than 250,000 *Heart Truth* brochures (in English and Spanish) distributed;

- More than 20 corporate relationships secured and developed to reach tens of millions of women through promotional programming;

- Four national FSIs — Johnson & Johnson, REACH, General Mills, and Promise — with a combined circulation of 165 million;

- 14.6 million General Mills products feature the Red Dress on packaging;

- Working with partners, *The Heart Truth* Road Show traveled to five U.S. cities, exhibiting designer red dresses (including Mrs. Bush's) and offering free heart health screenings — more than 86,000 consumers were reached, with nearly 4,000 being screened for heart disease risk factors; and

- Core campaign programs, including the Single City Stop program, First Lady events, and health professional conference outreach, resulted in more than 50 events in communities around the country. In addition to these targeted campaign initiatives, organizations and individuals executed hundreds of local community events across the country to spread *The Heart Truth,* including more than 100 events registered in *The Heart Truth* activity registry.

Women's health experts and heart disease thought leaders have acknowledged that the tide is turning in women's awareness of the importance of taking care of their heart. Moreover, these experts believe that *The Heart Truth* is the engine behind much of this increased attention and awareness.

Of course, there is no greater reward for a public health campaign than proof that it has saved lives. An event in Kansas City, Missouri, featuring remarks by the First Lady, did just that for one woman: "A 54-year-old woman presented to our Emergency Department after being awakened several times during the night with chest discomfort . . . After our wonderful media coverage, the patient confirmed that the surrounding media about the leading cause of death in women and the seriousness of women's heart health prompted her to take personal action—what impact!"

EXHIBIT 10-1A *Red Dress Project*

HEART DISEASE IS THE #1 KILLER OF WOMEN

HEART DISEASE *doesn't* CARE WHAT YOU WEAR

THE RED DRESS PROJECT
Fashion makes a statement for women and heart disease at Mercedes-Benz Fashion Week

Heart disease is not just a man's disease—it's the #1 killer of women. The Red Dress Project makes the statement in high fashion introducing the "Red Dress" as the new symbol for women and heart disease.

The Heart Truth is a national awareness campaign on women's heart health sponsored by the National Heart, Lung, and Blood Institute (NHLBI), part of the National Institutes of Health, U.S. Department of Health and Human Services (DHHS). The campaign is being conducted in partnership with the American Heart Association, the Office on Women's Health (DHHS), WomenHeart: the National Coalition for Women with Heart Disease, and other organizations committed to women's health.

The primary message driving *The Heart Truth* campaign is: Heart disease is not just a man's disease—it's the #1 killer of women. The campaign pairs the message with an arresting visual—the Red Dress—as the national symbol for women and heart disease.

The Red Dress is the heart of the Red Dress Project debuting at Mercedes-Benz Fashion Week, February 7-14, 2003, in New York during American Heart Month. This groundbreaking project, supported by Mercedes-Benz USA and 7th on Sixth (the producers of Mercedes-Benz Fashion Week), launches the red dress icon to raise awareness of women's risk of heart disease. According to a national survey conducted in 2000, only a third of women know that heart disease is the leading cause of death for women.

Why a Red Dress?
The Red Dress has proved to be a positive image to convey heart disease awareness messages targeted to women. Focus group research across the country showed that most women:
- Were aware of most major risk factors for heart disease and knew about heart-healthy behaviors—but had not adopted a heart-healthy lifestyle.

(over)

 U.S. DEPARTMENT OF HEALTH AND HUMAN SERVICES ♥ National Institutes of Health ♥ National Heart, Lung, and Blood Institute

Dress illustration adopted from pin design created by Angela Cummings Studio for the Red Dress Project

Courtesy The National Heart, Lung, and Blood Institute

333

EXHIBIT 10-1A   *Red Dress Project (continued)*

- Underestimated their personal risk (most thought they had a low to medium personal risk for heart disease even though they had risk factors such as smoking, high blood pressure, and high cholesterol).
- Did not fully understand the devastating impact that heart disease has on one's life and one's family.

The Red Dress Project is designed to build awareness that women are at risk; give a sense of hope that women can reduce their risk, and empower them to do so; and provide a clear call to action coupled with a sense of urgency.

The Red Dress Project

The Red Dress Project of *The Heart Truth* campaign puts the issue of women and heart disease in the national spotlight through a partnership with the Mercedes-Benz Fashion Week and the fashion industry.

Leading fashion designers contributed red dresses from either vintage or current collections to be showcased in the Red Dress Collection at Bryant Park throughout Mercedes-Benz Fashion Week.* A Red Dress pin, specially designed for *The Heart Truth* campaign by leading accessory designer Angela Cummings, will be introduced during Mercedes-Benz Fashion Week.

Mercedes-Benz USA presents the exclusive Mercedes-Benz Fashion Week magma red C320 Sports Coupe to be displayed at Bryant Park. In addition, the display area features an illustration of Angela Lindvall, Cover Girl, wearing a Donna Karan red dress photographed by David LaChapelle. The Red Dress Project of *The Heart Truth* campaign will be unveiled at a media briefing when Mercedes-Benz Fashion Week opens on Friday, February 7.

After Mercedes-Benz Fashion Week, the Red Dress Project will make a stop in Washington, D.C. before heading on a national tour.

For more information about the Red Dress Project, contact Sally McDonough at (202) 452-7815 or by mobile at (571) 259-1481. Photography supporting the Red Dress Project is available at http://www.nhlbi.nih.gov/health/hearttruth/press/press.htm.

*Participating Designers:

Bill Blass	Anne Klein	Badgley Mischka
Chaiken	Calvin Klein	Oscar de la Renta
Diane von Furstenberg	Michael Kors	Vivienne Tam
Carolina Herrera	Ralph Lauren	Carmen Marc Valvo
Tommy Hilfiger	Luca Luca	Vera Wang
Marc Jacobs	Catherine Malandrino	
Donna Karan	Nicole Miller	

EXHIBIT 10-1B *Infographic*

THE HEART TRUTH IS: HEART DISEASE IS A WOMEN'S ISSUE

Heart Disease is the #1 killer of women, regardless of race or ethnicity. Although significant progress has been made in raising awareness among women about heart disease, from 34 percent to 57 percent in just 4 years, most women fail to make the connection between risk factors, such as high blood pressure and high cholesterol, and their personal risk of developing heart disease. Only 20 percent of women identify heart disease as the greatest health problem facing women today, and awareness levels are lower among African American and Hispanic women. Experts at the National Heart, Lung, and Blood Institute encourage women to talk to their doctors to find out their personal risk for heart disease and how they can take action to lower it. For more information, visit www.hearttruth.gov.

Leading Causes of Death for Women

Heart Disease 356,014
Stroke 100,050
Lung Cancer 67,542
C.O.P.D. 64,103
Chronic Obstructive Pulmonary Disease
Breast Cancer 41,514

Source: The Healthy Heart Handbook for Women, National Heart, Lung, and Blood Institute (2005) Based on 2002 data

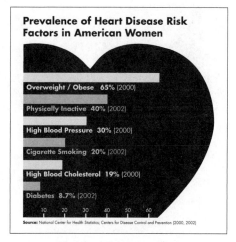

Prevalence of Heart Disease Risk Factors in American Women

Overweight / Obese **65%** (2000)
Physically Inactive **40%** (2002)
High Blood Pressure **30%** (2000)
Cigarette Smoking **20%** (2002)
High Blood Cholesterol **19%** (2000)
Diabetes **8.7%** (2002)

10   20   30   40   50   60

Source: National Center for Health Statistics; Centers for Disease Control and Prevention (2000, 2002)

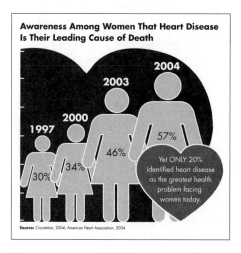

Awareness Among Women That Heart Disease Is Their Leading Cause of Death

2004
2003
2000
1997
30%   34%   46%   57%

Yet ONLY 20% identified heart disease as the greatest health problem facing women today.

Source: Circulation, 2004; American Heart Association, 2004

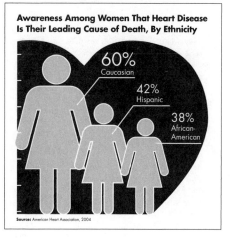

Awareness Among Women That Heart Disease Is Their Leading Cause of Death, By Ethnicity

60% Caucasian
42% Hispanic
38% African-American

Source: American Heart Association, 2004

The Heart Truth is a national awareness campaign for women about heart disease sponsored by the National Heart, Lung, and Blood Institute, part of the National Institutes of Health, U.S. Department of Health and Human Services.

To access camera-ready artwork, as well as photography and other creative materials for *The Heart Truth* campaign, visit www.hearttruth.gov. If you have questions, contact media@hearttruth.org.

Women & Heart Disease

Courtesy The National Heart, Lung, and Blood Institute

EXHIBIT 10-1C   *Fact Sheet for African American Women*

THE *heart* TRUTH
FOR WOMEN

THE HEART TRUTH FOR AFRICAN AMERICAN WOMEN: AN ACTION PLAN

When you hear the term "heart disease," what's your first reaction? Like many women, you may think, "That's a man's disease." But here's The Heart Truth: Heart disease is the #1 killer of women in the United States. One in three women dies of heart disease.

For African American women, the risk of heart disease is especially great. Heart disease is more prevalent among black women than white women—as are some of the factors that increase the risk of developing it, including high blood pressure, overweight and obesity, and diabetes.

But there's good news too: You can take action and lower your chance of developing heart disease and its risk factors. In fact, women can lower their heart disease risk by as much as 82 percent just by leading a healthy lifestyle. This fact sheet gives steps you can take to protect your heart health.

WHAT IS HEART DISEASE?
Coronary heart disease is the most common form of heart disease. Often referred to simply as "heart disease," it is a disorder of the blood vessels of the heart that can lead to a heart attack. It is a lifelong condition and will steadily worsen unless you make changes in your daily habits.

Risk Factors for Heart Disease
Lifestyle affects many of the "risk factors" for heart disease. Risk factors are conditions or habits that increase the chances of developing a disease or having it worsen. For heart disease, there are two types—those you can't change and those you can control. The ones you can't change are a family history of early heart disease and age, which for women becomes a risk

factor at 55. That's because, after menopause, women are more likely to get heart disease. Partly, this is because their body no longer produces estrogen. Also, middle age is a time when women tend to develop other heart disease risk factors.

But most of the risk factors can be controlled. Often, all it takes are lifestyle changes; sometimes, medication also is needed. Here's a quick review of these risk factors:

Smoking. About one in five black women smokes. Quit, and just one year later, your heart disease risk will drop by more than half. There's no easy way to quit but making a plan helps. You also can try an organized program or a medication—ask your doctor if either is right for you.

High Blood Pressure. Also called hypertension, high blood pressure increases your risk of heart disease, stroke, and congestive heart failure. Even levels slightly above normal—called "prehypertension"—increase your heart disease risk.

Black women develop high blood pressure earlier in life and have higher average blood pressures compared with white women. About 37 percent of black women have high blood pressure. Hypertension also increases the risk of stroke and congestive heart failure—and black women have high rates of both.

Lower elevated blood pressure by following a heart-healthy eating plan, including limiting your intake of salt and other forms of sodium, getting regular physical activity, maintaining a healthy weight, and, if you drink alcoholic beverages, doing so in moderation (not more than one drink a day). If you have high blood pressure, you also may need to take medication.

 U.S. DEPARTMENT OF HEALTH AND HUMAN SERVICES
National Institutes of Health
National Heart, Lung, and Blood Institute

 THE heart TRUTH

Courtesy The National Heart, Lung, and Blood Institute

One good eating plan, shown to lower elevated blood pressure, is called the DASH diet—for a copy of the plan, contact the National Heart, Lung, and Blood Institute (NHLBI) Health Information Center, which is listed in "To Learn More."

High Blood Cholesterol. Nearly half of black women have a total cholesterol that's too high. Excess cholesterol and fat in your blood builds up in the walls of vessels that supply blood to the heart and can lead to blockages. A "lipoprotein profile" tests your levels of the key types of cholesterol—total, LDL ("bad"), and HDL ("good") cholesterol—and triglycerides, a fatty substance in the blood.

Lower cholesterol by following a heart-healthy eating plan, being physically active, maintaining a healthy weight, and, if needed, taking medication.

Overweight/Obesity. Nearly 80 percent of black women are overweight or obese, increasing the risk not only of heart disease but also a host of other conditions, including stroke, gallbladder disease, arthritis, and some cancers. If you're overweight, even a small weight loss will help lower your risk. At the very least, try not to gain more weight.

Lasting weight loss needs a change of lifestyle—adopt a healthy, lower-calorie eating plan and get regular physical activity. Aim to lose no more than $^1/_2$ to 2 pounds per week.

Physical Inactivity. Fifty-five percent of black women are physically inactive. They do no spare-time physical activity.

Physical activity is crucial for good health, including heart health. Try to do at least 30 minutes of a moderate-intensity activity such as brisk walking on most, and preferably, all days of the week. If you need to, divide the period into shorter ones of at least 10 minutes each.

Diabetes. About 11 million Americans have been diagnosed with diabetes—and another 5.7 million don't know they have it. About two-thirds of those with diabetes die of a heart or blood vessel disease.

The type of diabetes that adults most commonly develop is "type 2." Diabetes can be detected with a blood sugar test. Modest changes in diet and level of physical activity can often prevent or delay the development of diabetes.

PAULA, age 45—"In 1991, I went to the ER with chest pains twice in one week...I had emergency surgery. But the damage was done; only 40 percent of my heart muscle functions. I am permanently disabled and had to quit a job I loved."

QUESTIONS TO ASK YOUR DOCTOR

1. What is my risk for heart disease?
2. What is my blood pressure? What does it mean for me, and what do I need to do about it?
3. What are my cholesterol numbers? (These include total cholesterol, LDL, HDL, and triglycerides, a type of fat found in the blood and food.) What do they mean for me, and what do I need to do about them?
4. What are my "body mass index" (BMI) and waist measurement? Do they mean that I need to lose weight for my health?
5. What is my blood sugar level, and does it mean I'm at risk for diabetes? If so, what do I need to do about it?
6. What other screening tests for heart disease do I need?
7. What can you do to help me quit smoking?
8. How much physical activity do I need to help protect my heart?
9. What's a heart-healthy eating plan for me?
10. How can I tell if I may be having a heart attack? If I think I'm having one, what should I do?

TAKING ACTION

Now that you know *The Heart Truth*, what should you do? Begin by finding out your "risk profile." See the Box above for questions to ask your doctor. Then begin taking the steps to heart health—don't smoke, follow a heart-healthy eating plan, be physically active, and maintain a healthy weight. Start today to keep your heart strong.

TO LEARN MORE
NHLBI Health Information Center
Phone: 301-592-8573
TTY: 240-629-3255
www.hearttruth.gov

American Heart Association
Phone: 1-888-MY HEART
www.americanheart.org/simplesolutions

WomenHeart: the National Coalition for Women with Heart Disease
Phone: 202-728-7199
www.womenheart.org

Office on Women's Health
U.S. Department of Health and Human Services
National Women's Health Information Center
Phone: 1-800-994-WOMAN
TDD: 1-888-220-5446
www.4woman.gov

U.S. DEPARTMENT OF HEALTH AND HUMAN SERVICES
National Institutes of Health
National Heart, Lung, and Blood Institute

NIH Publication No. 03-5066
September 2003

EXHIBIT 10-1D   *Pitch Letter*

THE .heart TRUTH

Women & Heart Disease

THE red DRESS is the national symbol for women and heart disease awareness

February 2005

Dear Media Representative:

Only 57% of women are aware that heart disease is the leading cause of death among women. Yet, one in three American women dies of it. This issue demands attention.

To increase women's awareness of the threat of heart disease, *The Heart Truth*—a national campaign for women about heart disease sponsored by the National Heart, Lung, and Blood Institute (NHLBI), part of the National Institutes of Health, U.S. Department of Health and Human Services—has planned a number of programs and events throughout February's American Heart Month. From new survey findings about women and heart disease and a Presidential proclamation declaring February American Heart Month to National Wear Red Day and a celebrity-studded Red Dress fashion show in New York, *The Heart Truth* will help bring nationwide attention to this critical health issue for women.

Since the campaign's launch in 2002, *The Heart Truth* and its partners have sparked a national movement to alert women about the dangers of heart disease. Although significant progress has been made in raising awareness among women about heart disease, from 34 percent to 57 percent in just 4 years, most women fail to make the connection between risk factors, such as high blood pressure and high cholesterol, and their personal risk of developing heart disease. Only 20 percent of women identify heart disease as the greatest health problem facing women today, and awareness levels are lower among African American and Hispanic women.

The good news is heart disease is preventable. Just by leading a healthy lifestyle, Americans can lower their risk by as much as 82 percent. We are asking for *your* help in promoting life-saving heart health messages among your audiences so that women do not continue to underestimate their personal risk of this deadly disease. The enclosed kit provides you with the following materials to help you give your audiences a red alert about the #1 health threat to women:

* Background information and data about women's heart disease
* Fact sheet about the Red Dress, the national symbol for women and heart disease awareness
* Red Dress Collection 2005 Fashion Show press announcement
* Infographics
* Calendar listings to help you craft local stories
* A listing of NHLBI's heart disease experts and resources

(over)

www.hearttruth.gov

U.S. DEPARTMENT OF HEALTH AND HUMAN SERVICES ■ National Institutes of Health ■ National Heart, Lung, and Blood Institute

Courtesy The National Heart, Lung, and Blood Institute

In addition, we are happy to coordinate interviews with female heart disease survivors and NHLBI experts. Please feel free to contact media@hearttruth.org or Sally McDonough at (202) 452-7815 for additional information, to set up an interview, and to receive the latest awareness data on women and heart disease. Campaign materials are also downloadable at ftp://207.41.116.200/. Thank you for your consideration.

Sincerely yours,

The Heart Truth team

To reduce the spread of tobacco use among teens, the New Jersey Department of Health & Senior Services sponsored a two-day "Kick Ash Weekend" planning session in which teens from all of the state's 21 counties created a youth antitobacco movement they called "REBEL," an acronym for "Reaching Everyone By Exposing Lies." The program effectively involved teens statewide through extensive use of the Internet, community activities, and the mass media. Exhibit 10-2a is the movement's "Not For Sale" document. Exhibit 10-2b is a news release from the governor's office, Exhibit 10-2c is a "Declaration of Independence from Tobacco," Exhibit 10-2d is a media alert used in the program, and Exhibit 10-2e is a photograph of the beach cleanup event.

REBEL: New Jersey's New Youth Antitobacco Movement

New Jersey Department of Health and Senior Services with Fleishman-Hillard International Communications

Overview

Each day, more than 3,000 kids become regular smokers—85 per day and more than 31,000 teens per year in New Jersey alone. More than 80 percent of New Jersey's adult smokers report that they picked up the habit before the age of 18. If current trends continue, 135,000 of today's New Jersey teens will die from tobacco-related illnesses.

In November 2000, the New Jersey Department of Health and Senior Services (DHSS) brought together 340 teens from all 21 counties in the state for a two-day "Kick Ash Weekend," where teens created REBEL (Reaching Everyone By Exposing Lies), New Jersey's youth antitobacco movement. DHSS brought Fleishman-Hillard (FH) on board to develop all public relations initiatives, to advance awareness of REBEL, and to help position the antitobacco movement as cool, hip, and exciting to teens.

Courtesy New Jersey Department of Health and Senior Services

Challenges

- Grow REBEL as an active, involved group with a program that appeals to all of New Jersey's teens throughout urban, suburban, and rural areas.

- Create a unified movement in a stratified state (north and south) with no central city or location.

- Counter-tobacco marketing. Although the 1998 Master Settlement Agreement (MSA) prohibited direct advertising to youth, the FTC reported that the five largest cigarette manufacturers spent $8.24 billion on advertising and promotions to teens in 1999, a 22.3 percent increase from the last pre-MSA year.

Research

- The 1999 New Jersey Youth Tobacco Survey found that 10.5 percent of middle school students and 27.6 percent of high school students smoke cigarettes.

- Market research conducted in 1999 by Just Kids, Inc., found that New Jersey teens want to associate themselves with peer-to-peer movement programs.

- A 2001 BPM: Beats Per Minute survey reported that teen-oriented service/volunteerism is the second most popular cocurricular activity among teens ages 14–18.

- DHSS focus groups among 8th- and 10th-graders showed that New Jersey teens are aware of the health risks associated with tobacco use and believe they are targets of the tobacco industry.

- A youth antitobacco movement audit, including Truth and Campaign for Tobacco-Free Kids, revealed that teens want to expose Big Tobacco's manipulative tactics.

- A 2000 Teen Research Unlimited survey revealed that it is an MTV world—teens spend most of their time listening to or watching music and hanging with friends.

- According to the U.S. Public Health Service, peer pressure and low self-esteem are the leading causes of teen smoking.

Strategic Approach

Objectives

- Reduce the spread of tobacco use among New Jersey teens and other members of their communities by 20 percent.

- Strengthen REBEL participation and grow membership to 5,000 teens from all 21 counties.

- Increase awareness of REBEL among New Jersey teens and other residents by generating 100 million media impressions.

Strategies

- Create a service component to REBEL that enables teens to join a group and participate in their community.
- Increase awareness of Big Tobacco's manipulation of teens and the dangers of tobacco use through the media and peer-to-peer communication.
- Use the Internet to deliver empowerment and independence messages while helping to create a unified program across a stratified state.
- Facilitate peer-to-peer messages to shift social norms against smoking, including: manipulation by Big Tobacco, peer acceptance, effects of tobacco on appearance (e.g., yellow teeth, smelly breath).

Primary Target Audiences

- New Jersey teenagers, ages 13–17
- General public (New Jersey/national)

Execution/Tactics

"Not For Sale" Launch

In February 2001, 758 REBEL members declared they were "Not For Sale" to Big Tobacco at a statewide youth rally at the Liberty Science Center (LSC). DHSS, FH, and BBDO (the advertising agency) launched the "Not For Sale" counter-marketing ad campaign and call to action, and introduced njrebel.com, the REBEL website.

Held in the shadow of the Statue of Liberty, the rally emphasized the theme of independence from Big Tobacco. REBEL teen leaders, who had been trained in public speaking and giving media interviews, hosted the rally and introduced the key speakers, DHSS Commissioner Christine Grant and Donald DiFrancesco, who made his first major appearance as acting governor of New Jersey. The presence of top political officials enhanced teens' sense of empowerment and the importance of their movement.

The "Not For Sale" TV ads were previewed on a big screen video, viewable from three floors in the LSC atrium, and teens were given the opportunity to try out the website at several computers.

REBEL leaders unveiled their "Declaration of Independence from Tobacco," printed on a large scroll, which the teens signed. Additional "Declaration" graffiti boards with a shortened message were placed throughout the science center for teens to sign and write about their commitment not to smoke as part of the rally. The boards were designed to provide an opportunity for teens to express themselves and get involved even if they did not sign up for REBEL membership. They also give DHSS another vehicle for measuring the impact of REBEL's empowerment messages on New Jersey teens.

Since the rally, the Declaration scroll and graffiti boards have traveled throughout the state, and the text has been posted on the website, collecting more than 4,200 signatures along the way. One graffiti board has even captured the signatures of the New York Giants football team, including Tiki Barber and Jason Sehorn.

The entire launch event was Web cast on njrebel.com. The rally resulted in coverage of more than 12 million impressions, the involvement of several hundred teens actively taking part in the event, the appearance and support of top state officials, and the many photo opportunities provided by chanting kids.

REBEL Online

New Jersey poses unique challenges in reaching a statewide audience.

The two primary media markets—New York and Philadelphia—are centered outside the state's boundaries and are among the most difficult and expensive to penetrate. Consequently, identifying and including alternative communications channels is essential.

DHSS and FH developed the njrebel.com website to provide a powerful communications media for teens to be heard statewide. In addition it addresses the campaign's need to establish a dialogue with teens in order to truly engage them in the REBEL movement and mission.

The website is an interactive forum to enable members to share ideas and information, alert them to upcoming meetings and events, and spread the REBEL message of empowerment. Teen opinions guided the content and look of the site. Following member suggestions, REBEL photos were used throughout.

For ease of navigation, the site was divided into five main components.

1. *Get Involved:* Teens reach out to other teens
    - *How We Began:* The story of REBEL told through pictures and captions
    - *Electronic Greeting Cards:* Hard-hitting e-cards to send to smokers
    - *Join REBEL:* A simple-to-use e-mail form
    - *Quitting Tips:* Tips with a teen-specific twist
    - *Be Heard:* Communication "how-to's," for reaching the press and elected officials

2. *The Lowdown:* The dangers of tobacco use
   - *Buyer Beware:* Graphic photos of the dangerous effects of tobacco
   - *Real Stories:* REBEL teens tell why they joined the fight against Big Tobacco
   - *Tobacco Facts:* Stats that give teens the whole, no-nonsense truth
   - *Get This:* Current event summaries to inform and motivate teens to take action

3. *What's Up?:* Features tobacco-related news and videos
   - *REBELS Making News:* REBEL newsmakers (a *Teen People* feature, for example, was downloaded more than 2,055 times)
   - *Screening Room:* "Not for Sale" ads and Channel One ads starring REBEL members
   - *Upcoming Events:* Tells REBEL members what's happening in their community
   - *Get This:* Current tobacco news for teens

4. *"Members Only" Download Center:* Enables teens to access artwork for REBEL posters, fliers, postcards, T-shirt iron-on designs, and other "fun stuff" for promoting REBEL at local events. Teens can also access resources for writing articles for their local and school newspapers.

5. *Press Room:* Provides journalists with both current and archived press materials and request-for-interview forms in a readily accessible location. The press room has helped generate national press for REBEL.

Everyone also has the opportunity to share their views about tobacco by submitting "Shout Outs," which scroll along the bottom of the screen. FH even recruited some celebrities to contribute shout outs.

Community Activities

Another important key to countermarketing REBEL's message of freedom from tobacco is providing opportunities for face-to-face interaction with their peers and a forum for expressing their views to adults. Teens want to have an impact on their friends and communities.

They want to matter, make a statement, and make a difference.

To create a framework for this interaction, DHSS established REBEL groups in each of New Jersey's 21 counties to spread their message to peers and promote tobacco control issues in their communities.

Community Outreach Toolbox

To help REBEL chapters create their own local recruitment efforts and plan events, FH developed template materials, including press releases and advisories, calendars, event planning guides, and "Declaration of Independence from Big Tobacco" signature boards. In addition, FH worked with DHSS to organize multicounty events for REBEL and conduct media outreach for each event.

African-American Day Parade

In May 2001, DHSS launched a new advertising campaign to emphasize the impact smoking has on the family and encourage smokers to quit smoking by using state-supported quit services. The campaign features an African-American baby's face with the caption, "Who Cares If You Quit Smoking?" DHSS and FH worked with J. Curtis and Company, a multicultural marketing agency, to promote this campaign in the state's multicultural communities. The agencies enlisted REBEL members to help achieve this goal by participating in Newark's African-American Heritage Festival, where they staffed a parade float and booth. REBEL teens handed out brochures and buttons informing smokers about New Jersey's free or low-cost quit-smoking services and encouraging their use. The teens also used this opportunity to expand REBEL's membership within the African-American community.

REBEL Day at Great Adventure

Three counties used the REBEL website to organize an antitobacco rally and recruitment effort at the Six Flags Great Adventure theme park. More than 225 teens participated in the rally, which included skits, rap music and dance, and antitobacco cheers. The rally succeeded in generating interest among scores of new teens at the park and gathered new signatures and commitments on REBEL's "Declaration" boards, which were posted throughout the rally site. FH prepared event coordination and media outreach materials to serve as a model for county-organized events.

Regional Summits

In May 2001, DHSS held two regional summits each attended by 300 teens. The summits provided an opportunity to educate new REBEL members regarding their manipulation by the tobacco industry and to motivate both new and current REBEL members on ways to combat tobacco industry tactics. FH produced a documentary short video on the birth of the REBEL movement, which was previewed at the summits to orient new members and generate excitement about being a part of the movement. FH provided teens with a recruitment handbook with hands-on tips for recruiting new members and held workshops to educate the teens' adult coordinators on media outreach techniques that they could pass along to the teens in their counties.

"Bust Your Butts on the Beach" Day

In August 2001, 696 REBEL members cleaned up more than 38,000 cigarette butts and other litter along the New Jersey shore. DHSS designed the event to deepen REBEL's involvement in community service.

The event was important to maintain REBEL momentum over the summer months and to fulfill the REBEL mission to conduct community-service initiatives.

The teens, known as the "REBEL Beach Patrol," combed eight beaches on the Jersey Shore from Sea Bright to Cape May, cleaning up cigarette filters and other litter. They drew attention to the damaging impact of cigarettes on the environment. Cigarette butts are the most common form of litter on beaches. The teens were joined by state officials, including the DHSS Acting Commissioner, the Deputy Commissioner for the New Jersey Department of Environmental Protection, and mayors of participating towns. Two IDVs (Interactive Display Vehicles) wrapped in the REBEL "Not For Sale" advertising message traveled from beach to beach, promoting the event along the way.

REBEL leaders received media training and gave interviews to print and broadcast reporters to inform the public about the environmental impact of butts on the beach as well as to promote their antitobacco messages.

To highlight the results, the cleanup was followed by a celebration at Ocean City where the 38,000 butts were displayed in clear bags to graphically underscore the teens' messages. FH shot B-roll footage at the event, sending it to TV stations to facilitate broadcast coverage. The event earned more than 40 million media impressions, including every major daily newspaper in the state and key TV stations. There is nothing like the combination of kids doing good works, an environmental issue, and lots of graphics to bring a news story to life and attract media attention.

Channel One

FH scripted and taped four 30-second documentary-style spots to air weekly on Channel One, a closed-circuit TV station aired in 308 New Jersey schools. In New Jersey's expensive media markets, Channel One offered a cost-effective way to get the message out to teens in their schools, where they spend the majority of their time. These ads reached a potential audience of 215,000 students every time they aired on Channel One.

All the spots featured REBEL members encouraging peers to join their movement and promoting their empowerment messages. One PSA featured New York Giants football star, Tiki Barber, praising REBEL and encouraging other teens to take part in the movement.

NJN Public Television's "Teen Smoking" Documentary

NJN, New Jersey's public television station, featured REBEL in a 30-minute documentary special on teen smoking. Eight REBEL teens participated as panelists. The show aired repeatedly throughout the fall of 2001. FH documented the making of this TV show to share the experience with teens throughout the state, extend the reach and impact of this broadcast, and demonstrate how REBEL's voice is being heard. The video footage has been incorporated in the "A Year in the Life of REBEL" documentary.

"A Year in the Life of REBEL" Documentary

Throughout this 18-month period, FH documented REBEL's activities on video, featuring many cameo appearances by REBEL members making personal statements about tobacco use and Big Tobacco's tactics to persuade teens to use their products. The video graphically portrays to New Jersey's teens the high-energy look and feel of the movement, the importance of its mission, and its accomplishments.

The video, distributed to all REBEL chapters, serves as an educational and motivational recruitment tool.

Evaluation

In 2001, all objectives were met and surpassed.

Reduce the Spread of Tobacco Use Among New Jersey Teens and Other Members of Their Community by 20 Percent

- The 2001 New Jersey Youth Tobacco Survey of 16,000 teens revealed a 42 percent drop in smoking among middle school students and an 11 percent drop among high school students over the past two years. These rates of decline in New Jersey exceeded the national rates of smoking reduction, which were 12 percent among middle school students and 9 percent among high school students.

Strengthen REBEL Participation and Grow Membership to 5,000 Teens from All 21 Counties

- REBEL membership grew from 340 to more than 7,000 members by the first quarter of 2002.
- More than 6,000 REBEL teens have signed the "Not For Sale" Declaration of Independence from Tobacco in the same time period.
- County REBEL groups host monthly meetings and communicate the dangers of smoking to their communities.

- By the first quarter of 2002, njrebel.com hosted 92,090 visitors, 90 percent of whom found the site through public relations advertising or by word of mouth.

Increase Awareness of Rebel Among New Jersey Teens and Other Residents Generating 100 Million Media Impressions

- By the first quarter of 2002, FH's media outreach had resulted in more than 155,000,000 media impressions, including features in all New Jersey dailies as well as national placements in *TIME for Kids, YM, Seventeen, Teen People,* and on CBS's *The Early Show, Good Morning America,* and *FOX & Friends.* Coverage included multicultural media outlets such as *La Voz, India Post,* and *El Especial.*

EXHIBIT 10-2A *"Not For Sale"*

NOT FOR SALE

Not For Sale
New Jersey's New Youth Anti-Tobacco Advertising Campaign

Every great movement needs a great rallying cry and this includes the New Jersey Department of Health and Senior Services' (DHSS's) youth anti-smoking movement. Not For Sale empowers the youth of New Jersey to stake their personal and collective claim against Big Tobacco. The youth of New Jersey are smart. They know the lies. They know the truth. They cannot be bought. Not For Sale is an expression of freedom from the addiction, manipulation and death caused by Big Tobacco.

The REBEL movement is a grassroots movement, created by and for the youth of New Jersey. The movement – <u>R</u>eaching <u>E</u>veryone <u>B</u>y <u>E</u>xposing <u>L</u>ies – speaks to their goal of changing social norms about youth smoking by connecting, on an individual and group basis, with people throughout the state. Each individual's decision to join the REBEL movement creates a stronger bond among the youth of New Jersey who have made the decision to be free from tobacco. The movement creates change through positive peer-pressure and community action.

Not For Sale empowers teens to:

- Educate communities about the dangers of tobacco;
- Make the choice to be free from tobacco;
- Encourage others to make personal choices based on knowledge;
- Accept accountability for individual actions;
- Promote good health and long lives for all New Jersey citizens.

Not For Sale builds upon the strengths of the national TRUTH campaign of the American Legacy Foundation giving New Jersey youth the strength and conviction they need to make the positive choice to be tobacco-free. The TRUTH campaign has taught them about the targeting, tactics, manipulation and lies used by Big Tobacco to influence their perceptions of tobacco and encourage them to smoke.

The brand will evolve as the needs of the REBEL movement change, but it will remain steadfast in the fact that New Jersey youth know the truth and that's why they are NOT FOR SALE.

Courtesy New Jersey Department of Health and Senior Services

EXHIBIT 10-2B   *News Release*

OFFICE OF THE GOVERNOR -- NEWS RELEASE

PO BOX 004
CONTACT: Jayne O'Connor
           Steffanie Bell
           (609) 777-2600

TRENTON, NJ 08625
RELEASE: Friday
February 16, 2001

New Jersey Unveils Anti-Tobacco "Not For Sale" Advertising Campaign
Teens of New Jersey REBEL Declare Independence from Tobacco

Acting Governor Donald DiFrancesco today joined 700 teens at the Liberty Science Center for a rally, sponsored by the New Jersey Department of Health and Senior Services (DHSS), to officially launch the new youth anti-tobacco "Not For Sale" advertising campaign. DHSS staged the event to support a youth led anti-tobacco movement called New Jersey REBEL (Reaching Everyone By Exposing Lies).

"My thanks to all the young people who have come from across the state to be here to kick off the 'Not For Sale' campaign," said Acting Governor DiFrancesco. "Through the Community Against Tobacco coalitions now in place in every county, you are taking a stand on a very important issue. I am very proud of you."

"Back in the 1950s, when I was a youngster, there was a very popular film called 'Rebel Without a Cause.' It starred James Dean, and was considered one of Hollywood's best films about rebellious youth," said DiFrancesco. "Like most movie actors in those days, James Dean was a smoker. Smoking was cool. Today, you are 'Rebels with a Cause,' and it's a very good cause indeed."

Based on the national TRUTH campaign, the new "Not For Sale" ads focus on manipulation by tobacco companies and the importance of young people making decisions that are informed. The advertisements, which have been airing since the beginning of February, can be seen in a variety of television spots from MTV (i.e., Real World and Road Rules) to the WB network (i.e., Buffy the Vampire Slayer, Felicity and Dawson's Creek) to NBC (i.e. X-Games), on radio, on billboards, at movie theatres, and will soon appear on special sports utility vehicles that will travel around the state. The advertisements can also be viewed on the new REBEL website at www.njrebel.com.

"It is exciting and encouraging to see New Jersey teens take hold of this critical issue – to stand up to Big Tobacco and say they are "Not For Sale," said Christine Grant, Commissioner of Health and Senior Services. "The Not For Sale" campaign provides the

Courtesy New Jersey Department of Health and Senior Services

REBEL movement with additional strength and conviction to make positive choices related to tobacco use."

Leaders of the newly formed REBEL movement urged teens throughout New Jersey to join them in their fight to prevent the spread of tobacco use. During the rally, teens viewed the "Not For Sale" advertising campaign and discussed tobacco industry tactics that influence teens to smoke. Working within New Jersey's 21 counties to roll out community-based initiatives, the REBEL teens hope to empower youth to stake a personal and collective claim against smoking.

"Through my involvement in REBEL, I learned that tobacco companies look for 'replacement smokers' to make up for 13,000 people who die in the state each year," said (name deleted), REBEL youth leader from Denville, New Jersey. "We are determined not to be in this group. We are letting the Tobacco Industry know that we are not for sale."

REBEL leaders read their *Declaration of Independence from Tobacco* and asserted their mission to: educate communities about the dangers of tobacco; make the choice to be free from tobacco; and promote good health and long lives for all New Jersey citizens. These leaders then signed the Declaration to mark their commitment and announced that they will seek additional signatures at the community level as the program rolls out. REBEL teens will distribute copies of the Declaration in their communities to foster recruitment and help build awareness of their goals.

"I think it is important to spread the word to other teens about the dangers of smoking, and how the tobacco industry lies to us," said (name deleted), REBEL youth leader, Manville, New Jersey. "The REBEL movement and the 'Not For Sale' advertising campaign will help us do this."

Over 80 percent of existing adult smokers become addicted before the age of 18. A 1999 New Jersey Youth Tobacco Survey states that nearly two in five high school students and nearly one in five middle school students had used tobacco products in the last month. If current trends continue, 135,000 New Jersey teens will eventually die of a tobacco related disease. But, if this cycle is successfully broken, the single most preventable cause of death and disease in New Jersey could be eliminated.

The REBEL Web site, www.njrebel.com, has been created to assist with building awareness and recruitment. Also introduced at the youth rally, the Web site provides steps for getting involved in local REBEL chapters and highlights specific ways to help expose the marketing tactics of the tobacco industry that attract teen smokers.

Following the Kick-Ash Bash in November, the founding members of REBEL began working in their communities to create local advocacy plans. They will continue to work throughout the year with a state-funded youth coordinator in each of New Jersey's 21 counties. Youth coordinators are based in the Communities Against Tobacco (CAT) coalitions, a grassroots network of local coalitions in each county that have joined together to change community norms, attitudes and behaviors about tobacco use.

EXHIBIT 10-2B   *News Release (continued)*

REBEL teen leaders will team up with their youth coordinators and the DHSS to organize and lead nine regional summits across the state over the next 18 months to strengthen their cause and recruit new teens for the movement. The DHSS has secured a $2.2 million, three-year grant from the American Legacy Foundation (Legacy) to fund these regional initiatives. Legacy is the national, independent, public health foundation established under the Master Settlement Agreement (MSA).

The "Not For Sale" advertising campaign is just one of many initiatives sponsored by DHSS and funded with money from the 1998 Master Tobacco Settlement Agreement (MSA) between 46 states and the tobacco industry. New Jersey is one of only 15 states, which are directing a substantial portion of these funds -- $30 million in the first three years of the program -- toward smoking prevention and cessation. New Jersey's Comprehensive Tobacco Control Program is designed to reduce the sickness, disability and death among New Jerseyans associated with the use of tobacco and exposure to environmental tobacco smoke.

In October 2000 the state launched two new free cessation services, New Jersey Quitnet^{SM} (www.nj.quitnet.com) and New Jersey Quitline at (1-866-NJ-STOPS/1-866-657-8677). New Jersey Quitnet is an innovative online resource that provides a comprehensive, individually tailored smoking cessation plan. New Jersey Quitline is a toll-free hotline offering personal counseling to state residents six days a week. The services are open to all age groups. With New Jersey Quitnet, the Department of Health and Senior Services is particularly targeting young adult smokers, who are comfortable with the Internet. This program is being funded from $6.3 million appropriated from the MSA funds for a media public awareness campaign.

###

EXHIBIT 10-2C *"Declaration of Independence"*

Reaching Everyone By Exposing Lies

Declaration of Independence From Tobacco

We the teenagers of New Jersey officially declare our independence from tobacco.

We have been influenced by tobacco marketing for too long. Now it's time to clear the smoke and take back our lives.

Therefore, we join with **New Jersey REBEL** in Reaching Everyone By Exposing Lies. We have the power to:

- Educate our communities about the dangers of tobacco;
- Make the choice to be free from tobacco;
- Encourage others to make personal choices based on knowledge;
- Accept accountability for our actions;
- Promote good health and long lives for all New Jersey citizens.

We will not allow Big Tobacco to affect our choices. We declare to Big Tobacco and to the world: We are

NOT FOR SALE !

Courtesy New Jersey Department of Health and Senior Services

EXHIBIT 10-2D *Media Alert*

MEDIA ALERT

NEW JERSEY REBEL Beach Patrol Declares August 20 "Bust Your Butts on the Beach" Day

WHAT: Hundreds of members of REBEL (<u>R</u>eaching <u>E</u>veryone <u>B</u>y <u>E</u>xposing <u>L</u>ies), New Jersey's youth anti-tobacco movement, will take part in a Beach Butts Clean-up, an initiative sponsored by the New Jersey Department of Health and Senior Services. REBEL members are using the opportunity to call particular attention to tobacco-related litter and the long-lasting problems associated with cigarette butts, the most prevalent form of litter on New Jersey beaches. Data collected during the Beach Butts Clean-up will contribute to an ongoing federal study conducted by DEP.

Photo ops:
- REBEL members from your community in action, cleaning NJ beaches (call for beach assignments by county.)
- **NJ officials taking part in the clean up (To be confirmed)**
- Recruitment table, teens signing on to "declare independence from tobacco." (all participating beaches)
- Trash bag "pile up" (Ocean City)
- Awards presentation (Ocean City)
- Anti-tobacco sand sculpture contest (Ocean City)

WHEN: Monday, August 20, 2001, 9 -11a.m. (Beach Clean-up)
    11-12 (recruitment/information table)
    2-5 p.m. Beach Celebration/Awards presentation

WHO: **Acting DHSS Commissioner George T. DiFerdinando, Jr., M.D., M.P.H.**
REBEL Beach Patrol participants

WHERE: **Clean up:**

Sea Bright	Island Beach State Park
Ocean Grove	Cape May
Wildwood	Ocean City
Belmar	Atlantic City

Celebration: Ocean City

CONTACT: For additional information, or beach sites, please contact Lisa Holmes at Fleishman Hillard Inc. at (212) 453-2489 or holmesl@fleishman.com.

Courtesy New Jersey Department of Health and Senior Services

EXHIBIT 10-2E *Photograph*

REBEL teens cleaned 38,000 cigarette butts from eight New Jersey beaches on "Bust Your Butts on the Beach Day," August 2001, to highlight the environmental impact of cigarette smoking.

Courtesy New Jersey Department of Health and Senior Services

To introduce a new photo service to young women, an organization used the culture of scrapbooks. It says much about the ability to target a specific audience using a specific value system — sharing memories with friends is important. Exhibit 10-3a is a news release, Exhibit 10-3b is a recap of the trip to Rochester, N.Y., and Exhibit 10-3c is a postevent message strategy.

The Shutterfly Soirée

Shutterfly with Maloney & Fox

Overview

How do you persuade an audience to trust an online photo service with their most treasured memories? How do you introduce a new, intimidating, technological service that requires some advanced knowledge of computers and digital photography before it can be used effectively and enjoyed? How do you educate this audience about the numerous benefits and features of the service and THEN get them to become subscribers and proselytizers? The Maloney & Fox answer: The Shutterfly Soirée — an upgraded version of the Tupperware Party with a high-tech twist. Small gatherings of 7–10 women hosted by a Shutterfly representative in strategic markets — competitors and potential partners' "backyards" — helped women understand and buy into the new service; catapulted Shutterfly's new registrants to 70,000 per month — double its pre-Soirée level; increased its print volume by 63 percent and has led Shutterfly, with no advertising support, to two successive profitable quarters on an EBITDA (Earnings before Interest, Taxes, Depreciation, and Amortization) basis.

Research

Maloney & Fox (M&F) began the research phase by combing through results from the annual Shutterfly User Survey, conducted November 2001. These statistics revealed that 63 percent of Shutterfly users are women, many with children, and a median age of 39. Primary research included one-on-one interviews to explore the best way to get women to overcome their aversion to "going digital" with their photography and learn about new exciting online photo applications. M&F determined that "hand-holding" support would be a determining factor in our audience's willingness to learn; nearly 80 percent of the 64 women inter-

Courtesy Shutterfly

viewed admitted that they'd be more eager to try the service if someone walked them through the Shutterfly "experience." Responses also included initial aversions to online banking until, as one respondent noted, "a friend showed me how easy it really is." This research finding, in particular, helped drive the creative approach to creating the Soirée.

Also, M&F conducted in-depth, secondary research about shopping trends, women and the Internet, market penetration of digital photography, and competition among online photo services. Much of this research (e.g., women are three to six times more likely than men to become frequent Internet users within two years according to data from Content Intelligence, 9/27/01) supported our decision to target women with kids, knowing too that women are more than likely to be the family "historian" and manage the family photo albums. And with household penetration of digital cameras and online shopping on the rise, the opportunity for Shutterfly to make its mark with this audience became very apparent.

Planning

Before M&F began its idea generation, several issues needed to be taken into consideration: Talk in language that women would understand. Create an experience where women would feel comfortable asking even the most basic questions. Conduct Shutterfly demos that didn't feel like a hard sell. With these points in mind, M&F created a program to (1) create awareness of the Shutterfly service and its range of photo products; (2) demystify the Shutterfly experience and educate women about the site's ease of use; and (3) stimulate trials and sign-ups, and increase monthly photo uploads.

Based on our research and understanding of the audience and its critical implications, M&F designed the Shutterfly Soirée to: (1) reach women on a personal level in a comfortable environment; (2) provide practical and useful advice about Shutterfly and its features that translates not only to "produce more creative photos" but also to saving time and hassle; and (3) capture local and national press attention. And, a major caveat—achieve these results with a budget of $15,000/ market, including agency fee.

Execution

What could be a more personal and conducive learning environment than someone's own living room? M&F conducted get-togethers for 7–10 women led by a staff representative and the Shutterfly director of communications, who walked the guests through current issues and limitations of how family photos are managed (usually taking up space in a shoebox) and the basic Shutterfly features. When guests leave the Soirée, they are equipped with resources needed to help spread the ease of use and convenience of Shutterfly, including product information (including a step-by-step "How To" Guide), a branded T-shirt and frame, and a promotional code to use on their first Shutterfly order.

Soirées have also been customized for specific audience segments. For example, M&F conducted Soirées for expectant mothers showcasing Shutterfly baby announcements; for brides-to-be, providing tips to personalize thank-you cards and wedding keepsakes; and for "groovy" grannies who learn about creating special mementos for their kids and grandkids (a double-punch opportunity here for spreading the Shutterfly word).

The location of the Soirées was another key strategic decision that helped gain significant industry and media attention.

M&F suggested the first three Soirées to be conducted in Kansas City, Rochester, and Cleveland—the homes of Hallmark, Kodak, and American Greetings, respectively. Soirées have also been conducted in Las Vegas, Seattle, New York, and Charlotte. One is currently being planned in San Francisco.

Targeted media outreach is a major component of the Soirée program. Armed with a localized pitch letter, press release, Soirée photo invitation created on Shutterfly, video B-roll (including actual Soirée and product and Shutterfly website shots), M&F offers in-studio or phone interviews with the Shutterfly spokesperson and desk-side Shutterfly tutorials. The media is also invited (and encouraged) to attend and cover local Soirées.

Evaluation

The Shutterfly Soirée received the MeirComm "Gold Galaxy Award" for excellence in education/awareness and has achieved unprecedented success on three levels:

> **Created awareness for Shutterfly through word-of-mouth and national media coverage.** The Shutterfly Customer Service Department indicated a significant increase in inquiries from consumers living in Soirée cities, many of them call/write with interest in attending or hosting a Soirée on their own. The Soirées have also received extensive national and local print and broadcast coverage in addition to favorable coverage from photo industry trades, including *Photo Marketing News* and *Photo Trade News*. Some highlights include in-person broadcast interviews with our spokesperson (e.g., WDAP-TV Kansas City, FOX; WHEC-TV, Rochester, NBC; KTNV-TV, Las Vegas, ABC; WDOK-FM Cleveland); in-depth print features (*Cleveland Plain Dealer, Rochester Democrat & Chronicle*); and a nationally released news story by Gannett News Service. Overall, the Shutterfly Soirée and general Shutterfly consumer public relations initiatives have generated more than 200 million media impressions with a total advertising dollar equivalent of more than $4 million.

Demystified Shutterfly's technology and educated women about Shutterfly's ease of use. Of those who attended the Shutterfly Soirées, 40 percent expressed an interest in the new technology but are put off by the "learning curve." Although 86 percent of attendees had never used an online photo service, through post-Soirée questionnaires, M&F determined that 91 percent agreed that they would be more likely to use an online photo service having attended the Soirée. Follow-up calls with attendees six weeks after the Soirée revealed that 72 percent of them are using Shutterfly on a regular/occasional basis and 88 percent have referred someone else to the site.

Stimulated trials and sign-ups, and increased monthly photo uploads. Most importantly, the Soirées have generated bottom-line sales results for Shutterfly. The Shutterfly Soirées have helped Shutterfly gain:

- A 63 percent increase in print volume (the critical component for company growth)
- Two straight quarters of profitability, a full year ahead of projections
- 70,000 new members per month
- A 100 percent increase in all of Shutterfly's most significant metrics (new members, photo uploads, print orders, revenues)

And—another note important to consider—M&F achieved all of this with no advertising support. Most gratifying for M&F is the satisfaction from our client, Shutterfly CEO Andy Wood. "The Soirées have injected enthusiasm into the company, and they've allowed us to get a real sense of who our customers are and what they're looking for from our service, so that we can do everything better."

EXHIBIT 10-3A *News Release*

FOR IMMEDIATE RELEASE

USING TECHNOLOGY TO GET MORE FROM TREASURED PHOTOS
Five Easy Tips for Women to Kick the Shoebox Habit

REDWOOD CITY, Calif. – As primary family communicators, women often take on the role of household photo-organizer. However, with free time at a premium these days, keeping up the family photo collection usually gets shunted to the bottom of the to-do list. Most women live with a messy stash of photo-filled shoeboxes filling closet shelves or taking up space under the bed.

Whitney Brown, Director of Corporate Communications for online photo service Shutterfly, is convinced that once women become familiar with the online tools available to them, their world becomes a much simpler and organized place. Ms. Brown advises using technology to help save time and to get a handle on managing all those photos. "Shutterfly is perfect for helping women easily organize pictures and share them with loved ones. Shutterfly is amazingly easy to use, and eliminates the "digital fear factor" that so often holds women back from trying new things."

To get started, Ms. Brown offers "Five Easy Tips to Kick the Shoebox Habit," a primer that will make any former photo hoarder feel like a qualified photo archivist in no time.

1. **Go Digital:** Consider investing in a digital camera and/or a scanner. Resolve to spend two hours a week scanning old family photos and uploading them to www.shutterfly.com, where you can tap into unlimited storage capacity or archive pictures onto a CD.

2. **Edit, Edit, Edit:** Be ruthless when sorting your photos: toss unflattering or "meaningless" pictures. Take advantage of online editing software to fix red-eye, crop or enhance the photos you really love.

3. **Get Personal:** Create your own custom stationary with favorite pictures of a pet, landscape or ancestral photo. Enclose extra prints in cards or notes you send to family and friends.

4. **Organize By Occasion:** Make event and holiday-themed online albums with Shutterfly Snapbooks (up to 40 photos with captions) to send milestone memories to far-away friends and family.

5. **Think Ahead:** Establish a "Creative Calendar" that will remind you in advance when it's time to start thinking about photo prints and cards for birthdays, events and anniversaries.

About Shutterfly
Shutterfly, the leading online photo service, leverages its proprietary technology and understanding of its customers to develop personalized, quality photo products and services that make it simple and fun for people to stay connected to those who matter most. Film and digital photographers alike can enjoy the benefits of Shutterfly's photo services, including high-quality prints, image enhancements, personalization, free online storage and picture sharing. Customers can custom back-print and transform their pictures with special effects and borders as well as create photo cards, invitations, calendars, note cards and Snapbooks ™, all of which can be mailed anywhere in the world. Shutterfly is consistently recognized for its photo quality and innovative features, and was most recently rated best overall online photo service in a field of twelve by MacWorld in its June 2002 issue. Shutterfly is based in Redwood City, CA. For more information, visit www.shutterfly.com.

Shutterfly, Shutterfly.com and the Shutterfly logo are trademarks of Shutterfly, Inc.

###

Courtesy Shutterfly

EXHIBIT 10-3B *Recap of City Visits*

MEMORANDAUM

DATE:

TO:

FROM:

RE: **Shutterfly Soirée Recap & Next Steps**

CC:

M&F was charged with the objective of raising awareness and buzz for Shutterfly in the backyards of American Greetings (Cleveland), Hallmark (Kansas City) and Kodak (Rochester) by early February 2002.

The agreed upon strategy of combining *Shutterfly Soirées* – intimate gatherings of local women for a hands-on tutorial about Shutterfly – and a spokesperson tour with Whitney Brown, proved to be highly successful because the initiative encouraged both grass-roots interest and generated substantial media coverage of Shutterfly in every market. Media highlights include:

- A lengthy article and photo in the *Cleveland Plain Dealer*
- Two taped radio segments (CNN & ABC affiliates) of 10 and 30 minutes in length that aired February 17th in Cleveland
- Pending story in the March issue of *Cleveland/Akron Family* magazine
- Live FOX noon news interview in Kansas City
- Live NBC noon news interview in Rochester
- Feature business story and photo in the *Rochester Democrat and Chronicle*

Please see the following pages for a complete summary/description of each Soirée and media opportunity.

LESSONS LEARNED

While in-market, we were able to gain some valuable insights and learn first-hand why the Soirée strategy was so effective.

Media Tour:
- Local angle of Soirée provides compelling reason for coverage
- Nature of news story is more commercial with Shutterfly spokesperson
- Celebrity or third-party expert spokesperson not necessary in small, local markets
- Anchors, producers, reporters become proselytizers of Shutterfly

Maloney & Fox, LLC
Page 1 of 9

Courtesy Shutterfly

EXHIBIT 10-3B *Recap of City Visits (continued)*

Soirées:
- Generate excitement about Shutterfly and digital photography among target female audience in key local markets
- Ensure loyalty by teaching one-on-one; sign up new users on the spot
- Spread awareness via word-of-mouth from recent converts
- Provide "focus group" type research; insights about potential users
- Support thesis that women need extra help adopting new technology
- Place branded totes, hats, t-shirts in market
- Plant the idea for women to host their own Shutterfly Soirées, thus continuing the groundswell of interest

SOIRÉE NEXT STEPS

We strongly recommend building on the momentum we generated in Cleveland, Kansas City and Rochester and continue this initiative in other markets targeted for strategic business objectives and awareness.

With Mother's Day (Sunday, May 12) approaching, we propose to complete two Soirées by the end of April. Markets discussed for consideration (and cities where we have contacts to host Soirées): Raleigh-Durham, Phoenix and Boulder/Denver. We also suggest investigating the following media-friendly markets: Indianapolis, Minneapolis/St. Paul, Memphis and Las Vegas.

With the bulk of our media and Soirée materials written and approved, we would develop in-depth media lists for the new Soirée markets and start pitching in early March. Having additional lead time would give us more opportunity and flexibility in booking Whitney on local news programs. Also, we would immediately begin to make arrangements to secure hostesses for the Soirées.

By working in advance, we expect to gain efficiencies in travel costs and we can pair down expenses associated with the hostesses; however, materials will need to be duplicated/recreated and hours needed to secure media remain constant.

Per market	Hours @ Avg. $200 per hour	cost
Co-ordinate with hostess	6.0	$1,200
Media outreach/follow-up	35.0	$7,000
Materials, duplication, postage		$800
In-market (2 10-hour days)	20.0	$4,000
Hostess gift		$200
Food/drinks/flowers		$400
Air travel, taxi (1 person, non-refundable)		$700
Hotel, meals (2 people, 1 night)		$500
Estimated Costs per Soirée Market		**$14,800**

ADDITIONAL FUTURE SOIRÉE CONSIDERATIONS

- Develop a strategy for the Soirée program to be self-generating

- Outreach to power Shutterfly users to encourage them to host Soirées

- Determine incentive for hosting Soirée – free product, cash, camera, etc. (Investigate working with partner/camera manufacturer to offset expense)

- Create how-to booklet and/or CD Rom with tutorial

- Explore holding Soirées where women gather to learn about technology: public libraries, community centers, learning centers, women's clubs; offer Whitney as guest speaker

- Consider market-wide special offer for all local residents

EXHIBIT 10-3C *Talking Points*

Post Soiree Talking Points

SHUTTERFLY GENERAL

Shutterfly is the leading online photo service that makes it fun and simple to get prints and creative projects from your film or digital camera.

Online photo services – such as Shutterfly – are fun, easy to use and can help you organize and share your pictures.

Shutterfly makes it fun and easy to stay connected to your family and friends.

Once people see that using Shutterfly is almost as easy as email, they are true converts.

You don't need a digital camera to use Shutterfly. You can send us your undeveloped film, scan in photos or use a Photo CD to get your pictures to us.

Shutterfly is free to join, to store an unlimited number of photos and to share your pictures online. You only pay for the prints and projects you create and order.

ANYTHING TO ADD?

Shutterfly is a fun and easy to use service that saves time and money and allows you to send personalized gifts to your friends and family around the world.

WOMEN SPECIFIC

We have witnessed a big change in our user base from mostly male "early adopters" to a more "mass market" consumer, where 63% of our users now are women.

Women tend to be the ones most likely to manage the family archives – taking family pictures, compiling baby books and vacation photo albums, and mailing important prints to loved ones. And if we're not doing it, then chances are the pictures (and the guilt) are piling up.

SOIREE SPECIFIC

The Shutterfly Soiree is the Tupperware or scrapbooking party for 2002. They are casual, social gatherings where women can learn from each other. It is a treat your friends to a hands-on, private lesson

Anyone can use Shutterfly. We have built our Soirees for women because traditionally, they are the digital archivist of the family (i.e. handles sending reprints to family and friends) and because our research has shown us that

2.12.02

Courtesy Shutterfly

Post Soiree Talking Points

women prefer to learn in groups with their friends. Men typically like tinkering around and figuring out new technology on their own.

The Soirees are a pilot program that we are testing in several mid-sized cities where the majority of our users were women and the majority of the women had classified themselves as new to digital and wanting to learn more.

We are hoping that as more and more women recognize the benefits of online photo services, they too will want to host their own Soiree to share it with their family and friends.

Our Soirees have been extremely successful in helping grow awareness about Shutterfly in these cities, acquire new customers and gather additional information about new and future users to supplement our focus groups, market research, usability tests and customer surveys. They are also very helpful for understanding consumers in different parts of the country (especially outside Silicon Valley) and their comfort level with technology and demands from an online photo service.

2.12.02

PART III

Emergency Public Relations

CHAPTER 11   **Emergency Public Relations**

Emergency Public Relations

In preparation for emergencies, the practitioner should be generally aware of the four aspects of the process model, although its use in this form of public relations will be limited.

RESEARCH

Some research will be helpful in reaching a state of readiness for an emergency. The three types of research used for other forms of public relations are appropriate.

Client Research

Client research should focus on preparing as many "worst-case" scenarios as possible. What can go wrong? Is the organization's physical plant vulnerable to fire, explosion, or other crises? Is dangerous equipment located on the premises? How will you respond if the organization's president is indicted for fraud? All division heads in the organization should be asked by the director of public relations to prepare a list of potential trouble spots that could erupt in their respective areas. Whenever possible, corrective action should be taken to neutralize these problems before an emergency can occur. Research may also examine the client's handling of past crises.

Opportunity or Problem Research

Emergency public relations is generically reactive in nature. Some practitioners argue that it is impossible to really get ready for a sweeping disaster. Emergency planning, however, must be proactive in order to be prepared for a proper reactive response to an emergency.

Audience Research

The practitioner should make a list of internal and external publics to be immediately notified in case of an emergency. Internal publics would include the chief executive officer and other top organizational officials on a "need-to-know" basis at first. As the emergency progresses, the entire workforce can be notified through existing internal channels of communication. External audiences in an emergency should include, in priority order, law enforcement officials; the next of kin of the injured or dead, notified before the public release of their names; the mass media; governmental agencies, if appropriate; and trade publications. These internal and external audiences are a suggested starting point. The practitioner needs to be much more specific in creating an emergency contacts list designed to notify all concerned parties in a timely fashion.

OBJECTIVES

Because of the exceptional nature of emergencies, objectives for this form of public relations cannot be carefully planned. Nonetheless, some general guidelines are applicable:

1. To provide accurate, timely information to all targeted internal and external audiences

2. To demonstrate concern for the safety of lives

3. To safeguard organizational facilities and assets

4. To maintain a positive image of the organization as a good corporate or community citizen

These guidelines will serve the practitioner well in preparing for the two areas of responsibility involved in programming.

PROGRAMMING

Programming for emergency public relations should focus on two major actions or areas of responsibility: establishing a public relations emergency headquarters and a media information center. Anticipate the necessary resources for a crisis—it may take additional people within the organization or even will require hiring a public relations agency to support expanded operations.

The Public Relations Headquarters

The public relations emergency headquarters (PR HQ) will probably be the regular public relations office itself. If more space is needed, other offices may also be designated as part of the PR HQ. This office will be responsible for notification of all internal and external emergency audiences, for preparation of material for the media, and for the establishment of a public information center to answer inquiries and to control rumors. The director of public relations should remain in the PR HQ to supervise these three functions.

Notification, the first function of PR HQ, will be the top priority of this office as soon as a crisis occurs. The internal and external audiences were discussed above and will be reviewed in Exhibit 11-a, the "Emergency Public Relations Checklist." Names of the injured or dead should be withheld from public release until the next of kin are notified or for 24 hours, whichever comes first.

The second function of the PR HQ will be preparation of materials for the media. A company or organizational backgrounder, fact sheet, biographies of major officers, and their captioned photographs should already be prepared and on the organizational website. Along with assembling these background materials, the public relations staff should immediately begin the task of preparing its first basic news release on the crisis. A good rule of thumb is that this should be ready for release *no more than one hour* after the occurrence of the emergency. The release should include all known facts, such as what happened, how, when, where, who, and how many were involved. The question of why may be omitted since the organization may run the risk of involving itself in litigation through an admission of fault. This matter should be handled by the legal department. The release should be cleared as quickly as possible with senior management, the legal department, and possibly the personnel department. Then the news release should be issued immediately to local and national mass media, specialized publications, employees, community leaders, and pertinent government agencies. In addition to the first basic release, PR HQ should issue frequent statements to the media in ongoing crises and should coordinate media interviews with the CEO as warranted.

Through all of these emergency public relations procedures, two principles are recommended: a *one-voice* principle and a *full-disclosure* principle. Above all other considerations, the organization should *speak with one voice*. All employees should be briefed to give information to the media or other concerned parties only from official organizational statements, issued by PR HQ. The full-disclosure principle refers to giving all known information, with the exception of why the emergency occurred if this might involve admission of fault.

The third function of the PR HQ is to establish a *public information center (PIC)*. The responsibilities of the PIC include responding to telephone inquiries with accurate information, providing information to groups to combat rumors, and holding meetings with groups as needed to clarify misinformation. The organization's switchboard should be briefed in advance to refer all calls in an emergency to the PIC, and the one-voice and full-disclosure principles should be observed at all times in its operation.

The Media Information Center

If media people will be gathering at the site of an emergency or disaster, the director of public relations should set up a *media information center (MIC)* at some location near the crisis area but away from the PR HQ. Public relations staff members at the PR HQ must be allowed to perform their required tasks without the interruption of news people wanting information. The MIC should, if possible, designate some staff people to escort media representatives if there is a hazardous disaster area. Reporters should not be permitted to wander freely through a dangerous zone, although they usually want unrestricted access to everything. The MIC should be a suitable room, preferably an auditorium if available, where journalists can remain to receive news releases about the emergency. A high-credibility spokesperson and several alternates should be designated in advance and, once chosen, a single spokesperson should be on duty as long as necessary at the MIC to read news releases. Directors of public relations should never be designated MIC spokespersons. They should remain at the PR HQ to supervise all operations. The spokesperson, however, should be a high-ranking officer in the organization; otherwise, the organization's credibility could suffer. Needless to say, the one-voice and full-disclosure principles should be stringently applied in the operation of the MIC.

Uncontrolled and Controlled Media

In an emergency situation, most of the communication will be uncontrolled in the form of news releases, interviews with organizational officials, and perhaps photographs, although the media representatives will usually take their own photos.

Controlled media will be used sparingly, usually as prepared background material or e-mail, voice mail, or in-house bulletins for employees. The organization's website can become an important resource in emergency public relations. Ongoing news of the crisis, along with a wealth of other information about the organization, can be posted on the website. After the crisis, the website can be used to clarify the organization's situation and to provide a record of the course of the crisis itself. Some organizations prepare a special website that is "hidden" on the server but can be activated immediately during a crisis. The sites provide additional background material and interactive features to handle exchanges with both the media and the publics most affected by the crisis.

Effective Communication

Two-way communication and audience participation may assume greater than usual importance in a crisis. The targeted audiences, especially the media, will want to be involved and interact with the spokesperson as much as possible. But, in general, all the previously discussed principles of communication should be observed.

Programming for emergency public relations, then, concentrates on the two major responsibilities of creating a public relations emergency headquarters and a media information center (see Exhibit 11-a). Beyond that, customary use of uncontrolled and controlled media and principles of effective communication are appropriate.

EXHIBIT 11-A   *Emergency Public Relations Checklist*

I. Public relations emergency headquarters (PR HQ). The PR director stays in PR department or designated PR HQ and supervises:

A. Notification and liaison

   1. Internal: Notify the CEO and other top officials on immediate "need-to-know" basis

   2. External: Notify the media; law enforcement officials; governmental agencies; next of kin of injured or dead, before public release of names (24-hour rule suggested)

B. Preparation of materials for media

   1. Have company backgrounder, fact sheet, and bios of officers already prepared and on the company website

 2. Prepare basic news release on crisis as soon as possible (one-hour rule suggested)

   a. Include all known facts—what happened, how, when, where, who, and how many involved—not why (fault)

   b. Be certain all information is accurate; never release unconfirmed information

   c. Withhold names of victims until next of kin are notified (or 24 hours, whichever comes first)

   d. Clear release with senior management, legal department, personnel department

   e. Issue release immediately to local and national mass media, specialized publications, employees by e-mail and phone, community leaders, insurance company, pertinent governmental agencies by fax and e-mail. Be sure to post the release on the company website.

 3. Issue timely statements to media in ongoing crises

 4. Use *one-voice principle*—information only from official organizational statements

 5. Use *full-disclosure principle* (except admission of fault)

C. Public information center (PIC)

 1. Establish and announce a public information center in PR HQ

 2. Respond to telephone and e-mail inquiries with accurate information

 3. Provide accurate information to groups where rumors are circulating

 4. Hold meetings with groups as needed to clarify misinformation

 5. Have switchboard refer all pertinent calls to PIC

 6. Direct company employees to make no unauthorized statements to media people

 7. Use *one-voice principle*—information only from official organizational statements

 8. Use *full-disclosure principle* (except admission of fault)

II. Media information center (MIC)

A. Designate a place for media people to gather, if necessary

B. Locate MIC at site near crisis area, but away from PR HQ. (Media people admitted to disaster site must be *escorted* by PR personnel)

C. Have sole spokesperson on duty day or night at MIC

 1. Use *one-voice principle*—information only from official organizational statements

 2. Use *full-disclosure principle* (except admission of fault)

EVALUATION

The evaluation of emergency public relations will be less precise than for other forms of the discipline. Since emergencies are unplanned, the PR objectives must be, at best, general and nonquantitative guidelines. In a quiet period well after the organization's recovery from the emergency, it will be appropriate to review the general guidelines previously mentioned and informally assess the PR department's degree of success in meeting them. Such a review should also include analyzing media coverage; tracking complaints from consumers, community, employees, and other relevant publics; holding internal meetings on the crisis plan and its implementation; and assessing damage to the organization's image. Of course, a formal survey of all participants can also be taken. The results may be used for a variety of purposes, possibly including improvement of emergency public relations procedures.

SUMMARY

Although the ROPE process has limited applicability in emergency public relations, it should not be forgotten or discarded.

Research is useful in preparing for emergencies. Worst-case scenarios should be prepared to determine what problems could possibly develop. Although emergency public relations is inherently reactive, planning for such crises should be proactive. Emergency contacts lists should be made, including all internal and external individuals, groups, and agencies that are to be notified in a crisis.

Objectives for emergency PR tend to be of an impact nature. They usually concentrate on providing information to important audiences as needed; safeguarding lives, facilities, and assets; and protecting the credibility of the organization.

Programming should include establishing a public relations emergency headquarters and, if necessary, a media information center. The functions of the emergency headquarters include notification and liaison and preparation of materials for the media. If reporters will be gathering at the site of a disaster or crisis, a media information center should be established near (but usually not on) the site, and an organizational spokesperson should be designated to be on duty to read statements to the journalists as long as the crisis lasts.

Evaluation for emergency PR is usually less formal than for other types. If objectives have been set before a crisis occurs, each should be appropriately evaluated. If not, the organization should, after the emergency, review its notification functions, its general accessibility and service to the media, and, of course, its media coverage during the event.

READINGS ON EMERGENCY PUBLIC RELATIONS

Adams, William C. "Responding to the Media During a Crisis: It's What You Say and When You Say It," *Public Relations Quarterly* 45 (spring 2000): 26 ff.

Barton, Lawrence. *Crisis in Organizations: Managing and Communicating in the Heat of Chaos,* 2d ed. Florence, KY: Thomson Learning, 2000.

Benoit, William L. "Image Repair Discourse and Crisis Communication," *Public Relations Review* 23 (summer 1997): 177–186.

Brown, Timothy S. "Powerful Crisis Communications Lessons: PR Lessons Learned from Hurricane Isabel," *Public Relations Quarterly* 48 (winter 2003): 31–35.

Budd, John F., Jr. "The Downside of Crisis Management," *Public Relations Strategist* 4 (fall 1998): 36 ff.

Caponigro, Jeffrey R. *The Crisis Counselor.* New York: McGraw-Hill/NTC, 2000.

Chyi, Hsiang Iris, and Maxwell McCombs. "Media Salience and the Process of Framing: Coverage of the Columbine School Shootings," *Journalism and Mass Communication Quarterly* 81 (spring 2004): 22–25.

Coombs, W. Timothy. "An Analytic Framework for Crisis Situations: Better Responses from a Better Understanding of the Situation," *Journal of Public Relations Research* 10, no. 3 (1998): 177 ff.

———. "Helping Crisis Managers Protect Reputational Assets," *Communications Quarterly* 16 (November 2002): 165–186.

———. *Ongoing Crisis Communication: Planning, Managing, and Responding.* Thousand Oaks, CA: Sage Publications, 1999.

Duke, Shearlean, and Lynne Masland. "Crisis Communication by the Book," *Public Relations Quarterly* 47, (fall 2002): 30–36.

Fearn-Banks, Kathleen. *Crisis Communications: A Casebook Approach,* 2d ed. Mahwah, NJ: Erlbaum, 2002.

Fearn-Banks, Kathleen, Richard J. Symmes, Mike Murphy, Shayan Amir-Hosseini, et al. "A Snapshot of How Organizations Responded to Tragedy," *Public Relations Tactics* 9 (September 2002): 30–32.

Fienberg, Bob. "Communicating in a Crisis," *Asian Business* (Hong Kong) 35 (May 1999): 70 ff.

Frazier, Douglas. "Crisis Planning for Digital Disasters," *Public Relations Tactics* 5 (July 1998): 16.

Gaschen, Dennis John. "Crisis—What Crisis? Taking Your Crisis Communications Plan for a Test Drive," *Public Relations Tactics* 10 (May 2003): 12.

Green, Walter G., III. "The Future of Disasters: Interesting Trends for Interesting Times," *Futures Research Quarterly* 20 (fall 2004): 59–68.

Hearit, Keith Michael. *Crisis Management by Apology.* Mahwah, NJ: Erlbaum, 2005.

Kimmel, Allan J. *Rumors and Rumor Control.* Mahwah, NJ: Erlbaum, 2004.

Kruvand, Marjorie, "Two Decades of Crisis Response," *Public Relations Strategist* 8 (fall 2002): 26–27.

Lerbinger, Otto. *The Crisis Manager: Facing Risk and Responsibility.* Mahwah, NJ: Erlbaum, 1997.

Logan, Dever. "Swissair Flight 111 Crash Tests PR Crisis Plans," *Public Relations Tactics* 5 (December 1998): 4.

Long, Richard K. "Benchmarking as Crisis Planning," *Public Relations Tactics* 7 (February 2000): 10.

Lukaszewski, James E. "Establishing Individual and Corporate Crisis Communication Standards: The Principles and Protocols," *Public Relations Quarterly* 42 (fall 1997), 7ff.

————. *Executive Action Series: Vol. I: War Stories and Crisis Communication Strategies, A Crisis Communication Management Anthology; Vol. II: Crisis Communication Planning Strategies, A Crisis Communication Management Workbook; Vol. IV: Media Relations Strategies During Emergencies, A Crisis Communication Management Guide.* New York: Public Relations Society of America, 2000.

McLaughlin, Shane. "Sept. 11: Four Views of Crisis Management," *Public Relations Strategist* 8 (winter 2002): 22–29.

Millar, Dan P., and Robert L. Heath, eds. *Responding to Crisis.* Mahwah, NJ: Erlbaum, 2004.

Mitroff, Ian, and Gus Anagnos. *Managing Crises Before They Happen: What Every Executive Needs to Know About Crisis Management.* New York: AMACOM, 2000.

O'Donnell, Jayne. "Damage Control: Handling Public Relations Disasters," *Working Woman* 24 (April 1999): 83ff.

Ogrizek, Michel, and Jean-Michel Guillery. *Communicating in Crisis.* Hawthorne, NY: Aldine de Gruyter, 1999.

Pinsdorf, Marion K. *Communicating When Your Company Is Under Siege: Surviving Public Crisis,* 3d ed. New York: Fordham University Press, 1999.

————. *All Crises Are Global: Managing to Escape Chaos, Communication and Organizational Crisis.* New York: NYU Press, 2004.

Preble, John F. "Integrating the Crisis Management Perspective into the Strategic Management Process," *Journal of Management Studies* 34 (September 1997): 769.

Profolio: Crisis Planning and Management. New York: Public Relations Society of America, 1998.

Richards, Barry. "Terrorism and Public Relations," *Public Relations Review* 30 (June 2004): 169–176.

Roach, Thomas. "The NIMBY and Goliath Phenomenon," *Rock Products* 107 (May 2004): 8.

Ropeik, David, and George Gray. *Risk! A Practical Guide for Deciding What's Really Safe and What's Really Dangerous in the World Around You.* New York: Houghton Mifflin, 2002.

Shin, Jae-Hwa, I-Huei Cheng, Yan Jin, and Glen T. Cameron. "Going Head to Head: Content Analysis of High Profile Conflicts as Played Out in the Press," *Public Relations Review* 31 (September 2005): 399–406.

Surowiecki, James. "In Case of Emergency," *New Yorker* 81 (June 13, 2005): 70.

Wiser, Nancy. "After the Storm: PR Efforts Help Quell Public Frustration in Kentucky," *Public Relations Tactics* 11 (January 2004): 11.

CASE 11-1

In a crisis, the public often weighs personal risk by how close the event comes to their own lives. Anything that threatens the food chain becomes very personal. The public doesn't want to hear officials discuss "low risk" or "negligible threats" to the health of their families; they expect "no risk" and perfect quality in food products. Exhibit 11-1a is a statement by the National Cattlemen's Beef Association, and Exhibit 11-1b is an announcement on the origin of the contaminated beef.

Protecting Consumer Confidence in U.S. Beef: A Success Story

National Cattlemen's Beef Association

Situation Analysis

The U.S. Department of Agriculture announced on Tuesday, December 23, 2003, that a cow located in Washington State tested positive for BSE. The test was confirmed by the International Reference Lab in the United Kingdom and the cow was traced back to Canadian origin. Even a single case of BSE had proven destructive in other countries. BSE was first identified in the United Kingdom in 1986 but when it was linked to a new human neurological disease (variant Creutzfeldt Jakob Disease — vCJD) in 1996, the effects crippled that country's beef industry. Before the United Kingdom was able to get the disease under control, more than 2 million bovine animals were destroyed and sales plummeted. In 1996, the consumption of beef dropped 9 percent in the European Union and didn't rebound to pre-BSE levels until 2000. When the first case hit Germany, beef sales tumbled almost 70 percent compared to the year earlier. The Canadian cattle industry lost its export markets when its first case was found — devastating considering that more than 65 percent of Canadian beef production was exported. Would the U.S. beef industry be next?

Courtesy National Cattlemen's Beef Association

Research

The National Cattlemen's Beef Association, on behalf of America's beef producers and their Checkoff Program, began market research with U.S. consumers in 1996 following the BSE link to human illness. Research included focus groups, quantitative tracking surveys (a total of 29 tracking surveys have been conducted since April 1996), and BSE media coverage monitoring and analysis. The research findings fueled the development of BSE response strategies, including:

1. added focus on scientific spokespersons;

2. focused message development to ensure effective communications;

3. added emphasis on "local" response plans at the state level, working with the 45 state beef councils and 46 state cattlemen's associations;

4. an aggressive media response plan to handle heightened interest; and

5. an issues-response strategy to correct misinformation.

Planning

The overall goal was to maintain beef demand by sustaining U.S. consumer confidence. In order to accomplish this, it would be imperative to:

1. ensure science-based facts were broadly available for consumers to use when making beef purchase decisions;

2. provide a unified, respected voice for the beef industry; and

3. correct misinformation.

The **audiences** were:

- Consumers: uncertainty about what BSE meant for them and their families

- Media (consumer, agriculture, and industry trade): since 1996, media found this story enticing and jumped at opportunities to share the latest assumption or image; their hunger for new information created potential for misinformation

- State and national beef industry organizations: highly motivated to reassure consumers and members of the beef industry

- U.S. government agencies: U.S. consumers viewed government safety experts as being the most reassuring and credible on BSE

- U.S. beef export markets: unwilling to jeopardize their own and consumer confidence; under pressure from domestic beef industries to potentially use this as a trade barrier over the long term

- Beef marketers (retail, food service, wholesale, etc.): interested in serving customers what they want and not necessarily interested in defending beef when other options (poultry, fish, pork, vegetarian) were available

Research findings drove the implementation of several preparedness tactics including: creation of BSE Crisis Response Plan; development of online scientific resource (located at bseinfo.org); creation of model for electronic issues advisories to inform stakeholders of BSE issues and talking points; crisis drills; contingency communications materials; development of a crisis section of www.bseinfo.org to be activated in the event of a U.S. case; and extensive media training for NCBA staff, producer leaders, and experts.

Execution

Immediately upon the announcement of the first U.S. BSE case, the first priority was to communicate a unified message to the media. Initial coverage was bound to be widespread and would set the tone for the long term.

The key **tactics** were:

- Aggressively communicate to domestic and international consumers, primarily through domestic and international media (print, broadcast, and Internet), the actions being taken by the U.S. government to ensure that BSE is not a health risk. Fifteen minutes after the USDA announcement, NCBA hosted a telephone news conference in which 160 consumer news and trade reporters participated. NCBA's experts quickly became among the most quoted on the topic. Trained NCBA spokespeople conducted hundreds of national and international news interviews during the first few days. Third-party experts were briefed on the facts so that they could reassure consumers of the science in media interviews. Tele-news conferences for the media were conducted frequently to amplify and clarify facts as the story developed. Video footage and photos that accurately portrayed the U.S. beef industry were provided to news organizations.

- Activate the beef industry crisis response section of www.bseinfo .org. This website became a key source of information for industry, media, beef marketers, governments, and consumers. In the month following the BSE announcement, this site averaged 40,000 unique visitors weekly.

- Work diligently with state beef councils and cattlemen's associations, food service companies, retailers, and other industry stakeholders to present a unified and science-based message to all audiences through daily, and sometimes hourly, e-mail advisories. The advisories were praised as a "must read" in the industry and significantly reduced speculation. A password-protected extranet site for state associations and allied organizations was created, providing a clearinghouse for key messages, Q&As, and media requests. Teleconferences were conducted with state organizations and allied groups to gain their input and keep messages on track.

- Insist that the U.S. government keep the process transparent and science driven.
- Counteract misinformation posted to the Internet by ensuring accurate information was broadly available on the Web.
- A special Super Bowl radio promotion was implemented to keep beef moving through the channels. NOTE: This was included to show the breadth of programming to address the situation.

As the issue continued, difficult situations surfaced. As the mainline story began to lose steam in the summer and fall of 2004, secondary stories began surfacing. Tactics were developed to address a variety of topics that became entangled in the BSE issue, including international trade and country of origin product labeling.

Evaluation

Consumer Demand

In 2004, beef demand rose 7.74 percent. This is the largest increase in decades, and by itself eclipsed the Beef Promotion & Research Industry Long Range Plan goal to increase demand by 6 percent between 2000 and 2004.

Confidence

Consumer confidence that U.S. beef is safe from mad cow disease was at 88 percent in September 2003, prior to the announcement of the U.S. BSE case. The January 2005 tracking survey showed that consumer confidence in U.S. beef was at 93 percent. In fact, in the 13 tracking surveys since December 23, 2003, consumer confidence hasn't dropped below where it was prior to that date.

Consumer Spending

The Cattle-Fax "2004 U.S. Consumer Spending on Beef" estimate is $70 billion—an $8 billion increase from last year and a $24 billion increase from the average of the 1990s. This is remarkable. The data indicate that the BSE case has not impacted consumer spending on beef.

Media Coverage

BSE generated a historic-high volume of beef industry media coverage. During the year of reporting that followed, BSE was referenced in 5,389 articles in the 154 top-tier consumer media outlets monitored by

NCBA—nearly four times the number of BSE-related articles in the previous year. Overall favorability remained near neutral throughout the coverage period, a remarkable outcome considering that misinformation was being delivered by a wide range of groups. According to the media-monitoring data, officials from USDA and NCBA were the most quoted sources on BSE. This served to mitigate some of the negative attacks against the government's BSE safeguards, which have protected consumers from this disease. Government and industry spokespersons helped set the tone of the coverage by speaking to the media early and often.

Most of the countries in the world that have diagnosed BSE cases have experienced a significant drop in consumer confidence and sales of beef. This didn't happen in the United States.

We had the science, messages, spokespersons, and communications systems in place to successfully manage this issue.

Together with the Cattlemen's Beef Board, state organizations, and producer leaders, NCBA maintained consumer confidence in beef safety and demand for beef.

EXHIBIT 11-1A   *Statement*

NATIONAL CATTLEMEN'S BEEF ASSOCIATION

1301 Pennsylvania Ave., NW, Suite #300 • Washington, DC 20004 • 202-347-0228 • Fax 202-638-0607

NCBA Statement Regarding
USDA Announcement of Suspect BSE in a Dairy Cow in Washington State

Terry Stokes, Chief Executive Officer, National Cattlemen's Beef Association
December 23, 2003

The U.S. Secretary of Agriculture announced today the diagnosis of a possible case of Bovine Spongiform Encephalopathy (BSE, also known as mad cow disease) in a Dairy Cow in Washington State.

The U.S. has conducted a BSE surveillance program since 1990 and this is the first possible case that has been found.

The Harvard Center for Risk Analysis has conducted a comprehensive multi-year assessment of the risk of BSE in the U.S. While the Harvard study noted there was some level of risk, the analysis concluded that "In summary, measures taken by the U.S. government and industry make the U.S. robust against the spread of BSE to animals or humans should it be introduced into this country."

While this one case is unfortunate, systems have been built over the past 15 years to prevent this disease from spreading and affecting either animal health or public health.

NCBA has fully supported an aggressive surveillance program in the U.S. to assure that if BSE were introduced it would be detected and eliminated. We applaud the swift action taken by the U.S. Department of Agriculture to announce the finding of this possible case and its aggressive investigation of the circumstances. The U.S. cattle industry remains committed to eliminating this disease from North America. As such, we will work closely with the USDA to carry out a full investigation and determine what additional preventive measures, if any, need to be taken to continue to protect animal and public health.

This case was found in a federally inspected plant. The central nervous tissue from this animal, which scientists recognize as the infective material, did not go into the food supply.

Consumers should continue to eat beef with confidence. All scientific studies show that the BSE infectious agent has never been found in beef muscle meat or milk and U.S. beef remains safe to eat.

Americans can be confident in the safety of U.S. beef for a number of reasons:

The BSE agent is not found in meat like steaks and roasts. It is found in central nervous system tissue such as brain and spinal cord.

All U.S. cattle are inspected by a USDA Inspector or veterinarian before going to slaughter. Animals with any signs of neurological disorder are tested for BSE.

Courtesy National Cattlemen's Beef Association

EXHIBIT 11-1A *Statement (continued)*

-        BSE affects older cattle, typically over 30 months of age. The vast majority of the cattle going to market in the U.S. are less than 24 months old.

-        The U.S. began a surveillance program for BSE in 1990 and was the first country without the disease within its borders to test cattle for the disease. The surveillance system targets all cattle with any signs of neurological disorder as well as those over 30 months of age and animals that are non-ambulatory.

-        The U.S. banned imports of cattle and bovine products from countries with BSE beginning in 1989.

-        The only way BSE spreads is through contaminated feed. The U.S. Food & Drug Administration in 1997 instituted a ban on feeding ruminant-derived meat and bone meal supplements to cattle. This is a firewall that prevents the spread of BSE to other animals if it were present in the U.S.

       Currently this is a suspected case in one animal and the USDA is aggressively investigating this case. We want to reiterate that we support a full investigation and the necessary steps to eliminate this disease from North America and protect the health of U.S. cattle.

###

For additional information go to <u>www.BSEinfo.org</u>

EXHIBIT 11-1B   *Statement on Origin of Problem*

NATIONAL CATTLEMEN'S BEEF ASSOCIATION

1301 Pennsylvania Ave., NW, Suite #300 • Washington, DC 20004 • 202-347-0228 • Fax 202-638-0607

NCBA Statement Regarding
USDA Announcement of the Origin of the BSE-positive Dairy Cow in Washington State

Terry Stokes, Chief Executive Officer, National Cattlemen's Beef Association
December 27, 2003

Based on today's announcement from the U.S. Department of Agriculture showing records indicate that the Washington state dairy cow that tested positive for BSE was imported from Canada, the National Cattlemen's Beef Association strongly urges our trading partners to reopen their borders to U.S. beef exports.

In five short days and despite the holiday, USDA has traced this animal through ear-tag identification to Canadian records. These records suggest this cow is more than six years old and entered the United States with 73 other animals that are being traced by USDA.

Again, USDA authorities have confirmed the central nervous system tissue from this animal **never** entered the human food chain. Rather, it was sent to rendering for non-human food uses. In new developments, the Food and Drug Administration also announced today that they have "under control" all the rendered product from this Washington state cow.

Scientists agree these central nervous system tissues, such as spinal cord and brain, are the carrier of BSE. The BSE agent is not found in muscle meat, like steaks, roasts or ground beef.

We applaud USDA for their rapid progress on this investigation and their collaborative efforts with the Canadian Food Inspection Agency to seek its swift conclusion. We also applaud and appreciate the Washington state dairy and cattle producers who have cooperated fully with U.S. investigators.

This investigation must be USDA's top priority. To that end, we are requesting an indefinite extension of the final comments on the proposed rule regarding the opening of the Canadian border to live animal trade until the investigation is complete. This will allow us to gather all the information from the investigation so we can comment accordingly on behalf of our members.

Just like we expect from our trading partners, importation into the United States from Canada of boneless beef from animals under 30 months of age presents no public health risk and should continue.

All decisions concerning re-establishment of trade for beef exports must be based on sound science. As USDA announced today, standards set by the international animal health body (OIE) recognize that meat can be safely traded from countries that have identified cases of BSE.

Courtesy National Cattlemen's Beef Association

EXHIBIT 11-1B   *Statement on Origin of Problem (continued)*

Subsequent to the Canadian announcement of BSE on May 20, 2003, USDA implemented a voluntary Beef Export Verification program for U.S. trading partners requiring additional and precautionary assurances. The Beef Export Verification program allows our trading partners to be assured that U.S. beef products remain safe for their consumers, just like it is for American consumers.

The National Cattlemen's Beef Association expects trade to be the Administration's top priority. Beef and variety meat exports represent approximately 10 percent of U.S. beef production and were valued at $3.5 billion to the U.S. industry in 2002.

###

For additional information go to www.BSEinfo.org.

*Natural disasters of short duration may have long-term conse-
quences to the economy. San Diego, an area known for tourist
attractions and a favorable location for national conventions,
fought hard to limit economic losses from disastrous wildfires in
the region. Exhibit 11-2a is a news release, Exhibit 11-2b is an
e-blast used to keep convention planners updated, and Exhibit
11-2c is the Convention Center's action plan for the crisis.*

San Diego Wildfires 2003

San Diego Convention Center Corporation

Summary

In 2003, the most destructive wildfires in California's history erupted in
San Diego. The fires began on October 25 in rural San Diego County.
By the next day, the fires were raging out of control within the city limits, only 20 miles away from the San Diego Convention Center, the
largest public facility in the region. The Convention Center aggressively
reached out to 15 groups scheduled to hold their multimillion-dollar
conventions and trade shows worth $109.7 million in economic impact
and $2.3 million in anticipated tax revenues for the city. The goal was
to avoid loss of business or diminished attendance, alleviate client concerns, and ensure the safety and well-being of convention attendees.

Overview

The San Diego Convention Center Corporation (SDCCC) is a public
benefit corporation established by the City of San Diego to manage and
market two public facilities, the San Diego Convention Center and the
San Diego Concourse. The SDCCC's primary mission is to attract national conventions and trade shows that generate significant economic
benefits for the San Diego region.

Located alongside scenic San Diego Bay, the San Diego Convention
Center is one of the region's strongest economic engines. This year it
held 230 events that attracted over 800,000 visitors and produced $1
billion in regional economic impact. The facility supports 8,000 jobs
countywide. Most recently, the Convention Center opened a $216 mil-
lion expansion that doubled the size of the building to 2.6 million
square feet, making it the 21st largest among some 380 facilities in the
North America.

Courtesy San Diego Convention Center Corporation

In late October 2003, the most destructive wildfires in California's history erupted in San Diego, making world news and having an extraordinary impact on the region. The fires killed nearly two dozen people, destroyed 3,600 homes, and scorched more than 750,000 acres throughout Southern California. The SDCCC aggressively reached out to several groups scheduled to hold their multimillion-dollar conventions and trade shows at the Convention Center to keep them abreast of the latest fire developments and to assure them that the building was not threatened and open for business. Fifteen groups were identified as potentially being affected with 35,000 estimated attendees. Collectively, the groups were worth $109.7 million in economic impact and $2.3 million in anticipated tax revenues for the City of San Diego.

Goal: Launch an immediate, coordinated communications campaign targeting 15 meeting planners who were holding conventions and trade shows at the San Diego Convention Center between October 25 and November 15. The purpose was to alleviate their concerns about the wildfires, provide them with up-to-date, factual information that could be funneled to attendees, assure them that the Convention Center was safe and open for business, and most importantly, avoid loss of business or cancellations.

Research

- An immediate analysis of business was conducted by in-house staff to identify which conventions and trade shows would likely be affected; 15 clients were identified who were the target audience.

- An immediate analysis of the 15 groups was conducted to quantify attendance. Attendance is the key element that greatly influences economic benefits to the City of San Diego.

- Information was gathered from local and state law enforcement and fire protection agencies for the most up-to-date information.

- Information was gathered from SDCCC partner hotels to gauge what impact, if any, the fires would have on out-of-town guests staying at hotels.

- Information was gathered from San Diego International Airport, Lindbergh Field, to determine what impact, if any, the fires would have on arrivals and departures for visiting convention delegates.

- Staff gathered information from the Air Pollution Control District of the County of San Diego for the latest information about air quality. Health tips for attendees with health concerns and breathing problems were collected from the American Heart Association website.

- One-on-one phone calls were placed to 15 meeting planners that served a twofold purpose of alleviating concerns, but more importantly, to gauge their perceptions about the fire in relationship to their event.

Planning

The SDCCC worked with the San Diego Convention & Visitors Bureau to coordinate a plan to produce consistent, timely, and factual information. Designated SDCCC staff and Convention & Visitor Bureau staff met to develop key message points and to determine how the information would be delivered and by whom. It was essential to have "one voice" and determine the best way to share vital information.

Electronic updates would be developed and sent out daily. They would come from the president and CEO of the SDCCC and the president and CEO of the Convention & Visitors Bureau—again consistent message and "one voice."

SDCCC would take the lead in responding to media calls. The vice president of public affairs would be on call 24/7 to respond to media requests.

Based on research, there was potential for 15 events to be impacted. The president and CEO from both the SDCCC and the Convention & Visitors Bureau would place personal phone calls to these customers offering assurances.

E-blasts would be sent to the 15 clients, and other stakeholders, on a regular basis to keep them well informed with up-to-date information. E-blasts would be formatted in such a way to be easily forwarded by meeting planners to attendee databases electronically.

Senior staff would reach out to the meeting planner for the American Society of Plastic Surgeons (5,000 attendees), the group in the building when the fires erupted.

The research gathered from the state and local law enforcement and fire protection agencies, the airport, local hotels, and the Air Pollution Control District of San Diego County and other factual information would be used to update clients. The communication would be concise and factual, no speculation.

E-blasts and news releases would be placed on both the SDCCC and SDCVB websites for easy reference.

Local news would be monitored on an ongoing basis to track changing circumstances.

Communication would continue until the wildfires subsided.

Execution

The fires began late Saturday evening, October 25, 2003, in rural San Diego County. By Sunday afternoon, October 26, the fires were out of control and within the city limits, 20 miles away from the Convention

Center. Communication between the SDCCC emergency chain of command that includes the president and CEO, the vice president of public affairs, the COO, and other senior executives was in full swing by Sunday afternoon. Communication with staff from the San Diego Convention & Visitors Bureau also took place on Sunday. The plan was executed on Monday morning.

- As our clients were on Eastern Standard Time (EST), 15 personal phone calls were placed so that meeting planners began receiving their calls no later than 8:30 a.m. EST. Clients were relieved at receiving the news that the fires were over 20 miles away from the Convention Center, and there was no threat of danger to the facility. Timely calls from the top people at each organization strengthened customer relations.

- Five electronic e-blasts with up-to-date information were e-mailed to clients.

- Electronic e-blasts were used by meeting planners to funnel information to their attendees immediately by simply forwarding the e-blast to their registration data base.

- Electronic e-blasts were posted on the website for easy reference.

- Local media was notified that the center was open for business.

- Incoming media inquiries were funneled to designated spokesperson to stay on message.

- The meeting with the American Society of Plastic Surgeons (ASPS), the group in the building when the fires started, also went well. The ASPS president ended up donating several thousand box lunches to local area shelters for distribution to those affected by the fire, as well as a financial contribution to the American Red Cross. ASPS members attending the plastic surgeon convention volunteered to provide medical services as needed.

- The immediate response to our clients was shared with the mayor and City Council members, demonstrating that the SDCCC values business and takes our role as one of San Diego's strongest producers of city tax revenues seriously.

Evaluation

Our ultimate goal was to avoid loss of business and to ensure that both meeting planners and their attendees received accurate information. Because high attendance drives economic impact, it was important that estimated attendance levels for each event not be impacted by the fires.

- No loss of business or events cancelled.

- Attendance levels for each event were met or exceeded expectations.

- The one-on-one personal phone calls from president and CEO strengthened customer relations and demonstrated that we value our clients' business and well-being.

- News media that called were immediately directed to SDCCC spokesperson as planned. The *Union Tribune* article was positive and prominently noted that we were reaching out to our customers with information and that no business had been cancelled as a result of the fires.

- Feedback was excellent on the e-blast method of disseminating information. Clients liked being able to funnel electronic information to their attendees immediately and to access our website.

- The experience garnered from this campaign was invaluable to public affairs staff.

EXHIBIT 11-2A   *News Release*

N E W S   R E L E A S E

SAN DIEGO CONVENTION CENTER CORPORATION
CORPORATE COMMUNICATIONS

FOR IMMEDIATE RELEASE
Monday, October 27, 2003

Contact: **Fred Sainz**
619-525-5251 (o)
858-442-8914 (c)

San Diego Convention Center and Downtown San Diego Open for Business

California Fires NOT a Threat to Downtown Establishments

SAN DIEGO - The San Diego Convention Center remains open for business and is NOT threatened by fires in the region. The harbor side Convention Center, the city's airport and hotels at which delegates will stay, are located in the city's compact Downtown, 25 miles west of the communities impacted by the fires. The Santa Ana winds that incited the fires are expected to subside by Tuesday. The only impact to the Downtown area has been regional air quality and that is expected to have a noticeable improvement by the end of the week as the fires subside.

The Center is presently hosting the 6,000 delegates of the American Society of Plastic Surgeons (ASPS)/Plastic Surgery Educational Foundation (PSEF) "Plastic Surgery 2003" Meeting. This meeting has gone on as regularly planned and without interruption. The Center's award-winning staff of 400 all reported for work as scheduled this morning to service the ASPS/PSEF delegates.

ASPS/PSEF have distinguished themselves as visitors to our community by donating thousands of box lunches to fire evacuees. In addition, CenterPlate, the Center's exclusive food and beverage provider, has also provided food and beverage for 5,000 evacuees located at Qualcomm Stadium.

"We are open for business as usual," said Carol Wallace, President/CEO of the San Diego Convention Center Corporation. "While the fires have had a devastating effect on portions of our community, San Diegans will continue to greet our convention visitors with broad smiles and open hearts."

###

Courtesy San Diego Convention Center Corporation

EXHIBIT 11-2B *E-blast Update*

A PARTNERSHIP BETWEEN THE SAN DIEGO CONVENTION CENTER CORPORATION AND THE SAN DIEGO CONVENTION & VISITORS BUREAU

San Diego Update

Tuesday, October 28, 2003

CONVENTION CENTER AND DOWNTOWN HOTELS OPEN FOR BUSINESS

Dear Friend:

The national media coverage regarding the fires has understandably concerned many of our near future convention clients -- and their attendees. In order to deliver the most **accurate and timely information**, the San Diego Convention Center Corporation and the San Diego Convention & Visitors Bureau are **aggressively outreaching to our clients and through them, to their attendees**, to assure them that the **Convention Center, the airport and Downtown San Diego are all safe and open for business**.

It is incredibly important that our clients hear from us -- first and often. We are in the best position to offer them accurate information, frank advice and positive reassurance. We began our outreach activities yesterday and **will continue them through the time the fires subside**. We thought you might want to know what we are doing to not only save conventions but almost as important, to keep attendance levels high. Click here to see the DAILY UPDATE that we will be issuing to our clients and through them, to their attendees.

There are 15 events scheduled to take place at the Convention Center between now and November 14 with 34,500 projected out-of-town visitors. These events will have a cumulative economic impact of $109 million on our region and generate $2.4 million in taxes for our city. Our San Diego Update Campaign is intended to make sure we realize all of these numbers.

Sincerely,

Carol Wallace
President/CEO
San Diego Convention
Center Corporation
619-525-5101

Reint Reinders
President/CEO
San Diego Convention &
Visitors Bureau
619-557-2831

Provided by the San Diego
Convention Center Corporation
and the San Diego Convention
and Visitor's Bureau.
For information on events in
the San Diego area please
email carol.reint@sdccc.org

Courtesy San Diego Convention Center Corporation

EXHIBIT 11-3C *Firestorm 2003 — Crisis Communication Plan*

San Diego Convention Center Corporation
Firestorm 2003 – Crisis Communication Plan

GOAL: Diminish risk for loss of business, alleviate client concerns about San Diego wildfires, and assure the safety and well-being of their attendees.

DAY 1 SUNDAY, OCT. 26	DAY 2 MONDAY, OCT. 27	DAY 3 TUESDAY, OCT. 28	DAY 4 WEDNESDAY, OCT. 29	DAY 5 THURSDAY, OCT. 30	DAY 6 FRIDAY, OCT. 31
• Immediately reach out to the client presently holding their convention (American Society of Plastic Surgeons.) • Identify future conventions and trade shows that could be affected; include all groups through Thanksgiving. • Quantify attendance, economic impact, direct delegate spending; & room nights. • Determine method for contacting each meeting planner. 　• Personal phone calls. 　• Electronic news blasts • Identify spokesperson to respond to media. 　• Notify media that the convention center was not in danger and open for business • Gather the most up to date information from local & state fire protection agencies; airport, partner hotels, Air Pollution Control District; tourist attractions.	• Place phone calls to meeting planners to offer assurance that the fires were not threatening the building and attendees would be safe. • Craft and disseminate e-blasts. Include factual information that would be disseminated to meeting planners & other stakeholders. • Post e-blasts and other news developments on web site. • Issue statement that the convention center was safe and open for business to local media. • Media contact on call 24/7. • Track local news for late-breaking developments.	• Issue daily e-blast with up-to-date information. • President and CEO available 24/7 to respond to clients or other stakeholders if necessary. • Media contact on call 24/7. • Reach out to the Mayor, city councilmembers and other leaders to inform them that we were in personal communication with meeting planners. The goal was to ensure that the economic impact and attendance not be effected by the wildfires.	• Issue daily e-blast with up-to-date information. • President and CEO available 24/7 to respond to clients or other stakeholders if necessary. • Media contact on call 24/7. • As the fires subsided within city limits, re-asses timeframe for client reach out effort.	• Issue daily e-blast with up-to-date information. • President and CEO available 24/7 to respond to clients or other stakeholders if necessary. • Media contact on call 24/7.	• Issue daily e-blast with up-to-date information. • President and CEO available 24/7 to respond to clients or other stakeholders if necessary. • Media contact on call 24/7. • Based on current information from local and state fire protection agencies, the fires were under control and clients were informed that last update would be sent today.

Oct 2003

PART IV

Beyond Public Relations

CHAPTER 12   **Integrated Marketing Communications**

Integrated Marketing Communications

Public relations has long been used as a tool for marketing products and services to consumers, but in the past, public relations was segregated or departmentalized as a function separate from product advertising. Public relations advertising was strictly defined as that advertising used to accomplish public relations objectives, such as image enhancement, not the sale of products or services.

During the past decade, integrated marketing communications (IMC) has become popular in promoting the products and services of corporate America. IMC simply combines the operations of traditional public relations with traditional marketing and advertising. One pioneering definition of IMC is the following:

> What is integrated marketing communications? It's a new way of looking at the whole, where once we only saw parts such as advertising, public relations, sales promotion, purchasing, employee communications, and so forth. It's realigning communications to look at it the way the customer sees it—as a flow of information from indistinguishable sources. Professional communicators have always been condescendingly amused that consumers called everything "advertising" or "PR." Now they recognize with concern if not chagrin that that's exactly the point—it is all one thing, at least to the consumer who sees or hears it.[1]

Like the major forms of public relations discussed in this book, IMC can be clearly understood using the ROPE process.

RESEARCH

Research for IMC may include investigation of the client, the reason for the program, and the publics or "stakeholders"[2] to be targeted.

Client Research

The usual background information needed for other forms of public relations is also necessary in the research phase of IMC: detailed analysis of the client's product or service, its personnel, financial status, and general reputation in its field. A frequently used tool in marketing is the SWOT analysis. *SWOT* stands for strengths, weaknesses, opportunities, and threats. To begin, the strengths and weaknesses of the client's products or services in the marketplace versus those of the competition should be honestly appraised. With this analysis in hand, the practitioner should assess opportunities, or ways by which the client might best increase the market share of its products or services in competitive situations. Finally, an assessment of external threats, or factors that might work against the client, should be made.[3]

Opportunity or Problem Research

The most obvious reason for any marketing program is to sell the client's merchandise. The traditional product-oriented marketing model focuses on the four Ps: product, price, place, and promotion. This process begins with the underlying assumption that a company decides what product to manufacture; then prices it; distributes it in particular places, locations, or outlets; and finally promotes the product in an essentially one-way mode of communication, usually mass media product advertising.[4]

IMC, on the other hand, begins with the assumption that the needs of the consumer and other stakeholders should come first. This, in turn, calls for an audience-centered, transactional model. Instead of simply selling products, IMC attempts to create *relationships* with consumers and other stakeholders. In addition to striving to get consumers to purchase products, IMC strives to get support and loyalty from consumers and other stakeholders.

Audience Research

IMC audience research, or stakeholder research, consists of using both nonquantitative and quantitative research methods to learn as much as possible about the groups to be targeted for communication. These stakeholder groups include:

Customers

New customers

Old customers

> Potential customers
> Employees
>> Management
>> Nonmanagement
> Media
>> Mass
>> Specialized
> Investors
>> Shareowners and potential shareowners
>> Financial analysts
>> Financial press
> Suppliers
> Competitors
> Government regulators

Attitudes, behaviors, media habits, and other demographic data about stakeholders are important research information in IMC.

OBJECTIVES

IMC may use both impact and output objectives.

Impact Objectives

Impact objectives may affect stakeholders by informing them or by modifying their attitudes or behaviors. Examples might include the following:

1. To increase (by 20 percent) the stakeholder's knowledge and awareness of the company's new product (during the next six months)

2. To enhance (by 15 percent) positive attitude formation toward the company's product (during the current year)

3. To increase customer purchases of the client's product (by 50 percent) during the current year

Output Objectives

Output objectives for IMC consist of measurable efforts for the client's program:

1. To increase print advertising in major metropolitan dailies by 10 percent during the sale period

2. To schedule five special events for the client's sales campaign during August

PROGRAMMING

As with the various forms of public relations, IMC may begin with planning the theme and messages. The uniqueness of IMC programming is that it combines the activities of traditional advertising with traditional public relations.

    Theme and Messages
    Advertising
        Print
        Broadcast
            Radio
            TV
        Direct Mail
        Telemarketing
        Point-of-purchase
        Specialty advertising
    Public Relations
        Uncontrolled
            Print
            Broadcast
        Controlled
            Print
            Audiovisual
            Interpersonal
            Websites
            Action or special events

Both advertising and public relations are combined in a seamless whole to accomplish essentially marketing goals.

Effective Communication

Since IMC seeks to establish interactive communication between client and stakeholders, the same principles of effective communication apply to it as to public relations. Of special interest to marketing communicators using IMC are the principles of source credibility, two-way communication, and audience participation. IMC is concerned with long-range consumer loyalty, not just the quick, one-shot sale of merchandise. The client's reputation thus becomes a matter of paramount concern. Customer involvement with the client or company is another major hallmark of IMC. Well-established interactive public relations techniques are a decisive advantage in such communication transactions.

EVALUATION

The success of IMC programs should be determined by tracking stated objectives. Impact and output objectives can be measured using the standard tools of public relations programs, as outlined in Chapter 2.

SUMMARY

Integrated marketing communications is a new combination of traditional advertising and public relations practices. The ROPE process is a convenient model for this relatively new field, which is making the old, separated categories of advertising and public relations obsolete.

NOTES

1.   Don E. Schultz, Stanley I. Tannenbaum, and Robert F. Lauterborn, *Integrated Marketing Communications* (Chicago: NTC Business Books, 1993), p. xvii.

2.   *Stakeholders* is the preferred term for IMC audiences. See Thomas L. Harris, *Value-Added Public Relations* (Chicago: NTC Business Books, 1998), p. 124, for a concise definition of stakeholders. Also see Tom Duncan and Sandra Moriarty, *Driving Brand Value* (New York: McGraw-Hill, 1997), chap. 4, for a more complete discussion of this concept.

3.   For discussions of SWOT, see Harris, *Value-Added Public Relations*, p. 235, and Duncan and Moriarty, *Driving Brand Value*, pp. 149–152.

4.   For a discussion of four-Ps theory, see Schultz, Tannenbaum, and Lauterborn, *Integrated Marketing Communications*, pp. 5 and 12.

READINGS ON INTEGRATED MARKETING COMMUNICATIONS

Caywood, Clarke L., ed. *The Handbook of Strategic Public Relations and Integrated Communications.* New York: McGraw-Hill, 1997.

Cobb, Robin. "Pointing the Way to PR," *Marketing* (March 12, 1998): 29.

Debreceny, Peter, and Lisa Cochrane. "Two Disciplines on the Same Road," *Advertising Age* 75 (November 8, 2004): 28.

Duncan, Tom, and Sandra Moriarty. *Driving Brand Value: Using Integrated Marketing to Manage Profitable Stakeholder Relationships.* New York: McGraw-Hill, 1997.

Eagle, Lynne, and Philip J. Kitchen. "IMC Brand Communications and Corporate Cultures: Client/Advertising Agency Co-Ordination and Cohesion," *European Journal of Marketing* 34 (May–June 2000): 667 ff.

Edmondson, Jan. "Come Together: Why Integrated Marketing Works," *Public Relations Tactics* 7 (January 2000): 12.

Elliott, Susan, ed. *Integrated Marketing Communications*. Houston, TX: American Productivity and Quality Center, 1998.

Fernando, Angelo. "Creating Buzz: New Media Tactics Have Changed the PR and Advertising Game," *Communication World* 21 (November–December 2004): 10–11.

Harris, Thomas L. *Value-Added Public Relations*. Chicago: NTC Business Books, 1998.

Henry, Rene A., Jr. *Marketing Public Relations: The Hows That Make It Work*. Ames: Iowa State University Press, 1995.

Heslop, Janet. *The American Marketplace: Demographics and Spending Pattern*, 3d rev. ed. Ithaca, NY: New Strategist Publications, 1997.

Jones, Susan K. *Creative Strategy in Direct Marketing*, 2d ed. Lincolnwood, IL: NTC/Contemporary Publishing, 1998.

Lundstrom, William J., and David Watkins. "Social Cause Dissemination and Feedback Using Multimedia and Internet-Based Techniques: The Case for Equality in Education," *Journal of Public Affairs* 5 (February 2005): 66–70.

Nash, Edward L. *Direct Marketing: Strategy, Planning, Execution*. New York: McGraw-Hill, 2000.

Page, Russell. "Michelin Americas Truck Tires with Jackson-Dawson Integrated Marketing Communications," *Public Relations Tactics* 10 (September 2003): 24.

Pickton, David, and Amanda Broderick. *Integrated Marketing Communications*, 2d ed. Englewood Cliffs, NJ: Prentice-Hall, 2005.

Ries, Al, and Laura Ries. *The Fall of Advertising and the Rise of PR*. New York: HarperCollins, 2002.

Samli, A. Coskun, and John S. Hill. *Marketing Globally: Planning and Practice*. Lincolnwood, IL: NTC/Contemporary Publishing, 1998.

Schmidt, Jack, and Alan Weber. *Desktop Database Marketing*. Lincolnwood, IL: NTC/Contemporary Publishing, 1998.

Schultz, Don E. "Outdated Approach to Planning Needs Revamping," *Marketing News* 36 (November 11, 2002): 6–7.

Schultz, Don E., Stanley I. Tannenbaum, and Robert F. Lauterborn. *Integrated Marketing Communications*. Chicago: NTC Business Books, 1993.

Sevier, Robert. "Solutions for Marketing Strategies," *University Business* 8 (July 2005): 35–41.

Spataro, Mike. "Net Relations: A Fusion of Direct Marketing and Public Relations," *Direct Marketing* 61 (August 1998): 16 ff.

Stevens, Joanna. "Yahoo! PR Events Sing with the Yodel Challenge," *Communication World* 22 (September–October 2005): 40–142.

Swain, William N. "Perceptions of IMC After a Decade of Development: Who's at the Wheel, and How Can We Measure Success?" *Journal of Advertising Research* 44 (March 2004): 46 ff.

Thorson, Esther, and Jeri Moore. *Integrated Communication*. Mahwah, NJ: Erlbaum, 1996.

Weiner, Mark. "Marketing PR Revolution," *Communication World* 22 (January–February 2005): 20–25.

Zarowitz, Janet R., and John T. Manna. "Using Technology to Maximize Marketing Opportunities: PR Management for the 21st Century," *Public Relations Tactics* 5 (November 1998): 18.

INTEGRATED MARKETING COMMUNICATIONS CASES

CASE 12-1

Even a local campaign may use all the elements of public relations and marketing to make an impact. A medical center developed a campaign targeted to those with diabetes through special events, media, and relationships with a corporate sponsor and a local television station. Exhibit 12-1a is a news release, Exhibit 12-1b is a brochure, and Exhibit 12-1c is a flyer for a special event.

Diabetes for Life Campaign

Washington Hospital Center with Donna Arbogast & Associates

Overview

In the spring of 2001, Washington Hospital Center (WHC), the 12th largest hospital in the United States, located in the nation's capital, launched the Diabetes for Life campaign in response to the overwhelming health care needs of Washington metropolitan area residents. Diabetes is a nationwide epidemic, and the link between heart disease and diabetes is also a major public health issue. This was of special interest to WHC, which offers a nationally recognized heart program and was well positioned to accept more cardiac referrals, particularly such complex cases involving diabetes. The communications challenge was this: How to create a simple, but compelling public health/marketing campaign "hook" that would provide valuable information, generate consumer response, and at the same time support the hospital's goal of expanding referrals to its heart program.

Hospital physicians gave us the answer. People with diabetes can significantly lower their risk of such life-threatening complications as heart disease by managing the "ABCs of Diabetes Care"—A1C test, Blood Pressure, and Cholesterol, yet most patients didn't know it. Here was a simple, and vital, public health message on which to build a campaign! After considerable research, WHC launched an integrated communications initiative called Diabetes for Life to accomplish two major goals: (1) to position the hospital as a leader on this increasingly critical health issue and (2) to expand its position as a referral center for dia-

---

Courtesy Donna Arbogast, Principal, Arbogast & Associates LLC

betes patients with difficult-to-manage heart disease and other serious complications.

Over its three-year lifespan, the campaign, in partnership with the local NBC station and a corporate cosponsor, reached 5 million people with a significant public health message, helped increase diabetes admissions to the hospital by 30 percent, generated a 12 percent increase in diabetes revenue, and in its final year, was instrumental in launching a unique, free diabetes education program with the DC Public Library System, which was funded entirely by contributions and grants and is now serving as a national model.

Research

Prior to launching the campaign, PR and Marketing Department planners:

- Interviewed 20 physicians and diabetes educators to collect data and fine-tune messages.
- Collected data on the incidence of diabetes among area residents through the city's Diabetes Control Center.
- Collected and analyzed financial, strategic planning, and medical coding data to determine the impact and scope of the disease within the hospital's patient population, particularly its correlation to heart disease.
- Conducted a market assessment survey in which 10.5 percent of respondents identified diabetes as one of the hospital's clinical strengths, much higher than any other area hospital, but with significant room for growth.
- Conducted a consumer literature search, finding almost no articles on the basic ABCs of diabetes care, particularly the vital A1C test, sometimes called such complex names as "glycosolated hemoglobin."
- Commissioned a national survey of 203 primary care physicians (PCPs) to assess their understanding of basic diabetes management. The results were astounding: 90 percent of the country's PCPS could not correctly name the top three tests that a person with diabetes should have regularly (the "ABC" tests), and they listed 29 different names when referring to the vital "A1C." These results became our news angle.

Planning

Primary Audiences

Men and women age 45+ with diabetes; internists, cardiologists, and other specialists.

Secondary Audiences

Civic, political, business leaders; employees; and associations and grant-making organizations—all in the Washington and mid-Atlantic areas.

Goals

- To position WHC as a regional and national leader on this important public health issue.

- To leverage this leadership position to increase the number of people who utilize the hospital for diabetes care, as well as for the serious complications associated with this disease, particularly heart disease.

- To generate cosponsorship dollars to support the campaign and improve patients' self-care.

Strategies

First, to ensure buy-in throughout the organization, an Advisory Committee of doctors was established to provide planning, guidance, and support throughout the initiative. Next, an existing advertising partnership was expanded with NBC4, the local NBC owned-and-operated station, which offers the area's top-rated TV news programs and has a major commitment to health.

Through negotiations, WHC secured the following comprehensive public education and advocacy package with an advertising budget of $200,000 per year over three years:

- Three station-produced, "public-service-style" ads per year to promote WHC's Diabetes for Life kit, plus station-produced "PSAs" to promote the diabetes seminars. While public service in style, they received paid air time.

- WHC sponsorship of the station's annual Health Expo, which draws 65,000 people to the convention center. Sponsors are recognized on TV promotions of the Expo, and during the three-year campaign, WHCs Expo-related promotions focused heavily on diabetes.

- In addition to the hospital's main sponsor's booth, NBC4 provided space and equipment for the establishment of a first-ever Diabetes Corner at the Expo for screenings, A1C testing, and education.

- A Diabetes for Life link on the station's website that incorporated hospital-written content. In addition, the campaign was implemented for three years for a total of $225,000, including the fees of a part-time campaign director, but corporate cosponsorship totaling $165,000 helped to offset some of these direct costs and to increase the TV air time.

Execution

1. A colorful and dramatic logo was created and a unique Diabetes for Life kit was developed to serve as the TV call-to-action collateral item.

2. All callers were directed to WHC's Physician Referral Line, whose staff codes and enters the information into a database. These callers can then be tracked to generate hospital utilization and revenue results.

3. The campaign was launched with a press briefing at the National Press Club to announce the results of the physician survey, and simultaneously, the ads began airing on NBC4 promoting the kit.

4. Four full-day diabetes seminars were held, attended by standing-room-only crowds, sometimes exceeding 350 people, and smaller sessions were offered throughout the region at such locations as the Jewish Community Center and the headquarters of Black Entertainment Television.

5. An important financial and promotional partnership with Care-First BlueCross BlueShield expanded the campaign's reach. Care-First reprinted campaign materials to distribute to thousands of their members, wrote articles for their publications, and helped support the Diabetes Corner at the Expo.

6. WHC included diabetes topics in existing hospital publications; sponsored continuing medical education programs for physicians; featured the Diabetes Team on TV and radio, in print, and on the Web; and expanded the campaign's reach through its sister hospitals in the MedStar Health system.

7. The campaign culminated with the launch of a unique program with the DC Public Library called the Diabetes for Life Learning Center, which offers area residents free diabetes classes and is now serving as a national model for hospital/library partnerships. The program is fully funded by grants and contributions. The honorary chairperson of the launch was NBA All-Star Jerry Stackhouse, founder of a diabetes foundation. Keynote speakers were former House Speaker Newt Gingrich, a long-time diabetes education advocate, Rep. George Nethercutt, cochair of the Congressional Diabetes Caucus, and Dr. Michael Richardson, deputy director of the D.C. Department of Health.

Evaluation

- More than 11,000 individual consumers called the hotline to request the Diabetes Kit; more than 1,600 people attended the seminars; 300 people have taken the two-day classes at the DC Public

Library; 400 physicians attended continuing education programs; nearly 4,000 people were screened at the Expos; more than 26,000 people viewed the diabetes page on NBC4's website in 2003 alone; and more than 100,000 people viewed the diabetes page on the Hospital Center website over the course of the campaign.

- The hospital saw a 30 percent increase in the number of diabetes patients admitted over the past three years, and these patients generated $257 million in revenue, a 12 percent increase over three years.

- Total revenue generated by those calling for a kit or registering for a seminar: nearly $8 million.

- A 2003 market assessment survey showed that 13.9 percent of respondents listed diabetes as a WHC strength, up from 10.5 percent three years earlier. The next closest hospital was recognized by just 3.4 percent of respondents.

- WHC received $165,000 from corporate sponsors to support the campaign and increase TV air time.

- The Diabetes for Life Learning Center received $100,000 in grants and contributions.

- The campaign generated tens of millions of media impressions in such outlets at CNN, the *Washington Post, U.S. News and World Report, USA Today, WebMD, Diabetes Forecast, AHA News, EPress*, BET, and Reuters.

EXHIBIT 12-1A *News Release*

Washington
Hospital Center
MedStar Health

For Immediate Release
Donna Arbogast (301) 261-3544
Meghan Stone (202) 877-7594

MOST PRIMARY CARE DOCTORS DON'T KNOW
BASIC TESTS FOR DIABETES

WASHINGTON, D.C., June 7, 2001 – In a recent national survey of physicians, more than 90% of the country's primary care doctors could not correctly name the top three tests that a person with diabetes should have on a regular basis – tests that could save their lives, experts say. More than 90% of Americans with diabetes receive their medical care from primary care doctors, rather than diabetes specialists.

In the survey commissioned by Washington Hospital Center in Washington, DC, one of the country's leading centers for diabetes treatment, nearly all of the physicians correctly named "hemoglobin A-1-c" as one of the most important tests for diabetic patients. However, only 24% mentioned cholesterol and just 5% mentioned blood pressure. These three tests have been identified by the National Diabetes Education Program as <u>the most important</u> in managing diabetes and reducing the risk of deadly complications.

"Diabetes is an epidemic in this country, affecting 16 million Americans," says Dr. Wm. James Howard, an endocrinologist and senior vice president and medical director for Washington Hospital Center. "We know that we can help these patients avoid serious complications with good diabetes management. This survey clearly shows that we need to more aggressively educate our physicians on the front lines of medicine. They must know how to effectively control diabetes to help their patients live as healthy and as long a life as possible."

- more -

Courtesy Donna Arbogast, Principal, Arbogast & Associates LLC

Other survey findings underscored the overall lack of understanding in this country about diabetes and how to effectively manage this disease.

- Despite the fact that most of the doctors could not name the top three tests for diabetics, three-quarters of doctors said they are spending more time with diabetes patients than they did 10 years ago, and nearly all said they could treat the typical patient with diabetes without the help of a specialist.
- Only 20% knew the target blood pressure goal for people with diabetes and only 40% correctly identified the goal for LDL (bad) cholesterol.
- When asked how they refer to the all-important "hemoglobin A-1-c" test when talking with patients (the three-month marker for blood sugar control), physicians gave 29 different answers.
- Only 17% of doctors correctly identified the upper limit for a normal fasting blood glucose.
- One-third of respondents said they do not have adequate time to care for patients with diabetes. They attributed this to managed care pressures, and that diabetic patients have an extensive need for education and are often elderly.

The survey results are all the more significant in light of the recent reports released by the Centers for Disease Control (CDC). According to an August 2000 CDC report, the incidence of diabetes increased 33% between 1990 and 1998. Just this past January, in a follow-up report, the CDC announced that this trend continued through 1999, with the incidence increasing another 9%. The CDC study linked the increase in diabetes with a rising rate of obesity, a major risk factor for diabetes.

As the incidence of diabetes increases, experts are focusing on diabetes as much more than a disease of blood sugar, says Dr. Howard. More than 75% of people with diabetes die of heart disease, one of the major complications of diabetes. Other complications include stroke, kidney disease and blindness. Studies show that by controlling blood sugar, blood pressure and cholesterol, patients have a much lower risk of developing these complications.

- more -

EXHIBIT 12-1A   *News Release (continued)*

3

The results of Washington Hospital Center's survey will serve as a guide for the hospital as it launches a three-year consumer and physician education campaign, *"Diabetes for Life."* The Hospital Center diagnoses and treats more patients with diabetes than any other hospital in the Washington/Baltimore region. In addition, one-third of the patients treated at the Hospital Center for heart disease, have diabetes.

Washington Hospital Center commissioned Professional Research Consultants (PRC) in Omaha, NE, to conduct this survey to help determine primary care physicians' level of knowledge about diabetes management. Between November 2000 and March 2001, PRC interviewed 203 primary care doctors – internists, family practitioners and general practitioners – from around the country.

A comprehensive package of information called the "Diabetes for Life" kit is available to those who call (202) 877-DOCS.

Washington Hospital Center is a 907-bed, not-for-profit, acute care teaching and research hospital based in Northwest Washington, DC. It is the largest private hospital in the nation's capital and has the thirteenth-highest patient volume in the United States. The Hospital Center is home to the nation's third-largest cardiac program, a comprehensive Cancer Institute, a nationally recognized diabetes treatment program, a full range of women's services, MedSTAR, one of the nation's top shock-trauma centers; an extensive organ transplantation program, and the most advanced burn center in the region. Washington Hospital Center is a member of MedStar Health, a not-for-profit, community-based health care organization comprised of 30 integrated businesses including seven major hospitals in the Baltimore/Washington area.

###

EXHIBIT 12-1B   *Learning Center Brochure*

Do You Have Diabetes?
If you have diabetes, you are not alone. More than 200,000 people in the Washington area have diabetes; 30,000 live in Washington, DC.

What Can I Do to Stay Healthy?
An important first step is to join us at the *Diabetes for Life Learning Center* for two free classes that will teach you the simple ABCs of diabetes — the basic building blocks that will help you control this disease.

When Are the Classes Offered and How Do I Register?
Each program consists of two, 2½-hour classes that are held over a two-week period. Classes are offered on different days and at different times. You can learn more about the schedule and also register for the program that is most convenient for you by calling (202) 877-7714.

What Will I Learn in this Program?
You will learn how to reach your goals for:
- Blood sugar,
- Blood pressure, and
- Cholesterol.

You will also learn:
- How to work with your doctor to reach your diabetes goals,
- How your diabetes medications work,
- How to choose healthy foods, and
- How to help prevent and treat diabetes problems.

The *Diabetes for Life Learning Center* at the Martin Luther King Jr. Library is a new and unique program for people with diabetes. Thanks to the support of nearly 20 organizations and government agencies, the Learning Center offers free diabetes classes at the library at a variety of times during the week. If you have diabetes, we want to teach you the ABCs of diabetes care to help you stay as healthy as possible.
We invite you to read more…

This is a portion of a three-fold brochure promoting a "Learning Center" event hosted by the MedStar Diabetes Institute at Washington Hospital Center held at the Martin Luther King Jr. Memorial Library.

Courtesy Donna Arbogast, Principal, Arbogast & Associates LLC

EXHIBIT 12-1C   *Event Flyer*

Diabetes for Life: Keys to Control
Saturday, November 17, 2001

SCHEDULE

8:15 – 8:55 am	Registration, Exhibits, Pre-Test: What Do We Need To Know?
8:55 – 9:00 am	Welcome
	Michelle Magee, MD, Morning Moderator
9:00 – 10:00 am	Keynote Address
	Diabetes **Does Not Have** a Psycho-social Issue;
	Diabetes **Is** a Psycho-social Issue
	Robert Anderson, PhD
10:00 – 10:30 am	The ABCs of Diabetes Care: Your Keys to Success
	Claresa Levetan, MD
10:30 – 10:45 am	Break
10:45 – 11:15 am	Nutrition: Tools You Can Use
	Barbara Howard, PhD
11:15 – 11:30 am	Cooking Demonstration: Practical Tips for Everyday Life
11:30 am – 12:30 pm	Lunch
12:30 – 12:35 pm	Afternoon Overview
	Meeta Sharma, MD, Afternoon Moderator
12:35 – 1:00 pm	New Technologies and Therapies
	Michelle Magee, MD
1:00 – 1:45 pm	The Expert Is In: Case Studies and Audience Interaction
	Expert Panel of Diabetes Specialists
1:45 – 2 pm	Post-test: What Have We Learned?
2:00 – 2:15 pm	Break
2:15 – 2:45 pm	Mental Health: Taking Control of Chronic Illness
	CareFirst BlueCross BlueShield Speaker
2:45 – 3:00 pm	Guided Imagery: A Relaxing End to a Busy Day

FACULTY

Robert Anderson, PhD
Educational Psychologist, Certified Diabetes Educator and Author
University of Michigan
Recipient of ADA's Outstanding Educator Award 2000

Cherrel Christian, RN, CDE
Diabetes Educator and Program Coordinator
MedStar Diabetes Institute at
Washington Hospital Center

Barbara Howard, PhD
President, MedStar Research Institute

Claresa Levetan, MD
Director, Diabetes Education
MedStar Clinical Research Center

Michelle Magee, MD
Director, MedStar Diabetes Institute
Medical Director, Diabetes Team
Washington Hospital Center

Claudia Morrison, RD, LD, CDE
Registered Dietitian and Diabetes Educator
Washington Hospital Center

Meeta Sharma, MD
Associate Director, Diabetes Team
Washington Hospital Center

DIRECTIONS AND PARKING

The Washington Marriott Hotel
1221 22nd St., NW

Driving & Parking:
The Washington Marriott is on the corner of 22nd and M Sts., NW, and 22nd St. is one-way north. The hotel will be on your right, and the parking garage entrance is off of the circle drive in front. The parking fee at the hotel if $6. On-street parking is also available and there is another garage next door to the hotel. However, the $6 rate only applies to the hotel's garage.

Metro:
The Washington Marriott is located near the Dupont Circle Metro stop on the Red Line and near the GWU-Foggy Bottom stop on the Orange / Blue Lines.

Please Note: Because parking is limited at the hotel, we encourage you to use the Metro if you can or to carpool with other attendees.

REGISTRATION

Registration for the seminar is free, but you must register in advance before November 14 by calling Washington Hospital Center at (202) 877-DOCS (3627). Thank you!

We gratefully acknowledge the support of the following organizations:

Gold Circle Partner
CareFirst BlueCross BlueShield

Silver Circle Partners
Aventis Pharmaceuticals
Roche Diagnostics Corporation

Bronze Circle Partner
Animas Corporation

Media Partner
NBC4

Courtesy Donna Arbogast, Principal, Arbogast & Associates LLC

Diet fads and public policy may dramatically impact the market for food products. The potato seems to fall in and out of favor depending upon the diet news of the day; therefore, the U.S. Potato Board developed a campaign to refurbish the image of the potato during the low-carb era. Exhibit 12-2a is campaign news release, Exhibit 12-2b is a letter to nutrition educators, Exhibit 12-2c is an advertisement, Exhibit 12-2d is a fact sheet, and Exhibit 12-2e is a "Get the Skinny" news release.

The Healthy Potato—Relaunching America's Favorite Vegetable in the Atkins Era

United States Potato Board with Fleishman-Hillard

Situation Analysis

In early 2004, the biggest weight-loss fad to hit America in a decade was at its peak: The low-carb diet. Spurred on by Atkins and *The South Beach Diet* book (70,000 copies sold each week in March, 2004[1]), and fueled by a slew of new, low-carb product introductions (586 were introduced in the first quarter of 2004, compared with 633 introduced in all of 2003[2]) and millions of advertising dollars to support them, it was the worst of times to be a potato. Hipsters from Hollywood to Manhattan were vocally avoiding potatoes, and their influence was pouring down to everyday folks who used to think, rightfully, that the potato was good for them. Media coverage of "carbs or low-carb and diet" peaked in the first quarter of 2004 with nearly 4,000 stories being reported, many of them including false nutrition information. Continued erroneous media coverage about potatoes could inadvertently predispose government policymakers against potatoes, as they were in the process of revising the official *Dietary Guidelines for Americans*. Negative attitudes about potatoes could lead to dramatic decreases in sales and business losses. Amidst this crisis, Fleishman-Hillard (FH) on behalf of the United States Potato Board (USPB) relaunched America's favorite vegetable as "The Healthy Potato" with an integrated campaign based

---

Courtesy U.S. Potato Board
[1] Nielsen Book Scan.
[2] Market Consumer Intelligence survey.

on research, influential allies, and a strategic mix of media and grassroots delivery vehicles to confront this "perfect storm" of spud bashing. As a result, the government's new *Dietary Guidelines* were favorable to fresh potatoes; consumer attitude and usage research showed positive gains; and 140 million consumers were exposed to key healthy potato messages.

Research

In this crisis environment, it was essential that campaign messages resonate with target audiences. Primary research was fielded in the form of focus groups. The studies showed that consumers universally underestimated the positive nutrition benefits of potatoes. When shown an FDA nutrition label for potatoes, the women were stunned at the exceptional nutrient profile. These women thought the information was too good to be true, and only believed it when they saw it came from the FDA. Specific messaging was later tested to find the most effective message to communicate the positive benefits of the potato. Next, a nutrition quiz was given in a nationwide survey, which confirmed that consumers were unaware of the positive nutrition profile of potatoes and that purchase intent was positively influenced by education. This research showed

1. the tremendous power of the official FDA nutrition label and
2. the importance of gaining third-party endorsements to be credible.

Planning

Timing was critical. Potato farmers wanted to take on directly the low-carb diets, which FH counseled strongly against to avoid providing an additional platform for low-carb proponents to promote their messages.

Target Audiences
- Women, ages 25–64, nutrition opinion leaders and policymakers, and food and nutrition media

Program Objectives
- Increase awareness and understanding of the positive nutrition benefits of potatoes (specifically, rich in vitamin C and an excellent source of potassium for only 100 calories)
- Make potato nutrition facts ubiquitous among consumers, opinion leaders, and policymakers

Communication Strategies
- Develop messages to balance and obviate anti-carb rhetoric without directly engaging in carb debate
- Formally relaunch potatoes to consumers via media and partnerships by emphasizing the nutrition facts

- Rely on FDA nutrition label to frame the healthy potato story
- Supply ideas for healthful potato preparation
- Provide nutrition opinion leaders with tools to help educate consumers

Budget

- Public Relations, $800,000; Advertising, $860,000

Execution

The misunderstood potato needed to be reintroduced to consumers as if it were an entirely new product. The Healthy Potato was launched in February 2004 through an integrated multimedia blitz.

Ad Campaign

FH recommended a limited print advertising buy to serve as the timely "hook" for securing media interest in The Healthy Potato. The ads featured the FDA nutrition label with key benefits highlighted and endorsements by leading nutrition experts. The launch ads ran the week of February 22, 2004, in the *New York Times, Washington Post,* and *USA Today.* A radio sponsorship on NPR in Washington, D.C., launched the same week to reach food/nutrition policymakers.

Media Outreach

A comprehensive press kit introducing The Healthy Potato was developed and distributed simultaneous to the ad launch. Extensive media outreach was conducted and an exclusive with the *New York Times* was secured. Food and nutrition editors were at the same time being briefed by nutrition expert and FH staff member Katherine Beals, Ph.D., R.D., and USPB client, Linda McCashion. Within one month, 1,000 press kits landed in editors' inboxes, a successful New York deskside tour was orchestrated, and a radio media tour and radio news release featuring one of the print ad's nutrition experts were delivered.

Consumer Tools

The USPB's website was revamped prior to the launch. Its URL was changed to healthypotato.com for brand consistency. Fresh new potato recipes were developed and featured on the website and in *The Healthy Potato* consumer brochure. The tools were used extensively during media outreach.

Weight Watchers Partnership

At the same time, a strategic alliance with Weight Watchers (WW), America's trusted name in weight loss, was announced. The potato was the first produce item highlighted in WW's new "Pick of the Season" program. Potato nutrition information and healthy recipes were distributed in WW meetings nationwide, touted in *Weight Watchers* magazine, and featured on the WW website. The valuable endorsement also was leveraged in 100 retail stores with displays, and packaging with special The Healthy Potato closure tags. To further publicize the partnership, WW and FH distributed a joint print release and coproduced a video news release.

Nutrition Community Outreach

FH enlisted an ambassador network of six regional registered dietitians as spokespeople to answer media inquiries and to write letters to newspapers correcting erroneous information about potato nutrition. FH nutrition experts created a series of nutrition fact sheets and a potato facts toolkit CD-ROM for dietitians and nutritionists to use in client education. The toolkit was provided to national ADA (American Dietetic Association) spokespeople and posted on the new website.

Policymaker Education

The Healthy Potato campaign also had to address the major review and revamping of the government's nutrition policy. Therefore, Dr. Beals provided formal written and oral testimony about the health benefits of potatoes to the Dietary Guidelines Advisory Committee (DGAC) in Washington, D.C.

Evaluation

Objective 1

Increase awareness and understanding of the positive nutrition benefits of potatoes.

A February 2005 Consumer Attitude Research Survey showed that, compared to 2004, there has been a 4 percent increase in the number of consumers agreeing that potatoes are "a good food for the health conscious" (33 percent vs. 29 percent); and, most importantly, after increasing each year from 2001 to 2004, this year fewer consumers hold negative attitudes toward the nutritional value of potatoes (31 percent vs. 35 percent). In addition, there has been a 4 percent increase in the number of consumers stating they served potatoes at home in the past seven days (86 percent vs. 82 percent).

Objective 2

Make nutrition facts ubiquitous.

Among consumers: More than 140 million consumers were exposed to key potato messages.

- Ad buy: 44 million.
- Weight Watchers partnership: 12.5 million.

- Website: Postlaunch visits per month more than doubled historical monthly click-throughs.

- Brochure requests: 250,000.

- Media placements: The *New York Times* included an editorial reprint of the ad to kick-off coverage. *USA Today, Newsweek,* and major daily newspapers followed, including multiple front-page food section features touting the healthy benefits of the potato. Later, the nationally syndicated column "Hints from Heloise" featured the brochure and drove consumers to the website. Media impressions totaled more than 84 million, surpassing the USPB's target goal by more than 200 percent.

- Low-carb media coverage: Compared to the first quarter of 2004, media coverage of "carbs or low-carb and diet" declined by 25 percent by the third quarter of 2004.[3]

Among opinion leaders: Former *Cooking Light* senior editor and registered dietitian, Jill Melton, praised the campaign during a presentation at the annual International Association of Culinary Professionals meeting, and Jane Brody of the *New York Times* mentioned it as an excellent nutrition education campaign at the Food Marketing Institute's annual convention. The USPB was also contacted by a publisher to include The Healthy Potato case history in a PR college textbook.

Among nutrition policymakers: The new *Dietary Guidelines for Americans* were released on January 12, 2005. Overall the recommendations were positive for potatoes and reflected the comments specifically submitted by the USPB:

1. Increasing the consumption of foods high in nutrients most likely to be consumed by general public in amounts low enough to be of concern, including potassium.

2. Starchy vegetable amounts were slightly increased and now equal those for green leafy vegetables and legumes.

3. Emphasizing that calories count—weight management depends on a balance of energy intake and energy expenditure, not the proportion of carbohydrate, protein, or fat; discounting the validity and practicality of fad diets.

Bonus Result: As of Saturday, March 19, 2005, the full grower Board of the USPB voted to increase the assessment rate levied on growers for marketing programs from 2 cents per cwt. of potatoes to 2-1/2 cents starting March 2007. Appreciation of the nutrition program was cited as the reason.

---

[3] Lexis-Nexis search by IFIC.

EXHIBIT 12-2A   *Letter to Editor*

Get the skinny on
America's favorite vegetable: The Healthy Potato.

February 22, 2004

Dear Editor,

When 96 percent of Americans don't know the main attributes of your product – a food staple that's served at roughly half of all at-home dinners in America – it's time to pull out all the stops and set the record straight.

We're talking about *potatoes*. America's favorite vegetable has been taking a bashing lately as a result of fad diets. In response to the food confusion sweeping the nation, The United States Potato Board (USPB) conducted extensive consumer research and found that **only 6 percent of survey respondents thought that potatoes were rich in vitamin C, when, in fact, one medium (5.3 ounce) potato contains 45 percent of the recommended Daily Value for this essential nutrient.** And, **only 34 percent considered potatoes with skins to be rich in potassium, when they are actually an excellent source of this mineral – higher than broccoli, spinach, or bananas.** And, only 4.2 percent of respondents thought that potatoes were BOTH rich in vitamin C and potassium.

But there is good news. When focus groups were shown the official FDA nutrition label for potatoes, they were thrilled to learn that one of their favorite foods was actually good for them. **They delighted in learning that one medium potato is an excellent source of potassium, rich in vitamin C and a good source of fiber for only 100 calories, with no fat and no cholesterol.**

To spread this good news, the USPB is launching a major education campaign. From advertisements in major news publications to a partnership with a major weight loss company, USPB is providing "the skinny" on potato nutrition focusing on the official FDA potato nutrition label, and featuring leading nutrition authorities who support potatoes.

We hope we can count on you to help set the record straight about potato nutrition. To assist with story ideas, we've enclosed the following materials:

- *Get the Skinny on Potatoes* release detailing consumer confusion about potato nutrition, and explaining detailed information about the USPB's new education campaign
- *The Healthy Potato* brochure and brochure offer information - includes new healthy recipes created by Robin Vitetta-Miller, M.S., contributing editor to *Health Magazine*
- A CD containing color images
- List of nutrition experts willing to answer specific potato-related questions

We sincerely hope that this information will be useful. Please feel free to call or email us at any time with questions. Thank you!

Cordially,

Margo S Kraus

Margo Kraus, MS, RD
Fleishman-Hillard, Inc.
503-221-2375

Linda McCashion

Linda McCashion
United States Potato Board
303-873-2326

United States Potato Board
7555 East Hampden Avenue, #412, Denver, CO 80231
www.healthypotato.com

UNITED STATES
Potato
B O A R D

Courtesy U.S. Potato Board

EXHIBIT 12-2B *Letter to Nutrition Educator*

Get the skinny on
America's favorite vegetable: The Healthy Potato.

February 2004

Dear Nutrition Educator:

Americans love potatoes – mashed, roasted, or baked. And rightly so, as the potato is a nutritional powerhouse, loaded with fiber and essential vitamins and minerals. Nonetheless, the low carbohydrate diet craze has left Americans wondering if potatoes should remain a part of their diet. With so much nutrition misinformation out there, it's time to set the record straight.

In August 2003, the United States Potato Board (USPB) conducted focus groups to find out what people know and don't know about potatoes. Participants said they loved potatoes in their myriad forms. But they knew very little about the important role potatoes play in a balanced diet.

Consumers in the focus groups were thrilled to discover that a medium-sized, 5.3 ounce potato is:
- A great source of Vitamin C
- An excellent source of potassium when eaten with the skin
- Only 100 calories
- Less than 10 percent of the daily value of carbohydrates
- A good source of fiber when eaten with the skin

Even the dieters and "potato misinformed" that had deprived themselves of potatoes began to rethink their decision.

We created "The Healthy Potato" nutrition tool kit to help you communicate to adult consumers some potato nutrition facts they may find surprising. Empower your clients, patients, and/or students with nutrition facts. Give them permission to enjoy their favorite vegetable and benefit from the nutrients it provides.

The presentation is suitable for a variety of populations because the potato is America's favorite vegetable, an integral part of most ethnic cuisines, inexpensive, versatile, and available year-round. The entire kit can be presented in one 30-minute class.

Included in the kit are:
- A CD with a PowerPoint presentation of 21 slides and presenter notes
- *The Healthy Potato* brochure
- *The Power of Potatoes – Positively Nutritious!* Nutrition Fact Sheet

- Recipe cards
- The Produce for Better Health Foundation's *Position Paper on Low Carb Diets* reviewed by Barbara Rolls, PhD, Penn State University
- Evaluation card

Copies of these materials will be available for downloading at www.healthypotato.com.

Thank you for allowing us to share "the Healthy Potato" nutrition tool kit with you - we hope you find it useful. If you have any questions or require further information, visit the USPB web site at www.healthypotato.com or contact Margo S. Kraus, MS, RD at (503) 221-2375 or krausm@fleishman.com. Please complete the evaluation card and let us know what you think. We look forward to hearing from you!

Warm regards,

Linda McCashion

Linda McCashion
The United States Potato Board

Margo S Kraus

Margo S. Kraus, MS, RD
Fleishman Hillard

United States Potato Board
7555 East Hampden Avenue, #412, Denver, CO 80231
www.healthypotato.com

Courtesy U.S. Potato Board

EXHIBIT 12-2C *Advertisement*

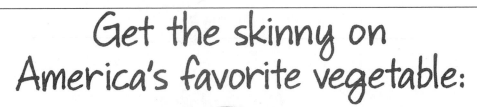

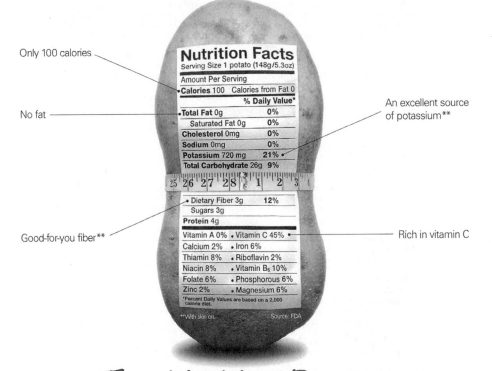

Only 100 calories

No fat

Good-for-you fiber**

An excellent source of potassium**

Rich in vitamin C

The Healthy Potato.

Potatoes aren't just good; they're good for you. Just check the label. America's favorite vegetable is naturally fat free, only 100 calories, rich in vitamin C and potassium and a good source of fiber. No wonder leading nutrition experts like Harvard Medical School's Dr. George L. Blackburn and Registered Dietitian Ann M. Coulston, past president of the American Dietetic Association, recommend potatoes as part of a healthy, balanced diet.

www.healthypotato.com

Courtesy U.S. Potato Board

EXHIBIT 12-2D *Nutrition Fact Sheet*

Nutrition
fact sheet

The Power of Potatoes— Positively Nutritious!

America's favorite vegetable is not only fat- and cholesterol-free, it is also high in vitamin C and potassium, and is an excellent source of fiber with the skin on.

In addition to being nutritious and delicious, potatoes are versatile. Potatoes can star at the center of the plate with beef, chicken or fish, or on their own as an easy vegetarian meal. Or, mash, bake or microwave potatoes for a tasty side dish. Leave the skins on your spuds for an extra nutritional boost since a wealth of vitamins, minerals and fiber are found in the peel.

Potassium

Potatoes with skin are an excellent source of potassium, which is great for cardiovascular health. In fact, potatoes qualify for a health claim approved by the U.S. Food and Drug Administration, which states: Diets containing foods that are a good source of potassium and that are low in sodium may reduce the risk of high blood pressure and stroke. Just one potato offers 21 percent of the Daily Value for potassium. Potassium also helps retain calcium, which is important to build strong bones.

Vitamin C

For vitamin C, don't just think oranges—think potatoes! Potatoes are one of the leading sources of vitamin C in the American diet. This vitamin is a potent antioxidant that helps stabilize free radicals, which may prevent cellular damage. Vitamin C also produces the collagen that helps hold bone tissue together.

Fiber

One medium potato (5.3 ounces) with skin contains three grams, or 12 percent of the recommended daily intake for fiber. Preliminary studies show that fiber is beneficial for a healthy digestive system and may help reduce the risk of some cancers and possibly heart disease. According to researchers at Pennsylvania State University, consuming adequate fiber and water helps increase satiety between meals.

Antioxidants

Antioxidants protect key cell components by neutralizing the damaging effects of "free radicals," natural byproducts of cell metabolism. Free radicals travel through cells, disrupting the structure of other molecules, causing cellular damage. Such cell damage is believed to contribute to aging and various health problems.
■ Potatoes contain glutathione, an antioxidant that may possibly help protect against some cancers. Per serving, potatoes, along with avocadoes, asparagus, squash, okra, cauli-

This fact sheet is sponsored by the United States Potato Board. The contents have been reviewed by the American Dietetic Association's Fact Sheet Review Board. The appearance of this information does not constitute an endorsement by ADA of the sponsor's products or services. This fact sheet was prepared for the general public. Questions regarding its content and use should be directed to a dietetics professional.

Courtesy U.S. Potato Board

EXHIBIT 12-2D *Nutrition Fact Sheet (continued)*

Information

The American
Dietetic
Association
Knowledge Center

*For food and nutrition
information or for a
referral to a dietetics
professional in your
area call:*

800/366-1655

or visit:
www.eatright.org

UNITED STATES
Potato
BOARD

For more potato nutrition information,
recipes and tips, check out:
www.potatohelp.com or write to:

United States Potato Board
7555 E. Hampden Avenue NW #412
Denver, Colorado 80231

AMERICAN DIETETIC ASSOCIATION
"Your link to nutrition and health"℠
216 WEST JACKSON BOULEVARD
CHICAGO, ILLINOIS 60606-6995

©2002 ADA. Reproduction of this
fact sheet is permitted for educational
purposes. Reproduction for sales
purposes is not authorized.
This fact sheet expires 9/1/2005.

flower, broccoli and raw tomatoes, have the highest glutathione content compared to other vegetables.

■ In a study comparing the overall antioxidant activity of potatoes, bell peppers, carrots, onions and broccoli, potatoes ranked second highest after broccoli.

Carbohydrates—The Meat and Potatoes of Healthful Eating

Foods that contain complex carbohydrates are the main source of energy for the body. Although some advocates of high-protein, low-carbohydrate diets recommend cutting back on or eliminating carbohydrate-containing foods such as potatoes, carrots and dried fruit, many nutrition experts believe that high-protein, low-carbohydrate diets are potentially unhealthy and are not beneficial for maintaining long-term weight loss. Because these diets tend to be high in saturated fats and low in fruits, vegetables and grains, they may increase the risk for heart disease and some cancers.

The Glycemic Index (GI)

The Glycemic Index (GI) is a system that assigns a number to foods, particularly carbohydrates such as bread, pasta and potatoes, based on their ability to increase blood glucose. The higher the GI, the more the food's ability to raise blood glucose levels. Several studies have examined the effects of the GI on appetite, but to date there have been no well-controlled, long-term human studies to examine the effects of GI on body weight regulation. In addition, there is no conclusive evidence that eating high GI foods will lead to obesity.

The practicality of the GI of individual foods in diet planning is controversial because combinations of foods can alter the total GI of a meal. In the case of

potatoes, for example, common toppings such as cheese, broccoli, butter, vinegar, or salsa may lower the combined GI.

Some of the foods that score high on the GI such as potatoes, also score high on the satiety index (SI). The higher the SI of a food, the more satisfied a person is between meals. More research is needed before health and nutrition professionals will recommend using the GI as a tool to help plan meals and snacks.

As always, it is recommended that you talk with your doctor or registered dietitian before starting any new diet or meal plan.

Tips for Healthy Living

To stay healthy, be sure to exercise, control meal portions and eat well. The best guide for eating well is the United States Department of Agriculture's (USDA) Food Guide Pyramid. Make sure to eat plenty of fruits and vegetables—a minimum of five servings of fruits and vegetables per day. Here are some tips on how America's favorite vegetable, the potato, can help.

Mexican Fiesta

Top a split baked potato with canned black beans, cooked frozen corn, nonfat sour cream and your favorite salsa.

Veggie Stir-Fry

Use a potato as a base for simple stir-fried vegetables. Stir-fry cut-up zucchini, carrots, green or red bell pepper and broccoli. Season with low-sodium soy sauce; spoon over a split baked potato.

Chili Potato

Spoon prepared chili over a split baked potato. Top with green onions, low fat shredded cheddar cheese and nonfat sour cream.

EXHIBIT 12-2E   *"Get the Skinny"*

Get the skinny on
America's favorite vegetable: The Healthy Potato.

Contact: Kris Caputo Hurley   Linda McCashion
           Fleishman-Hillard   United States Potato Board
           916-492-5337   303-873-2326
           caputok@fleishman.com   lindam@uspotatoes.com

GET THE SKINNY ON *THE HEALTHY POTATO*
Free Consumer Brochure Provides Fresh New Potato Recipes and Health Information

Denver, CO (February 6, 2004) – Great nutrition and healthy new recipes – now there's no reason to let anything come between you and the potatoes you love. The United States Potato Board is offering a free brochure, *The Healthy Potato*, to educate consumers about the healthful, versatile and delicious aspects of America's favorite vegetable.

Robin Vitetta-Miller, MS, contributing editor to *Health Magazine* and frequent contributor to *Shape*, *Men's Fitness* and CNN (and a lover of potatoes), has created numerous delectable preparation ideas using healthy ingredients for baked potatoes, mashed potatoes, roasted potatoes and potato salads. From Wasabi Mashed Potatoes to an Italian Potato Salad, the recipes included feature new ways to prepare potatoes that are healthy and delicious.

Potatoes are surprisingly full of essential vitamins and minerals. Nutrition authorities agree with Vitetta-Miller and are featured throughout the brochure proclaiming that potatoes fit naturally into a healthy diet and can be a great choice when losing or managing body weight. The FDA potato nutrition label is proof as well: With the skins on, potatoes provide nearly half the daily requirement of vitamin C, are an excellent source of potassium and a good source of fiber. One medium-sized potato contains only 100 calories and no fat, sodium or cholesterol. Potatoes are extremely versatile and satisfying, and pair deliciously with a variety of other vegetables and lean protein.

For healthy recipes and nutrition information, visit www.healthypotato.com. To receive a free copy of the *The Healthy Potato* brochure, send a self-addressed, business-sized, stamped envelope to:

Healthy Potato Recipes
5105 East 41st Avenue
Denver, CO 80216

###

United States Potato Board
7555 East Hampden Avenue, #412, Denver, CO 80231
www.healthypotato.com

Courtesy U.S. Potato Board

Public policy debates can require a multipronged campaign entailing public relations, advertising, and government lobbying. The Seneca Nation of Indians faced a new state law changing the tax structure on tribal lands and drafted a communication strategy for the situation. Exhibit 12-3a is a news release, Exhibit 12-3b is an advertisement, and Exhibit 12-3c and Exhibit 12-3d are scripts for television and radio advertisements.

Break a Treaty, Break the Law

Seneca Nation of Indians with Travers Collins & Company

Situational Analysis

The Seneca Nation of Indians has the distinction of being the only tribe that is party to the Buffalo Creek Treaty of 1842 with the United States. Buffalo Creek established, in part, that business conducted on Seneca territory would be immune from state taxes. In recent years, taking advantage of that rare treaty provision, the Senecas established $360 million in businesses selling products that normally carry heavy state taxes, like cigarettes and gasoline. By 1997, New York State lawmakers had begun to eye those growing sales as a potential source of tax revenue. The governor eventually abandoned the 1997 tax plan, citing a desire to maintain peace and friendship with the tribes. But the reprieve was short lived. The state legislature brought the issue to light once again when its 2003–4 budget included a plan to collect taxes on Indian territory.

By October 2003, with the latest tax regulations set to take effect December 1, the Senecas were growing increasingly concerned that their economy would soon be ravaged. Some Senecas were even making plans to protest the tax regulations by blocking a section of the state Thruway as they had done successfully in 1997. In part to forestall potentially violent protests and in part to bolster the existing lobbying efforts, the Seneca Nation Tribal Council enlisted Travers Collins & Company (TCC) to develop a communications strategy.

Research and Planning

With the state deadline looming, TCC was asked to launch the campaign by October 27, just three weeks after receiving the assignment. Time was of the essence, so the team turned to every source of secondary research it

Courtesy Seneca Nation of Indians and Travers Collins & Company

could find. TCC studied how the issue unfolded and was resolved in 1997, researched perceptions about the current issue, and listened to the opinions of Seneca business leaders on what messages they thought would be effective.

The research helped TCC conclude that state leaders would abandon the tax plan only if they perceived that most New Yorkers were against it. But TCC also knew that if structured as an economic debate, most voters would support the tax because it filled a budget gap. The solution was to frame the issue as one of ethics and integrity, rather than one of economics. If New Yorkers understood their elected officials were about to violate Indian treaties and a clause in the U.S. Constitution, they would be against the tax plan.

Objectives

- Convince state leaders to abandon or at least significantly diminish their plan to collect state tax on Indian territory.
- Demonstrate to Seneca Nation members that their elected leaders are pulling out all stops to fight the tax regulations.

Key Publics

- Governor Pataki, legislators, state tax department officials, registered voters in the major population centers of New York State, and Seneca Nation members.

Strategies

- Educate state citizens about the Seneca position in such a way that inspires their support.
- Demonstrate to state leaders that the majority of state voters favor the Seneca position.
- Consistently drive home the theme "Break a Treaty, Break the Law," making it very uncomfortable and unpopular for anyone to support the tax regulations—essentially to shame leaders into submission.

Execution

With only a few weeks to prevent the decimation of the Seneca Nation's economy, every viable tactic was put in play. TCC employed a blend of tactics, including advertising which ensured the campaign messages would reach the target publics in a timely and consistent manner. Every tactic—from news interviews to radio ads to bumper stickers—reinforced the "Break a Treaty, Break the Law" theme.

Media Relations

The editorial pages of the state's ten major daily newspapers are a key influencer of elected officials and public opinion. As such, securing favorable editorials was a major focus of the campaign. Supported by a comprehensive press kit, a fact-laden website, and a trained Seneca spokesperson, the campaign was launched with a press conference in Buffalo followed by dozens of news interviews and editorial board meetings throughout the state. Those tactics, combined with guest op-ed pieces submitted to all the major daily newspapers, helped achieve significant and consistent coverage across the state and several supportive or neutral editorials.

Advertising

Paid advertising was a must in order to make an impact on public opinion in such a tight window of time. Television, radio, and print advertisements were placed in key markets throughout the state. This was a true "saturation" campaign; in most markets the advertising message reached 90 percent or more of the target market up to ten times per person.

Website/Toll-Free Hotline

A simple website was created to serve as the campaign's online home base. A toll-free hotline was also established and staffed by Seneca employees. The website and the hotline staff encouraged supporters to contact Governor Pataki and send letters to their local newspapers.

Public Opinion Poll

Zogby International was commissioned to conduct a statewide poll two weeks after the campaign was launched. The poll revealed strong support for the Senecas' position on taxation. TCC planned to announce the results to help prove how unpopular the tax plan was. However, just after the poll concluded, the governor announced the postponement of the regulations. A second poll, yielding similar results, was conducted and released to the media during the campaign's second phase.

Lobbying

The Seneca Nation's lobbyists continued to press the governor's office, tax department, and key state legislators incorporating the campaign messages. In addition, Seneca members and businesses circulated petitions and distributed postage-paid postcards. The petitions and postcards were sent to Albany so state leaders would have tangible evidence of the public's support for the Senecas.

Evaluation

The approach TCC devised for the Senecas took everyone by surprise. Politicians, opposition groups, and journalists assumed the Senecas would resort to violent protests as they had done before; no one expected a sophisticated communications campaign. The Honor Indian

Treaties campaign educated New Yorkers about the effects of the proposed tax regulations and positively influenced the tax department's public comment period. The campaign captured the moral high ground of the issue by framing it as one of ethics and integrity. Uncomfortable with having to explain why they were willing to break Indian treaties, elected officials privately implored the Senecas to halt the campaign.

On November 7, just 11 days after the campaign started, the state postponed implementation of the tax regulations until March 1, 2004. The campaign went dark in November, and a second phase was launched in January 2004. On February 10, 2004, the tax commissioner announced he would indefinitely postpone the implementation of the tax regulations, providing a decisive victory and putting some much needed finality to the issue.

Return on Investment

By investing $4.8 million (actual total) in the campaign, the Seneca Nation blocked a $100 million hit to their economy; protected their priceless sovereignty; and prevented violent protests which in the past saw dozens of Senecas seriously injured and arrested.

1. Research Note: Two weeks into the campaign a stay was granted in the form of a postponement of the regulations. For the second phase of the campaign, TCC was able to incorporate additional research—such as statewide poll results, opinions expressed in editorials and letters to editors, and public feedback from the website and hotline—into the communication strategy. The new research showed that the public was very responsive to the ethical questions raised by the campaign, validating the team's original direction. TCC honed the campaign messages for the second phase to further emphasize that the tax plan proposed by the legislature was contrary to traditional American values.

EXHIBIT 12-3A *News Release*

Honor Indian Treaties

Treaties With The Six Nations

Fort Stanwix Treaty	Fort Harmar	Canandaigua Treaty	Buffalo Creek
October 22, 1784	January 9, 1789	November 11, 1794	May 20, 1842
7 Stat. 15	7 Stat. 38	7 Stat. 44	7 Stat. 586

For Immediate Release:
January 6, 2003

Contact: Beth Kelly
Travers Collins & Company
716-842-2222, ext 104

SENECA NATION RENEWS STATEWIDE ANTI-TAX CAMPAIGN
With March 1 Deadline Looming, Latest Effort Calls for Albany to Show Integrity

ALBANY, N.Y. – Today, the Seneca Nation of Indians announced it is renewing its statewide campaign to raise public awareness about New York State's plan to collect tax on goods sold to non-Indians on Indian territory. The new effort is the second phase of a campaign the Senecas began last October.

"We received a lot of positive feedback on the first phase of our campaign," said Rickey L. Armstrong, Sr., President of the Seneca Nation of Indians. "The citizens of New York were very supportive of our cause and expressed outrage that their elected leaders would enact such an unfair and unconstitutional measure."

Armstrong said that the feedback the Nation received inspired them to launch a second phase of the campaign that showcases the opinions expressed by Indians and non-Indians across the state. The Nation's latest advertisements depict a fictitious teacher, mechanic, and Vietnam veteran. Each of the characters expresses concern and frustration that Albany's tax plan is contrary to American principles such as fairness, truth, and honor.

-MORE-

Seneca Nation of Indians ° Honor Indian Treaties Campaign ° P.O. Box 1842 ° Irving, NY 14081 ° 1-888-665-5582

Courtesy Seneca Nation of Indians and Travers Collins & Company

"We were certainly glad that the implementation date of these regulations was postponed from December to March," said President Armstrong. "But we haven't forgotten for a moment that the deadline is still looming. This issue is a pivotal moment in Seneca history. Our sovereignty is at stake. It's imperative that we continue to highlight the public's opposition to this tax scheme."

The multi-faceted campaign utilizes paid advertisements on television, radio and in newspapers, incorporates a website (www.honorindiantreaties.org), a toll-free hotline (1-888-665-5582), and will have Seneca leaders canvassing the state to meet with local media outlets.

The Legislature passed a bill on May 2, 2003, which the Governor vetoed on May 14, 2003, as being in violation of the Federal Constitution, mandating that state tax regulations be adopted for the collection of taxes on sales conducted on sovereign territory of the Seneca Nation of Indians. The Governor publicly stated in his May 14, 2003, veto message that "The Legislature's language requires Indian Nations to collect taxes on all sales to non-Indians, even on shipments to states in which the Nations have no tax nexus. This runs afoul of the Federal Constitution."

Despite the Governor vetoing the bill, the State Legislature on May 15, 2003, overrode the Governor's veto. Pursuant to that state law, the New York State Tax Department issued on September 10, 2003, new regulations taxing the sales of goods on Indian territory which are scheduled to become effective March 1, 2004.

This action will devastate the Seneca economy, forcing hundreds of Indian-owned businesses to close and putting 1,000 Indians and non-Indians out of work. The Senecas maintain that the proposed law undermines a series of treaties between the Seneca Nation and the United States government, notably the Buffalo Creek Compromise Treaty of 1842. To further emphasize the inequity of the state's action, President Armstrong referred to article VI, Clause 2 of the United States Constitution which states that treaties are "the supreme Law of the Land; and the Judges in every state shall be bound thereby."

-MORE-

EXHIBIT 12-3A   *News Release (continued)*

Seneca Tax Ads Phase II
January 6, 2004
Page 3

President Armstrong said: "The tax scheme planned by the State of New York directly threatens the sovereignty of the Seneca Nation and compromises our free use and enjoyment of our land as promised in the Treaty of 1842 and many other treaties."

The Seneca Nation launched a media campaign October 27, 2003, to educate New Yorkers about how the tax regulations, set take effect December 1, 2003, would violate centuries-old treaties. On November 7, 2003, the state tax department announced that it would extend the public comment period on the regulations and postpone the implementation of the regulations until at least March 1, 2004.

For more information about the Seneca Nation's campaign visit: www.honorindiantreaties.org.

# # #

EXHIBIT 12-3B *Print Advertisement*

I risked my life fighting for ideals
that Albany doesn't seem to understand.

In Vietnam, the guys in my platoon were never
exactly sure why we were there. But, we knew it
had something to do with defending truth, justice
and democracy. That's what our Army oath was
all about: defending the U.S. Constitution from
all enemies foreign and domestic.

Now, New York State is breaking our Indian
treaties. Treaties the U.S. Constitution calls
"the supreme law of the land."

It's a sad irony. America's sons and daughters are
dying for truth, justice and democracy. And our
leaders in Albany don't seem to understand a
thing about truth, justice or democracy.

**Find out how you can let Governor Pataki
know you object to breaking treaties. Log
onto www.HonorIndianTreaties.org or call
1-888-665-5582.**

Break a Treaty, **Break the Law.**

PAID FOR BY SENECA NATION OF INDIANS

Courtesy Seneca Nation of Indians and Travers Collins & Company

EXHIBIT 12-3C   *Television Advertisement Script*

Honor Indian Treaties Campaign
Phase I (October/November 2003)

Television Script

:30 Television "Burning Treaty"

VIDEO	AUDIO
Open on a shot of an old-looking parchment, on which is written the Buffalo Creek Compromise Treaty of 1842.	ANNCR: When the United States enters a treaty, there is no higher law.
A hand reaches in and sets the treaty on fire.	ANNCR: And yet, New York state is about to violate a US treaty.
As fire burns, super images and type over the text of the document: *Rights guaranteed by 1842 Buffalo Creek Compromise Treaty.* *U.S. Constitution: Treaties are "Supreme Law."* *Over 1000 Indians and non-Indians will lose jobs*	ANNCR: By taxing sovereign Indian nations in our borders, a tax Governor Pataki has already called unconstitutional, the state will raise consumer prices and cost jobs throughout the state.
Type up over burning (and almost consumed) document: *Find out more at HonorIndianTreaties.com* add phone number: *1-888-665-5582*	ANNCR: Tell Governor Pataki to honor the supreme law of the land...
The document is completely burnt.	ANNCR: ...Before it's too late.
Fade to type: *Break a treaty, break the law.* Add disclaimer: *Seneca Nation of Indians*	ANNCR: Because if you break a treaty, you break the law.

Courtesy Seneca Nation of Indians and Travers Collins & Company

EXHIBIT 12-3D   *Radio Advertisement Script*

Honor Indian Treaties Campaign
Phase I (October/November 2003)

Radio Script

:60 Radio "Burning Treaty"

ANNCR: The U.S. Constitution calls treaties "the Supreme Law of the Land." Once we enter into one with another nation, no other law supercedes it. And yet New York State is about to violate US treaties that have lasted over 200 years. In a move that Governor Pataki has already called unconstitutional, the state is burdening the sovereign native nations within our borders with regulations and taxes they have no right to impose. Since 1784 the US has acknowledged Indian independence, and the Treaty of 1842 clearly says the Seneca Nation will not be taxed by any US government. Including New York State. The state's unconstitutional action will cause over 1000 Indians and non-Indians to lose their jobs, consumer prices to rise, businesses to close. Tell Governor Pataki to honor the supreme law of the land. Because if you break a treaty, you break the law. Find out more at HonorIndianTreaties.org or call 1-888-665-5582. Paid for by the Seneca Nation of Indians.

Courtesy Seneca Nation of Indians and Travers Collins & Company

Questions for Class Discussion and Case Analysis

The following questions can be used in class discussions of each of the cases in this textbook. Students can gain valuable experience by leading class discussions.

RESEARCH

Does the case give adequate background information about the organization itself? What was the major reason for conducting this program? Was the program proactive or reactive? Which audiences were targeted for communication? Should other audiences have also been targeted? How were research data about each audience obtained? Were the data as complete as necessary? Is there anything unusual about the research phase of this case? What are the research strengths and weaknesses of this case?

OBJECTIVES

Categorize this case's objectives. Which are impact objectives? Specify informational, attitudinal, or behavioral. Which are output objectives? Should they have been more quantitative? Should they have used time frames? Were output objectives used when the ultimate goal was really impact? What is your overall assessment of the objectives used in this case?

PROGRAMMING

Evaluate the theme (if any) used in this case. Is it short, catchy, memorable, to the point? What major message or messages are communicated in this case? Will the messages resonate with the publics identified by your research phase? Evaluate the central actions or special events in this case. Are they truly worthwhile and newsworthy? Are they "pseudoevents"? Evaluate the types of uncontrolled and controlled media that were used. Were any forms of communication omitted that should have been used? Was adequate use made of interpersonal communication? Did the communication achieve a sense of "grassroots involvement" through interpersonal communication, or was there overreliance on mass media publicity placement or impersonal forms of controlled media? Discuss the use of such communication principles as source credibility, salient information, effective nonverbal and verbal cues, two-way communication, opinion leaders, group influence, selective exposure, and audience participation. How effectively were these principles used? Explain.

EVALUATION

Was each of the case's objectives separately evaluated? Describe the evaluative methods used. How appropriate and effective were these methods? Did the program achieve its stated objectives? Was there a real *link* between the case's objectives and its evaluation?

OVERALL JUDGMENTS

As a whole, how effective was this public relations program? What are its major strengths? major weaknesses? Explain. What are the major PR lessons or principles to be learned from this case? What, if anything, would you do differently if you were assigned a public relations problem like this one?

PRSA Member Code of Ethics 2000

PREAMBLE

Public Relations Society of America

Member Code of Ethics 2000

- Professional Values
- Principles of Conduct
- Commitment and Compliance

This Code applies to PRSA members. The Code is designed to be a useful guide for PRSA members as they carry out their ethical responsibilities. This document is designed to anticipate and accommodate, by precedent, ethical challenges that may arise. The scenarios outlined in the Code provision are actual examples of misconduct. More will be added as experience with the Code occurs.

The Public Relations Society of America (PRSA) is committed to ethical practices. The level of public trust PRSA members seek, as we serve the public good, means we have taken on a special obligation to operate ethically.

The value of member reputation depends upon the ethical conduct of everyone affiliated with the Public Relations Society of America. Each of us sets an example for each other—as well as other professionals—by our pursuit of excellence with powerful standards of performance, professionalism, and ethical conduct.

Emphasis on enforcement of the Code has been eliminated. But, the PRSA Board of Directors retains the right to bar from membership or expel from the Society any individual who has been or is sanctioned by a government agency or convicted in a court of law of an action that is in violation of this Code.

Ethical practice is the most important obligation of a PRSA member. We view the Member Code of Ethics as a model for other professions, organizations, and professionals.

PRSA MEMBER STATEMENT OF PROFESSIONAL VALUES

This statement presents the core values of PRSA members and, more broadly, of the public relations profession. These values provide the foundation for the Member Code of Ethics and set the industry standard for the professional practice of public relations. These values are the fundamental beliefs that guide our behaviors and decision-making process. We believe our professional values are vital to the integrity of the profession as a whole.

PRSA Membership Code of Ethics 2000, reprinted with permission from the Public Relations Society of America, New York, NY.

Advocacy

- We serve the public interest by acting as responsible advocates for those we represent.
- We provide a voice in the marketplace of ideas, facts, and viewpoints to aid informed public debate.

Honesty

- We adhere to the highest standards of accuracy and truth in advancing the interests of those we represent and in communicating with the public.

Expertise

- We acquire and responsibly use specialized knowledge and experience.
- We advance the profession through continued professional development, research, and education.
- We build mutual understanding, credibility, and relationships among a wide array of institutions and audiences.

Independence

- We provide objective counsel to those we represent.
- We are accountable for our actions.

Loyalty

- We are faithful to those we represent, while honoring our obligation to serve the public interest.

Fairness

- We deal fairly with clients, employers, competitors, peers, vendors, the media, and the general public.
- We respect all opinions and support the right of free expression.

PRSA CODE PROVISIONS

Free Flow of Information

Core Principle. Protecting and advancing the free flow of accurate and truthful information is essential to serving the public interest and contributing to informed decision making in a democratic society.

Intent

- To maintain the integrity of relationships with the media, government officials, and the public.
- To aid informed decision making.

Guidelines

A member shall:

- Preserve the integrity of the process of communication.
- Be honest and accurate in all communications.
- Act promptly to correct erroneous communications for which the practitioner is responsible.
- Preserve the free flow of unprejudiced information when giving or receiving gifts by ensuring that gifts are nominal, legal, and infrequent.

Examples of Improper Conduct Under This Provision

- A member representing a ski manufacturer gives a pair of expensive racing skis to a sports magazine columnist, to influence the columnist to write favorable articles about the product.
- A member entertains a government official beyond legal limits and/or in violation of government reporting requirements.

Competition

Core Principle. Promoting healthy and fair competition among professionals preserves an ethical climate while fostering a robust business environment.

Intent

- To promote respect and fair competition among public relations professionals.
- To serve the public interest by providing the widest choice of practitioner options.

Guidelines

A member shall:

- Follow ethical hiring practices designed to respect free and open competition without deliberately undermining a competitor.
- Preserve intellectual property rights in the marketplace.

Examples of Improper Conduct Under This Provision

- A member employed by a "client organization" shares helpful information with a counseling firm that is competing with others for the organization's business.

- A member spreads malicious and unfounded rumors about a competitor in order to alienate the competitor's clients and employees in a ploy to recruit people and business.

Disclosure of Information

Core Principle. Open communication fosters informed decision making in a democratic society.

Intent
- To build trust with the public by revealing all information needed for responsible decision making.

Guidelines
A member shall:

- Be honest and accurate in all communications.
- Act promptly to correct erroneous communications for which the member is responsible.
- Investigate the truthfulness and accuracy of information released on behalf of those represented.
- Reveal the sponsors for causes and interests represented.
- Disclose financial interest (such as stock ownership) in a client's organization.
- Avoid deceptive practices.

Examples of Improper Conduct Under This Provision
- Front groups: A member implements "grass roots" campaigns or letter-writing campaigns to legislators on behalf of undisclosed interest groups.
- Lying by omission: A practitioner for a corporation knowingly fails to release financial information, giving a misleading impression of the corporation's performance.
- A member discovers inaccurate information disseminated via a website or media kit and does not correct the information.
- A member deceives the public by employing people to pose as volunteers to speak at public hearings and participate in "grass roots" campaigns.

Safeguarding Confidences

Core Principle. Client trust requires appropriate protection of confidential and private information.

Intent

- To protect the privacy rights of clients, organizations, and individuals by safeguarding confidential information.

Guidelines

A member shall:

- Safeguard the confidences and privacy rights of present, former, and prospective clients and employees.

- Protect privileged, confidential, or insider information gained from a client or organization.

- Immediately advise an appropriate authority if a member discovers that confidential information is being divulged by an employee of a client company or organization.

Examples of Improper Conduct Under This Provision

- A member changes jobs, takes confidential information, and uses that information in the new position to the detriment of the former employer.

- A member intentionally leaks proprietary information to the detriment of some other party.

Conflicts of Interest

Core Principle. Avoiding real, potential, or perceived conflicts of interest builds the trust of clients, employers, and the publics.

Intent

- To earn trust and mutual respect with clients or employers.

- To build trust with the public by avoiding or ending situations that put one's personal or professional interests in conflict with society's interests.

Guidelines

A member shall:

- Act in the best interests of the client or employer, even subordinating the member's personal interests.

- Avoid actions and circumstances that may appear to compromise good business judgment or create a conflict between personal and professional interests.

- Disclose promptly any existing or potential conflict of interest to affected clients or organizations.

- Encourage clients and customers to determine if a conflict exists after notifying all affected parties.

Examples of Improper Conduct Under This Provision
- The member fails to disclose that he or she has a strong financial interest in a client's chief competitor.
- The member represents a "competitor company" or a "conflicting interest" without informing a prospective client.

Enhancing the Profession

Core Principle. Public relations professionals work constantly to strengthen the public's trust in the profession.

Intent
- To build respect and credibility with the public for the profession of public relations.
- To improve, adapt, and expand professional practices.

Guidelines
A member shall:

- Acknowledge that there is an obligation to protect and enhance the profession.
- Keep informed and educated about practices in the profession to ensure ethical conduct.
- Actively pursue personal professional development.
- Decline representation of clients or organizations that urge or require actions contrary to this Code.
- Accurately define what public relations activities can accomplish.
- Counsel subordinates in proper ethical decision making.
- Require that subordinates adhere to the ethical requirements of the Code.
- Report ethical violations, whether committed by PRSA members or not, to the appropriate authority.

Examples of Improper Conduct Under This Provision
- A PRSA member declares publicly that a product the client sells is safe without disclosing evidence to the contrary.
- A member initially assigns some questionable client work to a non-member practitioner to avoid the ethical obligation of PRSA membership.

Resources

Rules and Guidelines. The following PRSA documents, available in *The Blue Book,* provide detailed rules and guidelines to help guide your professional behavior:

- PRSA Bylaws
- PRSA Administrative Rules
- Member Code of Ethics

If after reviewing them, you still have a question or issue, contact PRSA headquarters as noted below.

Questions. The PRSA is here to help. Whether you have a serious concern or simply need clarification, contact Judy Voss at judy.voss @prsa.org.

Action/special events. *See* Special events

Advocacy advertising, 37, 192

American Stock Exchange, 232

Annual reports, 228, 229, 231

Audience participation, 37, 42

Audience research, 15
- in community relations, 157–158
- in consumer relations, 267–268
- in emergency public relations, 379
- in employee relations, 95–96
- in financial relations, 228–229
- in government relations, 188–191
- in integrated marketing communications, 413
- in international public relations, 309–310
- in media relations, 52–55
- in member relations, 124–136
- methods, 16–25
- with special publics, 327–328
- for target publics, 15

Audiovisual communication, 36

Bacon's media directories, 54

"Barberton Citizens Hospital: Keep Barberton Healthy," 169–175

Bipartisan Campaign Reform Act, 193

Blogs, 6

"Break a Treaty, Break the Law," 424–433

Brochures, 35, 100, 125

"The Bucket Brigade: Creating Employee Loyalty through Corporate Philanthropy," 105–114

Bulletin boards, 35, 100

Burrelle's media directories, 54

Client research, 13–14
- in community relations, 157
- in consumer relations, 267
- in emergency public relations, 379
- in employee relations, 96
- in financial relations, 228
- in government relations, 191

in integrated marketing communications, 404

in international public relations, 300

in media relations, 53

in member relations, 125

with special publics, 327

Clipping services, 63

Coalition building, 188

Communication on political issues, 191

Communication principles, 38–42
- audience participation, 42
- group influence, 41
- nonverbal communication, 39–40
- opinion leaders, 41
- salient information, 38
- selective exposure, 41–42
- source credibility, 38
- two-way communication, 40
- verbal communication, 38–40

Community relations, 151–182
- evaluation of, 156
- objectives of, 154
- programming, 155–156
- research for, 152–153

Consumer relations, 250–273
- evaluation of, 254–255
- objectives of, 252
- programming, 252–254
- research for, 251–252

Consumer Reports, 250

Consumers Union, 250

Controlled media. *See* Media

"Convincing The World That Film Processing Matters—The Launch of Kodak Perfect Touch Processing," 284–298

Dale-Chall Formula, 43

"Dare to Care About the Air," 176–182

"Diabetes for Life Campaign," 403–412

Direct mail, 191

Displays, exhibits, 99

"Driving for Quality Care," 143–150

"Dr. Martin Luther King, Jr. Library—Check It Out!," 160–168

"The Electronic Product Code: From Concept to Commercialization in One Year," 299–308

Emergency public relations, 368–394
- checklist, 372–373
- evaluation of, 374
- objectives of, 369–370
- programming, 370–372
- research for, 369

Ethics, 6–8, 438–445

Ethnic groups. *See* Special publics, relations with

Evaluation, 43–45
- of attitudinal objectives, 44
- of behavioral objectives, 44
- in community relations, 151–152
- in consumer relations, 261
- in emergency public relations, 381
- in employee relations, 108–109
- in financial relations, 232
- in government relations, 195
- of informational objectives, 43
- in integrated marketing communications, 406–407
- in international public relations, 303
- in media relations, 63
- in member relations, 134
- of output objectives, 44–45
- with special publics, 330

Face-to-face, 23, 41, 151, 172

Farr-Jenkins-Patterson Formula, 43

"A Fashionable Red Alert Warns Women of the Heart Truth," 326–339

Feature stories, 32, 58

Federal Election Commission (FEC), 193

Federal Trade Commission (FTC), 250

Feedback, 38

Films, 36

Financial relations, 228–249
- evaluation of, 232
- objectives of, 230
- programming, 230–232
- research for, 229

527 groups, 193
Flesch Reading Ease Formula, 43
Food and Drug Administration, 250
Fry Formula, 43
Full-disclosure principle, 371

Government and ancillary publics, 185
Government relations. *See* Public affairs/government relations
Grassroots activities, 189–191
Group influence, 41
Gunning Fog Index, 43

"The Healthy Potato—Relaunching America's Favorite Vegetable in the Atkins Era," 413–423
Hospitality, 189–190
House publications, 35, 156
"How Will You Remember September 11?," 78–87

"IDRC Merges with NACORE: The Launch of CoreNet Global," 309–316
Information exchange, 189
Institutional advertising, 37
Integrated marketing communications, 396–433
  evaluation of, 400
  objectives of, 398
  programming, 399–400
  research for, 397–398
Internal communications, 95–150
  employee relations, 96–101
  member relations, 131–134
International public relations, 274–316
  evaluation of, 279–280
  objectives of, 276–277
  programming, 277–279
  research for, 275
Interpersonal communication, 37, 189–190, 331
Investor relations. *See* Financial relations
Issues management, 184
"It's Up to Us. It's Up to You," 136–142

Lay's Stax Challenge, 267–273
Likert scaling, 44, 194
Lobbying
  direct, 188–189
  indirect, 189–190

Management by objectives (MBO), 25

Media
  in community relations, 152–153
  in consumer relations, 259
  controlled and uncontrolled, 32–37
  in emergency public relations, 370–371
  in employee relations, 99
  in financial relations, 222
  in government relations, 193
  in integrated marketing communications, 399–400
  in international public relations, 303
  in media relations, 58–62
  in member relations, 133
  with special publics, 327
Media contacts list, 53–54
  in community relations, 153
Media directories, 67
Media information center (MIC), 371
Media interviews, 60–61
Media publics, 15, 55
Media relations, 52–94
  evaluation of, 63
  objectives of, 56–57
  programming, 57–61
  research for, 53–55
Member relations 131–150
  evaluation of, 134
  objectives of, 132–133
  programming, 133
  research for, 131-132
Message
  comprehension, 28, 43
  exposure, 28, 43
  retention, 28, 43

NASDAQ, 232
National Rifle Association (NRA), 190
"Navigating Through a Current of Uncertainty: Getting Aquila Back on Solid Ground," 242–249
"New Beginnings: Recovering from Tragedy; Unlocking the Value," 236–241
News conference, 35, 60
Newsletters, 35, 99, 133
News release, 35, 58–59
New technology, 5
New York Stock Exchange (NYSE), 232
Nonverbal communication, 38
Nonquantitative research, 16–23

Objectives, 25–31
  attitudinal, 28–30
  behavioral, 30–31
  in community relations, 154–155
  in consumer relations, 252
  in emergency public relations, 369–370
  in employee relations, 95–96
  in financial relations, 230
  in government relations, 186–187
  impact, 27–30
  impact and output, 26–28
  informational, 28
  in integrated marketing communications, 398
  in international public relations, 301
  measuring, 42–44
  in media relations, 56
  in member relations, 125–126
  output, 26–28
  with special publics, 327
  writing, 25
Ombudsman, 253
One-voice principle, 369, 371, 373
Opinion leaders, 40, 41
  in community relations, 153
  in international public relations, 300
  in lobbying, 189–190
  in relations with special publics, 332
Opportunity/problem, 14–15
  in community relations, 152
  in consumer relations, 251
  in emergency public relations, 369
  in employee relations, 96
  in financial relations, 229
  in government relations, 184
  in integrated marketing communications, 397
  in international public relations, 275
  in media relations, 53
  in member relations, 124
  with special publics, 326

Parent Teacher Association, 154
Pay inserts, 99
Photographs/photo opportunities, 35, 59–60
Podcast, 6
Political action committees (PACS), 191
Political support activities, 192–193

Press conferences. *See* News conference
Press release. *See* News release
Price/earnings (P/E) ratio, 233
PR Newswire, 68
Proactive and reactive programs, 14
Programming, 31–43
   in community relations, 155–156
   in consumer relations, 252–254
   in emergency public relations, 370–373
   in employee relations, 98–100
   in financial relations, 230–232
   in government relations, 187–195
   in integrated marketing communications, 399
   in international public relations, 277–279
   in media relations, 57–63
   in member relations, 133–134
   with special publics, 321–322
   theme and messages, 31
   uncontrolled and controlled media, 32–37
"Promoting and Positioning the Grand Opening of the National Museum of the American Indian," 69–77
"Protecting Consumer Confidence in U.S. Beef: A Success Story," 378–386
Public affairs/government relations, 183–227
   communication model of, 184
   evaluation of, 195–196
   objectives, 186–187
   programming, 187–195
   research for, 184–186
Public information center (PIC), 371, 373
Public relations advertising, 37, 192, 396
   and advocacy advertising, 37, 192
   institutional, 37, 192
Public relations process, 4, 12–46
   evaluation of, 42–45
   objectives of, 24–31
   outline of, 45–46
   programming, 31–43
   research for, 13–25
Public Relations Society of America (PRSA), 3–4, 438–445

member code of ethics, 438–445
official statement, 3–4

Quantitative research, 23–25

"REBEL: New Jersey's New Youth Antitobacco Movement," 340–355
"A Record Gift to NPR: Keeping Good News from Going Bad," 201–209
Research, 13–24
   for community relations, 152–154
   for consumer relations, 251–252
   for emergency public relations, 369
   for employee relations, 96–97
   for financial relations, 229
   for government relations, 184–186
   for integrated marketing communications, 397–398
   for international public relations, 275–276
   for media relations, 53–56
   for member relations, 131–132
   for special publics, 319–320
Response mechanisms, 40
ROPE formula. *See* Public relations process

Salient information, 38
"San Diego Wildfires 2003," 387–394
Sarbanes Oxley Act, 228
"Save our Doctors, Protect our Patients: The Maryland Miracle," 219–227
Schmertz, Herbert, 192
Securities and Exchange Commission (SEC), 228
Selective exposure, 41–42
Semantic differential, 44
"Shedd Sharks Go Wild," 88–94
"The Shutterfly Soirée," 356–365
Slogan, 31
Source credibility, 38
Speakers' bureau, 37
Special events, 31–32
   in community relations, 155
   in consumer relations, 253
   in employee relations, 99

in financial relations, 231
in government relations, 187–193
in integrated marketing communications, 399
in international public relations, 275–276
in media relations, 58
in member relations, 133
with special publics, 321
Specialized media, 17, 55
Special publics, relations with, 317–365
   evaluation of, 322
   objectives of, 320–321
   programming, 321–322
   research for, 319–320
Speeches. *See* Speakers' bureau
Spot news, 57
"Standing Up For Consumer Choice—The SB 1648 Battle," 210–218
"A Stronger Way to Sell Appliances," 258–266
Survey, 23–24

Target publics, 16, 17–22
Theme/message, 31
   in community relations, 155
   in consumer relations, 253
   in employee relations, 98
   in financial relations, 230–231
   in government relations, 187
   in integrated marketing communications, 399
   in international public relations, 277
   in media relations, 57–58
   in member relations, 133
   with special publics, 321
"Trinity Health Retirement Redesign: Communicating Benefit Changes," 115–123
24-hour rule, 370, 372
Two-way communication, 39–41

Uncontrolled media. *See* Media

Verbal cues/communication, 39
Viral messages, 6
Vocus media service, 68

Websites, 5, 37
"Wheel of Fortune," 124–130